Bert Williams : A Biography

BERT WILLIAMS

A Biography of the
Pioneer Black Comedian

by
Eric Ledell Smith

McFarland & Company, Inc., Publishers
Jefferson, North Carolina, and London

Frontispiece: **Bert Williams, c. 1910** *(Courtesy Hatch-Billops Collection, Inc.)*

British Library Cataloguing-in-Publication data are available

Library of Congress Cataloguing-in-Publication Data

Smith, Eric Ledell, 1949–
    Bert Williams : a biography of the pioneer Black comedian / by
Eric Ledell Smith.
        p.   cm.
    Includes bibliographical references and index.
    ISBN 0-89950-695-X (lib. bdg. : 50# alk. paper) ∞
    1. Williams, Bert, 1875–1922. 2. Afro-American entertainers –
Biography. 3. Theater – United States – History – 20th century.
I. Title.
    PN2287.W46S55   1992
    792.7'028'092 – dc20
    [B]   91-50947
                                                              CIP

Manufactured in the United States of America

McFarland & Company, Inc., Publishers
  Box 611, Jefferson, North Carolina 28640

To my parents:
Warren and Henrietta Smith

Contents

Acknowledgments

T he following libraries were very helpful in permitting me to use their interlibrary loan services to secure newspaper microfilm: Bobst Library of New York University, the University of Michigan Graduate Library, and the Detroit Public Library.

In connection to general theater research, I am greatly indebted to the following individuals: Maryann Chach, Shubert Archive (New York City); Barbara R. Geisler, San Francisco Performing Arts Library and Museum; William Swafford, Riverside (California) City/County Library; H. Vincent Moses, Riverside (California) Municipal Museum; Robin Chandler, Stanford University Archives; Diana Lachatanere, Schomburg Center for Research in Black Culture (New York City); Lofton Mitchell, State University of New York at Binghamton; Martha S. DeMonaco, Wagner Labor Archives, New York University; and Brigette Kueppers, Theatre Arts Library, University of California–Los Angeles.

The staff of the following institutions contributed much in time and service to the research of this book: New York City Municipal Archives, Theatre Collection, Museum of the City of New York; Shubert Archive (New York City); Registrar General's Office, Nassau, the Bahamas; Special Collections Department, UCLA Library; Theatre Arts Library, University of Texas at Austin; and the E. Azalia Hackley Collection of the Detroit Public Library.

The following individuals and institutions contributed to my knowledge and understanding of Bert Williams's music and its milieu: Diana Haskell, Newberry Library (Chicago); John Graziano, City College of City University of New York; Music Library, University of California–Berkeley; Mercer Cook, ASCAP (New York); William C. Parsons, Library of Congress; David A. Jasen, Long Island University; Thomas Riis, University of Georgia at Athens; Samuel Floyd, Columbia College (Chicago); and Morris Lawrence, Jr., of Washtenaw Community College, Ann Arbor, Michigan.

The following institutions and individuals assisted me with film material: Wisconsin Center for Film and Theatre Research; Henry T. Sampson, Film Department, Museum of Modern Art, New York; Jim Limbacher, and especially James Wheeler.

I wish to thank the following institutions for their research assistance and courtesy in granting me permission to reproduce photographs of Bert Williams and the Walkers: the Hatch-Billops Collection, Inc., New York City; the Wisconsin Center for Film and Theatre Research, Madison, Wisconsin; and the Beinecke Rare Book and Manuscript Library, Yale University, New Haven, Connecticut.

Among my many friends, the following gave me support and help in their own ways: Ken Brown of New York City, X. Ted Barber, Alvan Uhre, Bob Thomas, Stephen Skelly, Barbara Robinson, Edward Hunt, JoAnn Jager, and Silvia Williams. I am also indebted greatly to my former high school English teacher, Nettie Kravitz; my adviser and thesis director at NYU, Brooks McNamara; and my clerical assistant, David Heider, who was a great help to me. Finally, I must thank my family for guidance and support.

Preface

Black musical comedies, operettas, revues, and minstrel shows were part of the broad spectrum of American popular entertainment at the beginning of the twentieth century. These shows, with their provocative music and dancing, contributed both performers and material for what was to become the standard Broadway musical. One of the primary entertainers during this era was the incomparable Bert Williams (1874–1922).

During a dark period of American history, when many Americans condoned racial segregation, lynchings, and prejudice toward nonwhites, Bert Williams amassed an astonishing number of achievements. Williams was truly the first black superstar comedian – the first of his race to command universal respect for his talents. Williams starred in the first black musical comedy to open on Broadway – *In Dahomey* – also the first black show to give a command performance before England's King Edward VII in 1903. In 1901, along with his partner, George Walker, he became the first black recording artist and was among the first blacks to become a best-selling artist. Bert Williams was also a songwriter; he wrote at least seventy songs, many of them for his own shows. Bert Williams was the first black to be regularly featured in a Broadway revue: the *Ziegfeld Follies*. He is credited with opening the door for other blacks (most notably lyricist Noble Sissle and composer Eubie Blake with their successful show, *Shuffle Along*, in 1921). Bert Williams remains to this day the most famous black performer of pantomime. Although his movie appearances were brief, Williams in 1910 became the first major black star to be featured in a motion picture.

A large part of Bert Williams's success as an entertainer was due to his business guidance from and comedy partnership with George W. Walker (1872?–1911). In their heyday their act, known as Williams and Walker, had many imitators, including Miller and Lyles (stars of *Shuffle Along*). Williams played the woeful, dour bumpkin, while Walker played the straight, dapper role. They were joined in their shows by Walker's wife, Aida Overton Walker (1880–1914), who is regarded as the third wheel. A pioneer black choreographer and dancer, Mrs. Walker is clearly a predecessor of Katherine Dunham. Aida Overton Walker choreographed many of the Williams and Walker shows, as well as routines for her own vaudeville dance groups. The Walkers' contribution to Bert Williams's early successes cannot be denied.

Bert Williams's popularity in his day was enormous; his influence on fellow comedians – black and white – was widespread. Something of the pathos and self-pity of Williams's comedy can be seen in the work of such comics as Buster Keaton and Eddie Cantor, some of whom worked with him. Ironically, it was partly the success of such white entertainers as Al Jolson, Frank Tinney, and Eddie Cantor using blackface – whether in minstrel shows, vaudeville, or movies – that contributed to the demise of Williams's career.

It was white American entertainers, in the early nineteenth century, who started the use of burnt cork or blackface on stage. At first their goal was simply to "look like a black person." As time went by, however, the more ingenious entertainers incorporated different details based on social observation. The stage caricature became grotesque and bizarre. Blackface minstrels made up with thick, red painted lips and outlandish clothes. The Sambo stereotype was a result of this minstrel caricature. Joseph Boskin, in his book *Sambo: The Rise and Demise of an American Jester,* noted that during the twentieth century, "Sambo was found everywhere, in every nook and cranny of the popular culture,"[1] from sheet music to newspaper and magazine ads to grocery products like Aunt Jemima's pancake mix and Uncle Ben's rice. Aunt Jemima, Uncle Ben, and Bert Williams's stage characters drew on the antebellum image of the Negro: bred on the slave plantation, uneducated, and victims of their color. When the civil rights movement started after World War II, civil rights organizations began a campaign to abolish the Sambo image from popular culture. Minstrel shows are now socially unacceptable. Performing in blackface is professionally taboo. And in terms of scholarship, there began to be almost a form of censorship about the lives of people like Bert Williams.

Allen Woll, in his book on black theater history, points out that "white authors have tended to dismiss or underestimate black contributions, and black critics have found the stage persona of [Bert] Williams, [Ernest] Hogan, or Miller and Lyles to be something of an embarrassment."[2] Until very recently, no academic studies on Bert Williams's period were available. The first break in this trend came in 1970, when Ann Charters published a biography called *Nobody – The Story of Bert Williams.* It had been preceded by *Bert Williams – Son of Laughter,*[3] edited by Mabel Rowland in 1923. While Rowland's book was an anthology of tributes to and anecdotes about Williams, Charters's book chronicled Williams's life, noting his accomplishments and disappointments and his theater, music, and film contributions. Other studies of the period appeared, most notably books by Thomas Riis, Henry T. Sampson, Allan Woll, and James Haskins.[4] Drawing on these sources, as a New York University graduate student in 1983, I wrote what is believed to be the only thesis or dissertation available on Bert Williams. Though my thesis was on the show *In Dahomey*, I quickly became aware of how little information about Williams's life was known. Since there was no published biography on Williams or his times, I undertook to prepare my own. The result is included in this book in a scaled-down version. Primary source materials consulted included a copy of a Bert Williams "diary," letters written by Williams preserved at the Shubert Archives in New York, letters by Williams published in the press, autobiographical newspaper and magazine articles by Bert Williams, George Walker, and Aida Overton Walker; and original librettos and sheet music. Legal briefs and theatrical contracts were obtained from the Municipal Archives in New York.

Secondary source materials include national newspaper reviews of all of Williams's shows. Primarily New York-based reviews included those from both the black and white press. The biography goes substantially farther than Charters's or Rowland's in exploring Williams's career in vaudeville and the *Ziegfeld Follies*. Throughout the book, testimony from both Williams and his associates is utilized to tell the story. The author has not been able to verify some of the information cited by Williams or previous biographers. Where the alleged facts were erroneous, I point this out to the reader. Where the evidence is unclear, I present both sides of the issue as now known.

The appendix materials include short biographies of George and Aida Overton Walker. They also include a list of sixty-nine documented songs composed by Bert Williams, listed alphabetically by title.

Finally, an annotated bibliography is provided. For those who wish to explore more about Bert Williams and his times, it may be a useful tool. I make no claim to be an expert on music or film history. Those aspects of Williams's life are simply reported as part of his career. Though much about the music and film worlds of Bert Williams is not known, the reader will find several good studies that treat those topics intensely.

A word of caution to the reader: The language used in this book is not meant to be offensive. It is, however, meant to be an attempt to represent Bert Williams and his times accurately. Words like, *nigger, coon, darkey, colored, Negro* recur often in the text. This is indicative of the social times Williams lived in the early twentieth century. For those unused to such terminology, this book may be something of a shock.

Nevertheless, the real surprise of this biography lies in the immense talent and achievement of a remarkable entertainer. Bert Williams was truly a great comedian.

Chapter 1

I was born in New Providence, Nassau, in the Bahamas Islands," began Mr. Williams, with a distant, dreamy look in his kindly eyes, "and migrated at the tender age of two years. How's that for a beginning?"[1]

With these remarks to a Chicago newspaper in 1910, Bert Williams left no doubt about the fact that he was from the Bahamas and proud of it. West Indians have a quiet dignity that is sometimes mistaken for arrogance; the black experience of West Indians has been somewhat different from that of their North American counterparts.

In the eighteenth century the Bahamian government, like its North American counterpart, was anxious to start a plantation economy to spur colonial revenue. For this slaves were needed, and it is recorded that "the Yoruba, Congo, Ibo, Mandingo, Fulani, Hausa and other tribes were all represented among Bahamian blacks.... Slaves were brought in annually until 1804 when the last arrivals were recorded."[2]

Slavery was abolished in the Bahamas on August 1, 1834, about thirty years before it ended in the United States.

Bert Williams's immediate ancestors were not slaves. His paternal grandfather was Frederick K. Williams, Sr. Bert Williams claimed that his grandfather had been born in Copenhagen, Denmark, and had come to the Bahamas in the early nineteenth century as a Danish diplomat.[3]

Bert Williams wrote of his grandfather: "He left Copenhagen some years ago and became Danish consul in Nassau."[4] At another time, Williams suggested that his grandfather had represented the Spanish government in Nassau as well.[5]

There is evidence that Frederick Williams was also involved in various types of business. One source gives his occupation as "jeweler" in Nassau. Bert Williams's niece, Charlotte Tyler, once told a reporter that her uncle said that Frederick Williams, Sr., had been "a Danish orange grower."[6] Another journalist claimed, "The grandfather was a manufacturer of salt, which he shipped to Newfoundland in a fleet of eight schooners that he owned himself."[7]

The last two accounts are quite plausible. Before the founding of the citrus fruit industry in Florida, the Bahamas was a major world exporter of such fruits as oranges, lemons, limes, and pineapples. Salt was also an important product:

> Before refrigeration, salt had a much wider use than today. It was essential and much in demand for the preservation of meat and fish.... There were salt works in Eleuthera and on New Providence and nearby islands.... From the Bahamas, many shiploads were exported annually.[8]

Frederick Williams, Sr., married a mulatto named Emiline (or Emma) Armbrister from the West Indies.

Ann Charters points out that a description of his grandmother that Bert Williams once gave a reporter was inaccurately recorded.[9] Williams stated: "He married my [grand]mother who was half Spanish and half African."[10] Grandmother Williams was fluent in Spanish, as Williams recalled from his childhood. When he was a little boy, Williams once brought a crawfish into his grandmother's sickroom. Williams said: "The Spanish things she hollered out about me were many and loud and they brought results when my mother rushed into the room."[11]

Emiline Williams's only child, Frederick Williams, Jr., was born October 7, 1850, in the district of St. Agnes, Nassau, the Bahamas. He seems to have been very fair complexioned for a black man. Charlotte Tyler described him as "a fair man with red hair and a 'Buffalo Bill' mustache."[12]

The Williamses lived in an era when the Bahamas were just beginning to invite tourism. In the mid-nineteenth century, when steamships were becoming a major form of transportation, the Bahamas saw an opportunity to diversify its economy,[13]

> offer[ing] an annual bounty of £1000 to any person or company who would provide a "good substantial and efficient" steamboat service between New York and Nassau.... It was only after it was increased to £3000 ... that a contract could be signed for a monthly service with Mr. Samuel Cunard. The first ship, a paddle-wheel steamer named the *Karnak,* took five days to make the first voyage from New York to Nassau in 1859.[14]

In anticipation of tourism, the Bahamian government built a new hotel, the Royal Victoria, in 1861. One Bahamian historian wrote that, with the coming of the American Civil War, the Royal Victoria Hotel prospered, largely due to the patronage of people allied with the Confederacy. Nassau could thus "sumptuously entertain their southern friends – the daring and dashing wearers of the gray."[15]

During the American Civil War, the war at sea became almost as important as the war on land. In 1861 President Abraham Lincoln ordered a blockade of the Confederate seaports, a move aimed at preventing the Confederacy from receiving supplies. Soon it became evident to Federals and Confederates alike that only a certain type of ship was likely to get through, and then only under certain conditions. A fast steamer with shallow draught and a low silhouette, burning smokeless coal, camouflaged with paint, and under expert pilotage, stood a very good chance on a dark night.... Nassau became important as a trans-shipping port where good from ocean steamers were transferred to blockage runners and vice versa. And it was then that the Bahamas experienced a boom far surpassing anything in its previous history.[16]

Thus, as a result of the Civil War, not only Nassau's Royal Victoria Hotel but the Bahamas as a whole experienced economic expansion.

Blockade running culminated in 1864 and the early part of 1865.... In January and February, 1865, twenty steamers ran the blockade, and landed at Nassau 14,182 bales of cotton, which were of the total value of two and three-quarter million dollars. Everyone was wild with excitement. Fortunes were made in a few weeks or months. Gold eagles, and twenty dollar gold pieces were pitched instead of pennies, by fickle fortune's new favorites in the court of the Royal Victoria Hotel.[17]

Frederick Williams, Sr., was among those Bahamians who participated in the blockade-running business. Although it appears that he was able to make money from this enterprise, some have argued that he eventually suffered financial losses. According to one account: "At the time of the Civil War, these schooners were converted into blockade runners and the family fortune rapidly dwindled."[18]

However, Bert Williams told Booker T. Washington that his grandfather "made considerable money during the Civil War, which he lost later in investments in the United States."[19]

In 1870, Frederick Williams, Jr., was twenty years old. He found employment as a waiter at the Royal Victoria Hotel at an opportune time, for the hotel was doing a brisk business.[20] "The season of 1870 was very successful with the Royal Victoria filled to capacity. And in 1873, Nassau had its best tourist season up to that time with nearly five hundred arrivals."[21] Then as now, the tourists were the rich who could afford to vacation in the Bahamas. They tipped well.

Soon Frederick junior was able to think about starting a family. He married a young black woman from Antigua named Julia Monceur. She is said to have been "sister to the Episcopal clergyman of the Church of England in Antigua."[22] The marriage probably took place in the early 1870s in the Bahamas. Unfortunately, no photograph of the Williamses has ever been found. But friends of Bert Williams recalled how physically distinctive they were. Eubie Blake, the famous ragtime pianist and composer, said

Bert Williams ... was only seven or eight years older than me, but he was a star when I was a kid.... Big, handsome man. Come from big, *strong* people. I met his father and mother in 1915. They were both very big. Very strong.[23]

Photographs of Bert Williams bear out the fact that he inherited his parents' physical stature, growing almost six feet tall as an adult.

The Registrar General's Office in Nassau records that on November 12, 1874, an "unnamed male of mixed race" was born to Frederick and Julia Monceur Williams, in the parish of St. Matthews in Nassau. Later this boy, christened Egbert Austin Williams, was destined to become famous as Bert Williams.[24] (Bahamian authorities in those days classified race on birth certificates in three categories: European, African, and Mixed. The classification Mixed was reserved for offspring of interracial marriages as well as those born to black parents but who had light or fair complexions.)

Years later, Williams confessed that Willams was not his real name. "Williams, of course, is obviously not a Danish name. Nobody in America knows my real name and, if I can prevent it, nobody ever will. That was the only promise I made to my father."[25]

This is not the language of an entertainer who has merely adopted another name for the stage. Whether from shame or fear, Williams appears to be concealing some family secret. Why? On his birth certificate as well as his father's, the family name is Williams. If Bert Williams was implying that his real family name was Danish, then Frederick K. Williams, Sr., had changed his name after coming to the Bahamas. It was common practice among people of European ancestry to Anglicize their names or adopt different ones after immigrating. Thus there is nothing unusual about what Frederick Williams, Sr., did. But Bert Williams's concealment of his grandfather's true name is rather unusual.

It seems that Bert Williams was also very secretive about his family. Though he represented himself throughout his lifetime as an only child, this may not have been the case. In 1933 an obituary surfaced about a man in Illinois who was purportedly Bert Willliams's older brother. The *New York Times* reported the death of an Ivory (or Ivery) Williams, who had been a janitor at the Vermillion County, Illinois, courthouse:

> He was a brother of the late Bert Williams, famous Negro comedian of the Williams and Walker duo and inherited most of Bert's personal effects. Born near Kingston, Jamaica, he came to this country at the close of the Civil War and was naturalized here in 1902.[26]

I investigated this story and found it to be dubious. Ivery Williams's death certificate states that "[he] was born in Henderson, Kentucky, May 15, 1853."[27] However, the state of Kentucky did not begin keeping central vital records until 1911. It is therefore impossible to tell which report is a hoax or erroneous. But it is certainly possible that Bert Williams had a brother.

More solid evidence, however, is available about a possible sister. Bert Williams himself supplied an anecdote about his older sibling, whom he did not name:

> My sister had a baby, that when it was about three years old, could hardly talk and yet it used to understand what we said so well that we had to use the utmost precaution in our conversation. We never dared to speak the word "candy" in its presence, so we used to spell the word out to each other. The next day, that child memorized the letters and repeated them in a preemptory tone.[28]

In all the interviews Williams ever gave, this was the only time he spoke of having a sister.

In 1876, when Bert Williams was two years old, his father took him and his family aboard a Cunard steamship and sailed for New York City. According to Booker T. Washington, Frederick Williams, Jr., was interested in learning a trade. "Here he learned the trade of papier-mâché maker and this brought him into connection with the New York theatres."[29] Papier-mâché was a common material used to make stage props.

The Williamses stayed in New York for only a short time. They returned to the Bahamas and did not come back to the States until about ten years later.[30] Religious people, the Williamses were Episcopalians. As a boy Bert Williams was required to attend Sunday services; like most children, he was restless in church. His recollections of these early days show that even then he had a sense of humor:

> I used to find myself getting so sleepy; and what with the nudges from my mother on the right and my grandmother and grandfather on the left, I just knew that I had to keep awake. The monotony of the preacher's tone soothed me, and to avoid its soporific effect, I would glance about until I found something unimportant like some old gentlemen's bald spot or a fly buzzing around some old sister's ear, upon which to fasten my attention. ... Even such simple subjects would suggest whole slapstick comedies to me and I would find myself shaking the pew with uncontrollable mirth, while dotted lines from the eyes of my relatives on both sides were aimed at me.[31]

About 1885, when Bert Williams was eleven, the Williamses again came to the United States. They first settled in Florida, close to the Bahamas. The Williamses were part of a large migration of West Indians to Florida during its economic expansion after the Civil War:

> A remarkable building boom was on and any Bahamian who wanted a job could find it. Bahamians left their home islands by the scores and hundreds and came to Nassau to find passage across the Gulf Stream. ... One Bahamian in every five left home [during that time].[32]

One of Bert Williams's favorite anecdotes was about his days in Florida and how he would "perform" in order to get a treat:

In Florida, along the street where we lived, there were outdoor booths, where old colored mammies sold sweet potato pie. It used to be a favorite haunt of mine, for I loved the pie they made, but I never had any money to buy any. So I would begin at the first booth in the row and go up and gaze at the counter of pies. My mouth would begin to water and my eyes would get big and sad-looking and I'd try to mesmerize a pie. Why, I guess I almost cried with internal longing and mental hunger. But after I had begged with my eyes long enough, the owner of the pies would say:

"Bless yo' heaht, honey, ain't yo' had no suppah?"

"No'm," I'd say, still looking starved and pathetic.

Then I'd get a big piece of good old sweet potato pie, but I'd have to give each of the fellows a bite or I wouldn't get to play with them.

I repeated the performance at each booth, never getting enough pie until I had gone the length of the row. But one night I got too much, and when I went home, I was desperately sick and my mother asked me what I had been doing.

"Playing," I said, trying to conceal my agony. "I guess boys don't get sick just playing [said Bert's mother]. What's left on your face looks like sweet potato pie. I know what's good for that!"

At this point, the reporter interviewing Williams asked if his mother had given him paregoric, a type of sedative. Williams replied: "Yes, but not in the liquid form." Then Bert Williams smiled as he remembered the spanking he got.[33]

From Florida, Williams says he traveled "with my parents by way of Panama to San Pedro, California, now Los Angeles Harbor."[34] Eventually, when Williams was about eleven or twelve, they settled in the small town of Riverside, California.

Ann Charters claims that in Riverside, Frederick Williams, Jr., was a railroad porter, but no evidence has been found to substantiate this. It is far more likely, however, that Bert Williams's father was connected with the citrus fruit industry in Riverside because Frederick Williams, Sr., had been a fruit grower in the Bahamas. One California historian records: "Early Riverside settlers were mainly farmers; citrus fruits their major crop. Once the irrigation problems were solved, income was soon three thousand dollars an acre in Riverside, from the citrus crops."[35]

In order to supplement the family income, Julia Williams also worked. A former classmate of Bert Williams said that Mrs Williams worked as a laundress: "She took in washing and lived in a little shack over by the Santa Fe depot."[36] Bert Williams discovered that he had a voice and spent much time singing in the church choir in Riverside. But he had no formal musical training, and later he regretted this: "When I was a lad, I thought I had a voice, but I learned differently in later years. I did not take proper care of it, and now I have to talk all my numbers."[37]

In the late nineteenth century, Riverside had separate high schools for boys and girls. Bert Williams most likely attended the Riverside Boys High School. According to his father, however, Bert was not a scholar:

> Bert never stood out as a shining light at school. He studied just enough so that he passed and his reports were good. But I am inclined to think that all the joy he ever got out of studying came from his own observations. Indeed, he seemed delighted with each new achievement in mimicry and he developed this gift to a degree while only a child. . . . We punished him for this at first, but soon discovered that punishment was of no use.[38]

Charlotte Tyler told a different story about her uncle's school days. She once displayed to an interviewer Bert Williams's seventh-grade report card, which had "Excellent" ratings in all subjects.[39]

Williams himself admitted that:

> I was always doing something funny, and my teachers didn't know what to do with me. They couldn't spank me for being funny, and I wasn't a mischievous boy. Once when I was in the sixth grade, I got tired of having lessons, so I got out my almanac from my desk and buried myself in it. I was always reading every joke I could find and I remember on this particular day, I had read some good ones. The class was reading in geography and pretty soon I was called upon. "Bert, you may recite," the teacher said. Well, I hadn't the least idea what to say. But I got up and told the class a joke I had just read.[40]

It was not long before Bert Williams realized that he was attracted to show business. But since he was still a teenager, the only way to be an entertainer was to run away from home. Charlotte Tyler said that Frederick Williams, Jr.,

> got mad when his boy Bert quit high school at 16 to get a job barking with a medicine show. Trailing his boy, he found him, hid behind a tree listening to the long-legged, long-armed kid "spiel" from a platform, then edged up and told him to come home. But the boy, even then a mesmerizing talker, gave his father such a story about the show inside that the parent smoothed down his red hair, went in – and was lost. His boy had sung well in the Episcopalian choir, but he never knew he was funny too. So, Father Williams told his boy to go ahead.[41]

Nonetheless, after the father-son confrontation, Bert Williams went home with his father. Years later Williams told the *Chicago Record-Herald* that he graduated from high school "when he was nineteen years old" (in 1893). There are, however, no extant school records for the year 1893 in the Riverside Unified School District Office. Therefore, Williams's claim to be a high school graduate cannot be documented.[42] About this time, too, it seems that Bert Williams worked as a singer/waiter at the Old Mission Inn in Riverside. The *Riverside Press* reported that he had been a member of an all-black quartet of waiters who performed in the inn's dining room.[43] It would have been Bert Williams's first job as an entertainer. According to Booker T. Washington, Williams also worked as a bellboy at the Hollenbeck Hotel in Los Angeles.[44]

About this period of his life, Bert Williams wrote: "I had not the slightest idea of going on the stage at first, nor any very definite ambition to get an education. I went through high school in Southern California and was going to Leland Stanford University."[45]

Although Williams claimed that he attended Stanford, a check of the registrar's records there for the period 1888 to 1896 reveals that he never attended that school.[46] Apparently Williams was *planning* to go to Stanford with the intention of studying civil engineering. Even after he broke into show business, he still thought about eventually getting an engineering degree. A diary of Williams's in the collection of the San Francisco Performing Arts Library and Museum, lists civil engineering textbooks that he wanted to buy and study. On one page, he noted the following books:

> The Elements of Civil Engineering
>
> Volume   1 – Mathematics & Mechanics
> Volume   2 – Bridge Engineering
> Volume   3 – Railroad Engineering
> Volume   4 – Municipal Engineering
> Volume   5 – Hydraulic Engineering
> Volume   6 – Steam Engineering
> Volume   7 – Electrical Engineering
> Volume   8 – Natural Science
> Volume   9 – Tables & Formulas
> Volume 10 – Answers with Questions
> Volume 11 – Answers with Questions[47]

At the bottom of the page, however, Williams wrote not the name of Stanford, but "International Correspondence Schools, Scranton, Pa."

The so-called diary from which this information is quoted is really a combination address memo book, despite the fact that its brown leather cover carries the inscription (typical of its time) "My Travels Abroad." The "diary" also refers to such songs as "My Little Zulu Babe," from the 1900 musical comedy *The Policy Players*, and ostensibly dates from that period.

In 1893 Williams joined a show that toured the West Coast – possibly the show that Frederick Williams, Jr., told his son "to go ahead" and join – adding credence to Williams's niece's claim that her uncle quit high school at age sixteen. Speaking of the show years later, Bert Williams contended that he joined it with the purpose of earning money to attend Stanford University: "A bunch of us, three white boys and myself[,] thought it would be nice and easy to make spending money by touring through the small towns on the coast on a bus and giving entertainments."[48]

It is not clear whether the show was a minstrel show, but it was run by Lew Johnson, one of the many important minstrel-show-company managers of the late nineteenth century. The story about Williams joining the Lew Johnson show comes from Booker T. Washington:

> One day, a colored man named Lew Johnson, who kept a barbershop in San Francisco, asked Bert Williams if he did not want to join a little company that he intended to take up along the coast to play the lumber camps between San Francisco and Eureka, and then come back by way of the mining camps at the western edge of the mountains.[49]

But the experience with Johnson's company was a horrible one. Williams later recalled:

> We got back to San Francisco without a stitch of clothing, literally without a stitch, as the few rags I wore to spare the hostility of the police had to be burned for reasons that everyone will understand who has read of the experiences of the soldiers in the trenches.[50]

It was the first time Williams had encounted racism. With much anger, Williams complained:

> It was then that I first ran up against the humiliation and persecution that have to be faced by every person of colored blood, no matter what his brains, education, or the integrity of his conduct. How many times have hotel keepers said to me, "I know you Williams, and I like you, and I would like nothing better than to have you stay here, but you see, we have Southern gentlemen in the house and they would object."[51]

After the Lew Johnson show Williams thought of creative ways to utilize his talent. Because he was light skinned, he got a job impersonating a Polynesian. According to Mabel Rowland:

> A group of Hawaiians heard him sing and they told him that if he could consent to become a Hawaiian wearing the white blouse with the yellow lei around his neck and learn to play the guitar and sing their songs with them, he would have steady work for some months. This he did.[52]

Finally, sometime in 1893, Williams got a job offer from William Selig,[53] who owned the Martin and Selig's Minstrels. Selig later became an important figure in the early motion picture business. Terry Ramsaye recorded a version of the meeting between Williams and Selig:

> Selig paused on the street one day to observe a lonely, forlornly, idle darky. He was a yellow boy. He yawned a deep, wide open watermelon expanse of mouth and settled himself to let the sunshine soak in. He saw Selig looking at him and smiled. The smile was approxmiately one foot on its major axis. Selig admired it greatly.
> "Boy, want a job?"

"Whut at, boss?" the yellow boy was casually interested.
"In a minstrel show—just stand up and open your mouth, that's your act."
"I most suttinly kin, boss. When does we start?"[54]

When Williams accepted the job from Selig, he did not know it would be a turning point in his life. In fact, this job would bring him into contact with the man who would be his partner and ticket to fame: George William Walker.

Chapter 2

I was in San Francisco with Martin & Selig's Mastodon Minstrels, composed of five whites, one Mexican and four colored minstrels. The Mexican drove the four-horse team and played trombone.[1]

The minstrel show is the key to understanding the format of what became Williams's stage persona – the burnt cork makeup, or blackface. Although black professional minstrels did not appear until after the Civil War,[2] the history of minstrelsy itself dates back to the early nineteenth century.

> Blackface minstrelsy was a form of theatrical performance that emerged during the 1820s and reached its zenith during the years 1850–70. Essentially, it consisted of an exploitation of the slave's style of music and dancing by white men who blackened their faces with burnt cork and went on the stage to sing "Negro songs" (also called "Ethiopian songs"), to perform dances derived from those of the slaves, and to tell jokes based on slave life. Two basic types of slave impersonations were developed: one a caricature of the plantation slave and his ragged clothes and thick dialect; the other portraying the city slave, the dandy dressed in the latest fashion, who boasted of his exploits among the ladies. The former was referred to as Jim Crow and the latter as Zip Coon.[3]

Although one of the original purposes of minstrelsy was to imitate the black man as closely as possible, before long, white minstrels stopped presenting realistic stage characterizations of blacks. "Entertainers and songwriters began to treat the black man less sensitively than earlier, presenting him instead as a comic figure to be ridiculed."[4] Stage makeup – especially the use of burnt cork, enormous painted lips, and popping eyes – became the standard minstrel man's appearance. Minstrels played in many places where people had never seen slaves or free blacks and wanted to believe that these people were different from themselves. Therefore some minstrels called themselves "Ethiopian delineators."

But since some minstrel troupes included black religious songs, which had been given wide recognition by the Fisk Jubilee Singers and the Hampton Student Singers, these features also attracted an audience:

> A minstrel show lasted for an hour and forty-five minutes. The bandsmen sat

11

on an elevated platform on the stage. In front of them were the performers in the traditional semi-circle formations, soloists in front and supporting company behind.[5]

Most minstrels knew how to play a musical instrument or at least sing and dance. The instruments frequently used in shows were banjos, tambourines, fiddles, and bone castanets.[6] In the center of the semicircle sat the interlocutor, or master of ceremonies:

> On the ends of the semi-circle sat the greatest stars of most companies, the comedians, Brudder Tambo and Brudder Bones — named from their instruments. Made up to give the appearance of large eyes and gaping mouths with huge lips set apart by brighter, more flamboyant dress, and using heavier, more ludicrous dialects, the endmen contorted their bodies in exaggerated gestures and twisted their words in endless puns in order to keep the audience laughing.[7]

It is important to note that the minstrel show, from its inception up to its demise, evolved in different forms. But it is agreed that,

> in its established form, the minstrel show consisted of three parts, the first contained songs and jokes, the second, called the *olio*, comprised a variety of specialty acts and ensemble numbers. Typically, a performance concluded with a "walk around finale," an act in which some of the performers sang and danced up front (on the stage) and the remainder of the company gave support from the back.[8]

When Bert Williams stepped onto Martin and Selig's minstrel stage, he suffered an acute case of stage fright:

> This was, incidently, Bert Williams' first appearance on any stage. Being light of hue, fifteen-sixteenths white in ancestry, he was ordered into burnt candle makeup. Stage fright overtook Williams in the first ensemble number, and the sweat of distress poured down his face. His makeup ran in streaks of alarming perpendicular zebra effect. When the end man fired his funny question at Williams, the novice's eyes opened in terror and beads stood out on his forehead. He couldn't remember his lines. In dismay, his mouth flew open. The house roared. "If Ah says anything, those folks'll laugh at me." Williams backed out into the wings. His hit was made, in spite of him.[9]

It would be several years before Williams again attempted to wear blackface on stage.

After this episode, one of the end men in the minstrel show quit. Though legend has it that Williams and Walker met when this spot in the minstrel show became open, according to Bert Williams, that was not quite so. George Walker had arrived in San Francisco with Dr. Waite's medicine show from Lawrence, Kansas. Williams claimed: "George Walker was in town. He could dance and I was taking dance steps from him."

Thus the meeting between the two men was not the fortuitous street meeting biographers have portrayed. The men were already acquainted, and when Martin and Selig's show needed a replacement, Williams naturally turned to Walker for help:

> I asked him where I could find a certain fellow that I wished to get for the opposite end to me. We could not find him, and then I turned to George and said, "What's the use of looking any longer? You're the right man anyhow!"[10]

Thus began one of the most significant partnerships in American show business history. Walker said that the members of Martin and Selig's Minstrels were each paid seven dollars a week.

Around this time, claims theater critic Lester Walton, the team was joined by a third person: "While appearing with minstrel shows and theatrical companies of various kinds, a new partner was taken in the name of "Griff" Wilson, contortionist[,] and the new turn was named Wilson, Williams and Walker."[11]

Though contortionists were in demand for minstrel and vaudeville shows, neither Williams nor Walker in any of the interviews they gave or articles they wrote spoke of Griff Wilson. Furthermore, it is difficult to document any performances of Wilson, Williams, and Walker, since "the trio worked for quite a stretch in the West, but Williams and Walker began to long for the East."[12] Walter here implies that when Williams and Walker left California, Wilson remained behind. Walton was a lifelong friend of Bert Williams and knew him better than most people, but his assertion that Williams was originally part of a trio is dubious though interesting.

Life with the minstrel show was grueling. Bert Williams said:

> We were with that minstrel troupe for five months, getting our salary off and on. When we got it, his [Walker's] salary was $8 per week and cakes. I received $1 more for acting as stage manager. I think that we had three paydays that season. Once, we were stranded in Bakersfield. Tired and tried, we returned to Frisco, where for two years, we were at Halahan Horman's Midway.[13]

In an article published in the *New York Age*, George Walker wrote about "the Midway": "If you have ever been in San Francisco and can remember the old Creemore or the Midway, then you know the place of our maiden effort. It stood at 771 Market Street – but that was before the [1906] earthquake."[14]

The Midway Plaisance was once described by a San Francisco historian as

> a place on Market Street between Third and Fourth streets, which was opened originally as the Cremorne and later was called the Midway Plaisance. This was the first melodeon or music hall in San Francisco to make a special feature of hoochy-coochy dancers, or as the theatrical weekly *Variety* calls them, "torso-tossers and hip-wavers. . . ."

Virtue among its female entertainers was considered very detrimental to the best interests of the establishment. Like practically all of the other melodeons, it had a mezzanine floor cut up into booths, before which hung heavy curtains. A visitor who engaged a booth for the evening was entertained between acts by the female performers, and his conduct was not questioned as long as he continued to buy liquor.[15]

Williams and Walker found not only that the clientele was rough but so were the working hours for performers: The demanding schedule required a thirteen-hour day. Walker recalled: "We went on at 1:30 P.M. and were quite satisfied if permitted to come off at 4:00 A.M. We gave a continuous performance by ourselves."[16]

In 1893 the United States was experiencing an economic depression. One of California's largest cities at the time, San Francisco felt the economic squeeze. People were spending less, and the question was how to get them to spend more. A San Francisco newspaperman came up with an idea: "San Francisco should announce its intention to prosper despite the depression by presenting a 'Mid-Winter Fair,' advertising the climatic advantages of the city and California."[17]

Businessmen thought that San Francisco might be able to duplicate the success of Chicago's World's Columbian Exposition.

The Mid-Winter Fair opened officially on January 1, 1894, even though many exhibition buildings were not completed. More than eight thousand people thronged through the gates to see the various exotic exhibits:

"Step right in an' see the sea lions! ... Dancing gir-rls! Performance now begeens Ze Turkeesh dancing girls – danzing girls – danzing gir-r-rls! Only two beets, twenty-vive zents or a quarter of a dollar! Here ve haf de only – Animals trained to stand on their heads, turn somersaults, walk on rolling barrels and whatever else they are told to do. Wild and ferocious animals made as docile as the performing dogs and acrobatic monkeys! Only four bits, six bits and $1. The performance will begin in five minutes. Step inside. . . ." Thus the cries were heard as the visitors at the Fair walked about among the partially constructed buildings and along the picturesque driveways.[18]

Walker related:

In 1893, natives from Dahomey, Africa, were imported to San Francisco to be exhibited at the Mid-Winter Fair. They were late in arriving in time for the opening of the Fair, and Afro-Americans were employed and exhibited for native Dahomians. Williams and Walker were among the sham native Dahomians. After the arrival of the native Africans, the Afro-Americans were dismissed.[19]

By May 1894 the Dahomey Village had broken up, due to "tribal tension," the *San Francisco Examiner* reported. The chief, who was Afro-American, couldn't get along with the other "Dahomians":

"This man," said the *Examiner*, "used to own a whitewashing establishment on Brannan Street, but he abandoned that to become chief in the late Dahomey Village. Some of the other Dahomians happened to be men that he didn't care to associate with, even in disguise, and the Village broke up."[20]

Williams and Walker, however, had a different experience with the Africans. Walker continues the story:

Having had free access to the Fair grounds, we were permitted to visit the natives from Africa. It was there, for the first time, that we were brought into close touch with native Africans, and the study of those natives interested us very much. We were not long in deciding that if we ever reach the point of having a show of our own, we would delineate and feature native African characters and still remain American, and make our acting interesting and entertaining to American audiences.[21]

Bert Williams was also impressed by the Africans. He became an avid reader of African history and anthropology. An interviewer reported:

He has devoted some research to the history of the negro race and his copy of John Ogilby's *Africa*, published in 1670, is, I believe, one of the five still extant. . . . In showing it to me one day, and commenting upon the numerous kingdoms that flourished in Africa centuries ago, Williams said: "I suppose that with this volume, I could prove that every Pullman porter is the descendant of a king."[22]

After performing at the fair, Williams and Walker must have returned to the Midway Plaisance, since Williams claimed that the team played there for a total of two years. Although both men later described these times as fallow, they were in fact fertile. About 1895, the duo began composing songs. At first they published them with whatever Tin Pan Alley publishers they could find – usually firms like Howley, Havel and Company, and M. Witmark and Sons. They were among the first to recognize the marketability of black composers. In a time where there was as yet no recording industry or radio, the sale of published sheet music *was* the music industry.

By the turn of the century, a substantial amount of Williams and Walker's music was being published by Joseph W. Stern, a front-runner among Tin Pan Alley publishers in introducing new black music. Music scholar David Jasen notes:

The Stern Company was the first New York publisher to latch on to that captivating, toe-tapping piano music from Missouri called ragtime, when they bought the rights to Tom Turpin's 1897 St. Louis publication "Harlem Rag" in 1899.[23]

Among the Williams and Walker songs Stern published were "I Don't Like No Cheap Man," "He's Up Against the Real Thing Now," "The Ghost of a Coon," and "When It's All Goin' Out and Nothin' Comin' In."

A turning point for Williams and Walker occurred one day when another black vaudeville act, Joseph Hodges and Nina Lauchmere, saw them perform. According to vaudevillian Tom Fletcher:

> Hodges was so impressed with the kind of act they were doing that he had a talk with them and asked them if they would like to come east. Bert Williams said, "O.K. by me," and turned to his partner and asked, "How about it, Nash?" Nash was the name he called his partner, George Walker, because that had been the name of George's father.[24]

Sometime close to the end of 1895 or perhaps the beginning of 1896, Williams and Walker left San Francisco. According to Bert Williams:

> Gustave Walters, who formed the Orpheum [vaudeville] circuit, sent us to Los Angeles, where another act had made a failure. Clifford and Heath were the headliners. Our eyes popped out of our heads when Billy Clifford showed us $300 in gold. We stayed four, at $60 a week, and went from there to Denver. At Denver, a medicine man engaged us to go to Cripple Creek.[25]

George Walker had been in a medicine show, but Bert Williams had not. Biographers have claimed that Williams and Walker traveled in a medicine show in Texas or in Georgia. But the only autobiographical statement referring to a Williams and Walker appearance with quack doctors comes from Bert Williams's own testimony.

Because of the "wild frontier" atmosphere of Cripple Creek, Colorado, in 1895 and its history of labor strife, it is very probable that the medicine-show experience occurred there. Cripple Creek was a bustling gold rush town located about twenty-five miles west of Colorado Springs. Gold had been discovered there in 1890. By 1893 there were at least forty mines in the area, with new ones being prospected daily. The greed for gold soon pitted the mine owners against the miners:

> When the mine owners moved to extend the working day to ten hours with no increase in wages, the miners rebelled and demanded the restoration of their former wage-scale and recognition of their new union, the Western Federation of Miners. By February, 1894, most of the mines and many of the smelters around Cripple Creek had been closed down. Soon the area became an armed camp, the union men facing the local police and the state militia. . . . Tempers cooled, however, and in June, 1894, the strike was settled in the union's favor.[26]

Although the strike had been settled, tension among Cripple Creek people remained high. A historian of the area reported that Cripple Creek was a typical "Wild West" town: "Life at the camp was generally rough. Men were many and women few. Saloons and dance halls were numerous. The roads were poor and the city streets even worse."[27]

Mining towns like Cripple Creek were prejudiced against such recent immigrants as Italians, who wished to work in the mines. Some black people did manage to make a living in the Colorado mining districts, but they were a tiny minority. Miners were typically out-and-out "frontiersmen – the rough, hardy, fearless, independent, restrain[t]-hating type of manhood."[28] It was into this environment that Williams and Walker's medicine show traveled. On their arrival, they were attacked by a crowd of miners.

Mabel Rowland described the incident in her biography of Williams: "They were approached and questioned [about] their apparel, which struck the natives of this particular city as too good for them. They forced the men to disrobe, gave them some burlap sacking and drove off."[29]

Williams said of the medicine man:

> He got scared when he saw the miners and jumped his own show, but as we were already into his debt for $80, we did not care. With that money, we went to Chicago, reaching there with an outfit of music and in rags.[30]

In Chicago in 1895 Williams and Walker heard that black people were doing exciting things in theater. A few years before, a man named Sam T. Jack had had the genius to use black women in a musical. Only black males were allowed to perform in minstrel shows, but in Jack's *Creole Show*, black women were very prominent. There was even a chorus line of sixteen black women.[31] The *Creole Show* inspired a similar show, *The Octoroons*:

> Jack's advance man, John W. Isham, took the idea a step further. While preserving the overall three-part shape of the minstrel show, he eliminated the minstrel semi-circle, the formal introductions of an interlocutor, and the farci[c]al or punning wit of the endmen. Isham's new format amounted to a series of songs, dances, and specialty acts either preceding or following a thinly-plotted playlet, and the finale was a military drill and dance for the entire company.[32]

If it is true that Isham's *The Octoroons* broke with the prevailing minstrel influence, it is also true that it did not do so with its title. Moreover, pictures of the performers reveal that almost all the women were fair-skinned, or "yaller gals." Minstrels often parodied them in their skits:

> The alluring "yaller gal" . . . had the light skin and facial features of white women, combined with the exoticism and "availability" of Negroes. Almost always described as extremely beautiful and highly desirable, she, like the desirable white woman, was hard to win and harder to hold, but never coarse or mannerless. Only black women had these undesirable traits – never the sweet, graceful yellow girls. These were not comedy parts. Black women furnished the laughs. Yaller gals, generally called "octoroons" outside minstrelsy, provided coquettish, flirtatious, happy romances, and sad, untimely deaths.[33]

So while Isham consciously broke with some of the minstrel traditions, the *Indianapolis Freeman* praised *The Octoroons*, calling it "a well equipped company of colored artists" and describing "many in the company [as] superior to the average white performer."[34]

It was this innovative show for which Williams and Walker auditioned and were hired. They had never been with a large black show like this before. Williams and Walker's act was rough and worn from performing in dives like the Midway Plaisance and before audiences like gold miners.

"Much to their disappointment, however, Williams and Walker's act left the Chicago audience cold. They faced a major setback: they were dropped from the *Octoroons'* bill."[35] Jesse Shipp, later to become closely associated with Williams and Walker, was the stage manager of *The Octoroons*. He said that it wasn't because they had no talent, "because I knew they had; but with us . . . they had not even pleased."[36]

Bert Williams told what happened next:

> Walter J. Plummer gave us a start in Chicago. Montgomery and Stone [a blackface vaudeville act] had been booked for the Musee, Pittsburgh. They refused to fill the engagement and we took their place. That helped us to more work.[37]

Coming back west from Pittsburgh, Williams and Walker played in Detroit. They were booked into the Wonderland Theatre, a vaudeville house on Woodward Avenue. Williams had tried blackface before, while in his first minstrel show. But at that time he was so gripped by stage fright that he never gave himself a chance to feel comfortable with blackface. Now, with experience under his belt, Williams felt more confident. He had begun to experiment with songwriting and had finished his first song:

> One day at Moore's Wonderland in Detroit, just for a lark, I blackened my face and tried the song, "Oh, I Don't Know, You're Not So Warm." Nobody was more surprised than me when it went like a house on fire. Then I began to find myself.[38]

Nevertheless, Williams gradually became the comedian of the duo and Walker played the straight man. Although the original name of the act was Walker and Williams, somewhere along the line they decided to reverse the billing. Williams's emergence as a comedian may have had something to do with this. The timing was ominous, however, for their next engagement would lead to their big break. As George Walker described it:

> We had gone from Chicago to Louisville and were trying to make it a round trip without being at all impeded by accumulated treasure. Now, we were long on leisure and found some white professionals who were also the possessors of some spare golden moments; so . . . we all decided to devote a week to mending our health at West Baden [Indiana] and to give a "common wealth" show one night during the week to meet the bills incident to the mending. It was this show that Canary saw when he "rediscovered" us.[39]

William Foster gave a different account of the Indiana trip. According to Foster, Williams and Walker were desperate for work:

It was about this time when a Chicago agent got an order to rush a vaudeville show to West Baden, Indiana. Unengaged acts were scarce in Chicago, and to make up the bill he had to take on Williams and Walker. The show was being staged for the entertainment of a session of the Show Managers of America.[40]

Thomas Canary was the manager of *The Gold Bug*, a musical set to open in New York in September 1896. Canary was impressed with Williams and Walker. Williams said that Canary offered at first to engage them for a revue called *The Passing Show*:

> "But before that came off," said Williams, "we got a telegram from him saying that 'if we could get to New York by September 14th, we could have an engagement in *The Gold Bug*.' If we could get there! As if we wouldn't have crawled there on our knees!"[41]

Chapter 3

*T*he *Gold Bug* was the third operetta by Irish-born Victor Herbert (1859–1924), who was raised in England and Germany. Today he is remembered as the composer of such beloved operettas as *Babes in Toyland* and *Naughty Marietta*. According to operetta historian Richard Traubner, Herbert's music was characterized by

> an unmistakable wistfulness and charm, whether the setting of the operetta was in Hungary, New Orleans or Toyland. . . . But Herbert was also guilty – with his librettists – of lapsing into the childish triteness and quaintness so unfortunately popular at the turn of the century.[1]

Herbert had immigrated to the United States with his wife in the early 1890s to take a job as a cellist with the Metropolitan Opera in New York City. But before long he had embarked on a career as a composer.

Herbert's first operetta, *Prince Ananias*, ran only for 55 performances in 1894. But his second, *The Wizard of the Nile*, which ran for 105 performances, made him "a name to be reckoned with."[2]

The Gold Bug had a controversial libretto about miscegenation, by Glen MacDonough. Gerald Bordman records that the plot "revolved around Willetfloat, the Secretary of the Navy. . . . The skeleton in his closet is the Indian wife he deserted. His daughter by her, Wawayanda . . . appears and blackmails him into abetting her romance." The play was in two acts.[3] "The first act unfolded in Washington . . . the second on the deck of the cruiser *Gold Bug*. Hence, the name of the operetta."[4]

The Gold Bug was plagued by numerous production problems. "Much of the show's troubles stemmed from delaying the opening night several times. Even on that first night, many costumes were not ready."[5] It also featured a lackluster cast – Max Figman, Molly Fuller, Henry Norman, Robert Fisher, and Marie Cahill. (The last was the only performer who was applauded by critics and emerged from obscurity.) With these problems on his mind, producer George Lederer decided to audition Williams and Walker. Years later, Lederer wrote about that audition:

> In seeking material to build up some bad spots, someone brought word to me of a team of natural colored minstrels who had been encountered in a honky

tonk cafe in West Baden, Indiana. Reaching out for straws, I sent for the team. It was Williams and Walker. We gave them a hearing a day or so before "The Gold Bug" was to open, but the consensus of opinion of the invited audience was that not only were they mediocre material, but also that their color would be found to mediate against their chance of success on a legitimate stage. I bowed to the will of the majority.[6]

The failure of Williams and Walker's audition was also due to the fact that *The Gold Bug*'s orchestra couldn't play Bert Williams's ragtimelike song: "Oh, I Don't Know, You're Not So Warm." To musicians trained to play European music, black music was foreign. George Lederer explained:

> When the orchestra had been given the Williams and Walker music to play at the preliminary rehearsal, it had all but declared a strike. The musicians couldn't interpret it. It was a new kind of music for them. Syncopation wasn't new to the musicians of a score years ago, but the kind of cut-back and criss-cross harmonizing the Williams and Walker music sheets carried was a jigsaw puzzle to the men in the orchestra.[7]

The Gold Bug opened Monday, September 21, 1896, at the Casino Theater – without Williams and Walker. The Casino, at Broadway and Thirty-ninth Street, was for many years one of New York's most popular musical theaters.[8] But the Casino's popularity could not overcome the deficiences of *The Gold Bug*. The opening night reviews in the September 22, 1896, newspapers were awful.

Faced by the specter of a box-office failure, Lederer was desperate. He wrote: "Discouraged by *The Gold Bug*'s opening night fiasco to a point where I was considering its abrupt closing before a second performance, I decided at the last minute to give the show with the two wayfarers from Indiana."[9]

The major problem was getting the orchestra to learn Bert Williams's music. The conductor rehearsed the orchestra before the second night's performance until they gave a passable rendition:

> "Max Hoffman . . . had done the orchestration for the team," said Lederer. "And in my opinion, Hoffman should be put down as the first musician ever successfully to interpret the instinctive melodies of the coon music that Williams and Walker were among the first to introduce."[10]

Although Williams and Walker were not named in the theater program of *The Gold Bug*, they did their own number in one of the "variety turns" listed. Lederer was delighted with them:

> The second night's show of *The Gold Bug* proved as spiritless as the premiere, but the audience couldn't get enough of Williams and Walker. It was the first time I had ever seen a musical muke [sic] team stop a show, and they stopped *The Gold Bug* that night until they eventually gave out physically. Their *gem de resistance* was, "Oh, I Don't Know, You're Not So Warm."[11]

Victor Herbert's operetta music, including the now-famous "Gold Bug March," was virtually ignored by the critics: "This piece," said the *New York Dramatic Mirror*, " is neither a farce, burlesque or comic opera, but an incongruous blending of all three . . . The show is a pretentious variety show, thinly and transparently disguised."

In an apparent reference to Williams and Walker, however, the critic was gentler: "The success of the performances . . . depended in large measure upon the cleverness of the people brought together by the management for the purpose of galvanizing the piece with their individual humor."[12]

The kind remarks of critics about Williams and Walker were not enough to save the production, and after a week's run, it closed.[13] The *New York Times* critic breathed a sigh of relief:

> The Casino follies have never before put forth a show so stupid. Somehow, the mere suggestion of political satire depresses people in a playhouse, perhaps because all the possible jokes about lobbying, office-seeking, and vote-buying have been done to death.[14]

Out of a job, Williams and Walker took whatever they could get. About a week after *The Gold Bug* closed, Williams joined a new show out of town. He recalled: "We were with Peter F. Dailey in 'A Good Thing at the Hollis Theatre.'"[15] It was advertised as "a musical farce in three acts by John J. McNally."

McNally was famous for his popular revival of the musical *Evangeline*. The program for *A Good Thing* named "Bert A. Williams as servant" and "George W. Walker as waiter." Although these were stereotypical roles, at least Williams and Walker were given official credit. In terms of plot, *A Good Thing* seemed to be difficult to grasp. The *Boston Globe* complained that "there is the faintest outline of story exploited. . . . What little story the play contains runs about."[16]

The plot ostensibly has to do with an auctioneer and his clerk and their involvement with a "female seminary." The theater program lists specialties from Flora Irvins, Williams and Walker, and Peter F. Daily in the third act. It was this act, said the *Globe*, that "sets matters right to the satisfaction of the audience."[17]

When *A Good Thing* closed in Boston, after a weeklong run, Williams and Walker returned to New York.

Bert Williams recalled that next "We got one week with the Sandow show, in which were El Captain and Wood and Shepard and others."[18] The "Sandow Show" starred a German-born strongman, Eugene Sandow (?–1925). A muscle-builder, Sandow created a sensation in the American entertainment world due to Florenz Ziegfeld's management.

In his book *The Vaudevillians*, Anthony Slide summarized the Sandow attraction:

It was Ziegfeld who starred Sandow at the Chicago World Fair in August of 1893, when the strongman was said to have held a grown man on the palm of his hand, lifted a piano with several men on it and finally had three horses walk across a plank over his stomach. In addition, Ziegfeld had the idea of exploiting Sandow's body by having him appear in the briefest of shorts (thus creating a sensation with the ladies).[19]

But by 1896 Ziegfeld had stopped managing Sandow in favor of singer Anna Held. Thus it is unlikely that Ziegfeld would have met Bert Williams at the time.

The Sandow show opened in New York's Grand Opera House at Eighth Avenue and Twenty-third Street on October 10, 1896. Nothing is known of Williams and Walker's act in that show. Perhaps the closest description of their act at that time comes from George Walker. Early in their career, Walker wrote:

> We thought that as there seemed to be a great demand for black faces on the stage, we would do all we could to get what we felt belonged to us by the laws of nature. We finally decided that as white men with black faces were billing themselves "coons," Williams and Walker would do well to bill themselves the "Two Real Coons," and so we did.[20]

In other words Williams and Walker did their best to clown and joke as authentic "darkies" or "coons." But Sandow's vaudeville show was built around *him*; young unknown performers like Williams and Walker couldn't compete against a freak attraction like strongman Sandow. However, even Sandow was vulnerable. The *Dramatic Mirror* reported the only noteworthy item about the show: "Sandow's right eye was bruised one night last week at the Grand Opera House. The platform which he holds wobbled and struck him in the eye, causing a painful wound."[21]

Almost on that disastrous note, the show closed. It had run only a week, just like *The Gold Bug*.

The *Dramatic Mirror* said that the show had been losing money: "The company was booked on first-class theatres, but business did not warrant its continuance."[22] By this time Williams and Walker were discouraged. Within three weeks' time, they had appeared in three shows. All had been failures, and all had placed them in minor roles. They approached George Lederer, the producer of their first outing–*The Gold Bug*. Later Walker said that Lederer's suggestion resulted in a break for him and his partner: "George Lederer induced Will A. McConnel to put us on at Koster and Bial's. Then came thirty-six consecutive weeks of what you may call 'velvet.'"[23]

Chapter 4

Moving to vaudeville at Koster and Bial's was significant for Bert Williams and George Walker because in doing so, they were entering the mainstream of American entertainment of their day. During the late nineteenth century, vaudeville became a major form of American theater and, as one historian notes, the first to have standardized formats.¹ Many of the country's best-known entertainers would get their start in this medium. But what was it?

Although the term *vaudeville* is of decidedly French origin (the word derives from the French *Val de Vire*–sometimes *Vau de Vire*–the valley of the Vire River in Normandy, where quaint and sprightly songs and ballads were sung),² its evolution has a definite American flavor. Circuses, riverboat shows, dime museums, minstrel shows, medicine shows–all offered in their own way a type of "variety" bill. In England variety took place in music halls. A variety show implied a type of circus affair; various acts were presented onstage. These might be acrobatic acts, magic acts, jugglers, comedians, singers, and dancers. Early variety establishments provided liquor and coarse entertainment for mostly male audiences. In 1881 Antonio ("Tony") Pastor became the first vaudeville manager in the United States to break with the tradition of bawdy material and to offer "clean" variety. B. F. Keith and E. F. Albee conceived the idea of a "continuous performance" of vaudeville. In order to increase revenues, they adopted Pastor's dictum. Keith said to his performers: "Clean up your acts! Make them in all respects fit for decent women, and you will draw larger audiences and make more money."³

A typical vaudeville bill usually had a "dumb act," one with no talking, which could be a group of acrobats or tumblers. The number two act might be a singing and dancing act, but it could be anything. The third spot on the bill was varied:

> The main purpose was to wake up the audience [a comedy, dramatic sketch, or a magician]. . . . Then came a "corker" of an act, a big name, something elaborate. . . . Number Five had to be a big act, another big name, a star as important as any other on the bill.⁴

After a short intermission, an act was needed to sustain the audience's attention but not to "wow" them. This was reserved for the following act, next to closing: "Next-to-closing was the most important act of all. The last act was universally referred to as the 'chaser,' one designed to clear the house quickly and yet be the type that would delight those patrons who would remain seated."[5]

At $1,500 a week, the star or next-to-closing act was the highest-paid variety bill feature, while the opening act often received as low as $150 a week.[6] These fees were fixed by the vaudeville circuits run by managers like Keith and Albee.

> These circuits divided into what was usually identified as either "bigtime" or "smalltime." . . . In the main the "bigtime meant only two shows a day," an afternoon then an evening performance. "Smalltime" could mean anything from three to a dozen shows a day.[7]

The home of the big time before 1913 was Oscar Hammerstein's Victoria Theater at Broadway and Forty-second Street. After 1913, B. F. Keith's Palace became the mecca of vaudeville.

The music hall at Sixth Avenue and Twenty-third Street was one of the major vaudeville houses in New York City during its twenty-four year history. The managers, John Koster and Rudolf Bial, were primarily saloonkeepers who sought to increase their profit by offering entertainment for their patrons: "The partners skirted the existing laws against serving alcoholic beverages in a theatre by substituting for the theatre curtain a folding fan which would rise from the small stage to reveal the succession of performers."[8]

In this respect Koster and Bial were continuing the pre–Pastor variety show tradition of serving liquor. But by including ethnic humor in their shows, they were very much in keeping with contemporary trends:

> Vaudeville comedy was socially sanctioned fun-making. . . . From the earliest beginnings of variety, vaudeville acts reflected and re-enforced Irish, Black, Jewish, Dutch-German stereotypes, to name a few. . . . Ironically, many of the actors who promoted the stereotypes were themselves from the group in question.[9]

In the November 7, 1896, issue of the *New York Dramatic Mirror*, the opening of Williams and Walker at Koster and Bial's was reviewed:

> Williams and Walker made their first Eastern appearance in high class vaudeville here and scored an immediate success. The dude member of the team (Walker) does various funny walks, and the common everyday nigger (Williams) has only to open his mouth to bring laughs. He has a deep voice and sings a song called, "Oh, I Don't Know, You Ain't So Warm," with the greatest possible unction. The song would not be much use to anyone but him, and he makes the most of it. Their act is rather crude, and if it were properly fixed by an expert farce writer, it would be an immense hit.[10]

Through the end of 1896, Williams and Walker received good reviews, leaving Koster and Bial for Proctor's Theatre in December. By now, the *New York Dramatic Mirror* had learned to expect quality performances from the duo, and it said the pair "scored a hit as usual with their song, 'You Ain't So Warm.'" In January 1897, however, they were back at Koster and Bial's, making "their big hit with real 'coon' business."[11]

During the second week of January, they revised their act. Playing on a bill headlined by French actress Yvette Guilbert, Williams and Walker sang "You Ain't So Warm," and they performed a cakewalk, in which they were joined by two young women. They were Stella Wiley, who became the wife of Bob Cole, and Aida Reed Overton, who became George Walker's wife.[12]

The story of Aida Reed Overton is an interesting one, given later in this book. Here it is sufficient to note that Aida Overton (originally she spelled it Ada, changing it after she achieved stardom; Reed was her stepfather's name) was a member of the Black Patti Troubadours in 1896, when Bob Cole and other blacks had a dispute with the company's managers. William Foster records that when the disagreement between the Black Patti company and the managers began, Aida retired temporarily from the stage.[13]

Sometime late in 1896, the American Tobacco Company approached Williams and Walker and requested that they pose with some women in an advertisement for one of their products: Old Virginia Sheroots. George Walker persuaded his girlfriend, Stella Wiley, to find another girl to pose with her for the tobacco advertisement. Stella Wiley found Aida Reed. Aida posed for the photos, collected twenty dollars as pay, and went back home.[14]

> Some time later, the manager of Williams and Walker saw the cakewalking pictures in a show window. He decided to produce the dance on the stage, but to get the value of the publicity of the tobacco industry, he insisted on the same costumes and the same girls. When Walker sent for Miss Reed this time, she refused to come. Her experience on the stage had not been any too pleasant, and she had decided to give up a theatrical career for good. When his messenger returned with Aida's refusal, Walker decided to go see her for himself. Several visits were required to obtain Aida's consent, and then she agreed to join the show only so long as the company played in New York.[15]

The American Tobacco Company granted permission to John Stark & Sons, a music publishing company, to copy the photograph poses used in their advertisement for Old Virginia Sheroots. A line drawing was made for the cover sheet music of Scott Joplin's "Maple Leaf Rag." "It depicts two black couples in decorous dress as if engaged in or on their way to a cakewalk."[16] Music scholars have christened this edition of "Maple Leaf Rag" the St. Louis edition. (There is no evidence that Williams ever met Scott Joplin.) David Jasen says that there is no doubt that the couples depicted on this edition of "Maple Leaf Rag" were Bert Williams, George Walker, Stella Wiley, and Aida Overton Walker.[17] Bert Williams appears in similar costume on the sheet music cover of the 1897 song "Oh, I Don't Know, You're Not So Warm."

The origin of the cakewalk can be traced back to the walkaround part of the minstrel show. The white minstrel show performers attempted to imitate "slaves who dressed up in high fashion and mimicked the formal dances of their masters."[18] White minstrel players, and later black minstrels, made the dance the grand finale of the show. Though the precise choreographic evolution of the dance is unclear, several theories have been offered.

According to Lynne Fauley Emery, the cakewalk started in slavery as a "chalk-line walk."[19] Terry Waldo claims that the dance evolved through a process of socialization. During the ragtime era, he says: "The cakewalk was being performed by blacks imitating whites who were imitating blacks who were imitating whites."[20] Although these theories are debatable, it is certain that there were a number of interpreters and versions of the dance. Charlie Johnson and Dora Dean, the Black Patti Troubadours, and John Isham's Octoroons were a few of the interpreters.

So by 1898, when Williams and Walker performed the dance, their version was simply one of many. The vaudeville dancer Jack Donahue remembers that "Walker did a neat cakewalk, much like the strut of today." Carl Van Vechten recalled: "How the fellow did prance in the cakewalk , throwing his chest and his buttocks out in opposite directions, until he resembled a pouter pigeon more than a human being!"[21]

Bert Williams's style of dancing was original as well as funny, and in fact it was the disparity between Williams's and Walker's dancing that made their rendition unique. The dancer James Barton describes how Williams danced: "Williams brought down the house with a terrific Mooche or Grind – a sort of shuffle, combining rubberlegs with rotating hips."[22] Another observer said of Williams: "He had ... a trick step I'll never forget – he'd raise one knee waist-high with his foot back underneath him and then hitch the other foot up to it, traveling across the stage."[23]

Not everyone cared for cakewalks, however; the black sociologist W. E. B. DuBois, self-appointed leader of the "Talented Tenth" or black middle class, frowned on the dance. He considered it a form of recreation fit only for lower class people. In the *Philadelphia Negro: A Social Study* in 1899, Dubois wrote:

> The most innocent amusements of this class are the balls and cakewalks, although they are accompanied by much drinking and are attended by white and black prostitutes. The cakewalk is a rhythmic promenade or slow dance, and when well done is pretty and quite innocent.[24]

But since their cakewalking was successful, Williams and Walker could afford to ignore critics like DuBois. They expanded their act until it became practically a cakewalk ball, delighting the critic of the *Dramatic Mirror*:

> Williams and Walker put on a big cakewalk last week, which made an instantaneous hit. After they had finished their songs, a drum major appeared, juggling a baton. He was followed by a master of ceremonies, who was full of life and action, and who led on the seven couples who took part in the walk. Each couple got a chance to show their steps, and as they stalked or pranced around the stage, the audience was kept in constant laughter. Finally, Williams and Walker appeared and their two girls with the café au lait complexions. Their actions were more eccentric than any of the others, and it is to be presumed that they won the cake. The walk had been well rehearsed, and was full of colored fun.[25]

The *Indianapolis Freeman* also reviewed the act, giving a graphic description of the cakewalk dance. First George Walker danced:

> The airy man's attire is gorgeous. Pointed shoes, tight trousers, red and white striped shirtfront, and shining silk hat that are not out of harmony with mock diamonds that are as big as marbles. ... Away up stage, he and his partner meet and curtsey, she with the utmost grace, he with exaggerated courtliness. Then down they trip, his elbow squared, his hat held upright by the brim, and with a mincing gait. ... With every step, his body sways from side to side, and the outstretched elbows see-saw but the woman clings to the arm, and this grandest of entities is prolonged 'til the footlights are reached. Then, a turn at right-angles brings another curtsey before the two pass parallel to the footlights.

Next Bert Williams danced: "The other chap's rig is rusty, and his joints work jerkily, but he has his own ideas about high stepping, and carves them out in a walk that starts like his companion's but ends at the other side of the stage."

Finally, George Walker walked off with both women:

> Then the first fellow takes both women, one on each arm, and leaving the other man grimacing, vengefully, starts on a second tour of grace. Even then, he walks across the front of the stage with that huge smile wide open, and goes off, leaving the impression that he'd had a pretty good time, too.[26]

In March 1897, Williams and Walker appeared at the Bijou Theatre in Philadelphia. Their vaudeville act was lauded by the *Dramatic Mirror*, which stated that they were "the greatest comedy act ever witnessed in this city."[27] In April 1897 the comedy team were back in New York appearing with famous actor Maurice Barrymore, who often played vaudeville in the 1890s. The vaudeville bill was esoteric. It included "a man of the world" by Augustus Thomas, the biograph (a movie), the male Patti (a countertenor), Morris's educated ponies, and T. W. Eckert and Lillie Bug.[28] In her memoirs, Ethel Barrymore attributed the performance with Williams and Walker to her brother Lionel, although it is clear from the reviews that it was her father, Maurice, who was involved:

> Once when Lionel was playing in vaudeville, he was standing in the wings to watch Bert Williams' technique, as he did at every performance. One of the stagehands said, "Like him, huh?"
> Lionel said, "Yes. He's terrific."
> And the stagehand said, just as Williams came off stage and passed him, "Yeah, he's a good nigger, knows his place."
> And Williams mumbled, "Yes, a good nigger knows his place. Going there now. Dressing Room One!"[29]

The New York reviews of both Barrymore and Williams and Walker were positive:

> Maurice Barrymore played the second and last week of his engagement, and attracted many of his audiences to this cosy home of vaudeville. Williams and Walker, the two "real coons," had their first appearances here and scored a genuine hit with their unique speciality, "You Ain't So Warm," and the cake walk was applauded to the echo. They made their last appearance on Friday evening, as they had to leave for Europe on Saturday.[30]

Williams and Walker appeared for one week in April 1897 at the Empire Theatre in London, which was basically a music hall. The London newspaper, *Pall Mall Gazette*, advertized the big draw of the show as the Monte Cristo Ballet. Years later Williams recalled that disastrous engagement: "I was at the Empire in London and went on immediately after the ballet, and promptly died. That taught me to know better than to try to follow a ballet."[31]

During the summer of 1897, Williams and Walker continued to play vaudeville at Koster and Bial's, as well as other variety houses in New York and Boston. In July they appeared at Keith's Theatre in Boston to the following advertisement:

> Return of the "Real Coons" Cleverest Colored Men on the American Stage, Williams and Walker in the Greatest Negro Comedy Act Ever Given in Vaudeville. New Dialogue, New Songs, New Dances and the Most effective closing act ever witnessed.[32]

The bill included the opera baritone Thomas E. Clifford and a Biograph film showing the Harvard College varsity team taking a boat from the water. The *Boston Daily Globe* noted the improvement in the Williams and Walker act over the prior season, saying, "These colored artists are funmakers in the highest order."[33]

The following week the Boston press gossiped that the comic duo "will present something new this week." The "something new" seems to have been new coon songs. One ad named them: "I'll Make That Black Girl Mine" and "I Don't Have to Stand No Nigger Foolin,'" but it is not known whether Williams and Walker were the authors of the songs.[34]

By the autumn of 1897 Williams and Walker had joined Hyde's Comedians – a vaudeville traveling troupe headlined by the famous blackface comic team of McIntyre and Heath, white entertainers. The variety show drew wide praise, as evidenced by this San Francisco review:

> At the Orpheum . . . they have had one of the best collections of vaudeville talent that we have seen here for some time. There is not a dull feature on the programme, and business has been exceedingly large. . . . Williams and Walker do a cakewalk that is excellent and sing many funny songs.[35]

However, a review of Williams and Walker with McIntyre and Heath at New York's Proctor Theatre showed that the black comedians had to work hard to compete with the established white comics:

> McIntyre and Heath and Williams and Walker presented black-face turns. The former was made up, and the latter were the real thing. The make-believe coons made the audience laugh more than their dusky brethren, but the latter made a big hit with their songs and dances. Williams sang a new song called "I Doan' Want No Cheap Man." It parodied the young girl who demands the high life from her suitors.[36]

By 1898 Williams and Walker were recognized as unique cakewalkers. James Weldon Johnson recalled that they tried to capitalize on this reputation. On January 16, 1898, they visited the home of one of New York's wealthiest men, William Henry Vanderbilt, the son of Cornelius ("Commodore") Vanderbilt, who had made his fortune in the railroad and shipping industries. As a publicity stunt Williams and Walker left Vanderbilt a letter, challenging him to a cakewalk contest. The letter read:

> To Mr. William K. Vanderbilt
> Corner of Fifty-Second Street and Fifth Avenue
> New York
>
> Dear Sir:
>
> In view of the fact that you have made a success as a cakewalker, having appeared in a semi-public exhibition and having posed as an expert in that capacity, we, the undersigned world-renowned cakewalkers, believing that the attention of the public has been distracted from us on account of the tremendous hit which you have made, hereby challenge you to compete with us in a cake-walking match, which will decide which of us shall deserve the title of champion cake-walker of the world.
>
> As a guarantee of good faith, we have this day deposited at the office of the New York *World* the sum of $50. If you purpose proving to the public that you are really an expert cake-walker, we shall be pleased to have you cover that amount and name the day on which it will be convenient for you to try odds against us.

Very truly yours,

Williams and Walker[37]

There is no record that Vanderbilt accepted the challenge.

It was around this time, when they were teaming with Hyde's Comedians, that Williams and Walker met the man who was destined to make them famous: Will Marion Cook.

Chapter 5

Will Marion Cook (1869–1944) was one of the pivotal figures in the history of early black musical theater. Unlike many of his peers, Cook had trained to be a classical musician. Eileen Southern writes that Cook

> revealed musical talent early and was sent to study violin at Oberlin when he was only fifteen. During the years 1887–89, he worked with the great violinist Joseph Joachim in Berlin, Germany, and in later years (1894–95) attended the National Conservatory of Music, where he studied with Dvořák and John White, among others.[1]

Like many other talented blacks, Cook found the intellectual climate and tolerance of blacks in Europe suited to his creativity. On his return to America, therefore, Cook was far more militant and demanding in his expectations than were other black musicians. One music historian noted:

> He had received cultured and humane treatment in Europe and refused to tolerate anything less in America. Faced with American prejudice and the normal frustrations and competitions of the professional music world, Cook became ever more suspicious of people's motives and more ill-tempered. Cook was not a loner by nature, but he tended to isolate himself, often moving quickly to insult or call into question others' motives. He was bound to run into trouble in a business that relied heavily upon personal contacts, friendship, and mutual trust.[2]

It was common practice for critics to be restrained in their praise of black performers during the 1890s. For example, Bert Williams was frequently referred to as "the greatest colored comedian." When similar accolades were given Cook after his debut at Carnegie Hall, he was offended. Duke Ellington gave the following account:

> When he first returned to New York and did a concert at Carnegie Hall, he had a brilliant critique the next day in a newspaper. The reviewer said that Will Marion was definitely "the world's greatest Negro violinist." "Yes, Mr. Cook," the man said, "And I meant it all. . . ." With that, Dad Cook took out his violin and smashed it across the reviewer's desk. "I am not the world's greatest Negro violinist," he exclaimed. "I am the greatest violinist in the world!". . . He never picked up a violin again in his life.[3]

This incident and a dispute with composer Antonín Dvořák eventually led to Cook's association with Williams and Walker. In an autobiographical article Cook explained: "I was barred ... from the classes at the National Conservatory of Music because I wouldn't play my fiddle in the orchestra under Dvořák. ... Dvořák didn't like me anyway; Harry T. Burleigh was his pet."[4]

The argument with Dvořák was a serious setback for Cook. There were very few opportunities for trained black classical musicians, and it was almost impossible to advance professionally without the support of important musicians like Dvořák. There was nowhere for Cook to turn to except the world of black theater.

In 1898 Bert Williams and George Walker lived together in a flat on West Fifty-third Street in New York City, in an area known as "Black Bohemia." Many black theatrical people lived in the hotels and boardinghouses in the area, the most famous being the Marshall and Maceo hotels.[5]

George Walker said that when he and Williams first moved to New York in 1896,

> The first move was to hire a flat on Fifty-Third Street, furnish it and throw our doors open to all colored men who possessed theatrical and musical ability and ambition. The Williams and Walker flat soon became the headquarters of all the artistic young men of our race who were stage-struck. Among those who frequented our home were ... Will Marion Cook.[6]

Cook said: "I met Williams and Walker and gave them my ideas on creating a story of how the cakewalk came about in Louisiana in the early 1880's." Since Williams and Walker were then associated with the cakewalk, they were thrilled at Cook's proposal. Cook continued: "Williams and Walker made a few suggestions to me ... It was for them that I wrote the show."[7]

Paul Laurence Dunbar (1892–1906) became Cook's partner on the project, which was known as *Clorindy, or The Origin of the Cakewalk*. By 1898 Dunbar was already established as one of the country's leading poets. Like Williams and Walker, he was attracted to the stage and consented to work with Cook on *Clorindy*. After Cook and Dunbar had composed the music and lyrics for the show, Cook said, "Williams and Walker came through Washington with the Hyde and Behman show, on their way to the coast."[8] Williams and Walker lent Cook money to go to New York to play the music for a Tin Pan Alley publisher. But the music publisher wasn't interested. "He thought I must be crazy to believe that any Broadway audience would listen to Negroes singing Negro operas,"[9] Cook said. Finally Edward Everett Rice, manager of the Casino Roof Garden at the Casino Theater, allowed Cook to perform his *Clorindy*. The problem now was to get hold of Williams and Walker, whom Cook wanted to star in the piece. Unfortunately they were still in Chicago with Hyde's Comedians (the Hyde and Behman show). Cook had to settle for comedian Ernest Hogan as his star. On July 5, 1898, *Clorindy* opened to wild acclaim. It enjoyed a modest run throughout the summer of 1898. Cook was ecstatic about his first theatrical success. "Negroes were at last on Broadway and there to stay," he proclaimed.[10]

But *Clorindy* was a disappointment for Dunbar: Williams and Walker were unable to perform in the piece, and Dunbar's libretto had to be scrapped because it would have made the late-night performance too long. "Dunbar and his wife were present on opening night. . . . As Dunbar listened to the lyrics he had helped to write, he felt a sense of embarrassment. The musical was in the worst of the minstrel tradition."[11]

Clorindy was the beginning of a number of artistic differences between Cook and Dunbar that eventually led to their separation. However, the men did agree to collaborate on another venture, which would star Williams and Walker. It was called *Senegambian Carnival*, "Senegambian" referring to a region of West Africa. But the show's plot had nothing to do with Africa. A review of the show's opening in Boston on August 29, 1898, said that, "the vehicle for the introduction of the two stars and their support is a two-act African musical novelty entitled, 'The Origin of the Cakewalk.'"[12] This strongly suggests that *Senegambian Carnival*'s plot was simply a recycling of *Clorindy*. Since the original librettos of both *Clorindy* and *Senegambian Carnival* are now lost, the critics' summaries are the only source of information about the show.

The *Cincinnati Inquirer* said: "The first act is a plantation scene in the South. The darkies are supposed to depict the primitive slave days with the sunset festivities in the slave quarters. They dance and sing to their hearts' content."[13]

The *Boston Globe* gave a somewhat different report about the first act, stating that "the carnival opens at a steamboat landing on the Mississippi, where an excursion is to be taken north by 'Silver King' [George W. Walker] and 'Dollar Bill' [Bert Williams]."[14]

The Globe later described the Williams character as "a returned Klondiker with plenty of newly-acquired gold," while Walker played "a natural-born confidence man." Like *Clorindy*, *Senegambian Carnival* had a cakewalk finale: "The closing act shows them in New York at the home of a rich colored woman and the finale is a grand cakewalk."[15]

However, the critics thought the *Carnival* was nothing but a variety show of "songs, choruses and specialties." The specialties featured were buck-and-wing dancing, acrobatics, twin-brother comedians, Aida Overton's dance group, Edward Johnson as Black Carl the Magician, and cakewalk dancers. The *Boston Globe* said that the plot of the *Carnival* was weak: "There is a suspicion of a plot, but the audience soon loses sight of it and watches for the next specialty."[16]

Since the critics found little to comment on regarding the production, they focused their attention on the performance of Williams and Walker. Bert Williams was recognized as a true comedian. The *Washington Post* observed: "Bert Williams is one of the cleverest delineators of Negro characters on the stage, and has no trouble at all keeping his audience in tears of laughter. In George Walker, he has an able co-worker."[17] And the *Cincinnati Inquirer* agreed: "Bert Williams has a happy part as Dollar Bill and is the same humorous Williams. He is genuinely funny, and is besides a comedian of no mean attainments."[18]

What Williams and Walker did was essentially adopt the familiar characters of the "rural coon," or darky, and Jim Dandy, or "coon dandy," into musical format. Walker's character acted "wearing skin-tight 'trousaloons,' a long-tailed coat with padded shoulders, a high ruffled collar, white gloves, an eye-piece and a long watch chain."[19] On the other hand, Williams's character was "an update of the loyal plantation darky. They were ignorant, malaprop-speaking low-comedy types."[20]

The *Boston Globe* sensed this minstrel heritage in the show and stated that "each ... [has] that fund of humor and eccentricity which has made them famous in minstrelsy." Of the two actors, Walker stood out as strongly conforming to the minstrel roles of Jim Dandy. "Walker simply revels in silks and satins," said one critic, adding that they were "something gorgeous in their makeup and yet faultless in fit."[21]

One of the songs (originally from *Clorindy*) that critics of *Senegambian Carnival* liked was "Jump Back, Honey."[22] The *Boston Globe* said: "A good song and chorus in the first act was 'Jump Back,' with solo by Miss Lottie Thompson."[23]

Lottie Thompson was born Charlotte Louise Johnson in 1866 in Illinois. Eight years older than Bert Williams, she was the daughter of Lewis Henry Johnson and Emily Junior.[24] According to Ann Charters, Lottie Thompson had been married to a Chicago businessman, Sam Thompson. Sam Thompson must have died around 1899, the year that Lottie moved to New York City, since Rowland contends that "Mr. Williams married a widow."[25] It is likely that Lottie Thompson met Bert Williams around the time he was rehearsing *Senegambian Carnival*; she is cited in the first review of the show in Boston. Critics as late as March 1900 cited her name as "Thompson" but by November 1901 she was being referred to as "Lottie Williams." This suggests that her marriage most likely occurred between March 1900 and November 1901. Verification of the exact date of the marriage is difficult; the marriage was not announced in the press. And the Williamses apparently did not marry in New York – Williams's place of residence – nor in

Chicago – Lottie Thompson's hometown. One would conclude, therefore, that they married somewhere else or they were never legally married.[26]

Lottie Thompson was attracted to Bert Williams by his good looks as well as his personality. She once told an interviewer:

> I suppose a wife may be excused for thinking that her husband is good-looking. I did think my husband was the best-looking man I ever saw, and I could not help telling him so. It never made him conceited. Naturally, I hated the fact that he always appeared in cork makeup; I would have enjoyed having the whole world see him as he really looked.[27]

Another song from *Clorindy* that was interpolated into *Senegambian Carnival* was "Who Dat Say Chicken in Dis Crowd?"[28] Bert Williams sang the Cook-Dunbar song that spoofed rural black folks' ways. The *Cincinnati Enquirer* thought that "Chicken in Dis Crowd" was a "great song" for Williams.[29] It did not, however, believe that *Senegambian Carnival* was a great show for Cook and Dunbar:

> Viewed as a novelty [the show is] . . . a good thing just at this time when the songs and acts seen in the carnival are the rage. Treated seriously, however, the production is somewhat of a disappointment. Both Paul Dunbar, as a poet, and Will Marion, as a musician, have reputations that seem to warrant the belief that their little comedy would present a better picture of the frolics and eccentricities of their own race. This was the prime object of their collaboration, but they have fallen short of expectations, and the two-act comedy narrows down to a typical "coon" show.[30]

The *Washington Post* also thought the piece wasn't much of a play. It declared: "There is nothing to the '*Senegambian Carnival*' except an aggregation that affords an excuse for a long list of specialties."[31]

The sharp criticism of Cook and Dunbar's *Senegambian Carnival* did not prevent them from presenting Williams and Walker in a similar vehicle late in 1898. Around this time Williams and Walker came under the management of the Hurtig Brothers and Harry Seamon. The Hurtig Brothers – Benjamin and Jules – were originally merchants in Cincinnati. At one time they had a circus act with Barnum and Bailey; at that time they met their future partner, Harry J. Seamon, a juggler. The trio put together a vaudeville booking agency. Hurtig and Seamon's Music Hall on West 125th Street in Harlem was the first of a number of vaudeville houses they operated around the country.[32] Hurtig and Seamon also briefly ran a music-publishing house. Among the Williams and Walker songs published by Hurtig and Seamon were, "The Voodoo Man," "Blackville Strutters' Ball," and "If You Love Your Baby, Make Goo Goo Eyes."

In December 1898 *A Lucky Coon* played in New England theaters. In

Bert Williams and George William Walker in street clothes, probably around the turn of the century. (*Courtesy Beinecke Rare Book and Manuscript Library, Yale University*)

January 1899 it opened at the Dewey Theater on East Fourteenth Street in Greenwich Village, New York City, and it played in Brooklyn later that month before going on the road. The *Brooklyn Eagle's* review of the piece implied that it was a thinly disguised revival of *Senegambian Carnival*:

> The scene of the first act is in Louisiana. An excursion trip is made to New York and $30,000 is won by "Dollar Bill" [Bert Williams] in the lottery, falls into the hands of "Silver King"[George Walker], a confidence man who takes the party north. Dollar Bill is then introduced into the Darktown society of the metropolis with a very amusing effect.[33]

One reviewer reported that a cakewalk dance and the song "Hottest Coon in Dixie" concluded act one of the show.[34] George Walker, who was "dressed to the nines" as a "Jim Dandy" coon, sang the song. The tune's lyrics aptly describe the Jim Dandy character, a carryover from minstrel shows.[35]

Critics were overwhelmed by the eclectic range of music in *A Lucky Coon*. The music, said the *Dramatic Mirror*, "includes nearly everything in the 'coon line,' from buck dancing and ragtime melodies to selections from grand opera."[36]

As usual, the team of Williams and Walker attracted critics' attention. The *Cleveland Plain Dealer* cited Williams and Walker for "their clever character work." A special compliment came from the *Washington Post*, which compared the young comedy team to an older and more established vaudeville act:

> Williams and Walker are the Weber and Fields of their color. . . . Williams is genuinely funny in his delineation of the darky as he is often seen. While Walker provides the spectacular for the duo, Williams supplies the real humor.[37]

Curiously enough it was not Williams and Walker but Edward Johnson as Black Carl the Magician who gathered the most praise from critics of *A Lucky Coon*. For instance, the *Brooklyn Eagle* said:

> Black Carl the Magician performed some clever feats. . . . His trick with the rings which he borrowed from the audience almost caused one of the young women to burst into tears when she saw her jewel flattened out in front of her eyes.[38]

The reviews for *A Lucky Coon* were mixed. The *Cleveland Plain Dealer* admired the show:

> The performance gave general satisfaction, and rightly so, for it is one of the best of its kind seen in this city. There is a very plausible story running through it, an abundance of Negro comedy, some excellent singing and dancing. It is well staged also.[39]

The *Washington Post* also thought the staging was good, but it withheld its approval of the show:

> The piece was magnificently staged and well-presented, with a generous show of appropriate costumes and a close regard to the details of the stage effect. Nevertheless, it cannot be said to be a thoroughly satisfactory performance.[40]

Despite the mixed reviews, *A Lucky Coon* was important to Williams and Walker in that it gave them confidence. They had begun to make a name for themselves and to attract a following. In many of the theaters Williams and Walker played in, the house was filled to capacity. In Dayton, Ohio, for example, the theater was "standing room only." In Brooklyn, New York, "not a seat in the house was unoccupied when the curtain rang up."[41] The *Cleveland Plain Dealer* prophesied correctly about the show, calling it "a real novelty [which] . . . will be a popular one."[42]

Chapter 6

In May 1899, after *A Lucky Coon* closed in Washington, D.C., Williams and Walker tried their hand at writing a play. Still intrigued by the theme of gambling, Williams and Walker tried to write a play about the game of Policy.

Jim Fletcher once described the Policy game:

> The winning numbers were picked after a turn of a wheel, patterned after a roulette wheel. [You needed] three spins of the wheel [before] the winning digits were picked. Like this: 3-6-9, or like this: 3-11-33, or 19-29-39. If you had any of these digits on your slip you played, you were a winner. That was called a "gig." You were paid four dollars for five cents.[1]

Williams and Walker had picked a title, "4-11-44," but were having trouble writing the play because of their lack of training. They got Jesse Shipp, an experienced showman, to doctor up the script. Shipp had met Williams and Walker when they tried out for the *Octoroons* show in Chicago. He later recalled how he worked on "4-11-44":

> They called me in to see what was the matter with "Four Eleven Forty Four," and the first suggestion I made was that it be renamed "The Policy Players." After that, we made some changes in it, and when it was all revamped, it made some money.[2]

With *The Policy Players*, Jesse Shipp began writing a string of successful shows for Williams and Walker. A synopsis of the plot, quoted below from Henry T. Sampson's *Blacks in Blackface*, shows that *The Policy Players* had a much fuller plot than previous Williams and Walker shows, though it was build on formulaic story lines:

> Story: The first act shows Dusty Cheapman (Bert Williams), a lottery fiend from Thompson Street, who eventually wins a lot of money, and desires to enter high society and is introduced to Happy Hotstuff (George Walker) who engineers the scheme very successfully.

> The second act shows a very elaborate scene at the house of the Astrobilts on the Hudson River. Mr. Readymoney, butler of the Astrobilt family, is anxious to become one of the Black 400 and Happy Hotstuff agrees to furnish the means by which the coveted distinction is acquired for the sum of four

hundred dollars. Hotstuff induces the butler to allow an affair to take place at the residence of his employers on the Hudson by promising to have his personal friend, the Ex-President of Haiti (Bert Williams) stop by on his tour around the world and grace the grand gathering of the Colored 400 with his presence. The Ex-President of Haiti arrives at the affair amid much band playing and gaiety when many funny incidents occur.[3]

A theater program for the show commented on the gambling theme:

> Policy playing is almost a lost art in our community, for the subtle and enticing form of gambling has been . . . broken up by the police and United States secret detectives. People nowadays want to be sure of getting their money back when they make an investment.[4]

Critics were divided about whether *The Policy Players* had a coherent plot. The *New York Times* even went so far as to say that "the musical farce-comedy has little or nothing to do with policy playing, but serves an excellent means to present Williams and Walker."[5] Many thought the play had no plot whatever.

The *Louisville Courier-Journal* said: "The farce . . . is nothing more than a clothesrack on which to hang ragtime songs.[6] However, the *Boston Globe* critic did perceive a plot to the piece. He wrote: "The show comes very near to having a connected story, something truly remarkable."[7]

The "connected story" in Williams and Walker's latest show was simply a formula plot line they had used in their last two shows. Although the librettos are not available for comparison, it is clear from the reviewers' descriptions of the shows that *Senegambian Carnival*, *A Lucky Coon*, and *The Policy Players* had much in common. All three had as main characters a naïve dude who comes into money and a con man who tries to trick him. Two of the shows' plots originate in the South, and all three conclude in New York. All three stress gambling and a desire for social climbing.

In *The Policy Players* the playwright Jesse Shipp made an effort to include elements of social life that both blacks and whites could identify with. Blacks were probably familiar with the gambling game of Policy, and the "Astrobilt" family was an obvious allusion to the wealthy Astors and Vanderbilt families of New York. By having Bert Williams impersonate the "Ex-President of Haiti," Shipp was calling attention to blacks in position of political power, something unusual for 1899. Although *The Policy Players* seems to have been far from a "well-made play" or integrated-book musical comedy, many song titles explicitly made reference to the show's gambling theme.

The score of *The Policy Players* was not published. But theater program synopses provide some insight into the musical numbers.[8] Act 1 opened "on Thompson Street, Greenwich Village, in a policy shop." The opening choral number was called, "Who's Going to Make the Lucky Play?" Next was a

Chinese impersonation by a black man, George Catlin. The black vaudeville brother team of Ed and Frank Mallory then sang the song, "Dream Interpreter," a spoof on people who select betting numbers from their dreams. Aida Overton Walker and Grace Halliday, who had formed a dance duo, were next with a performance of "Honolulu Belles." They were followed by Ike McBeard and chorus in the gambling song: "Gwine to Catch a Gig Today." The closing number of Act 1 was "Kings of the Policy Shops," sung by Williams and Walker and chorus.

Incidental to Act 1 were the two most famous songs of the show, performed by Williams and Walker. Drawing on their experience with the medicine man in Colorado, Williams and Walker had written a whimsical song about "The Medicine Man."[9] Few in the audience knew that Williams and Walker meant every word of the humerous lyrics seriously.

The *Louisville Courier-Journal* cited "The Medicine Man" as "among the best things introduced during the farce."[10] Another Williams and Walker hit song in the first act was the tune "The Ghost of a Coon,"[11] also written by Williams and Walker, of which the *Boston Globe* remarked that it was "one of the weirdest coon songs sung in a long time."[12] They also sang a third number, called "The Band."

Act 2 was set at "Astrobilt's residence on the Hudson by moonlight." The act featured at least two songs by Williams and Walker. The *Brooklyn Eagle* said, "Their new topical song, 'The Man in the Moon Might Tell' . . . made an emphatic hit, no less than six encores being demanded."[13] The *Boston Globe* also found the tune "extremely catchy." George Walker had a solo with the song "Broadway Coon." Yet it was Bert Williams who was complimented for his singing. "Without exception," said one reviewer, "every one of Mr. Williams' songs are good."[14]

Musically Williams and Walker were very nearly upstaged by a black soprano in the company, Mattie Wilkes. Many critics admired her singing; in fact, the *Brooklyn Eagle* claimed that "next to the 'Real Coons,' Miss Mattie Wilkes, the prima donna of the company, was accorded the most favor."[15] Unfortunately reviewers did not name the songs Wilkes sang. On the whole the critics liked the music of *The Policy Players*. The *Baltimore Sun* noted that "the music is exceedingly good."[16] The *Brooklyn Eagle* made what might be construed as a racist remark when it said: "There was an agreeable absence of ragtime music that is a healthful indication of subsidence of what has been an unusually prolonged popular craze."[17] Louisville critics complained about the lack of choreography in the show. Oddly enough, it made no mention of the dancing of Aida Overton Walker and Grace Halliday:

> One thing about the farce is that there is almost no dancing in it of any description. It seems a trifle strange that there should be almost a dearth of

buck and wing dancing, which is peculiarly an African institution, but the
other features compensate for this lack.[18]

The *Courier-Journal*, however, had much to say about Bert Williams.
It is noteworthy that even as early as 1899, Williams was seen as ranking
above his white peers in talent: "Williams is a genuinely amusing Negro.
Williams possesses many of the elements of a comedian and his work is
decidedly cleverer than much of that foisted on the public by his white com-
petitors."[19]

The *Boston Globe* saw *The Policy Players* as essentially a vehicle for
Williams and Walker. Said its critic:

> Of course, Williams and Walker come very near to being a whole show. While
> they are on stage, the audience have eyes for no others. Williams will be
> remembererd as the tall, lean "cullard" gentleman with the large and hungry
> mouth. Walker is slick and sprightly, and together they are a pair of "warm
> babies!"[20]

But the *Detroit Free Press* thought that the popularity of Williams and
Walker was the result of a lot of hype. It claimed that "the two stars of the
organization are funny after a fashion, though their reputation exceeds
their achievement."[21]

In general *The Policy Players* received good reviews, especially for its
music. The *Cleveland Plain Dealer* said, "the musical features . . . are the
prominent feature, although the comedy spirit is strong."[22]

The *Detroit Free Press* thought the "entertainment . . . ambitious in a
musical way . . . the volume of sound . . . constitutes the chief feature of the
performance."[23] Another review thought the play had "the best sort of
Ethiopian fun and music."[24] *The Policy Players* was called "undoubtedly the
best of its kind on the road," and some thought "it . . . as good if not better
than last year's vehicle."[25]

In retrospect, the *Philadelphia Inquirer* concluded, "There is no doubt
that Williams and Walker have at last secured a fitting vehicle for their
peculiar abilities in *The Policy Players*."[26]

Sons of Ham, Williams and Walker's next musical comedy, had no con-
nection with the biblical character Ham, who was the second son of Noah
and is considered by some to be the ancestor of the Egyptians. In *Sons of
Ham*, "Ham" is the nickname of an old Southern black man, Hampton J. J.
Flam. Ham's sons, Jeneriska and Aniesta (played respectively by Green H.
Tapley and Richard Connors), are expected home from college shortly. By
and by, two characters, Tobias Wormwood (Bert Williams) and Harty
Lafter (George Walker), drift into Ham's town – Swampville, Tennessee –
and masquerade as Ham's long-gone sons. That is, until Ham's real sons –
accomplished acrobats – arrive, when the real fun begins. Even though the
mistaken-identity plot line seems threadworn now, it was a giant step for

black performers at the turn of the century. Clearly, one of the contributions of Bert Williams and George Walker was their ability to star in Broadway shows that constantly broke away from minstrel-show standards.

Sons of Ham was a huge success for Williams and Walker, playing to crowded houses for two seasons and firmly establishing the pair as the nation's leading black comedians. The first performance of Sons of Ham was on September 17, 1900, in Mount Vernon, New York. It then toured New England and played in Philadelphia and Brooklyn before opening in Manhattan on October 19, 1900. Of the show's New York opening, the Dramatic Mirror said:

> An overflowing house greeted Williams and Walker and their colored company last night, when their new production, Sons of Ham, was seen for the first time in this city. The piece was written by Stephen Cassin and J[esse] A. Shipp, and is an excellent vehicle for the introduction of specialties, songs and choruses, which are in the main deserving of much praise.[27]

The first song of Act 1, "Down Where the Cotton Blossoms Grow," was rendered by the soubrette, Anna Cook. The next song, "Old Man's Song and Dance," was written by Williams and Walker and performed by Peter Hampton. But it was the Cecil Mack-Tom Lemonier song, "Miss Hannah from Savannah," that first woke the audience. Aida Overton Walker performed the song, which is different from the better-known 1929 song, "Hard-Hearted Hannah."[28] The chorus went as follows:

> My name's Miss Hannah from Savannah
> Ah wants all you folks to understand
> Ah am some de blueblood ob de land
> And ah I'se Miss Hannah from Savannah.[29]

The New York Times said: "Ada Overton was applauded to the echo for a song and dance, "Miss Hannah of Savannah." Similarly the Salt Lake Herald noted that, "Miss Overton-Walker made a big hit with her song."[30]

The New York Telegraph had mixed feelings about Aida Overton Walker, however:

> A new departure is the dark soubrette, Ada Overton Walker, who has developed as a straightliness and comes close to being the farce comedy soubrette. This is something new in this class of show. ... Ada Overton reads badly, although she is commencing to acquire some skill in facial byplay. She appears to be afraid to let her voice come out.[31]

The "students of Riske College" next sang a Williams and Walker composition, "Calisthenics." Soubrette Alice McKay was next with a rendition of the tune "Josephine My Jo," written by R. C. McPherson and James T. Bryman.

In addition to the music, Sons of Ham was lauded for its scenery. Critics said the production was "more elaborate than before." The scene that fascinated audiences and critics alike was the final scene of Act 1, entitled "In Africa." In this scene, reproduced in a picture in the *Denver Post*, Bert Williams wore the costume of a Zulu warrior. Kansas City reviewers were baffled by the scene. "The scene, 'In Africa,' which accompanies a novel song and dance, 'My Little Zulu Babe,' . . . is grotesque and so very grotesque that it is interesting."[32]

During intermission Will Accooe played his new waltz composition, "Southern Blossoms." Act 2 showed the inside of Ham's house. Aida Overton Walker sang a song called "Leading Lady."[33] Then Bert Williams returned to the stage to perform a funny song dealing with the occult sciences – "The Phrenologist Coon":

> After feelin' of your bump
> And your face I've read
> By just feelin' in your pocket
> I can tell what's in your head
> Dat's de reason why they call me
> The phrenologist coon.[34]

The *San Francisco Chronicle* said: "The best hit of the last night was the 'Phrenologist Coon' which had many encores."[35] The *Detroit Free Press* agreed: "Williams compelled a general surrender last night by his rendering of 'The Phrenologist Coon.'"[36]

Williams's next number, a ballad called "My Castle on the Nile," was different in mood:

> In my castle on the river Nile
> I am gwinter live in elegant style
> In laid diamonds onde flo'
> A baboon butler at my do'
> When I wed dat princess Anna Mazzo
> Den my Blood will change from red to blue
> Entertaining royalty all the while
> In my castle on the river Nile.[37]

The *New York Telegraph* said the song was a hit:

> For an encore, he has "My Castle on the Nile," which is one of the best things he has ever sung. It was encored a half dozen times the other evening and there was not a dissenting voice when he came out a sixth time. It was good swing and is catchy.[38]

The third big number Bert Williams performed was "All Goin' Out and Nothin' Comin' In." It was one of three songs written by Williams and Walker for the show. (The others were "Calisthenics" and "Old Man's Song and Dance.") The chorus went as follows:

Dat am de time when de troubles begin;
Money's gittin' low
People say: "I told you so,"
And you can't borrow a penny from any of yo' kin
An' it's all goin' out and nothin' comin' in.[39]

Williams may have had this song in mind when he wrote:

There are three things beside the thing that a successful song must have, in
my opinion. It must have a humorous situation, it must have a clear story,
and a chorus that has a definite trick of words that is funny. The music is the
least part of the trouble. The lyrics are the important feature.[40]

Walker followed Bert Williams, doing three McPherson-Lemonier
songs: "Leader of the Ball," "Good Afternoon, Mr. Jenkins," and "Elegant
Darky Dan." "With these songs," the *Detroit Free Press* said, "Walker . . .
had a merry inning."[41] The *Philadelphia Inquirer* noted that "Walker is a
good feeder for his partner's fun-making proclivities and, incidently, is a
clever singer and dancer."[42]

Baritone Lloyd Gibbs followed with some unnamed "vocal selections."
The closing finale numbers were the Will Accooe songs "The Promoters"
and "Ragtime Schottische."

The general critical reaction to *Sons of Ham* was that it was superb. The
Brooklyn Daily Eagle called it "high class" and "one of the cleverest shows
of its kind now on the road." Cincinnati and Salt Lake City reviewers
thought the play was one of the best of the season. The *Denver Post* commented, "It is seldom that the theater-going public sees a genuine novelty,
but [*Sons of Ham*] is one in every sense of the word." The *San Francisco
Chronicle* saw the show as "proof of the rapid advancement of the colored
folks in all kinds of stage work."[43]

Bert Williams was singled out once more as a premier comedian. One
review decided:

It is hard to say which one of the stars made the biggest hit last night, but
one would have to see Williams to get any idea of the expressions of his face
when he changes from laughter into blank dismay whenever things to wrong
against him. As a comedian, Williams outclasses any of his race.[44]

The *Chicago Tribune* also reflected upon the chemistry between
Williams and Walker, declaring: "The colored stars of that company are
really remarkable."[45] The *Kansas City Star* struck a blow at white imper-
sonators of black people by saying that the coon/blackface business was absurd. Said the *Star*: "Nothing is attempted in the presentation [of *Sons of
Ham*] that Negro comedians or singers are not equally well, if not more fully
qualified to set forth than the white actors of the stage."[46]

Sons of Ham played for two seasons. Its run, however, was not without
problems. In its first season, the *Indianapolis Freeman* reported, "Smallpox

broke out in the company while it was playing an engagement in Pittsburgh, necessitating the cancelling of the play before its finish of the week and the disbanding of the company."[47]

Toward the end of the season, the show was back on the road drawing standing-room-only crowds in places like Boston and Brooklyn.[48]

In June 1901, after *Sons of Ham* had finished its first season, Williams and Walker played in vaudeville. The high point of their act, said the *Dramatic Mirror*, was the music: "The Blackville Strutters' Ball," written by Williams and Walker, and "Good Morning, Carrie," composed by R. C. McPherson.

> Williams and Walker returned to town to top the ticket with a new act that proved highly amusing and made a pronounced hit. Their work improves constantly, and the hearty reception that they received attested to their popularity. The new turn concerned trouble about the Strutters' Club of Blackville and served to project a good deal of bright comedy as well as some effective new songs, one of which, "Good Morning, Carrie!," looks like a probable winner. Walker wore clothes as well as ever, and Williams wore bad clothes in the same old absurd way.[49]

"Good Morning, Carrie" was a suitor's song for a Southern belle:

> Good morning, Carrie . . .
> How you do this morning
> Was you dreamin' about me
> My pretty maid
> Say look here, Carrie . . .
> When we gwine to marry
> Long spring time, honey
> Good morning, babe.[50]

"Good Morning, Carrie" was Williams and Walker's best-selling song. They included it in the *Sons of Ham* second season and recorded it in October 1901. They are the earliest documented black recording artists.

Victor announced the signing of Williams and Walker in its catalog:

> The most popular songs of the day are the "Ragtime" or "Coon Songs." The greatest recommendation a song of this kind can have is that it is sung by Williams and Walker, the "Two Real Coons." Their selections are always from the brightest and best songs with the most catchy and pleasing melodies. Although Williams and Walker have been engaged to make records exclusively for us at the highest price ever paid in the history of the Talking Machine business, and although their records are the finest thing ever produced, being absolutely the real thing, we add them to our regular record list with no advance in price.[51]

On October 11, 1901, Williams and Walker recorded ten songs together and solo. Bert Williams recorded the following songs solo: "My Castle on the Nile," "The Phrenologist Coon," "Where Was Moses When the Lights Went

Out?," and "All Goin' Out and Nothin' Comin' In." Walker's solos were "Junie," "Good Afternoon, Mr. Jenkins," and "Her Name's Miss Dinah Fair." The comedy pair dueted in "I Don't Like That Face You Wear," "Good Morning, Carrie," and "My Little Zulu Babe." On November 8, 1901, Bert Williams returned to the Victor studio and recorded "The Ghost of a Coon," "The Fortune-Telling Man," "My Little Zulu Babe," "She's Gettin' More Like the White Folks Every Day," and "If You Love Your Baby, Make Them Goo Goo Eyes."[52]

Although Williams was the first black recording artist, few of his recordings are available now. Between 1901 and 1922, Williams recorded about eighty songs, mostly with Columbia (a few more than once), generally on discs rather than cylinders. Brian Rust has compiled a five-page list of these songs in his *Complete Entertainment Discography*. Eight songs from the 1919–21 period were reissued in the 1940s, and others in 1981, but only a few of Williams's songs from the pre–Ziegfeld shows have been preserved.[53]

Williams's success in music was not, however, limited to his own shows. In August 1902, Williams and Walker enjoyed the distinction of having their song "All Goin' Out" interpolated into the Marie Cahill Broadway musical, *Sally in Our Alley*.[54] Interpolations were songs not originally composed for a musical, which therefore bore no relationship to the plot. It was a good way to promote sheet-music song sales. With "All Goin' Out and Nothin' Comin' In," and the *Sons of Ham*, nothing but money and praise was coming Williams and Walker's way.

Chapter 7

The show that was to make Bert Williams an international star was called *In Dahomey*. This production heralded the return of Will Marion Cook to the Williams and Walker Company. Since the *Senegambian Carnival*, Cook had worked with Paul Laurence Dunbar on several shows.

In 1900, though Dunbar and Cook wrote the musical *Jes Lak White Folks* and a one-act sketch called *Uncle Eph's Christmas*, they failed to recapture the critical success of *Clorindy*. It is conceivable that Dunbar, in failing health and writing a novel,[1] was disillusioned with the theater: He refused to work with Cook any more. A frantic Cook sent James Weldon Johnson to try to persuade Dunbar. Johnson says of the episode: "He told me with emphasis, 'No, I won't do it. I just can't work with Cook; he irritates me beyond endurance.'"[2]

Dunbar had quit in the middle of writing *The Cannibal King*. James Johnson could not convince him to go back to work on the show. So Rosamond Johnson, James Weldon Johnson, and Bob Cole completed the libretto.

The Cannibal King had limited success, never making it to Broadway. And although Cook would present a revised version of *The Cannibal King* years later, he used the original story and score as the basis for a new Williams and Walker show.

In her study of early musical librettos, Helen Armstead-Johnson concludes that *The Cannibal King* and *In Dahomey* had much in common.

1. Both are set in Florida.
2. In *The Cannibal King* there is a lost box containing gold. In *In Dahomey* there is a lost casket.
3. Both are satires on socially ambitious people, and the song "Leader of Colored Aristocracy" appears in both.
4. Each has two masters of chicanery sneaking up on a house to enter a window.
5. Each has an educated, eligible daughter being groomed for marriage and society.
6. In *The Cannibal King* the young girl says, "I'm going to be a stage lady

49

too." In *In Dahomey* Aida Overton Walker, as Rosetta, sings "I Wants to Be an Actor Lady."

7. The song "The Czar" appears in both.[3]

Will Marion Cook's son, Mercer Cook, says his father gave the following account of the creation of *In Dahomey.*

> On Christmas Day, 1902, Cook invited Williams and Walker's managers, Hurtig and Seamon, to dinner, whereupon he gave them the idea of the libretto and played the score. Hurtig and Seamon were enthusiastic about the work as a vehicle for Williams and Walker. The latter subsequently threw out the Dunbar-Cole-Johnson libretto.[4]

However, if Armstead Johnson's analysis is correct, then Mercer Cook is wrong about George Walker's dismissal of the original libretto of *In Dahomey*. Too many similarities remained. What Walker wanted was an authentic rendition of the African on stage. He and Williams had impersonated Africans at the 1894 Mid-Winter Exposition in San Francisco. Although there had been some African characters in *Sons of Ham*, Walker wanted to explore the African background on stage even further. With *In Dahomey* he saw a chance to make his dream come true.

On Broadway in 1902, there was a trend toward using the motif of Americans in an exotic culture. Tom Fletcher writes that white comedians were performing in these sorts of musical comedies. "There was *Rogers Brothers in Mexico* for instance, the team of Montgomery and Stone in *The Wizard of Oz*, and Weber and Fields in a burlesque which was called *Sapolio*."[5] Around this time, too, there were many newspaper stories about African colonization societies. Many of these groups used extravagant advertising that promised to send blacks to Africa. The press sensationalized reports of black immigrants who perished in Africa or returned home penniless. Although the Marcus Garvey movement did not appear until about a decade later, the "back-to-Africa" notion was very much in the air.[6]

Nonetheless, Williams and Walker were taking a risk by using an African theme in their musical comedy. Many black Americans in 1902 wished to disassociate themselves from Africa. Black performers and producers knew that although white people would be amused by onstage portrayals of African people, black people would be offended.

Until recently, many black people had been influenced by social indoctrination against Africa. Harold Issacs cited one example:

> The worst thing anybody could say to you in addition to calling you "black nigger" was "black African." You spent most of your time trying to disassociate yourself from Africa, being ashamed of it. You got this through the churches, through discussion at home, through talk of the racial patterns, lamenting our sad and sorry state, the slaves, and how they got here. Also, out of the white newspapers, magazines, books and pictures they gave of Africans.[7]

Despite the show's title, therefore, it was decided in the end that only part of the plot would take place in Dahomey.

The script, some critics thought, was a scenario that was truly American. As one of them put it: "It is . . . a perfect cinematograph of the 'negro life of New York, or of Boston, or of any northern American city today.'"[8]

The first documented performance of *In Dahomey* is that of September 22, 1902, at the Boston Music Hall. The show seems to have played at least one other theater – the Grand Opera House – in Boston during this period.[9]

The advertisement for the opening of *In Dahomey* at Boston's Music Hall gives a clue to what the producers promised theatergoers.

> Hurtig and Seamon Present the Pioneers of all Colored Organizations, the Comedians Williams and Walker and their company of fifty people. The Most Costly and Colossal Production ever given by a Colored attraction – 3 act musical comedy *In Dahomey*. Carload of Beautiful Scenery and Mechanical Effects, New Music, Pretty Girls, Funny Specialties, Gorgeous Costumes and A Large Chorus of Well-Trained Voices. One Continuous Laugh from Rise to Fall of Curtain.[10]

In Dahomey did impress the Boston critics. The *Globe* saw it as "a rather pretentious farce with music . . . written with the idea of getting the 'real colored show' out of extravaganza and into legitimate comedy." The *Herald* called it "a genuine theatrical novelty."[11]

The press could not follow the plot. A review of the show at the Grand Opera House stated that "the plot is inconsequential, but it bobs up persistently throughout the piece."[12] The critic for the *Globe* cited a peculiar source of the plot: "A well-known local character, who some time ago was up as a candidate for minister to Dahomey, evidently furnished the idea for the story."[13] Only the *Herald* perceived the African colonization motif in the play. "The piece has little plot, of course, and in the main is a sort of satire on the proposition advanced from time to time to colonize the negroes in Africa."[14] According to the *Herald*: "The first act is presented as taking place in Boston, when the Dahomey plan is hatched up. . . . In the first act, two or three chorus numbers are given, followed by a tenor solo of unusual merit, 'Molly Green.'"[15] The tenor was Henry Troy.

Troy's song in *In Dahomey* is an example of a nonragtime song in an early black musical. "Molly Green," the sentimental waltz-time ballad, popular in the nineteenth century, was preserved in *In Dahomey*. "Using neither dialect nor syncopation, Will Marion Cook produced a number very different from the swinging tunes of *Clorindy* or even the other songs of *In Dahomey*."[16] Since there is no Molly Green character in the play, the song appears to be an opportunity for the composer to display his versatility. The lyrics are innocent, as seen in this excerpt from the final chorus:

Molly, Molly,
Dear little dark-eyed Molly
Always so gay and jolly
Who can help loving you?
Molly, Molly
My heart is pledged to Molly
If Cholly loves Molly
I don't think it folly to love her too.[17]

"Molly Green" was followed by "a buck and wing skirt dance by five lithe and pretty girls and a noisy and extremely funny entrance of the two stars."[18] The delayed entry of Williams and Walker on stage is said to be typical of them. Because they were stars, they did not appear "until after the curtain had been up between forty and fifty minutes."[19] The *Globe* review details Bert Williams's entrance:

Mr. Williams on the scene is very funny. A Salvation Army marches across the stage, and after they have disappeared from sight, the sound of a drum is heard, and Williams, clad in the uniform of the army, wanders on beating the thing at random and very evidently lost.[20]

The *Herald* commented that the first act "closes with an operatic finale that is remarkably good, and shows fine training of an excellent chorus."[21] Unfortunately the review does not name the musical number.

Act 2 was described in the press as being so hilarious that the laughter frequently drowned out the comedians' jokes.[22] It is probable that in this act the Bert Williams specialty number "All Goin' Out, and Nothin' Comin' In" was sung. The *Globe* critic erroneously named the song as "That's the Time," obviously an allusion to the beginning of the chorus stanza.

Beside "All Goin' Out," other types of songs were heard in the second act. A review of *In Dahomey* at the Grand discussed this contrast of musical styles:

There is one chorus in the second act that is especially good and has a sort of grand opera flavor, which is in direct contrast to the rest of the music, which is of the light, fantastic and ragtime order.[23]

While the review does not name the song, the evidence suggests that it may have been "Society"; a musicologist has described the music as having "at times operatic dimensions."[24]

A performance cited as having "brought down the house" was that of Aida Overton Walker. She performed the song "I Want to Be a Real Lady,"[25] written by Alex Rogers and Roger Lemonier. Later during the run of *In Dahomey*, her specialty song had a different title: "I Wants to Be a Actor Lady."

Another member of the cast singled out by the *Herald* for her singing was Hattie McIntosh. Though the newspaper did not name the song, it is likely to have been "Leaders of the Colored Aristrocracy."[26] The song is arranged in a "call-response" pattern between soloist and chorus, as is evident from the verse.

> *Solo*: Now to establish swell society for
> colour'd folks
> I have a yearning
> *Chorus*: She has a yearning
> *Solo*: And from the high-ton'd 'ristocratic
> White folks how to lead, I have been learning
> *Chorus*: She has been learning[27]

The final act of the Boston production of *In Dahomey* was lauded for its scenery. The *Globe* remarked that "the last two sets are very spectacular."[28] The *Herald* critic found this act "the most pretentious in the way of scenery" and said that it was "mounted superbly, particularly the jungle scene."[29]

The *Evening Transcript*, however, was more interested in the actors' appearance. It observed: "The cast is unusually attractive. A noticeable thing about the women is the effort of most of them to look white. . . . There is not a kinky head on the stage."[30] [The white critic of the *Evening Transcript* was probably not familiar with Madame C. J. Walker's hair-straightening treatment. In 1900 Walker (no relationship to George Walker) started selling her hair and scalp ointments door-to-door, teaching women to care for their hair and skin.[31]]

In general, the show's music garnered much praise from the Boston newspapers. The *Herald* called *In Dahomey* one of the best black shows ever seen in Boston. The *Evening Transcript* said the music was so good that it made other musical shows look like trash. The *Globe* also liked the music but could not accept it. The reviewer complained: "One thing is missing. . . . There is not a real 'raggy' coon song in the entire show."[32] *In Dahomey* was helping to break the stereotyped image of black performance, but it would take time.

Chapter 8

The opening of *In Dahomey* as "the first full-length musical written and played by blacks to be performed at a major Broadway house," is regarded as an important event in American musical theater history.[1] It is clear that Bert Williams was aware of the significance of the occasion.

> The way we've aimed for Broadway and just missed it in the past seven years would make you cry. We'd get our beatings, take a good running start and land in a Third Avenue theater. Then we'd measure the distance again and think we'd struck the right avenue at last – only to be stalled in a West Thirty-Fourth Street music hall with the whole stunt to do all over again. We'd get near enough to hear the Broadway audience applaud sometimes, but it was someone else they were applauding. I used to be so tempted to beg for a fifteen dollar job in a chorus just for one week so as to be able to say I'd been on Broadway once.[2]

In Dahomey opened in a relatively new house, the New York Theater. Located at Forty-fifth Street and Broadway, the New York occupied the former music-hall section of Oscar Hammerstein's Olympic Theater. The other part of the building was given a separate entrance in 1898 and re-named the Criterion. The structure reportedly cost Hammerstein more than two million dollars.[3] It was that kind of financing, some say, that caused Hammerstein to lose the Olympic Theater several years after he built it.

The New York Theater was under the control of Klaw and Erlanger when *In Dahomey* played there. Abraham Erlanger had worked his way up the theater business as an agent, publicity man, and manager. His work attracted the attention of the son of Joseph Jefferson III, who hired Erlanger to arrange a tour for his actor-father. Marc Klaw, a lawyer and former drama critic, started in theater as lawyer for the Frohman brothers, who were theatrical producers. He later became a theatrical booking agent, and it was during this venture that he met Erlanger. After sharing their experiences and ambitions in show business, they decided to work together. In 1896 Klaw and Erlanger formed what was known as the Syndicate.[4]

The purpose of the Syndicate "was to get exclusive booking control of all the important theatres of the country ... and the stimulus behind the plan was the promise of very bounteous profits.[5] In the pursuit of this goal,

> charges for booking services were established at a flat rate of from $25 to $250 per year, depending on quantity. These fees were available to managers who agreed to do all of their business with the firm. For those who chose to distribute their booking arrangements, there were higher, contracted charges. This arrangement introduced the first exclusive booking contracts in the theatre and entertainment world.[6]

As the Syndicate gained a monopoly on the threater booking business and real estate, it began to have influence over actors. Actors or managers who refused to book through the Syndicate found it difficult to launch productions. In addition the Syndicate disciplined actors who broke their contracts. By 1903 at least seventy-three theaters in the United States were leased or owned by the Syndicate, nine of them in New York City.[7]

In 1902 the New York was considered one of New York's finest theaters. The *Dramatic Mirror* called its interiors "models of architectural beauty."[8] A large electric chandelier hung from the ceiling in the center of the auditorium. The interior was decorated in Louis XIV style.[9] On opening night of *In Dahomey* "the huge auditorium was packed to the doors."[10] Blacks vied with whites for the best seats in the house, some offering to pay more than the dollar price of the orchestra seats. But "representatives of Klaw and Erlanger stood at the entrance and obdura[te]ly barred the way. The way around the corner to the bleak and inhospitable gallery was vigorously pointed out."[11] Evidently several black customers complained, and feuds resulted. The next day the *New York Times* revealed that before the show "there [had] been times when the trouble-breeders ... foreboded a race war."[12] The manager of the New York Theater was quoted in the press as saying: "We'll stand the lawsuits, if there are any ... but the orchestra and boxes of this theatre are for our white patrons and no others."[13] The seating of the black members of the audience was explained by the *Mail and Express*: "Colored patrons of the performance are assigned to seats in the three upper balconies, leaving the body of the house and the two balconies above for the white folks. ... As there are a dozen boxes in the three upper tiers, the 'quality' among the colored people can easily be provided for."[14]

This left only the musical director and the boys who peddled water in the aisles as "the only persons of color on the floor or in the barnacle-like proscenium boxes."[15] "This arrangement," one paper claimed, "meets with the full approval of the two stars and their managers." Whatever the true feelings of Williams and Walker may have been, the white press was clearly satisfied. In giving equal coverage to both the segregation issue and the performance, the *Mail and Express* boasted that "the race problem was most successfully handled at the New York last night."[16]

However, once the performance began, the audience forgot the confusion of the early evening. The *Clipper* commented on the wildness of the audience's laughter.[17] The *New York Times* concurred by stating "the laughter was so incessant, so noisy, that it often drowned the voices of the actors and actresses. ... At intervals, one heard a kiyi of applause from above or a mellow bass roar that betokened the seventh heaven of delight."[18] The *Mail and Express* said that the insistent audience demanded so many encores that the performance was not over until midnight.[19]

The New York critics were not as interested in the *mise-en-scene* of the piece as were the Boston reviewers. Their main focus, like that of the audience, was on the star performers. The *Evening World* said that the audience yawned and was bored when Williams and Walker or Aida Overton Walker were not on stage.[20] The critics proclaimed them the main attractions. And it was not a good evening for the chorus members; several newspapers criticized them. The *World* was the most offensive:

> As for the chorus, the less said the better. It is composed of light-colored men and women who, even in comparison with the average white chorus of the modern musical play, make a pitiful exhibition. Their range and tawny dresses are altogether out of place. In spite of the drawbacks, the piece is a success because Williams makes it one.[21]

In no less scornful a manner, the *World* said the male quartet "ought to be choked with its own ragtime melody." The *Mail and Express* did not appraise the choral singing, but only the size of the chorus. The critic thought the singers paid more attention to their costumes than to their singing.[22] Nevertheless, one reviewer said the male quartets "went well" and singled out Henry Troy's "Molly Green."[23] The song was described by the *Mail and Express* as "being quite as catchy and melodious as anything now being sung in town."[24] Another musical number that was admired was "Broadway in Dahomey," which was sung by George Walker. With music by Al Johnson, the song had clever lyrics by Alex Rogers, exemplified in these excerpts from the verse:

> We'd git some large gorillas
> And we'd use them for police
> Then git a Hippopotamus
> For justice of the peace.
>
> We'd build a nice roof garden
> Somewhere along the line
> Serve Giraffe High Balls
> And Real Cokenut wine.
>
> We'd use Montana Diamonds
> To make electric light
> And then have Wagner sung
> By parrots every night.[25]

The other major song of Act 1, "When Sousa Comes to Coontown," was also performed by Walker. This song, composed by Alex Rogers and James Vaughn, "made a sensation," said one critic. The critics also liked Aida Walker, who "dances away with the whole show at times"[26]

Sylvester Russell of the *Indianapolis Freeman* was captivated by Mrs. Walker's stage presence:

> We behold, all full of female whimsicalities, the greatest coming female comedy star of her race – Ada Overton Walker, with a grand star reception from the audience, her sweet expensive, childish little dress; a few short words and all is over. This was the only real trance which caused me to sign, as I sat leaning my elbow on my knee, while resting my chin upon my hand.[27]

But the major accolades were reserved for Bert Williams. The *Clipper* proclaimed "To Bert A. Williams must be given the greater part of the night's success." The *World* said Bert Williams was the particular star ... he would rank among the leaders of his profession if he were of the Caucasian race."[27] The *Indianapolis Freeman* disagreed, proclaiming Williams as "second to none as comedian, of any race or color, in legitimate comedy."[28]

Williams's style of acting was intriguing to the New York critics, who gave various descriptions of it:

> Williams, in particular, had electric connections with the risibilities of the audience. He is of serious, depressed turn of countenance, dull but possessing the deep wisdom of his kind; slow and grotesquently awkward in his movements. He holds a face for minutes at a time, seemingly, and when he alters it, bringing a laugh by the least movement.[29]

The *World* observed that Williams "had little to say, but he talked eloquently when changing facial expressions." The *Clipper* perceived him as "a naturally droll comedian, making every humorous point by a quiet but effective manner, which is at all times irresistible."[30]

The press reflected on Williams and Walker's teamwork. The *World* reported that "George Walker was funny, but his business was principally that of a foil." The *New York Times* critic tried to place the pair within a certain comedy tradition:

> He has the genius of the comedy in full measure. Walker is an able second, but distinctly a second. The pair are not yet a Weber and Fields, but they are quite as funny as anything to be found lower down Broadway. Their methods, in fact, reveal a close study of the prime Yiddish comedians. They are a distinct notch above all the rest of those who have elected to trudge along behind in the Weber-fieldian path.[31]

The high point of the evening was Williams's song, "I'm a Jonah Man." The song, which "sent a huge audience into hysterics" and brought the house to its feet, was a definite hit.[32] Its verse, written in dialect, could

Left to right: George William Walker, Aida Overton Walker, and Bert Williams in a scene from the 1903 Broadway musical *In Dahomey. (Courtesy Daniel Blum Collection, Wisconsin Center for Film and Theater Research)*

be rendered in a declamatory fashion. Williams received seven encores for singing it.[33]

> My hard luck started when I was born
> Leas' so the old folks say.
> Dat same hard luck ben my bes' fren'
> Up to dis very day.
>
> When I was young my mama's frens
> To find a name they tried.
> They named me after Papa
> And the same day Papa died.[34]

The New York press thought *In Dahomey* had both good and bad points. The *World* saw the piece as "nothing but vaudeville, with a meaningless dialogue to hold it together." The *Mail and Express* also thought there was too much talk. *In Dahomey* was judged to be "livelier than most other entertainments of the same description securely anchored on Broadway and any of the others could learn valuable lessons in good taste from it." *Theatre Magazine* said the musical was "about on the same level as the average Broadway musical comedy."[35] *The Clipper* cited the sets and costumes, writing that "the staging of 'In Dahomey' will compare very favorably with similar productions in this city, and the management deserve to succeed for their liberality in scenic display and pretty costuming."[36]

The sole holdout was the *Mail and Express*, whose critic lamented the fact that *In Dahomey* "is not so distinctively a darky play." The *Mail and Express* resented this new direction of black show business, insisting that "when white folks are to be amused by the colored race, they want characteristic entertainment, and not an imitation of the musical comedy as it is now in evidence at a dozen theaters along the Appian Way."[37]

But as a whole, New York was delighted with *In Dahomey*. The show ran for fifty-three performances at the New York Theater. The *Evening Journal* celebrated the event by printing a whimsical poem about the show on its editorial page. Some of the verse went as follows:

> En' so Paul Laurence Dunbar (dar's a poet that kin sing!)
> En Bre'r Williams, en Bre'r Walker
> En our old frien' Buck and Wing
> Get dey kinky haids togedder,
> En dey writes dey notions down
> En de first thing dat we knows
> Oh Misto' Coon am come to town.[38]

Chapter 9

Hurtig and Seamon, Williams and Walker's managers, were so enthused over the Broadway success of *In Dahomey* that they made plans to book the show overseas, signing an agreement with Norman J. Norman, manager of the Shaftesbury Theater in London, to bring the musical comedy there. In addition to the Shaftesbury, *In Dahomey* would play theaters in Hull, Peckham, Newcastle, Sheffield, Oxford, Manchester, Edinburgh, and Glasgow.[1]

The Shaftesbury was located in Shaftesbury Avenue at the intersection of Greek and Nassau streets and Gerald Place,[2] in the West End theater district – the London equivalent of Broadway.

The Shaftesbury had the reputation of being a musical comedy house. Norman had brought *The Belle of New York* there in 1898. *The Casino Girl* played there in 1900, and *Are You a Mason?* played in 1901. This was an appropriate house for "the first all-black musical comedy seen in London," *In Dahomey*.[3]

But initially, Williams and Walker were very much upset about the idea of taking *In Dahomey* to England. Rowland argues that:

> In spite of their now established success, both Williams and Walker were very apprehensive. They had failed so completely over there with their ventures in the [music] halls ... However, in spite of their protest, their managers insisted that they go and they did so, sailing on the "Urania," April 28, 1903.[4]

For Williams the most alarming advice offered was that he should perform without blackface. Williams said that this advice came from some Tin Pan Alley publishers who had followed the show to London:

> They had decided that it would be fatal for me to appear in cork. At first, I thought that they meant Cork, Ireland, but they soon assured me that to blacken my face with burnt cork would be to puzzle the English theatregoers, who wouldn't *get me*. For about ten minutes, they had me going, but all of a sudden, I got sort of bullish myself and stopped listening to suggestions. I wore cork, just as I had done since the "Sons of Ham" days.[5]

Williams realized that his emergence as a comedian was inescapably linked to his adoption of blackface. He had been to England before and knew of the blackface entertainers who performed in London, so he probably sensed that this advice to drop the blackface was foolish.

The ten days of rehearsal were needed for the company for several reasons. The size of the company had been increased to about ninety. Jesse Shipp, the stage director, needed the time to direct these additional players in the numerous choral ensembles.

The Shaftesbury Theatre program for *In Dahomey* reveals a change in credits. Alex Rogers is named along with Paul Laurence Dunbar as lyricist of the show. Rogers wrote the following songs heard in *In Dahomey*: "I May Be Crazy But I Ain't No Fool," "Why Adam Sinned," "Me and' de Minstrel Ban'," "Broadway in Dahomey Bye and Bye," "I'm a Jonah Man," and "When the Moon Shines." His contributions to the show make him more important than Dunbar, who only wrote two songs.

Bert Williams wore blackface as usual on opening night at the Shaftesbury. Unlike his previous British appearance, this performance turned out to be a success. But audience response at the beginning of the show revealed that there was still hostility and skepticism about black performers.

The *London Mail* noted: "A welcome sensation of surprise was afforded visitors to the Shaftesbury Theatre on Saturday night. Those who had come to scoff remained to laugh." The last sentence seems to refer to "the offensive behavior of a negligible section of the occupants of the gallery."[6]

One London newspaper, the *Star*, articulated the public's initial skepticism about black actors, saying: "It is at first difficult to accept a chorus of black – or at least dark – ladies with equanimity, but they go about their business with such evident joy and high spirits that one soon forgets the little matter of color."[7]

The reviewers could not grasp the plot of the piece, however. *In Dahomey*'s story was said to be "shadowy," "hazy," and generally "not much in evidence."[8] According to the *Sunday Sun*, if it had not been for the story synopsis on the program, nobody would have been aware of a plot.[9] In fact, said the *Daily Mail*, even the program was no help. It seems that only one London newspaper, the *Sunday Sun*, did perceive the African colonization motif of the show.[10]

The composer of *In Dahomey* – Will Marion Cook – was mentioned in many reviews. In particular, his music and his performance as conductor of the orchestra were the topics of discussion. According to the *Times*:

> The composer conducted with much vigour, singing most of the tunes with his band and a kind of untrammelled spontaneity that finds expression in the whole action of the piece, and more particularly in the dancing.[11]

Other critics were perturbed by Cook. The *Star* noted that "his method of getting every ounce out of the orchestra is certainly effective if somewhat unconventional."[12] A key to this "unconventionality" might be found in the notice in the *Standard*. While Cook was not a performer on stage, the paper named him as

> one of the principal vocalists, for as he faces the audience to direct the over-ture, he sings all the airs, and so far as could be observed, warbles or hums throughout the score. In fact, Mr. Cook is rather disturbingly in evidence.[13]

The loudness of the music was criticized by some observers. Both the *St. James Gazette* and the *Globe* took the conductor to task for this. The *London Daily News* commented that "the chorus are at their best when they are least loud."[14]

Yet no one doubted Cook's musicianship. The *Era* reported that "in several of the numbers, one could listen to excellent orchestration . . . and in several of the concerted pieces in his score, his music displays true dramatic perception."[15] To the critic of the *Star*, Cook's "melodies are pleasantly original." The *Playgoer* cited the choruses as "very effective and the orchestration, sometimes bizarre, is full of vivid colour."[16]

While one journal decided that Cook's musical score was "utterly and completely Negro," other newspapers disagreed. The *Sphere* remarked that the lack of plantation songs in *In Dahomey* "seems to have been the inten-tion of Mr. Will Marion Cook." The *Globe* acknowledged that Cook's work was admirable. But it felt that the show lacked true black music. "Most of the music is by a negro composer, but by a negro writing under 'white' train-ing, influences and inspiration. . . . But where are the distinctive nigger tones?"[17] The *Globe* could not accept the eclectic nature of *In Dahomey*.

One example of this was the folk song "Annie Laurie," which was ap-parently sung early in the production. The *Times* described the scene in a critical manner:

> One characteristic feature of a certain class of American drama could easily be spared; a shoeblack, a lamplighter, and two other promiscuous street loafers meet in a well-managed street scene in Boston, and immediately sing "Annie Laurie," in parts, retiring after the inevitable encore without advanc-ing the action of the piece in any way.[18]

"Annie Laurie's" lyrics have a decided Scottish flavor.[19] The song, written by William Douglas, was introduced to British soldiers during the Crimean War. The tune had, therefore, been around Great Britain for some time. It is conceivable that the *Times* critic simply resented having to hear it again.

Another piece heard early in the show was entitled "Dahomian Queen." Its lyrics told of pining for a different kind of woman:

> My Dahomian Queen
> My dusky dove

What a beautiful scene
Me and my lady love

She's so sweet and serene
Fresh from the jungle green
She is my kaiokalonian
Royal Dahomean Queen.[20]

Chorus members Anna Cook and Morris Smith were the soloists. The *Times* described the song as "a kind of 'coon duet.'"

This number was followed by a tune composed by Cook: "The Caboceers' Entrance." The next number in Act 1 was one of Cook's best-known compositions. "Swing Along" is a choral number written in four parts: soprano, alto, tenor, and bass.[21]

"Swing Along" preceded a George Walker specialty number, "My Castle on the Nile." According to the *Playgoer*, Walker introduced the song in an exotic costume. "He poses as a prince from Dahomey and persuades hundreds of negroes to join them by singing of the glories of his 'Castle on the Nile' and 'Broadway in Dahomey.'"[22] This completed Act 1.

The first song of Act 2 was an Aida Overton Walker specialty – "I Want to Be an Actor Lady." The music was by Harry Von Tilzer,[23] and the lyrics were by Vincent Bryan. The song is significant because it is "rare conclusive evidence for the interpolation of a complete song by a white composer into a black show."[24]

"Actor Lady," with its moderate tempo and saucy lyrics, provided a vehicle for Mrs. Walker. She sang with a "low-pitched voice with a natural sob to it, which she knew how to use with telling effect in 'putting over' a song."[25] The lyrics contain allusions to popular entertainment of the day:

I wants to be a actor lady in the play
Up on Broadway
Spotlight for me
No back row shady
I'm the real thing
I dance and sing
Miss Carter she may play "DuBarry"[26]
But she can't sing "Good Morning, Carrie"[27]
I wants to be a actor lady too, indeed I do.[28]

Next was a performance by an important black actress and singer, Abbie Mitchell (1884–1960).[29] She was the wife of Will Marion Cook. It is likely that she met Cook while performing in the cast of his first show, *Clorindy, or the Origin of the Cakewalk*. Mitchell also was associated with the Black Patti Company. With her husband, Abbie Mitchell was involved in the musical *Jes Lek White Folks* and the choir group the Memphis Students.

Her other credits include *The Red Moon* (1909), *In Abraham's Bosom*

(1925), *Coquette* (1927), *Stevedore* (1934), *Porgy and Bess* (1935), and *The Little Foxes* (1939). In addition Mitchell was an original member of the Lafayette Players of Harlem. Her most memorable stage role was the part of Clara in *Porgy and Bess*, in which she introduced the Gershwin song, "Summertime."

Abbie Mitchell was one of the few players in *In Dahomey* who had training in classical music. Her expertise was appreciated by the critics. The *Times* reviewer wrote of Ms. Mitchell's performance:

> Another successful song, "Brown Skin Baby Mine," which is due to Mr. Cook, is sung by Miss Abbie Mitchell, whose voice, though exceedingly small in volume, is of great charm, and has evidently been well-trained. She is supported by a choir who sing with an amount of tone that is really tremendous.[30]

The *Daily Mail*, the *Globe*, and the *St. James Gazette* all cited the song as outstanding. The *Gazette* described Mitchell as having "a voice of excellent quality and a really refined method of production." The *Daily News* selected the song as "the best number of the piece."[31] "Brown-Skin Baby Mine" was simply a ballad with tender lyrics.

> She ain't no tulip rare
> Nor mornin' glory fine
> But 'mongst de flowers fair
> Kaint none compare
> Wid' brown-skin baby mine.[32]

The *Playgoer* commented that "the refrain of this song, 'I ain't no violet, I ain't no red, red rose' has a melody that should make it one of the most popular things about town."[33]

The next numbers in *In Dahomey* were "Leaders Of The Colored Aristocracy" and "Society." These were followed by a comic sketch by Williams and Walker. Although blackface performers were hardly new to England, the critics of *In Dahomey* were perplexed by Williams's use of burnt cork. Williams was a fair-complexioned black man and the only member of the cast to "blacken up," which may explain why the critics were confused. The reviewer of the *Sunday Sun* wrote: "Of what precise shade of brown he may be by nature, I am not aware."[34] Similarly, the *Times* observed: "Mr. Williams would appear to be 'not so black as he is painted,' for in his case, the makeup associated with the minstrels of the Moore and Burgess type is employed."[35] (The Moore and Burgess Minstrels were London entertainers.)

The scene that introduced the Williams musical number was described in the *Playgoer*:

> On the way [to Florida], the unhappy Williams, carrying his partner's baggage and kept under as usual, sings "The Jonah Man," a most comically

lugubrious ditty . . . after which the woes of nigger and white man alike are plaintively voiced in another melancholy song with a refrain of "It's all goin' out, an' nothin' comin' in." Williams, the comic pessimist, is good to listen to. He burlesques our woes and makes us laugh at them.[36]

This review suggests that Williams sang not one song, but a medley of "Jonah Man" and "When It's All Goin' Out and Nothin' Comin' In." The *Times* admired the Williams performance. "The 'Jonah Man' has a fine tune that must be a remnant of genuine folk music."[37] The song must have been popular with the audience, for one writer complained: "On Saturday, Mr. Williams took for his song one encore too many."[38]

"A Rich Coon's Babe," sung by Aida Overton Walker, was the next musical number in the show. The *Pall Mall Gazette* thought it was a song that showed Will Marion Cook "at his best." The *Gazette* added: "The tune is extremely pretty and delicate, the orchestration possessing too a very distinct character of its own."[39] The *Times*'s description of the number implies that Mrs. Walker danced while singing: "'A Rich Coon's Babe' has point and 'snap' of the right kind. The last is sung by Miss Aida Overton Walker, who as an *enfant terrible*, acts with much dash and dances with extraordinary vivacity."[40]

Mrs. Walker joined her husband in the next musical number, "The Czar." The Walkers were respected as accomplished dancers. Their performance of "The Czar" was encored, and the song was said to be one that could become popular. In the show the dialogue preceding the song refers to a portrait of a "Czar of Dixie," but it does not figure in the plot of the play.[41]

The lyrics were sung in a lively manner, with music written for four parts:

> He is the greatest thing, and known afar
> The black folks always sing
> He is the Czar
> His style is super fine
> He's always right in line.
> He says the world is mine.
> He is the Czar.[42]

The *Era* remarked that "the dancing of the pair was one of most delightfully free and graceful character."[43]

Two of the most important British theater critics of the day were in the audience for *In Dahomey*. Although they did not actually review the show, their reactions to the production are on record. One was Max Beerbohm, the drama critic for the *Saturday Review* from 1898 to 1910. Beerbohm replaced George Bernard Shaw, who was devoting more time to writing plays.

Beerbohm was the half-brother of famous actor-manager Herbert Beerbohm Tree. Max Beerbohm's writing on the theater was noted for its "shrewd common sense combined with a very personal style that often made the appearance of his dramatic criticisms into something of an event."[44] He was not always appreciative of the important plays of writers, choosing for example, to underrate George Bernard Shaw. The comment on *In Dahomey* was written in 1904:

> [The Irish] . . . have not merely their own charm but that charm also which belongs to all exotics. Many people went many times, lately to "In Dahomey," fascinated by the sight of a strange and remote race expressing through their own language things most strange and remote from us. Well, we are as far removed from the Irish people as from the negroes. . . . I admit that it was, in a way, more pleasant to see those negroes than to see these Irish folk. When we contemplate negroes . . . we are assuredly in the presence of an inferior race.[45]

George Bernard Shaw was the other major theater critic who saw *In Dahomey*. During this period Shaw was writing *Man and Superman*. He was also casting parts for the premier performance of *Caesar and Cleopatra*. Though this work had been given a copyright performance in 1899 by Mrs. Patrick Campbell's company in England,[46] it had not been given a professional performance in New York. This Shaw was anxious to do. A student production was mounted in Chicago in 1901 by the Anna Morgan Studios for Art and Expression. Shaw's correspondence with actor Johnston Forbes-Robertson reveals some of Shaw's ideas about the future American production. (Forbes-Robertson was Shaw's first choice for the role of Caesar.) Bert Williams's name was mentioned in respect to another role in *Caesar and Cleopatra*. Writing to Forbes-Robertson, Shaw says: "By far, the best acting now in London is that of Williams and Walker in 'In Dahomey.' I shall certainly ask Williams to play Ftatateeta."[47]

It is not known whether Shaw talked to Williams about the part, since Shaw's correspondence does not mention Williams again and there is no extant Williams correspondence. In the 1906 New York performance of *Caesar and Cleopatra*, the part of Ftatateeta – Cleopatra's maid – was played by Adeline Bourne.[48]

One of the most glowing reviews of *In Dahomey* in London came from the *Sunday Dispatch*:

> Mr. Williams has methods which are absolutely "sui generis." His facial expression can only be described as marvelous. Even when he allows himself to dance, it is executed with a quaint restraint which takes it entirely out of the category of anything ordinary. In a word, Mr. Williams must be seen to be appreciated. There is not a white comedian on our stage who could not profit by watching his methods. He is a combination of Coquelin and, well, of Williams. His singing of "Jonah Man" is the quintessence of art. His side partner, Mr. Walker, is equally gifted. Natural grace and refinement are his attributes. His cakewalk is absolutely irresistible. Aida Overton Walker's

singing and dancing were a revelation, as was the melodious chorus. The music of Will Marion Cook, the Negro musician, was of the very highest class, and his technique is racy of the soil, with finales which would not be out of place at Covent Garden.[49]

Other London critics had some reservations about the show. But they tended to agree on the quality of acting by Williams and Walker. The *Playgoer* said:

> It is the quaint humor of Williams and Walker, and the life, vitality, and "go" shown by the coloured company that constitute the chief attraction of *In Dahomey*. Not one of them seems to be acting. They are just expressing their joy in life and thereby making the audience feel its joyousness.[50]

The *Times* thought the piece should be "a great success." It credited Williams and Walker for trying to "impart new life into a number of dialogues that occasionally remind one of 'knock about artists' at the music halls."[51] The *Pall Mall Gazette* singled out Bert Williams: "All praise be given to Mr. Bert Williams's extraordinary amusing impersonation of the part of Shylock Homestead. For this alone, the work deserves to score a great popular success."[52]

The *Sunday Sun* critic did not like the choreography, though it is not clear whether he is criticizing a particular dancer or the whole company: "The singing and the costumes are good, as is also the incidental music. . . . The dancing was to me a disappointment. I had expected better things."[53]

The more severe comments by London critics are interesting from a social point of view. On the one hand, they questioned whether blacks could write and produce a musical comedy or any kind of nonminstrel show. On the other, some contended that *In Dahomey* was an example of a play rather than a musical.

The *Sphere* said: "Something too much has been attempted in the nature of a play."[54] The *Pall Mall Gazette* disagreed, however, saying: "There is no particular reason why the work should be called a musical comedy, because there is no sort of coherence or development of incident which justifies the name of comedy. A far more suitable phrase would have been 'a negro musical medley.'"[55]

The *Times* was disturbed about the show's attempt to imitate the current romantic comedies set in exotic lands. It said *In Dahomey*'s

> contrast between the dignity and picturesque surroundings of the African race in Africa and the absurd aping of the white man's ways . . . is perhaps the most pathetic thing in regard to the "colour problem" of the present day.[56]

The *New York Herald* and the *New York Clipper* were among the American newspapers that reviewed *In Dahomey* in London. The *Herald* said:

Cakewalk and lullaby make a hit. London audience delighted with performance of Williams and Walker. Find it quite irresistible. . . . The hit of the show was Williams. London audiences never saw his likes before. He was applauded to the echo for his quaint mannerisms.[57]

The *Clipper* concurred:

Bert Williams made an instantaneous hit . . . Mr. Walker, too, is a revelation of the smartness of the smart coon. His gleaming, dazzling teeth, his extraordinary vitality and humorous slyness, give him an attractive personality that will count for much in the success of the piece.[58]

The dialogue of the play was seen as "too long and too full of American slang."[59] One observer claimed that the problem with the long colloquies was compounded by the speech of the actors, who made no attempt to hide their use of black English. "The coloured performers speak so fast and accent their words so curiously, that it is difficult to follow them."[60]

Others, however, looked upon the American "accent" of the piece as an advantage. Several reviewers placed the production along side of other contemporary American shows. The *Globe*, for example, summarized *In Dahomey* this way:

In fact, when you have noticed Mr. Williams, and Mr. Walker, and Miss Mitchell, you have very little to note in "In Dahomey" (apart from the music), except the excellence of the stage-management and the verve and "go" of the chorus and the supernumeries. This is what impressed us all in *The Belle of New York*, and that is what impresses in this latest importation.[61]

The *New York Times* critic in London had this to add:

What seems like the beginning of a long-threatened invasion of the English theatre by American authors has just in a very quiet way had its beginning, says the London Mail. *In Dahomey*, at the Shaftesbury, and *Glittering Gloria*, at Wyndham's, are both American products.[62]

Chapter 10

The house did not immediately burst into applause when the final curtain came down at the Shaftesbury Theatre on the opening night of *In Dahomey*. Instead "The audience remained seated for some little while after the final fall of the curtain, unable to realize that the play was over."[1] The conductor and composer of the piece, Will Marion Cook, sensing a crisis, had the musicians play "God Save the King."[2] The audience then knew that there was "no more of 'In Dahomey,'" and began to applaud.[3] George H. Harris, a white man who claimed to be Williams's business manager, talked about the company's reaction in an interview:

> We all felt very nervous until next morning, and Jules Hurtig, Messrs. Williams and Walker and myself stayed up until the London papers came out, which we eagerly devoured. After reading them, we were satisfied that the show was a tremendous success. We all took [sic] hands together and patted ourselves on the shoulders that we had caught a fastidious public with a purely American production.[4]

The critics did not like the ending, however; they thought it was shocking. The *Sunday Sun* said: "The end was as flat as a pancake." The *St. James Gazette* called the conclusion so unexpected that it "had to be seen to be believed." The latter critic nevertheless admired the end. "It will be a pity," he said, "if the conclusion of 'In Dahomey' is made to undergo any change. At present, it is distinctive, in an age when distinction is rare."[5]

Yet the writers of the piece knew something was wrong. In their effort to break with the minstrel-show formula, they had omitted the cakewalk finale, or "walkaround." But in the papers the reason given was: "It was believed that the dance had had its day in London." This was obviously not true: Norman J. Norman received many letters requesting the cakewalk in *In Dahomey*.[6]

Soon afterward, the *Era* reported that "a real cakewalk has been introduced into *In Dahomey* at the Shaftesbury Theatre by the Negro comedians, Williams and Walker."[7]

In June 1903 the *Era* reported:

> At the Shaftesbury Theatre, on Wednesday, the cakewalk introduced into
> the successful entertainment *In Dahomey* was made more effective by the in-
> troduction of a huge cake over six feet in height, and illuminated by one-
> hundred electric lights. Mr. Hurtig, who shares with Mr. Seamon the
> management of the company, will present £ 10 to the person who wins the
> cake walk prize most times during the week.[8]

Ten pounds was a great deal of money in 1903 – about fifty dollars.[9] The
Playgoer noted: "Each week, the pairing is altered, so that all get a chance
of winning."[10] The scenery background was the house in Florida for the
scene called the darky's hall in Gatorville. "Dressed in fine clothes, each couple would march in, two by two, doing the high-stepping strut."[11] Then
"each couple was escorted into the limelight by Jesse Shipp, who *would ex-
ecute some different* little eccentric step by way of introducing them. Then
the cake would be awarded according to the plaudits of the audience."[12] One
review described the dancing: "These couples have no set form for the walk,
but trust a good deal to the inspiration of the moment. So they seldom dance
twice alike, and the destination of the cake is by no means a foregone conclusion."[13]

The cakewalk was a good publicity stunt as well. One paper said the
show was sold out: "Night after night, not a stall or a box can be secured."[14]

The cakewalk music of *In Dahomey* consisted of a number of interpolated compositions by various composers. These included selections composed by Harry Von Tilzer, Bert Williams, James Vaughan, and J. Leubrie
Hill. According to the published score of *In Dahomey*, all the cakewalk tunes
were played at the end of the show. It is likely that during the contest, they
were played as a medley, the different styles of syncopation tending to catch
the dancers off guard. The score also shows that all these numbers were instrumental except for one song, "That's How the Cakewalk's Done," whose
lyrics gave directions to the dancers similar to those in square-dance songs:

> Bow to the right
> Bow to the left
> Then you take your place
> Be sure to have a smile on your face
> Step high with lots of style and grace
> With a salty prance
> Do a ragtime dance
> Step way back and get your gun
> With a bow look wise
> Make goo-goo eyes
> For that's how the cakewalk's done.[15]

The composer of "That's How the Cakewalk's Done" was J. (John)
Leubrie Hill (1873–1916), who is known for three popular black musicals he
produced. In 1911 he produced the show *My Friend from Kentucky*, a

revised version of which was called *Darktown Follies*. That show, produced in 1915, was probably Hill's best-known production. In one scene, "to the music of a song called 'At the Ball,' the whole company formed a long chain that snaked around the stage, singing and dancing."[16] Presumably during this number, the black dance "Ballin' the Jack" was introduced.[17] Florenz Ziegfeld bought the rights to the number for use in the *Ziegfeld Follies*.[18] Besides the song, "That's How the Cakewalk's Done," Hill wrote one other cakewalk instrumental and the tune "Dahomian Queen."

The success of *In Dahomey* came to the attention of George Ashton, who acted as the theater ticket agent of King Edward VII of Great Britain. "At the height of his success, he was regarded as the most powerful individual in show business, for he could make or mar reputations – and did."[19] Ashton recommended to the king what type of entertainment was worth seeing, which often helped set the theatergoing trend of the British public. Ashton was responsible for selecting the play, booking the artists, and acting as host on the transportation that moved the company to the royal palace where it would perform. All this was done at royal expense.[20]

The king liked opera, musical comedy, and social dramas. He also loved entertaining his grandchildren, of whom David was his favorite. David (1894–1972) was the son of George V (1865–1936) and Princess Mary of Teck. When David's father died in 1936, David ascended to the throne as King Edward VIII but abdicated when he married an American divorcee: Wallis Simpson. Afterward, David was known as the Duke of Windsor. The Duke wrote in his autobiography: "I was christened Edward Albert Christian George Andrew Patrick David ... But my family have always called me David."[21] David's ninth birthday was June 23, 1903. Ashton advised the king that since *In Dahomey* was a musical comedy, it might be a good selection for entertainment. Arrangements were made with Norman J. Norman to bring the company to a royal palace to perform.[22] However, Norman stipulated that after the afternoon royal performance, the company had to be back at the theater in time for the evening show.[23] Edward VII usually preferred to be entertained at Sandringham or at Windsor Palace.[24] This time, however, it was decided that the entertainment would take place at Buckingham Palace.[25] Not only did this palace have spacious grounds that could accommodate a makeshift stage, but its London location would enable the company to be back at the Shaftesbury in time for that evening's performance.

According to Bert Williams, the stage was assembled at the rear of the palace. He described it as a large stage complete with fly gallery, lighting equipment, and parquet flooring. The musicians were seated at the foot of the stage.[26] All the scenery and costumes for the cast had to transported from the Shaftesbury Theatre, traveling "from Shaftesbury Avenue, through Piccadilly, and via the parks to the palace, although this distance was only a brisk ten-minute walk."[27] The *Era* remarked that "to transport some eighty coloured comedians, together with the scenery belonging to their show, is not an easy matter; but, then, it was the command of the King."[28] In any event, it was a real trial for the stage director. Jesse Shipp was kept busy "giving last-minute instructions to the carpenters and electricians, fixing props and adjusting the footlights." All the while, he counseled the actors to remember their parts and generally "bustled like a mother hen."[29]

Shipp was tense. When the British tried to make conversation with him while he was working, Shipp lost his temper. The episode was reported to Bert Williams who shared the account with Mabel Rowland.

> He said that he might have offended some of the people who had stolled down from the palace to ask questions. He confessed that he had not bothered to stop and talk, but had gone right on, wielding the hammer and screwdriver as he answered their queries about how he liked the country and so on. He said that he had not volunteered any information, but that one stout gentleman in a red vest, probably the head butler, had asked if he found anything wrong with the English way of doing things, and he said he had "let that fellow have it." He told him a dozen things that were wrong, from the handling of baggage, on down.[30]

More than 150 young guests had been invited to the birthday party for the little prince.[31] "The juvenile members of the Royal Family came out from the Palace a little before four o'clock, their curiosity being thoroughly aroused at the prospect of seeing real niggers on the stage."[32]

The cast members of *In Dahomey* were curious too. Bert Williams said: "I had just finished dressing and was standing in the wings. . . . The curtain was down. Suddenly, the strains of that inspiring anthem, 'God Save the King' filled the air."[33] The royal procession: "The King and Queen and the young Prince of Wales walked down the palace steps and terrace to the lawn chairs reserved for the King and Queen. The other members of the royal party found places on the grass."[34] Williams recalled:

> On this occasion, the King was attired in grey frock and topper, as were the other males in attendance. The ladies, following the lead of Queen Alexandra, were gowned in pastel silks and gauzes, with large picture hats and umbrellas.[35]

Though the members of the *In Dahomey* company were themselves celebrities, they reacted like ordinary people would, when they saw the King and Queen of England. Bert Williams said:

> I looked through the [theater] curtain and saw the royal family . . . There were several peepholes in the curtain; my company made several more! It was, actually, the *time of our lives* . . . Suddenly, Shipp came up to the peephole where I was and looked through with me. Slowly the procession was

approaching. "Lemme see the King," he said grouchily. "There he is," I said. "Where?" "In the front, there, see?" "Oh my, isn't the King a stunning figure?"–This from some of our ladies. "Danged if I see any King in that mob," said Shipp angrily. "There ain't a soul got on a crown nor a royal robe that I can see. Where is he?" I showed him the central figure, now well within our unobstructed view from the peephole. "That man?" he gasped. "My Gawd, that fat man with the red vest, is he the King? That's the man I was roastin' the country to. I was looking for a king to *look like a king*." After being presented to King Edward ... he told me of the incident and how much he enjoyed Shipp's unrestrained criticism.[36]

The royal command performance was a program of musical numbers from *In Dahomey*, Will Marion Cook conducting the orchestra. The press overheard a discussion between Edward VII and his brother Albert about whether the performers were black by nature."[37] Edward VII was also curious about whether the version of the cakewalk performed by Williams and Walker was authentic. He was assured that it was a standard rendition.[38]

Will Marion Cook's younger brother, John, had written a song for Williams to sing. Because of its title, which is echoed in the chorus, Williams was skeptical about its appropriateness in a royal command performance.[39] However, Williams presented the song, and apparently no one complained:

Evah darkey is a king!
Royalty is jes' de ting.
If yo' social life's a bungle
Jes yo' go back to yo' jungle,
And remember dat your daddy was a king.[40]

Afterwards, Williams said that he had had a bad case of stage fright. Nevertheless:

The kindest, most courteous, most democratic man I ever met was the King of England, the late Edward VII. I shall never forget how frightened I was before the first time I sang for him. I kept thinking of his position, his dignity, his titles: King of Great Britain and Ireland, Emperor of India, and half a page more of them, and my knees knocked together and the sweat stood out on my forehead. And I found the easiest, most responsive, most appreciative audience any [performer] could wish.[41]

Because the performance was scheduled to last only one hour, encores were discouraged. But an exception had to be made for Bert Williams, who reprised "I'm a Jonah Man." The audience liked Abbie Mitchell's "Brown-Skin Baby Mine," as well as George Walker's "Castle on the Nile."[42] A cakewalk contest was held. It was popular with the children, who attempted to mimic the dancers.[43]

After the performance, there was a reception for the company. The king asked Williams and Walker and Aida Overton Walker to show him how to cakewalk. Walker reminisced:

We were treated royally. That is the only word for it. We had champagne from the Royal cellar and strawberries and cream from the Royal garden. The Queen was perfectly lovely, and the King was as jolly as he could be and the little princes and princesses were as nice as they could be, just like little fairies.[44]

Bert Williams became friends with Edward VII, teaching him the cakewalk dance and the card game of craps. The King also tried to learn Williams's comic monologues or jokes. Williams recalled that: "I was lucky in that he liked my stories, and used to send for me to come to the palace once or twice a week to tell some story over that he had taken a liking to, and found he couldn't tell correctly."[45] Unfortunately, Edward VII's recollections of Bert Williams do not seem to have been recorded.

Aida Overton Walker found herself a favorite of British society because of her dancing ability. Many society matrons sought her out for lessons in cakewalking. One such request was published in the *New York Age*:

Dunrohm Castle,
Sutherland.

Lady Constance Mackenzie will be very much obliged if Mrs. Walker will give her a dancing lesson on Monday at five o'clock in the evening. She is sorry she was unable to have them before. Please let Lady Constance know if Mrs. Walker cannot come, otherwise she will expect her at Stafford House, St. James, at 3 on Monday next, the 5th.[46]

Aida Overton Walker was pleased to mingle with British nobility without the stigma of Jim Crow. In an article for *Colored American Magazine*, she wrote:

At these entertainments [we] were not screened off, nor were we slighted in any way. We have performed in the drawing rooms of Mrs. Arthur Paget, Miss Muriel Wilson, Mrs. Frank Avery, Lady Constance Mackenzie, and many others. At the entertainments given in London, England, English nobility were present and expressed pleasure and delight at being entertained as we entertained them. When Sir Thomas Lipton was presented with the silver service from the American Yacht Club, Williams and Walker entertained Sir Thomas and his party at the Hyde Park Hotel in London.[47]

In England during 1904 and 1905, Bert Williams recorded several songs on cylinders:

The British branches of the Columbia, Edison and Lambert companies issued cylinders by a comedian named Bert Williams. Judging by the titles – "It Wasn't His Turn to Laugh," "Bill's Whistle," and "Bertie in Love" – they were of an English type of comedy, different from anything he recorded in the States.[48]

While traveling with *In Dahomey* in Great Britain, Bert Williams and nine other performers joined the Masonic Fraternity in Scotland. They joined Lodge Waverly 597 in Edinburgh.[49] According to Mabel Rowland:

> While playing in Edinburgh, he took the first degree and then went on to Glasgow. When the time came for the second degree, they were about to depart for Manchester, so a special dispensation was granted and the second degree was taken at 8 A.M. on the day of departure. He then played a week in Glasgow, returned to London for three weeks, and returned to Edinburgh for the third degree. Williams and his friends then stayed on at Edinburgh and went to the Royal Arch, St. Andrew's Chapter 83. This was a very happy event for Williams.[50]

Although Oxford was not one of the original stops planned for the *In Dahomey* company, they were invited there by students of Oxford University. In one of the few reports about the British tour of *In Dahomey*, Mrs. Walker wrote:

> Messrs. Williams and Walker were invited to the renowned city of Oxford by students of the famous Oxford University, to attend a "stag party" given in honor of Williams and Walker. Every attention possible was shown to the distinguished colored actors. Students of Oxford entertained the visitors by giving performances from plays written by Oxford men.[51]

No other black theatrical company up to that time had been so honored by British royalty and society or been so warmly welcomed by the British people. Aida Overton Walker no doubt spoke for Williams and Walker as well as herself when she stated: "I am sure Williams and Walker's visit to Oxford reflected credit on the race and left a lasting impression in the minds of proud and highly cultured Englishmen."[52]

Chapter 11

What was the acting like in *In Dahomey*? For the most part we don't know. The press reviews concentrated on the musical numbers. During the American tour, however, several newspapers made special mention of one particular scene that featured Williams and Walker, in Act 2, Scene 2, of the play. The setting was referred to in the program synopsis as "road, one and one half mile[s] from Gatorville."[1] In one of the production photos, Williams and Walker are seen in front of what seems to be a painted drop depicting an outdoor scene. The drop includes a "signpost" pointing the direction to "Gatorville." According to the *San Francisco Chronicle*, "Walker starts to get some money out of Williams, who is seated on a suitcase."[2] Walker has a long monologue, "a thrilling story of Nick Carter and Old Sleuth."[3] "Nick Carter," a creation of the dime novelist John Russell Coryell,[4] was the detective hero in many of Coryell's stories, including *Nick Carter's Protégé* (1899) and *Nick Carter Down East* (1900). The Nick Carter, or Gatorville, sketch, cited by many — including the *San Francisco Chronicle*, the *Baltimore Sun*, and Mabel Rowland's book, *Bert Williams: Son of Laughter*[5] — matches the scene as written in the original script of *In Dahomey*. Therefore it is possible to reconstruct an actual scene from the show.

The *San Francisco Chronicle* noted that the scene was melodramatic. It included "illustrative punctuations in the orchestra and behind the scenes.[6] Rowland relates that "this description was told in Walker's most excited manner. ... Walker turned on that electric smile of his and, with wild gestures and many long words, he related the chase, quickening the tempo and becoming more eloquent every second."[7] The following is the "On the Roadside" sketch from the original script of *In Dahomey*.[8] ("Rare" refers to Rareback Pinkerton, the role played by George Walker. "Shy" refers to Shylock Homestead, the part portrayed by Bert Williams.)

> Rare: Come on, Shy – we're on the right road – here's a signpost. (Reads sign) GATORVILLE One – One –
> Shy: What's that, Gatorville, one hundred miles yet?
> Rare: (Laughing) No, no, Gatorville. One mile and some more.
> Shy: Some more miles!

Rare: Come on! It can't be much further. Look, you can already see the house tops.

Shy: I've been having that same bird's eye view of dem houses ever since I got off dat train.

Rare: A detective is never supposed to get tired. Why Nick Carter or Old Sleuth would laugh at the idea of a detective wanting rest. At the rate we're going, it will be plum dark before we get into town.

Shy: I ain't worryin' about gittin' into the town – if these people find out we ain't no regular detectives, the thing to figure on is now to get out of town.

Rare: You're just as much a detective as you're ever going to be. I can see now that you'll never be a Nick Carter or an Old Sleuth.

Shy: You always castin' up reflections. I never heard of dis man Nick Carter or Old Hoof either.

Rare: Never heard of Nick Carter or Old Sleuth? Why, Shy, they're the greatest detective in the world. Nick Carter is the only man living that's been shot through the heart 41 times, and Old Sleuth's been knocked in the head with his hands tied behind him and a gag in his mouth and throwed in every sewer in the country.

Shy: With that kind of treatment as a regular diet, how long is a man supposed to last?

Rare: Why say, Shy, that ain't nothin'. Old Sleuth and Nick Carter were both sent out to a Western town to trace up some bank robbers. The robbers got word of it somehow and waylaid the train about 30 miles from the town. Imagine . . . a mountain pass about 30,000 [feet] above the level of the sea [and] a bridge suspended in midair over a chasm one thousand feet deep. A stormy night. The snow falling thick and fast and not a ship to be seen. The robbers, after removing the middle span of the bridge, fled like spectres down the track to a curve a hundred yards away, and there, behind a huge boulder, lay in wait for the train. On rushed the fast mail. Every passenger was asleep excepting Nick Carter and Old Sleuth, and they were playing pinochle[9] in the smoking apartment of a car. Crack, crack, crack, and the whip-like report of a gatling gun rang out on the midnight air. Nick Carter was seen to rise suddenly to his feet and take from the hat rack a bottle of rye whiskey, take a drink and light a cigar and coolly raise the window to prevent the broken glass from entering the wounds made by the bullets of the bandits. Old Sleuth, always on the alert, threw a keg of beer[10] out the window, and the robbers ceased firing long enough to secure the beer, by which time the train was well on its way to the deadly bridge, little dreaming of the danger ahead. Nick Carter sat down to trim his corns, when Old Sleuth, whose hearing was wonderfully acute, said, "Nick, the middle span is out of that bridge ahead. I can hear the air sucking the broken rails. Something must be done at once." Quick as a flash, Nick cut the bell cord with his corn knife, plunged through the window, caught the telegraph wire, which broke with his weight, and swung him out over the chasm. Letting go the wire, he dropped to the bottom, attached the bell cord to the span that had been removed – which fortunately had landed on a bed of marsh

> and remained intact – passed the other end to Old Sleuth, who had by
> this time reached the cow-catcher of the engine, and with superhuman
> effort, the span was snatched into place and the lives of the sleeping
> passengers saved.
>
> Shy: How deep did you say that chasm was?
>
> Rare: One thousand feet.
>
> Shy: Then I suppose this Nick Carter, having rubber soles on his shoes, hit
> himself on top de head and bounced back in de smoking department
> of de car and played Peanuckle till he got to town.
>
> Rare: Nothing so unreasonable as that occurred. An artificial lake at the
> head of the gap used as a reservoir became flooded and burst its banks.
> The torrent of water swept through the chasm and carried Nick
> Carter to the town 30 miles away and landed him on the platform of
> the depot just as the train pulled in with Old Sleuth standing in the
> cab of the engine smoking a Childs cigar.

Rowland wrote that Walker as narrator did all the talking. The *San Francisco Chronicle* reported that "Williams sat there last night with only an interjection now and then for all of twenty minutes, while the waves of laughter came from gallery to the orchestra seats."[11] Shylock asked Rareback at the end, "Huh? wuz de robbers apperhended?"[12] The critics called the scene "an immensely funny sketch . . . as clear a bit of negro comedy as ever one could wish to see."[13] The song: "I May Be Crazy, But I Ain't No Fool" was sung by Williams after this.[14]

The *Baltimore Sun* said the tune was hilarious, while in San Francisco it was encored a dozen times.[15] This was another hit song produced by Alex Rogers. In the lyrics, a gullible person professes to be "street smart."[16]

When *In Dahomey* began its tour of the United States, it seems that "most of the original music was replaced by new numbers."[17] One explanation given for this is Will Marion Cook's departure from the show. "When *In Dahomey* returned to the states, Will Marion Cook dropped out of the show to work on another project, presumably *Abyssinia*. He was replaced by composer-conductor James Vaughn."[18]

James Vaughn (1870–1935) was musical director for the show on opening night at the New York Theater. Vaughn served as musical director for Williams and Walker's company until 1909. For the musical *In Dahomey*, he composed the cakewalk instrumental "Happy Jim" and the music to Alex Rogers's lyrics for "When the Moon Shines" and "Me an' de Minstrel Ban'."

The American tour of *In Dahomey* included two novelty songs[19] that appear to refer to the recent American takeover of the Philippines. "A Dream of the Philippines," sung by George Walker, was admired by the Brooklyn press. In Trenton, New Jersey, the song "Dear Luzon" was cited by critics.[20] The New York Grand Opera House's program for *In Dahomey* discloses that the latter song was sung by "Filipino Misses and Chorus." Both numbers were performed near the end of the show.

Two interpolated songs were cited from Act 1 by American critics.[21] One was performed by George Walker and concerned a boy's fantasy about joining a minstrel band. The chorus of the number describes the parade of the minstrel showmen as they entered a town.

> Away up front march de two main guys
> Who holds the sho in han'
> Then comes a bunch of the very best
> Performers in de lan'
> Then here I comes wid my face lit up
> Wid a smile serened blan'
> I'm a show man too for an hour or so,
> Me an' de minstrel ban'.[22]

The *Indianapolis Freeman* commented:

> George Walker seemed to have developed with time in his artistic element as a kid-glove comedian. . . . He showed more comedy in his dialogues with Williams than ever before. "Me and de Minstrel Band," with a minstrel parade chorus march was a very novel feature.[23]

The other featured tune in the act was also composed by Alex Rogers and James Vaughn. It was a sentimental love song sung by Richard Conners, "When the Moon Shines."

> When the moon shines, when the moon shines,
> And the sun's at rest
> If the night's hot, there's your choice spot
> That you both like best.[24]

The *Indianapolis Freeman* was satisfied with Conners, stating that "the singing of Richard Conners, who generally pays no attention to the orchestra, the audience and himself more than he does to his duty in the play, found favor. Conners has a pretty, light tenor voice which he uses with expression, as heard in his rendition of the song, 'When the Moon Shines.'"[25]

In Act 2, Mrs. Walker had a humorous song called "Why Adam Sinned," better known as "Adam Never Had No Mammy."

> Adam neber had no Mammy
> For to take him on her knee
> An to tell him what was right, and show him
> Things he'd ought to see
> I know, down in my heart,
> He'd a' let dat apple be;
> But Adam neber had no dear old Mammy.[26]

The dancing of *In Dahomey* was praised by some American critics. The Boston press cited Williams and Mr. and Mrs. Walker. The *Chicago Tribune* named them along with Jesse Shipp and Theodore Panckey. The *Denver*

Post, in an otherwise negative review, liked "the graceful dancing of one of the girls." This may have been a reference to Aida Walker. After the *In Dahomey* performance at the Grand Opera House, the *New York Evening Post* said the production had "improved since its stay in England."²⁷

But not all critics were happy about the choreography. Several complained about the lack of a cakewalk. The *Baltimore Sun* accused Williams and Walker of not conforming to racial stereotypes by omitting the cakewalk finale. "Attempts to portray 'swell society,'" said the critic, "would seem to be aiming at failure."²⁸ The *Brooklyn Daily Eagle* was also critical. Ironically, it welcomed the deletion of the cakewalk, but the *Eagle* argued that blacks could not act.²⁹

The music and comedy of *In Dahomey* gathered the most compliments from American newspapers. Referring to Will Marion Cook, the *Boston Transcript* critic wrote: "The composer has succeeded in lifting Negro music above the plane of the so-called 'Coon' song without destroying the characteristics of the melodies."³⁰

The *San Francisco Chronicle* agreed, adding that the musical has several numbers "in which the composer rises considerably above the average of the musical comedies."³¹ The *Denver Post* commented that the show has some "thoroughly good features." But it thought that these could be reduced to a vaudeville show. "The show itself," said the *Denver Post*, "is not up to any particular standard."³²

In his extremely racially chauvinistic review, the *Denver Post* critic was reluctant to accept Williams and Walker as entertainers. It admitted that in the eyes of many black people, Williams and Walker were the Edwin Booth and Lawrence Barrett of their race. Of Williams and Walker the critic noted: "They are a clever pair, this darky couple . . . their exaggerations are . . . presumed to illustrate the simple life of our colored brethren." Later in the same article, there was a change of mood. The critic decided that the acting of Williams and Walker proved that "in the delineation of negro character, the white man is much superior to the darky. . . . While they [Williams and Walker] may be funny, they have no particular or genuine merit."³³

The majority of the press and the public, however, enjoyed the comedy of *In Dahomey*. The *Brooklyn Daily Eagle* said the team was "really funny," providing "a rare opportunity to watch fooling of such spontaneity." Their interpretation of their material made them a hit. A Trenton, New Jersey, newspaper called *In Dahomey* "a rare exhibition of good-natured coon jollity." In the opinion of the *St. Louis Republic, In Dahomey* was "the best comedy they have offered."³⁴

The show was a "professional triumph for Bert Williams. He had really "arrived" as the leading black comedian, if not the foremost American comedian, of the day. Williams's achievement, later to be noticed by Florenz

Ziegfeld, was recognized by his peers. The Italian actress Eleonora Duse (1859–1924) is said to have commented on Bert Williams[35]:

> Seeing Williams do such things you know what Mme. Duse meant when she said that this man is a great actor. If great acting is to produce deep, sudden, unexpected and poignant effects in ways that seem utterly casual and unforced – then there is no doubt about the matter.[36]

In February 1905, amid the success of the show, there was tragedy. While *In Dahomey* played in Minneapolis, Richard Conners, the singer of the tune, "When the Moon Shines," was found shot to death in his dressing room at the Bijou Theater. Another member of the Williams and Walker company was charged with the shooting.[37]

In 1905 Williams and Walker became associated with another pioneer effort: they became among the first to sign with a black music publishing firm. David Jasen says that the Attucks Music Publishing Company was "the first black-owned-and-operated Tin Pan Alley firm."[38] Founded in 1903 by Shepard N. Edmonds, it was sold in 1905 to songwriter R. C. McPherson and Will Marion Cook. McPherson and Cook merged the Attucks Company with their own firm – the Gotham Music Company. Bert Williams's song "Nobody" had been published by Attucks. Gotham-Attucks "quickly signed Williams and Walker to an exclusive contract."[39] Walker, a stout believer in black self-help, was probably instrumental in cinching the deal. From 1905 to 1908, Gotham-Attucks published all of Williams and Walker's music. The arrangement somehow ceased around 1908. Although Gotham-Attucks lasted only until 1911, it broke ground for other blacks to get into the music publishing business. Early black publishers included the Pace and Handy Music Company, the (Clarence) Williams and Piron Music Publishing Company, and the Bradford Music Company.[40]

Bert Williams must have thought that with Gotham-Attucks he had finally found a publishing firm that would pay him his music royalties. Like many young songwriters, Williams learned about music royalties the hard way. He once admitted:

> I am beginning to learn a little about these things. I should have derived more revenue from my songs. I think I have paid for three or four of the pillars in the Joseph W. Stern & Co. Building, and I know that I put the clock in M. Witmark & Sons' Tower.[41]

But as late as 1912, Williams told a journalist that "his gross revenues in royalties from these sources has been less than $5,000,"[42] even though Williams is credited with writing no fewer than seventy songs.

"Nobody" was the most popular Bert Williams song published by Gotham-Attucks. The song – named in a *Chicago Tribune* review – was introduced during the 1906-7 season of *Abyssinia*.[43] It became so popular that Williams had to perform it all the time. Lottie Williams told an interviewer that she and her husband were surprised that the tune became a smash. She would listen to her husband compose music after he had got home late at night from the theater. Lottie Williams said that she was Bert Williams's main critic: "'I would sit by the piano, a drowsy critic,' said Mrs. Williams, 'and if I nodded, he was sure that the song must be no good. In that way, we decided that "Nobody" would never, never go big, but we were wrong, you see.'"[44]

Bert Williams confessed:

> Before I got through with "Nobody," I could have wished that both the author of the words and the assembler of the tune had been strangled or drowned or talked to death. For seven whole years, I had to sing it. Month after month, I tried to drop it and sing something new, but I could get nothing to replace it, and the audiences seemed to want nothing else. Every comedian at some point in his life learns to curse the particular stunt of his that was most popular. "Nobody" was a particularly hard song to replace.[45]

Williams complained that many songwriters tried to plagiarize or imitate his song "Nobody":

> At one time, it seemed to me that almost everybody in the United States was writing a song, "just like Nobody." It never occurred to any of them that to be "just like Nobody," a song would need to have the same human appeal of the friendless man. Most of these imitations were called "Somebody," and that was the only single solitary idea they had, just a feeble paraphrase of "Nobody," with the refrain swiched around to "Somebody."[46]

Charters tells how Williams put a bit of acting into his performance of "Nobody":

> To spark some enthusiasm in himself for his endless repetitions, Bert worked the song into a regular act. He pretended he found it difficult to remember Jesse Shipp's words, and he began to read them off a piece of paper, deliberately pulling a little notebook from his pocket and hesitatingly finding the right page, before half-singing, half-reciting the song.[47]

Why was "Nobody" so popular? A major key to the successfulness of the song lies in the unique lyrics of Alex Rogers. Rogers captured universal themes – human needs – in each of the stanzas. In the first stanza, the singer talks of the need for understanding and shelter from cold and hunger. In the second stanza, the singer longs for true friendship. In the third, the singer expresses the need for admiration and love. All these desires are universal – there is nothing specifically "black" or "white" about them. "Nobody" had a philosophical bent: It expressed the existential desire to be treated as a person. Audiences perceived Bert Williams at first as simply pleading for society to respect the black man. But by the end of the song, unwittingly, they were persuaded to identify with him.

Williams and Walker began planning for a new show, as soon as *In Dahomey* ended. *In Dahomey* had opened in a Broadway house – the New York Theater – and Walker naturally expected that their next show would also open on Broadway. But A. L. Erlanger, of the Syndicate that owned the New York Theater, disagreed. Williams and Walker should open at the Majestic, which was uptown on Columbus Circle. Because of its distance from Broadway, the Majestic Theater was called the "Arctic Circle" by performers, who knew that audiences stayed away from Columbus Circle. The Majestic was not regarded as a first-class theater.[48]

Erlanger argued that "a Negro show would never be accepted on Broadway and such absurd notions should be forgotten as soon as possible."[49] Walker was furious. He had begun planning for a "national Ethiopian theater in New York." "Ethiopian" was then a common term for black American that applied to churches, theaters, and the like. In his dream of an Ethiopian theater, Walker foresaw a place where black actors could appear in plays by black playwrights without fear of white interference.[50] To stop Williams and Walker from being on Broadway was unthinkable: It was discrimination, Walker decided.

Bert Williams was also progressive in his thinking, but he was inclined toward compromise. He confessed:

> In a business deal where the other party decided against us, I was usually willing to consider it settled rather than argue. Not so with Walker. He would talk on and on. "Arguing" he called it, and little by little, the other side would begin to be convinced. Eventually, you would have to believe that Walker was right.[51]

Walker was impatient with Williams and angry with his managers, Hurtig and Seamon, who supported Erlanger's view. He decided to work for another theatrical management that would concur with his production plans. Hurtig and Seamon sued. In an injunction filed June 19, 1905, with the New York State Supreme Court, the plaintiff, Hurtig and Seamon, asked the court to enjoin Williams and Walker from performing under other managers in any theaters, opera houses, or places of amusement in the United States and Canada. Specifically Hurtig, Hurtig and Seamon argued that "unless the defendants perform their said agreement with the plaintiffs, the plaintiffs . . . will sustain great loss and damage."[52]

Bert Williams later said: "With Messrs. Hurtig and Seamon, the plays in which we appeared, were not booked in what is termed first-class theatres, and we were very desirous of making a business arrangement with a manager who could play our productions in first-class theatres."[53]

It was not this legal point, however, but the financial status of Williams and Walker that caused an uproar in court. When Williams and Walker "disclosed that their earnings for one season totaled $40,000, the judge almost fell off the bench."[54] For black entertainers to earn that much money in 1905 was just unheard of. No court records survive of the hearing, but Lester Walton later reported that the case was settled on "what was declared to be equitable grounds."[55]

Williams and Walker were released from their contract with Hurtig and Seamon. At first the comedy duo had picked minstrel performer Lew Dockstader to manage them in their next show, *Abyssinia*. "But when Mr. Walker laid before Mr. Dockstader his payroll and the amount of money needed for the proper appearance of the company (in the first-class houses), the manager was thrown into a stupor." Williams and Walker held their ground, however, and when Dockstader refused to put up the money for the new show, they postponed the show indefinitely.[56] Late in 1905 a businessman named Melville Raymond agreed to finance the show. So, given the enormous success of *In Dahomey*, the future looked bright for Williams and Walker.

Chapter 12

I n December 1905 a surprising announcement was made in the entertainment newspaper *Variety*: Williams and Walker were about to separate. The short gossip item said:

> The rumor is current that next season, Bert Williams, of Williams and Walker, will offer himself as a monologue entertainer. There is said to be some feeling between the two members of the team, and Williams is reported to feel that he would fare better alone. It was impossible to verify the story, but some such development may be looked for before the opening of next season.[1]

Since *In Dahomey* Williams had been drawing more attention from fans and audiences than Walker had, and Walker may have resented this. There began to be a contest onstage to see who could dominate. One 1905 vaudeville review suggested that their act suffered as a result.

> Williams and Walker – with more Walker than Williams – held the stage some forty minutes to do about ten minutes of real work – which is Williams' rendition of "Nobody." The rest is a tiresome copy of the sort of act that was stale when Williams and Walker were new to New York. The last song is interminably drawn out and poorly done. However, they scored throughout.[2]

During another vaudeville engagement that same month at Hammerstein's Victoria Theater, "W. C. Kelly, who was booked at the Victoria Theatre, New York, refused to appear with Williams and Walker, who were headliners on the bill."[3] Hammerstein asked Kelly why he was boycotting, and Kelly said he was a Southerner. Hammerstein then asked why Kelly was complaining about Williams and Walker now when he had known weeks before that they were going to be in the show. Kelly didn't respond.

George Walker laughed when he was told of the incident. Then, after some serious thought, he said:

> The man is foolish. . . . The day is past for that sort of thing. Both white men and black men have a right to earn a living in whatever manner they find most convenient, providing that they injure no one else. We do not obtrude ourselves and they need have nothing to do with us if that is their desire. But if vaudeville performers are going to draw the color line, either they or we

will have to give up the work, for there is hardly a vaudeville show in which colored performers do not appear.[4]

Meanwhile, relations between Williams and Walker remained cool. Ann Charters says that Williams stayed away from his own company's rehearsals.

When *Abyssinia* was in rehearsal, Williams didn't participate until shortly before the opening performance, letting Walker settle the production details. Alex Rogers came over to Bert's apartment every few days to keep him informed about the progress of the show. But it wasn't until the first dress rehearsal that Williams came to the theater. He and Walker then clowned through their roles, so that Bert first saw what the rest of the company was doing only a day or two before the public got to judge the show.[5]

Williams's absence from rehearsals may have been interpreted as a way of avoiding Walker. But even years later, after Walker died, Williams never admitted that they had any differences. He told a reporter once: "From the day we became partners, we were never separated, never had any difficulty of opinion, and no harsh or unkind words passed between us."[6]

Abyssinia opened at the Majestic Theater in New York City on February 20, 1906.[7] It was a musical play in four scenes set against the background of Addis Ababa, the capital of Abyssinia, or what is now called Ethiopia. The play centers on two characters: Jasmine Jenkins, played by Bert Williams, and Rastus Johnson, played by George Walker. The pair escort a group of black Americans on a trip to Abyssinia, where they encounter danger:

Mistaken identities plague the visit of Rastus Johnson and Jasmine Jenkins to Abyssinia. Ras is mistaken for a rebel chief, and Jas, trying to protect his friend from the officials, grabs a vase from the market stall. The official then charges Jas with theft and explains that the penalty for such a crime is the loss of the offending hand. This dilemma allows Williams to sing "Here It Comes Again." "It," of course, is the inevitable trouble that always follows the beleaguered Williams. The emperor's daughter reveals the misunderstanding, and Ras and Jas are freed. As they leave, they sing to their newfound friends: "We wish you success, may you ever progress – Ethiopia goodbye."[8]

For this play Will Marion Cook and Bert Williams composed the music, with lyrics by Alex Rogers. Unfortunately we may only surmise as to how *Abyssinia* compared with *In Dahomey*. Musicologist Thomas Riis claims:

Unlike *In Dahomey*, *Abyssinia* was not published in complete score. Considering the documented luxuriance of the staging of the later production, with more or less the same personnel, it is tempting to assume that the musical score as a whole, particularly the structure of the choral numbers, would have been as impressive as [that of] *In Dahomey*.

Furthermore, although Cook was involved with *Abyssinia*, "nearly all of the individually published songs list words by Alex Rogers and music by Williams alone. Perhaps Cook contributed the orchestrations and the unpublished choral parts."[9]

Of the eight nonchoral numbers in *Abyssinia*, Bert Williams is known to have written the music for six. These were "Here It Comes Again," "It's Hard to Find a King Like Me," "Rastus Johnson, USA," "Where My Forefathers Died," "The Lion and the Monk," and "Jolly Jungle Boys." In addition Williams wrote the music for a later interpolated number, "The Isle of By and Bye." This suggests that Bert Williams rather than Will Marion cook was the chief composer for *Abyssinia*. In that many songs were interwoven into the story line, Williams anticipated what we now call a "book musical." Other songs, however, had no real connection to the plot or characters in *Abyssinia*[10]:

> He would sit quietly and smoke a cigarette, maybe two or three," said Lottie Wiliams, "one after the other until some idea away back in his brain had developed, and then he would go to the piano and work it out, very quietly. People said my husband could caress the piano keys. He found unusual chords as he played.[11]

Despite their unusual chord structures, most of Williams's songs exhibit the conventional AABA rhyme scheme, chorus structure and harmonies.

Like that of *In Dahomey*, the plot of *Abyssinia* was inspired by Africa. Scene 1 opened in the campsite of Boreman Springs, just outside Addis Ababa. The set was a mountain pass with a waterfall in the background. The *New York Times* said: "A property lion and camel and live asses were introduced to give atmosphere and local color." The opening choral number was "Ode to the Sun," followed by a rousing male choral number, "Jolly Jungle Boys," whose chorus featured African references similar to those of *In Dahomey*: "Kiddy come kick the coconut and kick it to Kanakree." Another choral number followed: "Ode to Menelik." The *New York Times* found Cook's choral numbers "especially pleasing" and complimented him on the well-trained chorus.[12]

These choral preludes were followed by a song and dance by Aida Overton Walker and a group of women. The song, "The Lion and the Monk" was "good," said the *Dramatic Mirror*.[13] Later in the production tour, this spot was apparently taken over by Bert Williams, who used it to introduce another song, "The Isle of By and Bye." The song was a departure for Bert Williams, who normally sang "Jonah Man" songs of frustration. Here, he reveled in a wistful, gentle ballad, as the lyrics demonstrate:

> The beautiful island of By and Bye
> Where ev'rything delights the eye
> Nice mild sunshine ev'ryday

Full moon shining ev'ry night they say
Flowers you pass by.
Bidding you welcome with a happy sigh
Oh 'Toil and Care'
Can't live over there
On the isle of By and Bye
On the Island of By and Bye.[14]

The closing number of Scene 1 was "Where My Forefathers Died." The song, introduced by Hattie McIntosh, contained quotes from Stephen Foster's "My Old Kentucky Home."[15]

Scene 2 opened with a choral performance of "Holiday in the Market." The first big number, however, was "Rastus Johnson, USA." An attempt to give the show a type of "George M. Cohan" patriotic number, it quoted from the "Star-Spangled Banner."[16] Bert's wife, Lottie, was next with a popular song, "Answers That You Don't Expect." With this song, the *Chicago Tribune* declared, "Mrs. Williams scores." The reception of the song was such that by the time *Abyssinia* was touring a year later, Lottie's husband was singing it. The *Brooklyn Eagle* said that the tune, "sung by Bert A. Williams, assisted by the chorus, made a tremendous hit."[17]

Aida Overton Walker returned to the stage with a number entitled, "I'll Keep a Warm Spot in My Heart for You." Her husband, George, followed with a song called, "It's Hard to Find a King Like Me." He used this occasion to show off his cakewalk steps, to the delight of the audience. This prompted the *Chicago Tribune* to note: "His cakewalk in the finale of 'It's Hard to Find a King Like Me' can but take the fancy of the audience."[18] Then Williams and the entire company joined Walker to sing "The Capture of Yaraboo."

The third scene focuses on Williams. The *Chicago Daily Tribune* graphically described the scene it called "the climax of the fun ... when Williams has his great chance of the evening." The scene takes place in King Menelik's chambers:

> Jasmine has been accused of having stolen a "vaise" – "we call it a jug in Kansas," is his comment – in the market place. He is arrested, brought before the king, tells his story, and is informed that the king will investigate. If, upon investigation, it is found that Jasmine is innocent, a gong will be struck four times; if guilty, the gong will sound but three times, and Jasmine will then be treated as all thieves in Abyssinia are treated – his right hand will be severed from the arm at the wrist. Jasmine seats himself at the council table and takes up a book, in which he tries to be greatly interested. His friend, Rastus [Walker], sits on a stool by the table and proceeds to dilate upon the hopelessness of Jasmine's nature – always getting into trouble and disgracing the rest of his associates – and refers repeatedly to the approaching loss of the hand. Jasmine endures until patience ceases to be a virtue even in his bovine makeup. He then orders Rastus to "go do something about it," and ends by singing a hard-luck song entitled "Here It Comes Again."[19]

(Chorus)

Here it comes again [spoken]. Plague take it!
Here it comes again!
But when that feeling comes astealing
It's no use to complain
I thought that Jonah spell had passed
But I was figuring too fast
My dream it was too good to last
[Spoken] Dod bust it! Here it comes again.[20]

The *New York Times* said "Bert Williams seemed to revive memories of the success of 'Nobody' when he sang "Here It Comes Again.""[21] The *Dramatic Mirror* also said the song was "likely to find favor" but did not have "the immediate success of 'Nobody.'"[22]

The *Chicago Tribune* described the climax of *Abyssinia*:

> The song itself is indescribably funny as Williams gives it, and at the close of the last stanza, the gong begins to sound. Three strokes and then a long pause. The look of fatalistic hopelessness on the face of the listening victim simply convulsed the spectators last evening. And when, after a pause, the fourth stroke was heard, Jasmine seized that good right hand of his and, his face broadened out into the inimitable Williams grin, the climax carried the house off its feet. The applause was deafening, and shouts came from every part of the house. The comedian returned and sang "Nobody," and this so increased the [en]thusiam that the hand-clapping and calls were kept up throughout all of the intermission that followed.[23]

Mabel Rowland said that "something in the modeling of Williams' features, something intangible as a shadow, communicated the tragic import of the moment as *he felt it*. It was in this scene that Williams' finest acting was done."[24]

Scene 4 was simply an anticlimax following Jasmine's pardon. The choreography of Aida Overton Walker and dancers was featured here in the numbers, "Menelik's Tribute to Queen Tai Tu," "The Dance of the Falasha Maids," and "The Dance of the Amhara Maids." Rastus, Jasmine, and friends then bid good-bye to Abyssinia.

The critics found Williams and Walker enjoyable: The *Boston Globe* reported that "they made big hits" in the show. But one journalist complained:

> There is altogether too much of Walker and too little of Williams in the performance. The latter is one of the most amusing Negro comedians on the stage. His only song last night was "Here It Comes Again," and it might have had a hundred verses had he complied with the demands of the audience.[25]

One wonders if this critic's complaint reflects the fact that Walker controlled the production's rehearsals during Williams's absence.

However, there was unanimous praise for Aida Overton Walker from all over the country. She had clearly "arrived" as a choreographer and dancer. Perhaps the most appreciative toast to her talent came from the *Chicago Tribune*. Referring to the women of the cast, the critic said:

> They move with a grace, a lightness and a swiftness that makes watching them a pleasure. Mrs. Walker is clearly responsible for this unusual quality in the work of the women of the company, for the same excellence marks her own performance, in a superlative degree. She is not only an attractive singer and pleasing comedienne, but her equal as a dancer is yet to be seen on the Chicago stage. The absolute grace, the abandon, and the modesty with which she does the most intricate steps, make her without a rival. And her excellencies have been communicated to the women of the chorus, with the result that the ensemble dances are far from being the least attractive features of the entertainment.[26]

The New York press gave *Abyssinia* favorable reviews: "A blithe performance of the piece affords considerable amusement," concluded the *New York Tribune*. The *New York Times* saw *Abyssinia* as an achievement for Williams and Walker: "The piece is far in advance of their last vehicle, 'In Dahomey,' in costumes, scenery, and effects, while the work of the singers, especially in the choruses, surpasses all their previous efforts." There was also positive reaction from the black community to *Abyssinia*. The show would have "a lengthy, pleasant and prosperous stay on Broadway," predicted the *New York Age*.[27]

Other critics were more cynical about the play's success. "While it was good in spots," said the *New York Herald*,[28] "it was on the whole disappointing." The *Evening Post* was more benevolent in its criticism:

> Had Williams and Walker been a little less ambitious, they might have scored an instant success with their new play. . . . They tried too much, however, and a good deal of trimming will be necessary to make the production interesting with a good deal more of Williams, there should be a long life for *Abyssinia*.[29]

The lengthy performance was also objected to by the *Dramatic Mirror*, but more brutally:

> The new vehicle is more pretentious than *In Dahomey* but little more can be said of it. There is a paucity of wit and interest throughout that makes it drag hopelessly. . . . Whether too many cooks spoiled the broth or the very meaning of the word Abyssinia, "Habesh, a mixture," got into the composition. The whole affair is a hopelessly jumble and the pruning knife, to be effective, must be an axe.[30]

Out-of-town critics, however, tended to be kinder to the Williams and Walker show. Most thought the show had "many good qualities" and was filled with "ginger, wit, and catchy melodies."[31]

The *St. Louis Globe Democrat* saluted not only Williams and Walker: "The general excellence of the production as a whole–all the work of colored men and women–is both amazing and diverting."[32] The Philadelphia critics probably came closest to accurately describing the musical when they wrote: "Perhaps Messrs. Shipp and Rogers have not written the cleverest book and lyrics, nor Cook and Williams' music that would startle this particular field of musical endeavor, but both are of sufficient merit to carry *Abyssinia*."[33]

During the run of *Abyssinia*, Bert Williams signed a contract with Columbia Records. He was to record for them exclusively for the rest of his life. In July 1906 Columbia issued a notice of Bert Williams's recording of "Nobody" in its record catalog. The advertisement for the record said: "The Ethiopian baritone, Bert Williams, sings his big hit, 'Nobody,' . . . in extremely funny way, the haunting melody being supported by the trombone and orchestra."[34]

In September 1906 Columbia's catalog described two more Williams songs:

> "Here It Comes Again" . . . by the chief of Ethiopian comedians, who is now featuring it in *Abyssinia* at the Grand Opera House, New York. A characteristic coon oddity, with orchestra accompaniment, unique and entertaining. Mr. Williams makes a tuneful plea for good home cookery in his song, "I'm Tired of Eating in Restaurants" . . . with orchestra accompaniment. Both of these songs are original, being the compositions of this celebrated comedian and recorded by him exclusively for the Columbia Phonograph Company.[35]

Financially and critically *Abyssinia* did very well in spite of only thirty-one performances on Broadway and its producer going into bankruptcy. Lester Walton of the *New York Age* revealed that:

> Early last season, Melville B. Raymond became bankrupt and Williams and Walker had the production put in the hands of a receiver. Last May, when the show closed, there was money on the right side of the ledger – an unusual ending for shows that are conducted at the instance of the court.[36]

Because of their experience with Raymond, Williams and Walker got another manager in 1907. Bert Williams revealed:

> On or about the 1st day of March, 1907, we entered into a business arrangement with F. Ray Comstock to be jointly interested in a theatrical company to be known as Williams and Walker Company. . . . My associate, George W. Walker, and myself were informed and led to believe by Mr. Comstock, that if we entered into a business arrangement with him, we could get into first-class theatres. And so we entered into a partnership and joint venture with Mr. Comstock.[37]

F. Ray Comstock (1880–1949) was a theatrical producer who teamed with Morris Gest and the Shuberts to produce numerous Broadway shows. One of his best-known productions was the 1915 Jerome Kern musical *Very Good Eddie*.[38] According to Jerry Stagg, sometime before Sam Shubert's death in 1905, Comstock became a business associate of the Shuberts, forming the F. Ray Comstock Company. "Mr. Comstock . . . was president, Sam [Shubert] was vice president, Lee [Shubert] the secretary. . . . It was Mr. Comstock's honor to become the first wholly owned Shubert subsidiary." In other words, the Comstock company was a branch of the Shubert Theatrical Corporation.

The Comstock-Williams contract stipulated that:

- F. Ray Comstock, Bert Williams, and George Walker are "jointly interested in the management of the company."

- The plays, music, lyrics, scenery, costumes, actors, and stage crew are to be selected by Williams and Walker.

- Comstock will advance money for the entire cost of rehearsals and first productions of the play. He will be reimbursed from the show's profits.

- Williams and Walker will stage the show and "have exclusive control of the stage management of the play."

- Williams and Walker will jointly receive $500 a week salary.

- Comstock agrees to book the play for a season of not less than thirty-five weeks per theatrical season.

- Williams and Walker and Comstock will collectively agree on a tour itinerary and theaters to perform in.

- The company shall be booked only in first-class theaters, for which the prices of seats shall range from at least twenty-five cents to one dollar and a half a seat.[39]

The contract also provided that if the Williams and Walker play did not make money in first-class theaters, Comstock had the option of booking the company into second-class houses. The name of the new Williams and Walker play was to be *Bandanna Land*.

Chapter 13

*B*andanna Land* would continue to feature George Walker as the slick, fast-talking dandy and Bert Williams as the droll, slow-witted bumpkin who constantly has bad luck. Audiences and critics found the dynamics of the comedy team irresistible. But some people believed that Williams and Walker ought to present stage characters that represented middle-class blacks. One such person was Albert Ross, a Kansas college professor who wrote to Williams and Walker in late 1907. Ross wrote:

> May I ask this question? Is it not possible that while at the same time you hold the old plantation Negro, the ludicrous darkey, and the scheming "grafter" up to entertain people, that you could likewise have a prominent character representative of [Alain] Locke,[1] the Negro student at Oxford, England, having an American Rhodes scholarship by reason of his superior ability, mentally, morally and physically? . . . Such would tend to lift the young Negro mind up to imitate and emulate these heroes. . . . *You* have the opportunity; can't you turn your tremendous influence more and more as you grow older and wiser along this line?[2]

In their reply to Ross, Williams and Walker admitted that "the progress, achievements, and possibilities thus far allotted to the Negro in this work is still in its infancy, but is growing very rapidly." But, they argued, up until recently, black performers had to condescend to holdovers from minstrel shows like buck-and-wing dancing and slapstick humor, "which might please the non-sympathetic, biased and prejudiced white man." Because the white man both financially supported and criticized black entertainers, the latter had not been in a position to alter significantly the image of black people onstage. But that was changing.

> We, Williams and Walker, proudly boast of the fact that all of our shows were written, staged and produced by Negroes, and which required some thought and very careful deliberation before attempting to present them before the public.

Williams and Walker pointed out that black performers were caught in a dilemma; in order to make money, they had to be able to please both black and white audiences:

93

Our task was no easy one, but rather difficult, because the colored threatregoer, taken collectively, only wants to see when he attends a Negro show such characters as remind him of "white folks," while on the other hand, the white patrons only want to see him portray the antebellum "darkey"; but our aim is to average and simply use characters most familiar today, and in doing so, we do it with every regard for art sake – for in true art there is no color line.

In closing, Williams and Walker thanked Ross for writing and expressed their regrets that there were so few black Ivy League college graduates:

We must not overlook character drawing; we must draw from the mass and not from a few; such characters as you mention are worthy examples, but in a public sense, they are obscure and surely away from the type, and consequently, would prove uninteresting [onstage].[3]

Bandanna Land, however, focused on what Williams and Walker considered to be "interesting" characters, in a small Southern town. The *Dramatic Mirror* outlined the plot of the piece:

The story relates the adventures of Skunton Bowser, heir to a legacy left by his father's old employer. Led by a scheming lawyer, Mose Blackstone, the colored citizens of a Southern community organize a realty syndicate for the purchase of a farm belonging to Amos Simmons, land desired by a street railway company for a park. The syndicate is not able to raise all the money necessary until Mose Blackstone discovers the missing heir, Skunton Bowser, stranded with a small minstrel company. He brings the young man South, and with him, Bud Jenkins, a slightly educated and very extravagant colored youth. Bud appoints himself Skunton's guardian and takes charge of his money. The land is purchased and half of it sold to the street railway company. Then Mose disclosed his scheme to turn the other half into a park for colored people and make so much noise that the white company will pay any price to get rid of them. The plan works successfully, but Skunton, at the last minute, decides to handle his own money and receives the benefit of the others' work.[4]

The name of the play was taken from the colored people's park – Bandanna Land. Playwright Jesse Shipp played the lawyer Mose Blackstone; composer Alex Rogers played farmer Amos Simmons; Aida Overton Walker played the farmer's daughter, Dinah Simmons; George Walker played Bud Jenkins; and Skunton Bowser was portrayed by Bert Williams. The play ostensibly calls for white characters, but it is not known whether these parts were played by white actors or black actors in whiteface.

Officially the play was advertised as composed by Will Marion Cook and Alex Rogers, but this is not quite the case. Cook and Rogers certainly did contribute a number of songs, mainly choral numbers. There remained, however, a substantial number of interpolated tunes by other songwriters. Some of the songwriting teams who contributed to *Bandanna Land* included John Leubrie Hill and Mord Allen; Jeff T. Branen and Evans Lloyd; R. C. McPherson and Chris Smith; Bert Williams and David Kempner; Bert Williams and John B. Lovitz; Bert Williams, E. C. Jones, and Alex Rogers; and Bert Williams and Alex Rogers. Williams therefore wrote music for this show, although not as many songs as for *Abyssinia*. The Cook-Rogers songs, it seems, were mostly introduced in Act 1.

Soubrette Bertha Cook sang the opening choral number, "Corn Song." Aida Overton Walker then sang a character song, "Dinah," which told of her fantasy about a potential suitor.

> Dinah, Dinah, my duskie shine, oh,
> You're my onliest, sweetest love
> Dinah, Dinah, you hear me whine, oh,
> Just say you'll be my little turtle dove,
> I make a good livin' an' I don't mind givin'
> It every bit to you,
> If you'll name the name and just softly say,
> That you'll be my little Dinah true.[5]

Mrs. Walker was followed by Alex Rogers and chorus in the tune "Tain't Gwine to Be No Rain," also known as "The Rain Song." Another Cook-Rogers choral piece – "Exhortation" – was rendered by baritone Lloyd Gibbs. As the purchase of the property for the park was settled at the end of Act 1, Williams and Walker sang "Until Then." The lyrics, with their reference to "Mr. Eddie," a name applied by Southern black folks to the white aristocracy, demonstrate that the song was integrated into the plot of the play.

> Tomorrow mornin', when the clock strikes ten,
> We'll go to Mr. Eddie's an' grab a pen,
> An' sign de lovin' papers, den look out men...
> Have a little patience, until then.[6]

In Act 2 the scene shifted from Amos Simmons's farm to the basement of the Odd Fellows Hall. First there was a minuet by Jesse Shipp and cast members. Then Lottie Williams performed the J. Leubrie Hill–Mord Allen composition "Sweet Sixteen." Aida Overton Walker sang a song of unrequited love: "It's Hard to Love Somebody."

> It's hard to love somebody, when somebody don't love you
> When you keep on doing little things, and proving
> That your love is on the level too
> Instead of wooing, it's a-fussing and a-stewing
> 'Til you almost lose your health
> It's hard to love somebody, when that somebody
> Is loving somebody else.[7]

"Just the Same" was another love ballad, composed by Cook and Rogers and sung by Henry Troy and chorus.

Then Bert Williams sang his big song of the show, "Late Hours." The *Dramatic Mirror* said the song was sung by Skunton Bowser (Bert Williams) "while under the influence of apple jack,"[8] accompanied by Williams's pantomime of a poker game. In the song Bowser regrets having drunk the applejack.

> Late hours, late hours,
> Retribution comes each morn,
> I swear off drinking just of dawn
> And start again as night comes on.
> Late hours, late hours,
> I feel so sick and forlorn,
> Sometimes, I wish I'd ne'er been born
> To keep late hours.[9]

The *Toronto Star* admired the Bert Williams song:

> He has a song in the second act entitled "Late Hours" that is the best thing heard here since Raymond Hitchcock sprung his famous "Ain't It Funny What a Difference a Few Hours Make." His pantomime poker game and his lack of control over his legs following it, is side-splitting.[10]

But in New York, black theater critic Lester Walton had harsh words about the tune. Walton wrote:

> True, "Late Hours" is a selection that permits him to do the most artistic work he ever did in his life. In it, he does some real pantomiming. But "Late Hours" is not a "Nobody" or "Let It Alone." . . . We would like to see Mr. Williams get a new song at the earliest possible moment.[11]

The pantomime poker game is the most famous stage act Bert Williams ever performed. Besides doing the pantomime in *Bandanna Land*, Williams did it numerous times in vaudeville and included it in a motion picture in 1916 – *A Natural Born Gambler*. Tom Fletcher says that Williams hit on the idea of the pantomime by accident:

> Bert himself told me, one night in the backroom of Matheney's Cafe on 135th Street and Seventh Avenue, where he got the idea of his pantomime poker game. He said that it was while playing in Lincoln, Nebraska, he went to see an old friend in a hospital. The guard said to him, "Would you like to walk around with me and see the place?" He accepted the invitation and the guard first took him to see the patients that were almost ready to leave the hospital. Then the guard took him to another part of the hospital where the patients were very ill. There was one fellow in a room alone. Evidently, his mental illness was due to gambling, playing poker. In his room was a table and a chair. He was there all alone, talking to himself and acting as though he were in a poker game, for he would go through the motions of having a drink,

looking around the table and smiling at the other players. He would reach in his imaginary pile of chips and throw in his ante, looking around to see if everybody was in, then smile again. He would shuffle and begin to deal around and after he had finished dealing, he would pick up his imaginary hand and look at each player after they had discarded, to see how many cards they wanted. All this time, he would have a smile on his face as if he believed he had the best hand, and as each player asked for cards, his smile would get broader. As each imaginary player would ask for cards, he would put up fingers to show he understood how many. Then, when one of the imaginary players stood pat, his smile would begin to vanish. When the deal was all over, the betting would start. Each player would call or pass. When it was up to him, he would look at his hand, put it down, pour a little drink from his imaginary bottle, and look again. Then he would push in the last of his chips and call. After the showdown, he had the second-best hand. He would stand up, brush off his pants, and go back to his bunk, place his elbows on his knees and, leaning on his hands, shake his head slowly.

Bert stood there and watched the man. Jesse Shipp, who was with Williams, broke the silence and said, "Bert, there you are."[12]

Williams confessed years later that it was only after some formal study of pantomime that he was able to replicate the imaginary poker on stage. In an article for *American Magazine*, Williams wrote that he went to Europe to learn pantomime.

> I used to go over every summer for a while and study pantomime from Pietro, the great pantomimist. He is the one artist from whom I can truthfully say that I learned. He taught me gesture, facial expression – without which I would not ever have been able to do the poker game stunt that was so popular. ... I played a good deal of pantomime in Europe. I did the Toreador in the pantomime version of *Carmen* and many other parts.[13]

George Walker closed the second act with a song that was forever to be identified with him: "Bon-Bon Buddie." The music was by Will Marion Cook, and the lyrics were by Alex Rogers.

> Bon-Bon Buddie, the chocolate drop, dat's me,
> Bon-Bon Buddie, is all that I want to be;
> I've gained no fame, but I ain't ashamed
> I'm satisfied with my nick-name,
> Bon-Bon Buddie, the chocolate drop, dat's me.[14]

The *New York Age* thought that "Bon-Bon Buddie" was "the song hit of the show," and the *Toronto Star* noted that Walker took six encores for the number. Walker was not cited as often as Williams for his singing, but the *New York Sun* said "'Bon-Bon Buddie' by Walker went unusually well."[15]

In some theater programs for *Bandanna Land*, "Negro Dances" was listed as the finale of Act 2. One dance was "The Merry Widow Waltz," performed by George and Aida Walker. The *New York Tribune* called it a "burlesque" of the dance. But the *New York Times* seemed to recognize the Walkers' version as authentic, reporting that the dance "was done with dash and spirit."[16] The "Negro Dances" also included a cakewalk by Williams and Walker. One reviewer observed:

> Walker, in one of his most gorgeous costumes, began with what might be decribed as a "high and mighty" cakewalk; then came Williams, his big body indescribably grotesque in a more "lowdown" way; then the two together, with a response from the audience that was utterly deafening. This cakewalk, with the accompanying dancing frills and shuffles, received at least a baker's dozen of encores.[17]

Act 3 opened in the park called Bandanna Land, George Walker and chorus led off with something called "Drill," no doubt a military march. This was followed by Bert Williams singing a song by Jeff Branen and Evans Lloyd, which he had adapted for himself: "Somebody Lied." The lyrics contain an element of political protest that is surprising for 1908.

> Somebody lied, somebody lied you see,
> There never was a President that ever resembled me
> Somebody lied,
> As plain as you can be
> Somebody lied as sure as you're born
> Somebody falsified to me.[18]

After this Aida Overton Walker introduced a ballet – "Ethiopia" – which she choreographed and performed. Mrs. Walker's dancing was appreciated by many audiences and critics.

The *Toronto Star* singled out Mrs. Walker: "Miss Aida Overton Walker deserves special mention. She is an attractive little person who can both sing and dance." The *Chicago Tribune* said: "Mrs. Walker is a dancer who, where skill and grace are concerned, would hunt vainly for her equal on the American stage."[19] Aida Overton Walker was credited on *Bandanna Land* programs as the show's choreographer. The grand finale of the show was the title tune, "Bandanna Land."

Praise for Bert Williams in *Bandanna Land* came from almost every review. The *Cincinnati Enquirer* called him "the funniest Negro on stage today." The *New York Herald* declared: "Mr. Williams plays this part to perfection." The *Dramatic Mirror* agreed: "There are few better comedians in the country than Bert Williams, whose methods of making his points are refined, apparently natural and thoroughly effective."[20] The *Baltimore Sun* compared Williams with white musical comedy star De Wolf Hopper.[21]

> Bert Williams is the principal funmaker. He is sort of a black De Wolf Hopper, and his humor is ever fresh and delightful. Last night, his grotesque dancing was the chief cause of the hurricane of howls of laughter. . . . Few more amusing burlesques have been seen on the stage.[22]

Aida Overton Walker, wife of George William Walker, in a publicity photo taken around 1908 during *Bandanna Land*. (*Courtesy Beinecke Rare Book and Manuscript Library, Yale University*)

Perhaps the highest compliment paid to Williams was from the *Chicago Tribune*, which said that Williams was not just a comedian, he was an artist:

> Artist is a large word to apply to any worker – a word of honor which, despite its careless use, means much – but it is a word which is merited by Bert Williams. He is an artist in his work, for there is never a moment when he does too little. His performance is perfectly balanced, perfectly proportioned, and an effect never is undertaken without being carried through to complete success. . . . In other words, there is art in everything Mr. Williams accomplishes.[23]

Critics could not find enough words to commend *Bandanna Land*. Some of the remarks made were: "It is one of the rare plays that one feels like witnessing a second time" [*Dramatic Mirror*]; "one of the best things seen in Toronto for years" [*Toronto Star*]; "better than half the pretentious imbecility that passes for comic opera" [*Detroit Free Press*]; "Few musical comedy or light opera companies before the public . . . are the equal of the Williams and Walker troupe" [*Chicago Tribune*].[24] The *New York Age* aptly summed up reaction to *Bandanna Land* when it stated: "*Bandanna Land* is not a good show. It is a great show."[25]

The man to whom many American blacks looked as the leader in fighting discrimination in 1908 was Booker T. Washington. Born a slave in 1856 in Virginia, he graduated from Hampton Institute and founded an institute of his own in Tuskegee, Alabama, in 1881. By 1895 his reputation as an educator and orator was such that he was invited to deliver an address at the famous Atlanta Exposition. Washington's plea for tolerance of the black man to whites, and self-improvement to the blacks, overnight made him the national spokesman for blacks. He published his autobiography, *Up from Slavery*, in 1901. Various calls for advice from both people and presidents led Washington to travel widely.

On one of these trips Washington stopped in New York to see *Bandanna Land*. He arrived at the theater while Williams and Walker were onstage and took an inconspicuous seat in the balcony. Soon, however, his presence became known and an ovation erupted in the theater. Williams and Walker stopped the show and sent a messenger to see what the commotion was about. When they learned that Booker T. Washington was sitting in the balcony, they invited him to sit in a better seat in a box near the stage. Washington declined the invitation, stating that he had only dropped by on his way to his hotel.[26]

While Booker T. Washington pursued a philosophy of tolerance and gradual change with respect to racism, George Walker was different. Bigots had to be put in their place and he would make no bones about it.

In February 1908 Walker wrote a letter to the *New York Age*, replying to a letter from white booking agent William Morris. Illness had prevented a black vaudeville team from fulfilling their contract to Morris, and Morris had denounced all black entertainers as "unreliable." In a letter dated February 6, 1908, addressed to Lester Walton, Walker wrote:

> My Dear Sir:
>
> There are many reasons why Mr. Morris should not receive such treatment as he was subjected to by Carter and Blueford, from the colored vaudeville artist, and [I] will further say on the other hand, there are many reasons why the colored artist should not receive such a letter from Mr. Morris. At this time, however, I have not the time to enter into detail relative to same.
>
> Yours truly,
>
> George W. Walker.[27]

Around the same time, Walker reprimanded his managers for their handling of a black reporter. When the theater critic presented his press card at the theater, he was seated not in the press box but in the gallery with other black people. In the *New York Age*, Walker wrote:

> Some of the white managers who earn their meat and bread by working for colored performers had better wake up. This is particularly true of J. Shoemaker who represents Willams and Walker and F. Ray Comstock. Like many white men, Shoemaker does not appreciate the fact that his actions toward colored people [are] not the best, [are] liable to cause his colored bosses to lose hundreds of dollars.[28]

Walker also published a letter to a New York private club, accusing them of racism by excluding blacks from a conference on racism:

> Gentlemen of the Thirteen Club—I have seen in the daily press an announcement of a dinner to take place at the Harlem Casino Cafe this evening the 13th of February, 1908, [at] which time representatives of the Hebrew race, the Japanese race, the Italian race, and the Irish race will speak on the subject, "Is Race Prejudice a Form of Superstition?"
>
> Gentlemen, please explain how it came to pass that your learned society failed to invite a representative of my race to speak at your dinner. Is it possible that you have members who are seeking to emancipate themselves from superstition and yet they fail to be broad (minded) enough to ask a man of African blood in his views to be present and to take part in your deliberations? . . . Gentlemen, please do not misunderstand me in the least. I am not a race agitator, and do not claim to thoroughly understand the questions with which your society deals. Williams and Walker seek to make people happy by giving them a clean-cut show, composed of and acted entirely by members of the African race. We seek to be natural. . . . Please do not seek to destroy this natural quality in us by telling us to emancipate all mankind from race prejudice which is due to lack of proper training and not from superstition.[29]

In an interview printed the following week, almost as a rejoinder to Walker's letter, Bert Williams expounded on what it meant to be a "natural":

> There is something about the darky character that appeals with peculiar force to pleasure-loving people, . . . and by the same token, the attempt of a colored player to go out of his native line is rebuffed. The American Negro is a natural minstrel. He is the one in whom humor is native, often unconscious, but nevertheless keen and laugh-compelling. He dances from the cradle stage almost, for his feet have been educated prenatally, it would seem. He usually has a voice, and there is not much necessity for schools of voice culture to temper with a natural voice. There is soul in the Negro music: There is simplicity and an entire lack of artificiality.[30]

Perhaps Bert Williams overstated his case in praising the black man as a "natural minstrel." He came dangerously close to reiterating old and familiar stereotypes, not realizing that these are often the basis of prejudice. The following week Williams and Walker were invited by George M. Cohan to headline a benefit at New York's Academy of Music for the Newsboys Home Club. The colored comedians consented and, telling the event in the newspapers, they were put ahead of every star act on the bill. The *New York Age* reprinted an article by the *New York Globe* that explained what happened.

> Walter C. Kelly, known as "The Virginia Judge," and who also had not even volunteered his services for the benefit, held a meeting in the Hotel Metropole and tried to influence a number of the performers not to appear on the stage with the colored comedians. He even went so far as to send out telegrams to several, requesting them not to give a performance. Only two acts withdrew: James J. Morton, and "That Quartette," neither of which was missed.[31]

Prominent performers at the benefit included Frank Keeney and Frances Cameron, the originators of the Merry Widow Waltz. The *New York Age* commented that "when Williams and Walker appeared, the galleries went wild." More than five thousand dollars were raised, making the Newsboy benefit a huge success. The Newsboys were delighted with Williams and Walker and angry with Walter C. Kelly. They voted to send letters to the major theaters in the country explaining how improperly Kelly had acted and suggesting that the theaters take this into consideration when Kelly wished to perform. Theater critic Lester A. Walton said that once before, at Hammerstein's Victoria Theater, Kelly had refused to appear onstage with Williams and Walker. At that time Walker said that Kelly was foolish for being prejudiced.

About a month after the Kelly incident, Williams and Walker celebrated their sixteenth anniversary as an entertainment act. The event was hastily arranged. The Williams and Walker company performed the first two acts of *Bandanna Land* but omitted the finale tune "Bon-Bon Buddie." This was replaced by "an operatic number" written and performed by Will Marion Cook on piano. An actor dressed as a "Conjure Man," or witch doctor, pranced and sang around the stage. Cook had not been able to complete the orchestration for the piece in time for the show and the music sounded peculiar. "One can readily imagine how different an operatic number would sound with a piano instead of a large orchestra." The music and the actor had no clear relationship, so "many of the people wondererd what it was all about when it was over," said Lester Walton. In place of the third act, Aida Overton Walker and Williams and Walker sang songs. Mrs. Walker sang a J. Leubrie Hill song, "Bill Simmon's Sister," and the *Bandanna Land* song "It's Hard to Love Somebody." Williams and Walker sang "See Yer Colored Man" and a medley of their hits. Bert Williams came back with his ever-popular "Nobody," while Aida Overton Walker gave encore after encore of her *In Dahomey* hit success, "Why Adam Sinned."

The gala event was packed. "Every seat in the two upper floors [was] occupied two hours before the performance. At 6 o'clock, so crowded was the gallery that the police were detained to prevent more from going on.[32]

In June 1908 Williams and Walker were kept busy giving a benefit show for Ernest Hogan and appearing in vaudeville at the Alhambra, Orpheum, and Colonial theaters in New York City.[33] In their new vaudeville act, the comedy team played part of one act from *Bandanna Land*, with full stage setting from the show. Walker sang "Bon-Bon Buddie" and Williams sang two new songs, "You're in the Right Church But the Wrong Pew," and "Sometimes in the Summertime." Walton said Williams and Walker were the highest paid black vaudeville entertainers of their day. Williams later said that he was paid better in vaudeville than in shows like *Bandanna Land*:

> I received in all during the first season $2,098, which for the season of 38 weeks, was at the average of $55 a week, and for the second season, I received for my share of the profits $2,125, which for the season of 35 weeks we played, averaged about $60 a week.[34]

As an example of how the public had learned to perceive Williams and Walker as successful entertainers, Lester Walton recorded the following dialogue overheard in the audience at a Williams and Walker vaudeville performance:

> *First young man*: It is a pity [about] these two fellows. I bet if they were white men they would make a barrel of money.
> *Second young man*: Yes, they are certainly clever, but I understand they make a very large salary in vaudeville if they are colored.

First young man: Well, I wonder how much they get?
Second young man: I understand about $3,000 a week.
An interested listener: No, they get $2,000.
Both young men in unison: Gee!
First young man: I don't think that's discrimination on account of color.[35]

Chapter 14

Williams and Walker's success in vaudeville was exceptional; not only did they make big money, but they made a reputation for themselves which drew young aspiring black peformers to watch their shows. Others were not so fortunate. For example, "the team of Sissle and Blake (composers of the show *Shuffle Along*) had had remarkably little contact with other Negro performers, as vaudeville managers made it a practice not to bill more than one black act per show."[1]

In order to combat this professional isolation, black entertainers made it a point to socialize with one another whenever possible. One popular way of socializing was through a black entertainment baseball league. Bert Williams was an avid fan of baseball. He organized his own team – Williams and Walker – and later joined the baseball team of the *Ziegfeld Follies* company.[2] Tom Fletcher recalled that Bert Williams's antics on the baseball field were fun to watch. Williams's position was first base.

> Bert Williams' baseball playing as a member of his company's team was always a great entertainment because it was generally known that Bert was especially concerned about injuring his feet. As a result, every time an opposing player came down the line to first base while Bert was playing, he would charge straight for Bert's feet. The famous comedian's interest would immediately switch from making a possible putout to protect his precious "dogs," and often he would leap clear away from the bag regardless of whether or not he had a chance to put the runner out.[3]

On May 28, 1908, the Williams and Walker team played the Vaudeville Nine for the black theatrical championship. Bert Williams "brought with him a bat with a hole in it which caused him on more than one occasion to do what Casey did at the bat – strike out."[4]

The scoreboard showed that "neither team scored in the first inning, but the Colored Vaudeville Artists made two runs in the second on errors made by their opponents. In the fourth inning, they made one more run."

Williams and Walker got on the board in the top half of the sixth inning by getting three runs, making the score 5 to 3 in favor of Colored Vaudeville. Then, "with two out in the first half of the seventh, Williams and

Walker scored two runs, thanks to some nice batting. In the eighth inning, they made the score standing in the last half of the ninth inning 6 to 5 in their favor."[5]

Now the Colored Vaudeville Artists came to bat. It was "do or die" and they knew it. Three strikes and one man was out. The Williams and Walker team was screaming with glee on the field. Meanwhile, the pressure mounted on the Vaudeville Nine—6 to 5 with one man out in the last half of the ninth. Who would win this championship? It was up to Bass Foster, the next batter for the Vaudeville Nine, to decide. Bert Williams waited anxiously down at first base. At the pitch, the crowd roared. "Bass Foster hit the ball near second, which should have been [Jesse] Shipp's, but the comedian [Williams] went after the ball, leaving no one on first to put the runner out."[6]

The score was tied—6 to 6—in the last half of the ninth with one out, one man on base, and the championship of the black theatrical baseball league up for grabs. This was the all-important moment. The Vaudeville Nine grew more confident as the Williams and Walker team realized that they were in trouble. Bill "Bojangles" Robinson came up to the plate to bat for the Vaudeville team. Foster waited nervously on first base. The pitcher threw; Robinson hit.

> A ball was knocked over first base, which made the first baseman [Bert Williams] and his team mates "feel so sick and so forlorn!" [He later said] he saw the ball coming toward him, but it looked like about the size of a marble, hence it made its way into left field uncaptured, and the bases were cleared.[7]

The Vaudeville Nine won the game, 7 to 6.

Another way in which black performers socialized was through fraternal organizations or clubs. On July 5, 1908, black theatrical men founded a club called "The Frogs." The club's name was inspired by Aristophanes' eponymous play. In the play the character Charon makes reference to "our minstrel frogs."[8] The *New York Age* announced the formation and goals of "The Frogs":

> An organization to be known as the "Frogs" was formed Sunday evening at the residence of George W. Walker, 52 West 133rd Street. The prime movers in forming such an organization are the leading actors of the race, and it is the intention of the incorporators to make the "Frogs" to the Negro performer, as well as to members of the race, what the Lambs' Club and the Players' Club mean to the white profession.[9]

In 1908 theatrical clubs such as the Lambs, the Players, and the Friars did not admit black members. The members of the Frogs included not only black actors but songwriters, musicians, and playwrights. At their first meeting the Frogs elected the following officers: George W. Walker, president; John Rosamond Johnson, vice president; Jesse Shipp, treasurer;

and R. C. McPherson, secretary. Bert Williams was elected head of the Art Committee.[10]

The Frogs saw their mission as promoting education of blacks about the race's achievements and providing a social group for discussing these achievements. The *New York Age* said:

> The Frogs have been formed for social, historical and library purposes with a view to promoting social intercourse between the representative members of the Negro theatrical profession and to those connected directly or indirectly with art, literature, music, scientific and liberal professions and the patrons of arts.[11]

One of the Frogs' most popular activities was their annual Frolic Ball; it became a social affair for New York blacks, where Bert Williams could sometimes be seen performing for his peers.

Bandanna Land toured throughout the spring and summer of 1908. When Williams and Walker signed with F. Ray Comstock as the manager of the show, the contract stipulated that "the company shall be booked only in first-class theaters."[12] But in 1907 developments occurred in the theatrical business that had an impact on whether Comstock would be able to live up to this contract clause. On April 28, 1907, the *New York Times* announced that a new theatrical booking combine had been formed by Klaw and Erlanger and the Shuberts. The new company was called the United States Amusement Company. Under the new organization the Shuberts agreed to convert some of their first-class houses into vaudeville houses. In exchange Klaw and Erlanger would book Shubert legitimate attractions in their houses.[13] Klaw and Erlanger issued a statement explaining the motive behind the new arrangement:

> Messrs. Klaw & Erlanger state that the arrangement . . . will at once clear the theatrical atmosphere, that there were altogether too many theatres devoted exclusively to high-class attractions, that while there was an enormous public to support "popular-priced" and vaudeville attractions, the higher-class theatres necessarily catered to a minority.[14]

Lee Shubert told the press "that in the cities where now only one first-class legitimate theater new remains, the public would be benefited, as the poor productions would be eliminated."[15] In other words, the true reasons for the new booking combine were to increase profits for Klaw and Erlanger and the Shuberts by concentrating on vaudeville or popular-priced houses and to give the Shuberts, mainly legitimate producers, a piece of the vaudeville pie.

What remained unexplained from the press discussion of the new booking deal was the criteria by which the Shuberts and Klaw and Erlanger decided whether a show deserved to be in a "high" or "first-class house" or in a "popular-priced" house. Lester Walton feared that the Syndicate and the Shuberts would immediately assign black performers like Williams and Walker to second-class theaters. Early in the 1907–8 season of *Bandanna Land*, Walton observed:

> So far, I have noticed that in such towns as Syracuse and Rochester, they held forth at the same popular price playhouses. Also in Cleveland, they appeared at the Lyceum Theatre – another popular price playhouse. Now, if in Cincinnati they go to Heuck's Theatre, the question will necessarily arise in my mind – When will they make their managers live up to their contracts and play them in the very best houses?[16]

George Walker got the message. Williams and Walker were successful in knocking down Jim Crow laws in several cities. Their company became the first black company to play at a first-class house in Philadelphia:

> Before opening in New York City, the company played in the Park Theatre – the most popular price theatre in Philadelphia. However, the comedians demanded better houses after their long run in New York. That is the reason they did not return to the Park Theatre.[17]

In July 1908 Williams and Walker were booked into the Belasco Theatre in Washington, D.C., again a first for a black theatrical company. Walker was pleased but firm in his intent for first-class theaters for himself and his partner. As he put it: "Either first-class houses or tents."[18]

Bert Williams's victory had some unforeseen consequences. During the second season of *Bandanna Land*, the show played in a first-class house – the Duquesne Theatre in Pittsburgh. The coincidence of racial segregation in the theater with high ticket prices left the house half vacant. The *Dramatic Mirror* editorialized on the incident:

> The booking of those two clever comedians, Williams and Walker, at this house last week certainly proved unprofitable. None of their race were allowed to occupy seats in the parquet, and the result was that this part of the house was almost vacant. Then, too, the high scale of prices was detrimental, as heretofore they had played at popular prices. This, . . . is indeed a plaintive tale, and seemingly bodes ill for the future of the team, through no direct fault of their own. The white people simply will not tolerate the black brother in their midst on the lower floor of these $1.50 houses, even if the colored people were able or inclined to separate themselves from that amount to see a show. It is an indisputed fact that the very sinew of support of a colored show comes more than one-half from the ranks of their own people. Whether or not any attraction can afford to offend or subject to humiliation one-half of its clientele in a vaunting effort to cater to the other half is a financial problem that will solve itself as the season wears on. Capacity business in the popular priced houses, it does seem, as compared to crowded balconies and galleries (and empty lower floors) in the high-priced houses is materially the better proposition for all parties concerned.[19]

On August 20, 1908, *Bandanna Land* officially began its second season at the Grand Opera House in New York City. There were changes in the program from the first season. Bert Williams sang two new songs, "You're in the Right Church But in the Wrong Pew," and "Peace with the World." George Walker introduced a tune entitled "Any Old Place in Dixieland Is Good Enough for Me," while his wife, Aida, had a new number in "Sheath Gown in Darktown."[20]

During the following week, a standing-room-only sign had to be erected at the front of the theater because of Aida Overton Walker's new feature, a version of the famous "Salome" dance. The dance was not new; white dancers such as Isadora Duncan, Marie Madeline, and Gertrude Hoffman had performed the dance as early as 1904. But Mrs. Walker was the first black woman to perform a version of the dance. Her choice was considered daring at that time: Black women simply didn't perform "modern dance," and in some quarters "Salome" was considered almost vulgar. However, Aida Overton Walker's choreography was praised for being "a cleaner dance and void of suggestiveness."[21]

Not to be outdone, Bert Williams came up with his own "burlesque version" of Salome, a week later when *Bandanna Land* played in New Haven, Connecticut.[22] Although Williams enjoyed the hectic traveling and constant changes involved with *Bandanna Land*, there was one change that he couldn't accept. His wife, Lottie, was not with him. Late in the spring of 1908, it was reported that Mrs. Williams had been feeling run-down and would leave the show to rest. It was anticipated that she would return for the second season in the fall. But *Bandanna Land* was to be her last show. Just before Christmas 1908, Lottie Williams announced her retirement "owing to ill health."[23] This means that Lottie Williams retired from show business before her husband joined the *Ziegfeld Follies* and not afterward, as Williams's biographer, Ann Charters, claims.[24] Williams's disappointment must have been considerable, as he liked to have "Mother" (his nickname for his wife) around him when he performed.

After playing New Haven, *Bandanna Land* went to Boston, opening at the Orpheum Theater, a Shubert house. The Orpheum was a high-price house, but orchestra seats were selling as low as a dollar for *Bandanna Land*. Williams and Walker protested. A compromise was reached. "As the show was doing 'big business,'" Lester Walton explained, "it was agreed to let the prices remain unchanged with a promise that in the future, the attraction would play to first-class prices."[25]

Something else happened in Boston, but it went unmentioned in the press. A cast member of *Bandanna Land*, Effie King Wilson (wife of actor Frank H. Wilson), told how George Walker became ill:

> While in Boston one night, George began singing "Bon-Bon Buddie." Suddenly, he began to sing in a thick-lipped manner, droning out the lyrics.

> Mrs. Wilson said she and the other cast members smiled, believing that George was improvising a new gag. Suddenly, however, they learned that he was actually ill, that he had a stroke.[26]

Walker was later diagnosed as suffering from paresis, or incomplete paralysis:

> General paresis is caused by damage to the brain by the syphilis-causing microorganism. . . . Early symptoms of general paresis may include personality changes, memory loss, speech defects, tremors, and temporary paralysis. Seizures may also occur. As the disease progresses, the patient deteriorates both physically and mentally.

The prognosis for Walker was poor because the present-day treatment for syphilis – penicillin – was not available until the 1940s.[27]

Despite his deteriorating health, Walker continued to perform in *Bandanna Land* and at special benefits. In December 1908 the *New York Age* tried to cheer fans of Williams and Walker by stating "George W. Walker is much improved in health and is playing the part of 'Bud Jenkins' with old-time vigor."[28] At Christmas, Walker took time to write an article about his career, which was published in the *New York Age*. At the conclusion of the article, Walker described his partnership with Williams as also a role model for future generations:

> Our payroll is about $2,300 a week. Do you know what that means? Take your pencils and figure how many families could be supported comfortably on that. Then look at the talent, the many-sided talent we are employing and encouraging. Add to this what we contribute to maintain the standing of the race in the estimation of the lighter majority. Now, do you see us in the light of a race institution? That is what we aspire to be, and if we ever attain our ambition, I earnestly hope and honestly believe that our children, that are to be, will say a good word in their day for "Bert and me and them."[29]

In the same vein of thought, Bert Williams expounded on the importance of the black actor in a Chicago newspaper interview. He foresaw a day when blacks could portray any character, comic or tragic, onstage with dignity and lack of discrimination.

> The day is not far off when the traveling negro dramatic company will come to town as often does the Negro musical or minstrel company. The negro actor will then take rank with the negro teacher in the negro school. Booker Washington will then have strong allies in his work of elevating the social standard of the black man. The tragedian or straight comedian will carry the words of Tuskegee Institute to every village and hamlet and into every home, white or black. Companies of purposeful players will, through the presentation of proper plays, aid a more perfect understanding among the races.[30]

Probably neither Williams nor Walker, when they spoke of their vision for black theater, realized that their participation in that vision was coming to a close. In January 1909 many members of the *Bandanna Land* company were struck down with illness. Aida Overton Walker's mother fell ill, forcing the dancer-actress to return home to New York. And George Walker struggled against the telltale symptoms of paresis that became more marked with every performance. Finally, the day came when he could not go on any longer. Walker gave his final performance in Louisville, Kentucky, in February 1909. His doctors and colleagues tried to downplay the seriousness of his illness, attributing it to "overworked nerves."

Walker's wife, Aida, was singing "Bon-Bon Buddie" in a special costume designed for her. Speaking of Walker, Lester Walton said: "During his absence, no one will attempt to play his part, as the show has been rewritten to provide Bert A. Williams with situations without his partner."

The question for Bert was: Could anyone take George's place?[31]

Chapter 15

G eorge Walker's illness forced Bert Williams for the first time to prepare seriously to perform as a solo comedian. He therefore decided to ask F. Ray Comstock for a new contract. Williams said he did so "as I was advised by counsel . . . as the inability of Mr. Walker to continue carrying on the business and to appear in the play, terminated the contract. This led to the making of the contract of May 8, 1909."[1] "This contract," said Comstock, had an unusual provision.

> Even though the old contract had not yet expired . . . I would agree that in case the said George W. Walker became well again, that he could come into the play and could take part in the contract as though he were a party thereto.[2]

Bert Williams absolutely refused to allow any speculation that this new arrangement meant that he and Walker were permanently separated. Late in May 1909 he told reporters "when my old pal is alright . . . we will be together again."[3]

Under this new contract, the company was to be known as "Comstock and Williams." Both parties were to be regarded as legal and financial partners. The old contract would run out on June 1, 1909, and the new one would begin September 1, 1909. It was to last for three consecutive theatrical seasons and "each theatrical season [was] to consist of not less than thirty-five weeks."[4]

Some of the responsibilities of the company were to be shared; others to be divided between the partners. Williams was to select the play, music, lyrics, actors, stage crew, and scenery. However, the details of the production "must be mutually agreed upon by both parties hereto." Williams would also be responsible for staging. He was to be advertised as the star, and if Walker should participate, both would be billed as the stars. Williams was to get $300 a week. If Walker performed, then Williams and Walker would each get $250 a week.

Comstock was responsible for advancing the money for rehearsals and the first production, which would "be repaid to him out of the receipts taken in from the production." Comstock was to book the company "only in theatres in which the prices of seats shall be not less than $1.00 for the first 10 rows of orchestra." Comstock was to keep track of the company's finances. "On the first day of each month, there will be an accounting of business done and profits made during the previous month. At the end of each season, there will be a final acounting." Both parties were to have "free and unrestricted access in person or by representative to the production's business accounting books and vouchers."

Finally the contract stipulated that Bert Williams could not perform for anyone else without Comstock's consent during the term of the contract, which was three years.

In May 1909 Williams appeared for the first time as a solo vaudeville performer in Boston, appearing on a bill that included the Four Keatons. Buster Keaton, who began his career with this family act, recalled an anecdote about a meeting between his father, Joseph Keaton, and Bert Williams. The story painfully illustrates how the stigma of segregation bore heavily upon Williams's personality.

> When Negroes were allowed in white saloons at all, they were restricted to the end of the bar farthest from the door. Pops ignored this the night he walked into the Adams Hotel bar in Boston, which was conveniently situated, being directly behind Keith's Theater. Bert Williams, who was again on the bill with us, was standing, as required, far down at the other end.
>
> "Bert," said Pops, "Come up here and have a drink with me." Bert looked nervously from one white face at the bar to another, and replied, "Think I better stay down here, Mr. Joe."
>
> "All right," said Pops, picking up his glass, "then I'll have to come down there to you."[5]

It was as though Williams was never completely out of character; with or without blackface, he was expected to be a Negro who knew his "place."

But for Williams and the theatergoing public, his real place was onstage in the limelight. When Williams appeared at Hammerstein's in New York, he was undeniably the hit of the bill. *Variety* described the act enthusiastically:

> Three new songs and "Nobody," with a bit of talk worked in between tunes, make up Williams' single specialty. Both songs and talk were highly amusing. Williams was never funnier. "That's Plenty" made a capital opening song. There followed a few minutes of talk adapted from his part of "Skunton" in "Bandanna Land." Even without a foil in his partner, George Walker, Williams' stupid darkey was a scream. His second song failed to keep up the first pace, but he picked up speed with a song about a dispute as to the naming of a baby, Williams' suggestion being something like George Washington, Abraham Lincoln, Booker T., and a lot more, until it was learned that the baby was a girl. The discussion ends when the mother

announces Carrie Jones as the name. "Nobody" served admirably as an encore, and Williams had to repeat his inimitable "loose dance" several times
before they would let him go.[6]

While Williams was playing at the Hammerstein, a legal dispute
erupted that threatened to cut short his engagement. According to the *New
York Age*, Hammerstein was under pressure from a group called the "White
Rats" to drop Williams from headline status.[7] The White Rats were founded
in 1900 as the vaudeville players' answer to the vaudeville managers' group:
the Vaudeville Managers' Protective Association (VMPA).

On June 4, 1909, Williams was the next-to-closing act at Proctor's Fifth
Avenue vaudeville house in New York, located at Twenty-eighth Street and
Broadway. *Variety*'s review of the act was favorable. It noted:

> The headline was Bert Williams,who appeared next to last. Mr. Williams
> registered a strong hit. ... Mr. Williams sang "Nobody" for a finish, going
> big with it, and also with "That's Plenty," which opened [the act]. "Next
> Week, Sometime," did not do much. The talk Williams uses is well-handled.[8]

However, a greater reception greeted Williams in his appearance at
Detroit's Temple Theatre on June 21. The *Detroit Free Press* admired the
performance:

> Williams, late of Williams and Walker, as a tall, dressed-up, shambling black
> gentleman, brought good things to a climax yesterday afternoon when he
> sang that excruciatingly pathetic effusion called "Nobody." No one can draw
> the quintessence of fun from this song like Bert Williams, who has a talent
> for extracting the remotest possibilities of a laugh from every line he utters.[9]

Other members of the old Williams and Walker organization continued
performing. For example, Jesse Shipp and Alex Rogers were hard at work
on a new production scheduled to open in the fall of 1909. Their company
comprised basically the same people who had been with Williams and
Walker earlier.

But in July 1909 came an announcement that shocked the theatrical
world. Aida Overton Walker was leaving the Williams company to perform
elsewhere. The *New York Age* said that Mrs. Walker "and the management
have not been able to agree on several items" in her contract.[10] To many
theatergoers, the unthinkable had happened. Within the short span of six
months, the three black entertainers regarded as inseparable – Bert
Williams, George Walker, and Aida Overton Walker – had separated. The
field was wide open for actors and actresses to replace George and Aida
Walker.

There was speculation as to which black performers would be selected.
Finally, it was announced in the *New York Age* that a successful black
vaudeville act called Brown and Nevarro had been signed to appear in the

piece. Tom Brown (1868–1919) was born in Indianapolis and appeared with the McCabe and Young Minstrels as well as the Richard and Pringle Minstrels. Around 1900 Brown, a light-skinned black man, hit on the idea of playing a Chinese man in his vaudeville act. A dancer, Siren Nevarro, soon joined him, impersonating a Chinese woman. The team toured in Europe, where they were well received. Brown later became a member of the Lafayette Theater company in New York.[11]

The selection of Brown and Nevarro was immediately thought of by many as a replacement for George and Aida Walker. But when questioned by *New York Age* critic, Lester Walton, Brown denied this, saying, "It would be almost impossible for anyone to try to fill their places."[12] In August 1909 the name of the new show in which Brown and Nevarro would appear was announced. It was to be called *Mr. Lode of Koal*.

Meanwhile, that summer Aida Overton Walker had signed a contract with the Cole and Johnson company, and a relative newcomer – Lottie Grady – had been signed as the female lead in the new Bert Williams play. Grady, an attractive black woman, had only a few credits to her name. In 1907 she appeared in the play *Captain Rufus*, and the following year she starred in Chicago's Pekin Theater productions of *The Merry Widower* and *Simple Mollie*. In early 1909 Grady had performed in a play called *The Husband*.[13]

Other than Lottie Grady and Brown and Nevarro, old familiar faces from the Williams and Walker company were in the company of *Mr. Lode of Koal*. Book and lyrics were by Jesse Shipp and Alex Rogers. Music was by J. Rosamond Johnson and Bert Williams. Williams starred as Chester A. Lode. Alex Rogers played the part of Buggsy, Lottie Grady that of Mysteria, and Brown and Nevarro played Gimlet and Gluter. Veterans of the old Williams and Walker company included J. Leubrie Hill as Buttron, Henry Troy as Cap, Hattie McIntosh as Woozy, and Charles Moore as Weedhead.

According to the 1909 contract between Comstock and Williams, Williams was to "have exclusive control of the stage management of the plays." But because of Williams's gentle personality or the tendency of people not to cooperate with him or both, his experience with managing *Mr. Lode of Koal* was a nightmare. He later described the various problems:

> The costumes were secured from the Eaves Costume Company. Mr. Jack Shoemaker obtained an estimate of the costumes and when he was ordered by Mr. Comstock to give the order, Comstock had no money, and Jack Shoemaker had to give his check for five hundred dollars.[14]

Williams said Comstock's carelessness in paying for production expenses caused the problems:

While the company was rehearsing, moneys had to be advanced to the members of the company, which is usual, and the contract provided that there should be advanced, during rehearsals, by Comstock, an amount not to exceed five hundred dollars a week, to be repaid out of the receipts taken in from the said production. All that could be secured from Comstock was four hundred and fifty dollars. I had to advance about six hundred dollars, and Jack Shoemaker, who was simply the manager . . . had to advance five hundred dollars himself of his own money.[15]

We had to have our dress rehearsals without scenery, because the scene artist had not been paid for his work and the scenery was only received the day before we left for Toledo.[16]

The play was to open in Toledo, Ohio, on August 29, 1909. As late as the first of the month, Williams didn't have a booking schedule for the play. Comstock was responsible for bookings. Williams complained:

When it came to about the first of August [1909], we could not get any route from Comstock. . . . This is to me the all-important provision of the contract. Comstock furnished me with no route, nor any contracts for performances to be given for my approval.[17]

When the play opened in Toledo at the end of August, Bert Williams still had no idea where he was going to perform next. But it was his first outing in a full-length show without George Walker, and he had to make the best of it.

The musical *Mr. Lode of Koal* utilized the musical comedy motif of adventures in an exotic setting. But unlike earlier Williams and Walker shows, there was nothing specifically "African" or "black" about the setting of the play. Because of this, the writers had more freedom with the libretto. Lester Walton observed:

Mr. Lode of Koal is a production entirely different from any other colored show every put on boards. In writing the book, Messrs. Shipp and Rogers were not in a serious mood, having put together a vehicle that is known on Broadway as a children's show. It is mythical in its thematic construction and appeals greatly to the imagination.[18]

The fantasy theme of the play was carried out through the dream of Chester Lode about being the king of a mythical kingdom on a mythical island called Koal, and what happened to him during his dreaming and awakening:

The opening scene of the play is laid in the courtyard of the king, Big Smoke, ruler of the mythical island of Koal. Poor Chester arrives just in time to take the place of the king who had been kidnapped by the political bandits of the island.[19]

In Act 1, Bert Williams entered with a monkey following him. It sat on the fence of the court while Chester talked to Buggsy (Alex Rogers). "Bert

Williams [as King Big Smoke] and Alex Rogers have some funny dialogue and exit amid screams of laughter, the monkey in close pursuit of Big Smoke."[20] This was followed by a song sung by Georgia Gomez, "The Harbor of Lost Dreams."[21] It was one of several Williams composed for the show. The lyrics by Alex Rogers told of yearning for faraway places.

Next Chester, alias Big Smoke, consulted a fortune-teller named Mysteria, played by Lottie Grady. Apparently a kind of clairvoyant, Mysteria asked Chester if he wished to have his fortune told. On his agreement,

> The fortune teller starts to tell Big Smoke's fortune. She runs her hand down on Big Smoke's hand, when Big Smoke looks up and says, "Tickle my curls." ... A moment later, Big Smoke is called a big, dark cloud. Big Smoke retaliates by saying, "Don't let dis cloud bust."[22]

According to Lester Walton, this scene "got the biggest laugh I have ever heard on Broadway." The following scene was also heralded as hilarious for Williams's clever use of pantomime. "Tom Brown, Leubrie Hill and Bert Williams next have a funny scene together. Williams sits on the steps and the monkey slips up behind him [unbeknownst to Williams]. When he turns and sees the monkey, the expression of his face is one long laugh and without a word, he exits."[23]

At the end of the first act, "the luscious, sleep-compelling fruit growing on the island and served exclusively to the king is eaten by Chester, who at once begins to enjoy one of the most satisfying and delightful dreams that he could have wished for. Big Smoke walks around the court in a nightgown, holding a candlestick, and looking for a place to sleep.[24]

> On getting near the fence, he sees the monkey asleep on top. The monkey, by the way, has also eaten some of those pretty red berries. ... Big Smoke proceeds to the fence and immediately pushes the monkey over the wall, sits down on a bench with his candle in his hand, and slowly lays down on the bench and goes to sleep as the curtain drops.[25]

At the beginning of Act 2, after a chorus sung by the company, Williams was carried in by four convicts. There was a toe dance performed by Siren Nevarro, and Williams sang another of his compositions, "That's a Plenty."[26]

The second act closed as Williams gurgled beer from a cask while Brown and Nevarro performed a Spanish dance. Williams fell asleep; then Chinese impersonator Tom Brown sang the tune "Chink Chink Chinaman."[27] Composed by Bert Williams and arranged by J. Rosamond Johnson, "Chinaman" offered yet another example of Williams's musical diversity.

When the third act opened, the audience saw a courtyard decorated with many flags and Big Smoke (Bert Williams) waking up shivering with cold. Then a group of confetti-throwing girls suddenly emerged. The Fete of the Seven Veils was on. Inspired by the biblical story of Salome and Herod, this was the same dance that Aida Overton Walker had performed in *Bandanna Land*. Williams danced with the group, and the *Indianapolis Freeman* said:

> Bert Williams dances that Williams comedy dance as only Bert Williams can dance it. He danced with three or four girls looking for Hoola. All girls are veiled. ... Big Smoke unveils the last girl he dances with and finds to his disgust that it is *a man*.[28]

Williams then sings another composition of his: "Believe Me."[29] The lyrics complained about being a scapegoat and were typical of Williams.

> But believe me, I'm gettin' tired of always
> being de dab
> Days worked on me so faithfully
> Til I'se wore most to a rub
> You all have heard about dat straw
> That broke de camel's back
> Well a bubble added to my load
> Would shelly make mine crack
> But believe me.[29]

At the end of the play, the real king, Big Smoke, is released by his kidnappers, and Chester is forced to become a royal servant.

Mr. Lode of Koal opened November 1, 1909, at the Majestic Theater in New York. Several weeks later the members of the cast gave Bert Williams a surprise birthday party (his birthday was November 12). The *New York Age* reported:

> The members of the company surprised him by making a number of birthday presents; the female members giving him a gold-headed umbrella and the men a beautiful vase. Refreshments were served on the stage, and several short presentation speeches were made; the comedian replying by saying, "Believe me, I highly appreciate the consideration you have shown, but as I am no speaker, I will close, for that's a plenty."

In fact, Bert Williams's thirty-fifth birthday celebration in 1909 was to be the only one the cast had. *Mr. Lode of Koal* achieved only forty performances at the Majestic, a very poor record by Broadway standards. And Williams was also upset about playing the Majestic again, far from Broadway. He lashed out at F. Ray Comstock:

> He played us at the Majestic Theatre in New York City ... although the Shuberts have a number of first-class theatres in the City of New York. He promised to play us at the West End Theatre, but did not. And when we were about to close at the Majestic Theatre, he told me that he did not know where he could play us after that engagement. This was several weeks before he did close the tour.[30]

A linoleum caricature of Bert Williams in vaudeville by the artist Alfred J. Früeh (1880–1968). (*Courtesy Wisconsin Center for Film and Theater Research*)

Broadway observers wondered whether Williams could succeed in a show without George Walker. The *New York Age* said:

> A question being asked by many is whether George Walker . . . is greatly missed. . . . When Bert Williams made his initial appearance in the first act, the writer at once thought of Walker, as he had been seeing the two make their first appearance together for years. But the writers [of the show] have so constructed the piece that as the moments fly, Bert Williams . . . proves that he is capable of starring alone successfully.[31]

The *New York Times* also thought Williams did well without Walker, noting that "Bert Williams is fully as amusing by himself as he was as part of the partnership of Williams and Walker in the least. "If the absence of his partner was noticed," said the *St. Louis Post-Dispatch*, "it was an agreeable change to many who found Walker's style of humor at times offensive."[32]

Critics gave Bert Williams high marks for his performance in *Mr. Lode of Koal*. "Williams is worth a trip to the Great Northern," declared the *Chicago Tribune*. "Mr. Williams makes the most of his part," noted the *Toledo Blade*, "and his apparent spontaneous funnyisms proved the magnet that caused much laughter." The *Quincy* (Illinois) *Daily Herald* said, "Bert Williams is the funniest colored comedian in the world." Observing that Bert Williams had developed a unique manner of physical comedy, the *Chicago American* critic wrote: "There is no other funny man on the stage who can do with his hands and feet what Williams can do with his."[33]

Perhaps the best toast to Williams's performance in *Mr. Lode of Koal* came from the theatrical newspaper the *New York Dramatic Mirror*. The *Mirror*, the authoritative show business journal in the country, departed from its cynical attitude toward blacks in its review of *Mr. Lode of Koal*.

> Bert Williams, with still the excruciating dance which is half lope and glide, and dangling arms tipped with white cotton gloves, and with the smile which is the more joyful because it comes only infrequently from the funny gloom with which the comedian in lugubrious tunes tells of his misfortunes; and last, but by no means the least important asset, the characteristic Williams method of singing – with all of these, Mr. Williams proves himself one of the best and most intelligent comedians we have. The test is that one forgets his color, and in the world of fun, color is not an important distinction.[34]

And Williams continued to express his unhappiness with Comstock's booking of the show:

> Comstock furnished me with no route, nor any contracts for performances to be given for my approval. We opened August 29, 1909, in Toledo. While in Toledo, I was informed that we were then to play at St. Louis, and so in that way I was led from place to place, never knowing two weeks in advance where we were going. Not a contract with a theatre was submitted to me for

my approval. In St. Louis, I was notified that we must play a week of one-night stands. Then I played in Kansas City, and [was] told we must go to Chicago. We played Louisville and Indianapolis, and were then jumped to New York, and I did not know until I was in Louisville that I was to play in New York.[35]

Even though Comstock and Williams were joint partners in the venture, communication between the two was almost nil, according to Williams.

> He paid no attention to the company and only visited the company once in Philadelphia when he went there in connection with another attraction ... once in Chicago, when he was out West to attend to some business for the Shuberts, and once, when he was in Cleveland. And there [he] did not even come to the theatre where I was playing to see me, but I went and called upon him at his hotel; I did not find him in, but saw him at his Colonial Theatre.[36]

Ironically Comstock was more than available to the press, and in January 1910 he answered reporters' questions about the show. When asked whether there was any truth to the rumor that George Walker was preparing to return to the stage to star with his wife, Comstock pleaded ignorance. "I have not heard from Mr. Walker for months, and I don't know his true condition. ... As to whether Mr. Walker contemplates appearing next season with his wife, Aida Overton Walker, I must say it is news to me."[37]

The *New York Age* then asked the all-important question concerning Bert Williams:

> Mr. Comstock was asked if there was any truth to the report that the show will close within a few weeks. He stated that he did not see any need of taking the *Mr. Lode of Koal* company off the road, as business has been very good since the first of the year, and charged that such rumors have been put into circulation by wags who know nothing of the affairs of the show whatsoever.[38]

But *Mr. Lode of Koal* did close abruptly in early March 1910. When Comstock made his statement to the press in January, the show had already lost money fourteen of the twenty-three weeks it had played. By March 1910 *Mr. Lode of Koal*'s profit-and-loss statements showed that out of the entire twenty-eight weeks of performances, the show lost money for nineteen weeks. When the "loss on weekly statements – $4,732.18 – is added to the production fees – $6,442.42 – the total loss [is] $11,174.60."[39]

Mr. Lode of Koal was an example of a musical comedy that was an artistic hit but failed at the box office. Lester Walton said that the show failed because Comstock had booked Bert Williams into second-class theaters that had low ticket prices. He cited the National Theater in Philadelphia and the Amphion in Brooklyn as examples. Since George Walker had previously seen to it that he and Williams were booked into first-class houses,

Williams's experience with Comstock was a professional step down. Walton concluded that

> The two persons responsible for the early closing of the production are F. Ray Comstock and Bert Williams. Mr. Comstock is to blame for his lukewarm interest, evincing very little concern in the affairs of the company, and Mr. Williams should be censured for not making the former give him and his show the attention to which both were justly entitled.[40]

Bert Williams needed a good vehicle for his abilities and a better sense of business savoir-faire, Walton decided. What Williams had learned from *Mr. Lode of Koal* was that as a performer he was strong enough to carry a show on his own. He also realized that in the area of business aptitude and management, he badly needed a George Walker.

Chapter 16

W hen *Mr. Lode of Koal* closed, Bert Williams told his company that he hoped to see them again in another all-black show next season.[1] But his future plans were not as clear-cut as he wished others to believe. Williams was also considering performing in music halls in London. The *New York Age* announced in March 1910:

> For over a week, he has been carrying about a contract to play over the Moss-Stoll circuit abroad at a salary of $1,000 a week; the contract calling for four consecutive weeks, with an option to increase the time to twenty weeks, if agreeable to all concerned. All the comedian has to do is to attach his signature to the contract and take passage for London, where he can open in one of the big variety halls.[2]

Simultaneously Williams was also considering a second proposition. "Another big offer is said to come from a Broadway manager, who is anxious to star Mr. Williams in a white show. Similar propositions were made him last year."[3] Williams felt uncomfortable. During the past two years, he had had to make business decisions concerning his career – decisions that George Walker had once made for him. As Sylvester Russell put it: "The serious lessons which Williams had never learned were taught to him during the season past and he will be able to build his new foundation upon his well-earned experience."[4] Russell added that Williams should recognize "that his popularity is still fresh, but as a businessman, he hasn't gotten his feet wet."[5]

In April 1910 Williams accepted an invitation to participate in a tribute to the popular showman George M. Cohan. Such an invitation was considered a form of acceptance by the established white theatrical world of New York. The Friars, who were hosting the dinner, were one of a number of actors' clubs in New York. Williams looked forward to appearing with the Four Keatons, whom he had met while in vaudeville, and with musical comedy star Victor Moore. At the Hotel Astor, part of the ballroom had been converted into a stage and dressing-room area. The Cohan dinner performers scrambled for the few dressing rooms, and Williams, feeling shunned, gradually inched his way into a corner of the stage.

123

The door opened after a few minutes and George Cohan walked in. He took a glance around the stage and spying Williams in the corner, Cohan grasped the situation immediately. He went up to him and shook his hand warmly. "Thank you for coming to help us out with the Frolic tonight," he told Williams. "Come on Bert, you're dressing with me."[6]

Kindhearted as Bert Williams was, however, he simply couldn't afford to play benefits all the time. Because *Mr. Lode of Koal* had been a financial disaster, he needed money badly. Williams stated:

I was left with no money, but a mass of obligations. . . . I was simply swamped with this mountain of debts, which will take me a season at least to pay off. . . . I made my arrangements to play in vaudeville through Mr. Morris Gest [the theatrical booking agent] . . . to whom I paid ten percent.[7]

Williams said that he did not ask F. Ray Comstock for permission to play in vaudeville. "He had nothing whatever to do with it. . . . Surely I would not play in vaudeville for the benefit of the partnership."[8]

On April 11, 1910, he began a brief engagement at Hammerstein's Victoria Theater. Williams was the headliner of the vaudeville bill, but efforts were made to stop this. The White Rats, agitating for equitable conditions for vaudevillians, also believed that "the progress of the colored vaudevillian should be retarded." When Williams's headliner status at Hammerstein's was advertised, the White Rats decided that "no colored artist [should] head a bill over a white vaudevillian." They persuaded the managers of the Victoria to stop promoting Bert Williams as featured star.[9]

Blacks were puzzled by the White Rats' action. In 1906 the White Rats had protested when George Walker helped form a union for black vaudevillians. The White Rats claimed at that time that blacks were able to join their union. In retrospect, when it is remembered that the White Rats had also harassed Williams in 1909, it appears that the White Rats were now "out to get" him: He was the only black vaudevillian so targeted, possibly because he was the highest paid.

The White Rats succeeded in forcing Williams to give up his headliner status, but the Hammerstein management came up with an ingenious plan to let the public know who the *real* star was. On the playbill that week, Maude Raymond was listed first as the headliner. Following her name, but in bigger type, was the name of Bert Williams, described as "the greatest and most original comedian in the world." Hammerstein made sure that "in electric lights in front of the Victoria Theater 'Bert Williams' [could] be seen at a distance, and in the lobby his pictures [were] conspicuous everywhere," said Lester Walton.[10]

Walton was furious, decrying the hypocrisy of the White Rats:

How discordant and irreconcilable do the expressions of white entertainers on the bill seem to the fair-minded, when it is recalled that the same people who crowded around the comedian, congratulated him and pronounced him "great" are responsible for the edict which seeks to draw the color line.[11]

Despite the harassment by the White Rats, Williams was a smash hit at Hammerstein's Victoria. *Variety* commented on Williams's comic monologues: "The yarn about the 'African Dodger' is a capital bit of humor, but the yarn about a colored circuit preacher is probably a more intimate bit of southern Negro story. Both are altogether delightful as told by Williams."[12]

Although the "African dodger" joke was not repeated by the critics, it appears to have been a humorous treatment of a current event. "African dodger" was a game in which white people, "at such amusement places as Coney Island, . . . indulged in the pastime of throwing balls at the heads of irresponsible Negroes." Not until 1917 did the New York state legislature pass a law banning this game.[13] Williams's jokes were frequently social satire based on incidents from real life.

During his nineteen-minute spot, Williams also sang six songs. He opened with "I'll Lend You Anything But My Wife." This was followed by "Believe Me," "Some Folks Call It Chantecler, But It's Just Plain Chicken to Me," "I'll Make You a Present of Her," and "Nobody" as an encore.

The sixth song, "Play That Barbershop Chord," was also a hit with the house. The *New York Age* commented that "even the ushers and waiters joined in the chorus and began to beat time with their feet." When Williams had finished, the applause was so intense that he was compelled to give a little speech thanking them. Through the laughter and applause, some members of the audience were heard to say: "Gee, it's too bad he's colored."[14]

Williams's "second banana" billing continued the following week, with a mind reader named Mrs. Eva Fay as the "featured attraction."[15] By his third week at Hammerstein's, Williams had overcome the stigma of being billed as a minor act. He proved he could draw big crowds no matter *where* he was on the bill. *Variety* said that thanks to Williams, Hammerstein's was breaking records: "The big drawing card is Bert Williams. . . . Hammerstein's hasn't seen the business it has enjoyed for the past three weeks in many a good moons."[16] Williams added a new monologue and introduced two new songs: "Late Hours" and "You're Going to Get Something You Don't Expect."

During the fourth week of his vaudeville stint, Williams appeared at two variety houses. At Hammerstein's Williams offered a shorter version of his act the previous week. He appeared early on the bill, played for twenty-one minutes, and then left to travel uptown to the Alhambra for another show. The Alhambra, part of the B. F. Keith vaudeville chain, was located at 126th Street and Seventh Avenue. Williams looked forward to playing the

Alhambra, one of the few New York theaters that allowed blacks to sit in the peanut gallery, "or as it was less delicately termed, 'nigger heaven.'"[17] At the Alhambra Williams performed songs and monologues. "After finishing his routine, he offered 'Nobody' to quiet the gallery and got away with the hit of the bill in twenty-three minutes."[18]

Bert Williams's stint in vaudeville gave him renewed confidence in his potential as an entertainer after the *Mr. Lode of Koal* fiasco. After overcoming the White Rats' boycott, he was a "hot ticket," and Broadway managers took notice. It must have been sometime during his vaudeville engagement in April 1910 that Bert Williams was approached by Florenz Ziegfeld. Since 1907 Ziegfeld had made his annual *Follies* the foremost revue on Broadway. There was a drawback, however. It was an all-white show and predominantly female. Williams had performed on vaudeville bills with whites before. But this was different. The advantages were that Williams would have steady employment: The *Follies* opened each June, and after the summer it toured the country. Furthermore, he would not have the stage management problems and responsibilities he had with *Mr. Lode of Koal*. Most of all, Ziegfeld offered him the opportunity to make history by becoming the first black entertainer to appear in a regular, full-length Broadway revue. The offer was tempting. Williams discussed the offer with David Gerber of the law firm Dittenhoefer, Gerber, and James in New York City. Gerber told Williams to accept Ziegfeld's offer, since he believed that F. Ray Comstock had not complied with his contract. Williams went to give Comstock the bad news; Comstock later told of the incident in a court affidavit:

> On or about the 22nd day of April 1910, the defendant called on me and advised me that he had an offer from Florenz Ziegfeld to appear in "The Follies of 1910" on the roof garden of the New York Theatre, to be starred and to go thereafter on a tour of the country.[19]

Comstock told Williams that "he had no right whatever to do this, and that if he attempted to make a contract with any other manager that he [Comstock] would be compelled to apply for an injunction to restrain him." According to Comstock, Williams said that "he had been to see David Gerber, his lawyer, and that he said David Gerber advised him that he could not be enjoined because he was practically a partner of the plaintiff." When Comstock heard this, he got angry. He said to Bert Williams: "Why did you agree with me that you would perform for nobody else for a period of three years? Do you think it is fair for you to throw me down after losing all this money and going with other managers?" Comstock reported that Williams declared: "My lawyer, Mr. Gerber, told me that I could break my contract with you, and that he was the lawyer for Mr. Ziegfeld, and that he would protect me, and that I could go in to work and that I am going to do so."[20] Williams himself gave a different version of the episode, however:

"It is untrue. . . ," said Williams, "that I told him that at any time I could break my contract. What I did state was that he had broken his contract, and in effect, that I had been advised that I could dispose of any time and services as I wished."

Williams said that he told Comstock that since "he had not kept any part of the contract . . . he surely could not expect me to continue under it." Williams said that the conversation took place May 7, 1910, "after I had been playing vaudeville engagements in the City of New York for four weeks."[21]

David Gerber filed a complaint against Comstock in New York State Supreme Court. The major issues Williams cited were:

1. That the defendant did not perform the said contract on his part and did not book the theatrical company giving the performances. . . . for thirty-five weeks.

2. That he made expenditures which were not mutually agreed upon, for scenery, costumes and property for the play. . . . Contracts were made, alleged expenditures claimed to have been incurred by the defendant, which were not agreed upon to by this plaintiff.

3. That a large amount of money was taken in from the performances given under the said contract, and no accounting has been rendered by the defendant to the plaintiff. . . .

4. That the parties hereto cannot agree upon the policy to be pursued, and have not and cannot agree upon any new play, and will not and do not concur in respect of the future business under said contract.[22]

Williams asked the court for termination of the 1909 contract and the Comstock-Williams business partnership; a final accounting of all business deals or transactions, contracts, profits and losses, and the like; and judgment in favor of Williams "against the defendant for the sum to which, on such accounting he may be found to be entitled, and other awards for damages that the court may see fit."[23]

On the same day that Bert Williams filed suit, a motion for a hearing was filed by Comstock's attorney, William Klein. Klein also filed an affidavit on behalf of F. Ray Comstock. The affidavit was a plea to enjoin Williams from working for Florenz Ziegfeld. Comstock alleged that Bert Williams had broken his contract. On May 10 Williams replied to Comstock, accusing the latter of breaking the contract himself. Three days later, Comstock filed another affidavit, refuting Williams's claims. On May 17 Williams issued a rejoinder to Comstock. The dispute between Williams and Comstock amounted to a suit and countersuit, each alleging that the other had broken the contract. The making of the contract between Comstock and Williams has been discussed earlier. What follows is a summary of the litigants' versions of what happened after the contract was signed.

According to Comstock, Williams was a risk:

Up' to that time, it was a physical impossibility to determine whether the defendant herein alone would be a good star or drawing attention, and I was advised by well-known managers that the defendant herein alone would not be a financial success. . . . I notified the defendant herein of that fact, and he requested me to make a contract with him for a year to see whether he would make such a financial success. I thereupon stated to the defendant that that would not be fair as I would be compelled to match my money against his talent and that it might take a year for him to become a thoroughly well-recognized star. But that perhaps if there was a loss, I would be compelled to retrieve during a long run and then I advised him that I would make a contract with him for a period of three years, taking my chance upon him being a success.[24]

With respect to the first-class bookings, Comstock argued that Williams was alluding to a certain clause in an old contract:

The contract under which I am claiming damages is the one which commenced with the season of 1908 and . . . was made May 8th, 1909. . . . The reference to that paragraph [which Williams cited] has also nothing whatsoever to do with this case, because it is a past contract that has expired. As a matter of fact, I did agree to give him exactly what is shown in the fourth paragraph of the defendant's affidavit, that is "to be booked in first-class theatres for which the prices of seats shall range from at least twenty-five cents to one and 50/100 ($1.50) dollars per seat," and I have carried out that contract.[25]

Comstock continued:

I deny that I promised the defendant that the bookings would be the best that the Shuberts could give . . . With reference to the theatrical season being not less than thirty-five weeks and the tour and list of theatres to be submitted to the defendant on or before August 1st. I allege that I did submit such tour and list to the defendant before August 1st.[26]

"Bert Williams is trying to con the court," Comstock added, "by his affidavit to show that he gave me fifty percent of the profits just for the booking of the play. This is untrue." Comstock cited social reasons for the apparent haphazard booking of *Mr. Lode of Koal*. He argued:

I endeavored to secure the best possible time for the defendant in which to secure the most money. In some towns, a colored company can secure great returns, and in others none, and that with this view, I caused the company to be taken in such towns and at such times where the most money would be obtained.[27]

Comstock stated that Williams asked him for permission to star in vaudeville after *Mr. Lode of Koal* closed. "Thereafter, the defendant called on me and we practically agreed upon a play for next season," said Comstock.[28]

Comstock concluded that the claims Bert Williams was making were absurd. "I deny that I owe moneys to Mr. Shoemaker for moneys advanced at various times when I had none. . . . I deny every allegation of the defendant that there was scarcely a line of the agreement which I performed."[29]

He pleaded with the court to honor his request to enjoin Williams from working for Ziegfeld:

> The defendant is an actor, performer and comedian of exceptional repute and character, has performed with great skill, he is unique, and extraordinary as a comedian and no one else can replace him. . . . It was part of the consideration that induced me to make the contract with him that he would appear for me only, and for no one else throughout the period of the said three years.[30]

"There was scarcely a line of this agreement, casting an obligation upon the plaintiff [Comstock], that he performed," Bert Williams declared to the New York State Supreme Court. "I was willing . . . to give the plaintiff fifty percent of the profits, provided that he would book the play as contemplated by the contract, but the plaintiff did not live up to any of the obligations which he assumed," said Williams. Comstock promised bookings "would be the best that the Shuberts could give."[31]

Williams's complaints about the booking of *Mr. Lode of Koal* focused on three issues: (1) the cross-country railroad routing, (2) the booking of the show into second-class houses, and (3) the booking of the show for fewer than thirty-five weeks. Although the court affidavits submitted by Williams mention other issues, a reading of the documents shows that Williams regarded the booking issues as the crux of the case. Williams said that Comstock did not use prudence in booking the show. He said that he was "jumped" from New Haven to Philadelphia and from Cleveland to Boston during the tour of *Mr. Lode of Koal*. "Naturally," said Williams, "that kind of booking resulted in a loss which the plaintiff now claims amounted to between eleven and twelve thousand dollars in the season. That sort of routing and booking necessarily would eat up all profits in railroad fares."[32]

Williams suggested that the reason Comstock never submitted a booking route to him before opening in Toledo was that Comstock was trying to deceive him. Williams said, "If he had one, [he] kept it concealed from me because he could not, or if he could, he did not book the attraction as contemplated by the agreement." Williams repeatedly called attention to the fact that he was booked in theaters where orchestra seats were sold for less than a dollar – a clear violation of the 1909 contract. He named the second-class theaters in which *Mr. Lode of Koal* had played:

> I was played in houses, such as Court Street, Brooklyn; the Amphion, Williamsburg; Grand Opera House in Philadephia; Great Northern, Chicago; and also the Lyceum in Cleveland; which were not first-class theatres, or

theatres in which any of the orchestra seats were charged as high as one dollar, [even] though in Cleveland, Comstock is the proprietor and lessee of the theatre called the Colonial, which is first-class, and in Philadelphia his associates, the Shuberts, have two theatres, the Adelphi and the Lyric, but I was only booked for the second-class theatres in those cities.[33]

Williams averred that being booked into these second-class theaters made financial losses of *Mr. Lode of Koal* inevitable. He said: "The result of this sort of treatment, and this method of booking the attraction resulted in practically loss after loss. In every second-class house that we were booked, we lost money."[34]

Williams challenged Comstock to prove to the court that he was booked for a thirty-five-week season.[35] "He does not, and cannot deny that I never got thirty-five weeks of booking," said Williams. Williams said that Comstock was lying when he claimed that the company played for only twenty-seven weeks because Williams wanted to perform in vaudeville during the balance of the time. Williams explained:

> Now, as a matter of fact, the company closed March 5th and I got no vaudeville engagement until April 11th. I only undertook to go into vaudeville after our tour was closed and the plaintiff could furnish me no other bookings.[36]

Williams said that he sensed that the show was in trouble early on but could not prove it because he had not seen the accounting books. He said that he continued performing nonetheless and stressed that it is bad business practice to close a show early:

> It is fatal to the prospects of a performer, particularly one who is part owner of a production, to close his tour in the middle of the season. This not only advertises the fact that he and his play is a failure, but it injures him in his profession and with owners of theatres where the play is to appear later in the season. It leaves the time of the theatres open, with the difficulty of filling the time, and all blame would fall upon me if it had gone out in the profession that I had refused to continue performing in the middle of the season.[37]

Williams refuted Comstock's allegation that they had picked a new play for production next season. "It is true," said Williams, "that at one interview, Mr. Comstock suggested taking a vaudeville sketch, to be padded and lengthened into a two-act play. But I did not and would not approve of that suggestion. No play was prepared."[38]

Williams said that the Comstock-Williams partnership was a financial mess. He cited the fact that his show lost money nineteen weeks out of a total of twenty-seven. "The firm owed over $11,174.60, in addition to some unstated amount for printing,"[39] said Williams. "I find myself indebted to the plaintiff for $5,500 and in liabilities to creditors of the firm of Comstock and Williams," Williams confessed to the court. Williams said that he had already started paying Comstock back. "To indicate my good faith, I paid the plaintiff ... three hundred and twenty-five dollars, out of my salary while in vaudeville, to apply toward my share of the losses."[40] He asked the court to force Comstock to give a final accounting of the business and to turn over all account books and vouchers. Williams said that the closing of *Mr. Lode of Koal* had caused him economic hardship. "I found myself heavily in debt, without sufficient money to pay even the premium on my life insurance which was maturing and all these obligations and losses to meet."[41]

Williams concluded his court affidavits by denouncing Comstock and his ways. "I am thoroughly dissatisfied with the plaintiff as a business partner and with his methods of doing business. ... We cannot get along in this business venture and I will not continue in business with one who has confronted me with nothing but losses."[42]

In December 1910 Judge McCall of the New York State Supreme Court denied the motion enjoining Bert Williams from appearing for Florenz Ziegfeld. Williams was free to explore new vistas.

Chapter 17

I n an interview with the *New York Age*, Bert Williams described his reasons for choosing to work for Florenz Ziegfeld:

> The colored show business – that is colored musical shows – is at the low ebb just now. I reached the conclusion last spring that I could best represent my race by doing pioneer work. It was far better to have joined a large white show than to have starred in a colored show, considering conditions.[1]

Williams was aware, however, that he was taking a risk: "When I became a member of the Follies of 1910, I well knew that my success would be due to the tact that I displayed. I realized that it was up to me to be a success or failure."[2]

The *Ziegfeld Follies* contract was for three years. It is not known what salary Williams earned. However, Williams had said he "could make twice the salary in vaudeville." If Williams was earning about $1,000 a week in vaudeville (what he received with George Walker in the act), he must have earned around $500 a week starting out with the *Follies*.

The contract also stipulated "that at no time would he be on stage with any of the female members of the company," and that the *Follies* tour would include no Southern towns. It was felt that Southern audiences would resent a show with an integrated cast.[3] Despite press reports of a contract signing, Williams claimed that the agreement between him and Ziegfeld was an oral one. He said: "There never has been any contract between us, just a gentleman's agreement."[4]

Florenz Ziegfeld, Jr. (1867–1932), was the son of a Chicago music teacher who sometimes served as music director for public concerts and vaudeville shows. For the 1893 Chicago Columbian Exposition, Ziegfeld helped his father recruit entertainment. The stunt man, Eugene Sandow, with whom Williams and Walker appeared early on, was Ziegfeld's first discovery. His next was French showgirl Anna Held (1875–1918). Held had worked the French revue stage without resounding success. She was not considered especially talented, "but her intimate style, her studied artifice, her tiny, exquisite body fascinated audiences."[5] Held, who became Ziegfeld's first wife, is sometimes credited with suggesting the idea of the *Follies* to Ziegfeld. However, Broadway librettist Harry B. Smith, in his autobiography, *First Nights and First Editions*, insists that the *Follies* was his brainchild.[6]

The first *Follies* in 1907 seems to have been a variety show. The major attraction was a chorus line of fifty women called "the Anna Held Girls." Although Anna wasn't in the chorus line, she did appear in the show. The "Ziegfeld Girls," as the chorus girls were later called, had to pass a rigorous audition. Ziegfeld once described it: "On days of inspection, the girls pass through my office in long lines. As they pass, I say 'Yes' or 'No.' That is all. Those to whom I say 'Yes' go down to the stage."[7]

On the roof garden of the New York Theater, the women were arranged according to height. Ziegfeld favored showgirls with both a figure *and* a personality. He explained that there was a difference. "Beauty," said Ziegfeld, "is something you *see*. Personality is something you *feel*."[8] Although Ziegfeld was said to have boasted that "you see on my stage every type of beauty," this was not the case. "He never said it," observed one theater historian, "but they had to be Caucasian. . . . There were no orientals and no Negroes."[9]

However, Ziegfeld had no compunction about hiring a Negro comedian – Bert Williams – thereby becoming the first major Broadway producer to hire a black as a regular in a revue. But in 1910 most white Americans weren't ready for integration. And when Williams showed up for his first *Follies* rehearsal, the other cast members revolted. Bert Williams later recalled the incident:

> When Mr. Ziegfeld first proposed to engage me for the Follies, there was a tremendous storm in a teacup. Everyone threatened to leave; they proposed to get up a boycott if he persisted, they said all sorts of things against my personal character. But Mr. Ziegfeld stuck to his guns and was quite undisturbed by anything that was said.[10]

Some of the cast members told Ziegfeld: "Either he goes or we go." Ziegfeld is said to have replied: "Go if you want to. I can replace every one of you, except the man you want me to fire."[11] Bert Williams believed that the attempts to slander him were provoked by jealous actors outside the *Follies* company. He said: "It was not people in the company, I since discovered, but outsiders who were making use of that line of talk for petty personal purposes."[12]

There is no record of any performer quitting the 1910 *Follies* to protest the hiring of Bert Williams. But though the company consented to his presence, they withheld their acceptance. As late as three weeks before opening night, the comedian had yet to be given a role in the show. Williams keenly felt the rejection, and when his absences from rehearsals were noted in the press, rumor had it that he would not be in the *Follies* after all.[13] Williams's pride had been wounded. To have come this far as a trailblazer for his people only to be pushed back out the door! When he had disagreements with people like Walker in 1906, Williams's reaction was to physically retreat.

It may have been during this time that Williams was considering another offer – from David Belasco.

David Belasco (1854–1931) was then reaching his peak as a dramatist and theatrical producer. Belasco started as a manager of the Madison Square Theater in New York and as stage manager of the Lyceum Theater before opening his own theater – the Belasco – in 1907. One of his major contributions to the theater was his naturalistic approach to drama.[14] Belasco was known for putting on such works as *The Heart of Maryland*. Like Ziegfeld, Belasco was a "star-maker." Among the actors he produced or "discovered" were Mrs. Leslie Carter, David Warfield, and Blanche Bates. Belasco hoped to add Bert Williams to this list of stars. He said: "It . . . occurred to me that a genuine Negro comedian of high class, properly directed and placed before the public in the right way, would become immensely popular and successful."[15]

Writing about Williams in an essay included in Mabel Rowland's book, *Bert Williams – Son of Laughter*, Belasco told of his meeting with the comedian. "I had seen Mr. Williams, then a young man, and had discerned in him the latent genius of comicality. I sent for him and proposed to take him under my management."[16]

Mabel Rowland retold the story from Bert Williams's viewpoint: "Belasco had sent for him, what should he do? Williams asked Rowland. He was elated and he declared then that that was the happiest moment of his life, all other professional and social honors to the contrary withstanding."[17]

For years Williams had yearned to break out of his darky stereotype characters and perform legitimate dramatic parts, but still in blackface. In 1909 he had issued a call to the theater community to give the black man opportunities in drama. Williams pleaded:

> Let some Shakespeare arise and write a drama; the story of the Negro to rise from meniality and servility to a position of independence, portraying the difficulties that seem almost insurmountable, keeping always in mind a certain omnipresent prejudice against him. . . . Has the dramatist appreciated his every opportunity? . . . Let us have a Negro drama such as Shakespeare might have written to help him out. And let us raise a Negro Booth to interpret it.[18]

Now it looked as though his dream might be coming true. When asked by his friend if he was going to see Belasco, Williams feigned modesty and declared he "guessed he just wouldn't go at all, he'd just be taking up the man's time."[19] Williams's friends wouldn't hear of this: "You have to go!" they told him. Williams bought a new suit and took a taxi to Belasco's office on the day of the appointment. As he was getting out of the cab, he caught his coat pocket on the door handle. His suit was torn. Williams laughed about it later as he recalled: "You know–me visiting Belasco. All dressed up. So warm now. I had had to tear the suit to get back to earth. As I tore it, I stood on the pavement and said to myself out loud–that's the ape part–tearing its clothes."[20]

When Belasco entered the office, he smiled and shook Williams's hand. "I have sent for you because you are ready for me," said Belasco. The theater producer complimented Williams on his past work and told him that he wanted to produce him in a play "in the not far-distant future."[21] At the time Belasco didn't have a play in mind, but he told Williams that he would probably write one or was willing to consider any play that Williams suggested.

Belasco contacted Williams apparently unaware that Williams had agreed to appear under Florenz Ziegfeld's management. Bert Williams admitted to his friends "that he had lacked the courage to tell Belasco the true state of affairs; that there [were] contractual difficulties. He wanted advice."

Some people felt that Williams should tell Ziegfeld of Belasco's offer and ask to be released from the contract. However, Williams recalled how Ziegfeld had defended him during the *Follies* cast revolt and "interposed an argument for loyalty and what he owed to the man who had taken a chance on him."[22] A lawyer present argued that Erlanger wasn't a person to take "chances" and if Bert Williams wasn't talented, he wouldn't have gotten a Ziegfeld contract at all. Williams agreed with the lawyer and decided to ask Ziegfeld to waive his option for a contract after the initial three years were up.[23]

Belasco frequently signed up stars for his productions without a specific play in mind. Williams didn't know that this was typical of Belasco's business practice. Belasco explained in his book *The Theatre Through Its Stage Door*:

> As I always have a number of plays in preparation, I must ever be on the lookout for chance talent. I make it a point to see as many would-be actors as my time permits. It does not take very long for me to gain a fairly accurate idea of their motives and possibilities. ... They may become useful to me, even if I have nothing in prospect at the moment.[24]

Williams looked forward to the time when he would be able to appear in a Belasco play, perhaps even be able to play Shakespeare! He thought he might write a play, which he hoped Belasco would consider producing. Mabel Rowland recalled:

> With our assistance, he wrote a play which he thought would suit him as a
> Belasco star, and called it "Bawndy." That was the name of the central figure
> and aside from its being the sort of nickname that adheres to every local
> youth in the South, the locale of the play, it spelled of the actor's initials and
> the contraction of his best-known song, "Nobody."[25]

Rowland claims that Williams never presented the play to Belasco.
Bawndy is now presumed lost, and Rowland's description is all we know
about it.

Williams faced the toughest decision of his life with the Belasco proposal. A number of factors were involved. The Comstock-Williams lawsuit
was still pending in New York State Supreme Court. Although Williams felt
that he had proved that F. Ray Comstock had broken his contract with him,
he had no way of knowing how the court would eventually rule. Technically
then, he was still under contract to Comstock. But he had also made an
agreement with Ziegfeld. To become involved with Belasco at this point
would be to compound his legal problems, especially if the court ruled in
Comstock's favor. Belasco also didn't have a play ready for him, and
Williams must have seen this also as an obstacle. He needed to work right
away because of the bills from *Mr. Lode of Koal.* As gratifying as it would
have been to his artistic ambitions to work with Belasco, Williams chose to
forego this in favor of economic survival with Ziegfeld.

Bert Williams had to tell Belasco that he could not work for him.
Belasco, unaware of the details of the situation, was mystified by Williams's
action. He wrote:

> At first, he was overjoyed and he immediately consented. But as we went fur-
> ther and further into the project, he became more and more fearful that he
> would be unable to perform what I had planned for him and would fail to
> fulfill my expectation. At last, overcome by diffidence and modesty, he came
> to me and begged to be released. I tried my best to reassure him, but after
> a week or two more, finding that apprehension and worry were making him
> literally ill, of course I consented – though with great regret – to cancellation
> of our agreement.[26]

It is interesting to speculate on how different Williams's career might
have been had he appeared in David Belasco's productions.

Eventually Williams returned to the *Follies* rehearsals, but with a wary
attitude. He reported later:

> I always get on perfectly with everyone in the company by being polite and
> friendly but keeping my distance. Meanwhile, I am lucky enough to have real
> friends, people who are sure enough of themselves not to need to care what
> their brainless and envious rivals will say if they happen to be seen walking
> along the street with me.[27]

Bert Williams was not the only newcomer to the 1910 *Follies*. The other was the legendary comedian Fanny Brice (1891–1951).[28] The daughter of a French-Jewish saloonkeeper, Charles Borach, as a thirteen-year-old New Yorker from the Lower East Side, Brice entered the amateur-night contest at Brooklyn's Keeney Theater. Later, during a stint singing and playing piano in a movie house, she changed her name to Brice.

When she was discovered by Ziegfeld, "she was earning eighteen dollars a week at Seamon's Transatlantic Burlesque," says Marjorie Farnsworth.[29] Brice proved to be a hit with the 1910 *Follies*, and she appeared in seven editions of the *Ziegfeld Follies* in all. The 1921 *Follies* was considered Brice's high point in the series, as she sang the songs "Second-Hand Rose" and "My Man."

When the Shubert brothers produced their own *Ziegfeld Follies* in 1934, Brice was the headliner. In this production she introduced the character of "Baby Snooks," which she later popularized on radio.

Ziegfeld was paying Brice more money than she got in burlesque: seventy-five dollars a week.[30] But at rehearsals she felt lost: No one had given her a song to perform in the show. Ziegfeld told her to "talk to the music boys." Brice approached the songwriters, who were swamped with performers fighting for a tune. The composers were Will Marion Cook, the composer of Bert Williams's hit show *In Dahomey*, and Joe Jordan (1882–1871), a ragtime pianist and composer for many black productions, including the 1928 show *Keep Shufflin'*. Fanny had a plan. After the rehearsal was over, Brice invited Cook and Jordan to her house for supper. When the songwriters had their fill of food, Brice talked them into writing a song for her.[31] The next day at rehearsal, she asked Ziegfeld and Erlanger to listen to her new song: "Lovey Joe." The chorus of the song went as follows:

> Lovey Joe, that ever-lovin' man
> From way down south in Birmingham
> He can do some lovin' an' some lovin' sho'
> An' when he starts to love me
> I jest hollers for mo'.[32]

Fanny Brice gave her rendition of "Lovey Joe" everything she had, right down to mimicking black dialect. However, this offended theater manager Abe Erlanger:

> "What," he demanded. "What's that? What did you say? What's that last line?" Fanny looked at Ziegfeld, who nodded. "I just hollers for mo'," she repeated. "Not for $2.50 a ticket, you don't holler for *mo'*, you're not in burlesque now, young woman. You holler for more. *More!*" "This is a coon song, Mr. Erlanger," Fanny explained. "I can't do it any other way, I always say mo'."[33]

An even more humorous version of this has Brice telling Erlanger: "I live on 128th Street. It's on the edge of Harlem. They all talk that way!"[34]

Erlanger was furious. "You're out! No one says 'mo' to me on stage!" Ziegfeld, Cook, and Jordan refused to look at Fanny. She ran offstage into the theater lobby. It was two nights before the Atlantic City opening, and now she was out of the show. When Ziegfeld walked up to her, she exclaimed: "What am I going to do, Mr. Ziegfeld? . . . I'm out." "You're in," he said. Then Ziegfeld cautioned her to stay away from Erlanger and to sit in the ladies' room on the train to Atlantic City. Only when she appeared onstage there could Erlanger see her.[35] Again Ziegfeld had gone to great lengths to keep a performer in the 1910 *Follies*. The debuts of Fanny Brice and Bert Williams made this edition of the *Follies* one of the most memorable.

A *Ziegfeld Follies* opening was usually scheduled for a night in June. The premiere always attracted a large crowd of society people, entertainment celebrities, and government officials. Ticket speculators asked as much as one hundred dollars a ticket for a *Follies* opening night. The 1910 *Follies* opened in the roof garden (or the Jardin de Paris, as it was called), of the New York Theater. "Roof gardens" were popular places of entertainment in the days before Manhattan theaters were air-conditioned. The *New York Times* reported that "the garden has been redecorated for the summer and new chairs have been installed." In the center of the roof was an electric-lighted platform that displayed the number 1910. Admission was one dollar. Ziegfeld employed a cast of 125, an orchestra of 42, and 60 "Anna Held Girls."[36]

The principal performers included Ziegfeld girl Lillian Lorraine, British comedian Billie Reeves, and comedian Harry Watson. But theater history remembers the 1910 edition of *Ziegfeld's Follies* for its two newcomers: Bert Williams and Fanny Brice. According to the program, early in the show Brice sang a song called "Goodbye Becky Cohn." While the song has been ascribed to Irving Berlin, this does not seem to be the case. In burlesque before she joined the *Follies*, Brice sang the Irving Berlin song "Sadie Salome," which had lyrics by Edgar Leslie. Her rendition of this song was in Yiddish, just like her "Goodbye Becky Cohn."[37] (In fact, this latter song was composed not by Irving Berlin but by Fred Fisher, with lyrics by Harry Breen. Conceivably early critics confused the two, and the confusion was incorporated into theater legend, giving Irving Berlin credit for the song. Fred Fisher [1874–1942] was a Tin Pan Alley composer who wrote numerous popular songs between 1907 and 1940, including two songs popularized by Al Jolson: "That Little German Band" and "Who Paid the Rent for Mrs. Rip Van Winkle When Rip Van Winkle Went Away?") *Variety* panned "Becky Cohn," claiming that this "Yiddish" number couldn't get over with the audience.[38]

The other newcomer to the *Follies*, Bert Williams, was paired with Billie Reeves in what the program called "A Scene in Reno." The reference to Reno is to the Jack Johnson–Jim Jeffries fight in Reno, Nevada, on July 4, 1910. At the height of his career, Jack Johnson was one of the most controversial black men in the world. He won the world heavyweight champion title from Tommy Burns in Australia in 1908. But the white boxing world would not concede that Johnson was champ. The search began for a "great white hope," or a white boxer to defeat Johnson. Veteran boxer Jim Jeffries was pulled out of retirement, pushed into the boxing ring, and was defeated by Johnson.

When the results of the fight were announced, Jeffries's supporters were outraged. Race riots started in more than fifty American cities.[39] The sensational fight and its aftermath were so overwhelming that the *New York Times* devoted its first four pages on July 5 to those topics. In New York City rioting broke out in the Hell's Kitchen and San Juan Hill districts and in Harlem. The Fifty-third Street area, home of the Marshall Hotel where black theater people gathered, also experienced trouble. The *Times* said that the uptown riot started when someone issued a call for lynching: "A cry of 'Let's lynch the first nigger we meet!' started a riot in front of a saloon in Eighth Avenue near 135th Street soon after Johnson was reported the winner over Jeffries."[40]

It may have been Bert Williams's idea to do a skit on the Jack Johnson fight, since he had taken boxing lessons from former lightweight champ Joe Gans in exchange for fixing Gans up with a date. "Gans was interested in a dusky belle attached to the Williams and Walker organization, and he depended on the star's courtesy for admittance. In order to curry favor with Williams, he undertook to instruct him in boxing."[41]

The skit was later added to the *Follies* program, and Williams rehearsed his role as "Johnson" with Harry Watson. Williams was apparently a pretty good boxer, as Abe Erlanger discovered during one rehearsal.

> He put on the boxing gloves and, without warning, dealt Williams a staggering blow on the jaw. For one moment, the latter was a trifle dazed and he contented himself with merely reaching down and tapping Mr. Erlanger frequently on top of the head, meanwhile protecting his face from attack. Erlanger, however, continued to rush and the members of the company were shocked a moment later, when Williams let fly his right hand and caught the chief squarely on the chin. Mr. Erlanger fell to the floor in a more or less comatose condition and rolled half way across the stage. He struggled to his feet, a little groggy and considerably chagrined, and turning to Watson, said: "There, that's the way I want it done."[42]

But it was Billie Reeves (1864–1943) rather than Harry Watson who portrayed Jim Jeffries in the show. The *Washington Post* admired the manner in which Reeves and Bert Williams burlesqued the fight, reflecting that "Williams and Reeves do a real legitimate imitation of what actually happened."[43]

Dressed as a gardener, Bert Williams appeared for a song specialty spot in Scene 8. One program described the background scenery as a picture of a "watermelon patch."[44] Although he was still wearing blackface, Williams was breaking new ground by acting such roles as gardener, porter, taxi driver, and so on. Because these jobs were typical of black laborers in 1910, Williams was breaking away from the minstrel image in order to portray a more realistic image of the black man onstage. Williams came on to wild applause.[45]

The *New York Times* did not think that the six songs Williams sang were of equal quality. Two songs, "Believe Me" and "Constantly," were written by Williams. Chris Smith and Jim Burris were the lyricists for "Constantly," a hard-luck song in the genre of "Nobody" and "Jonah Man." "Believe Me" was also a hard-luck song in the folksy Williams style. Alex Rogers wrote the lyrics, which are in dialect and meant to be partly recited and partly sung. Williams's lyricists, over the years, made up almost a who's-who of black songwriters. For instance, Chris Smith was a black Tin Pan Alley tunesmith who wrote songs like "I Want a Little Lovin' Sometime," for Marie Cahill.[46]

Ashton Stevens of the *Chicago Examiner* wrote:

> "Constantly" was another one of those "Nobody" classics, creaming with dismal fun, a minor epic of hard luck. It was slow-quoted, looper-jointed Williams at his deadliest. His funer[e]al joy in that song laid us out and we forgot that we were dead when we waked to applaud for more. "Believe Me" was another darktown ditty of fabulous humor – at least so Bert Williams made it sound and look.[47]

One song Williams sang, "The Black Cat," bombed. *Variety* said it "did a double somersault."[48] But the real crowd pleaser, according to the *New York Daily Tribune*, was "Play That Barber Shop Chord." It as a number "in which he revealed his exceptional powers as a comedian." The impact that Williams had on the audience with his song set was sensational. The *New York Sun* said: "Mr. Williams won the honors for humor. Although he came on late in the long first act, only two of his predecessors had succeeded in creating anything like the same degree of merriment."[49]

No *Follies* was complete without a "review," or travesty, of contemporary stage shows. In 1910 Ziegfeld chose the French play *Chantecler*, by Edmond Rostand, author of numerous plays, of which *Cyrano de Bergerac* is the most famous. *Chantecler* opened in New York in early 1910. The piece revolved around the character of Chantecler, a rooster who believes that he makes the sun rise. Because of its all-animal character cast and spectacular staging, *Chantecler* was considered something of a *succès de curiosité* on Broadway.[50]

In the *Follies* version, Bobby North played Chantecler, Lillian Lorraine

Bert Williams in the 1910 *Ziegfeld Follies* (Jardin de Paris roof garden, New York Theater). (*Courtesy Culver Pictures*)

played the Hen-Pheasant, Peter Swift played the Turkey, and Bert Williams played the Blackbird. Williams's costume was probably suggested by the original play, which called for a blackbird "in correct evening dress."[51] In one of the best known pictures of Williams from this skit, he is seen dressed in top hat and black tuxedo coat with black-feathered tail and webbed feet. If the costume alone had not been absurd enough, Williams created gales of laughter by making "an awkward entrance out of a large papier-mache egg."[52]

True to his style, Williams sang a song written by him and Andrew B. Sterling (1874–1955), a Tin Pan Alley lyricist. "White Folks Call It Chantecler, But It's Just Plain Chicken to Me," was a clever coon song that poked fun at white people's language.

> White folks call it chantecler
> But it's just plain chicken to me
> And the last time you were one of those
> You wore it fricassee
> They may call coffee demitasse
> And croquette is another name for hash
> You may call a barn fowl Chantecler
> But it's just plain chicken to me.[53]

Variety criticized Bert Williams, naming him as "another [actor] to strike the house wrongly at a later hour. . . . The house didn't just seem to take to him."[54] The *New York Dramatic Mirror* also thought the problem was the timing rather than the substance of Williams's performance.

> Bert Williams had his first innings in the last scene of the first half and his second in the Model Hennery where he appeared as a blackbird. It is needless to say that he was a great big hit, but had he been brought on earlier, when the audience would not have been as tired, he could have won even more favor.[55]

Later in the show, Fanny Brice sang "Lovie Joe," the song that almost cost her a place in the show. When she finished the song, Erlanger congratulated her by hitting her with his hat until it broke. He said, "You owe me a hat, Fanny," laughing at his own joke. "You owe me an apology, kid," she said.[56] Fanny Brice took a total of twelve encores that night for "Lovie Joe." But the songwriters were not able to share in Brice's triumph. Joe Jordan wept as he listened from outside the theater to the thunderous applause for the song's first performance – as a Negro, he had not been permitted to enter the theater. Segregation did not recognize talent: "If you're black, get back."[57]

The press was thrilled by Brice's singing. Her song "woke the audience up" and was the first to command "more than half-hearted applause." *Leslie's Weekly* proclaimed Brice to be "the principal hit . . . in the Follies this year."[58] At this early stage of her career, Brice was still influenced by other vaudeville comics. One critic observed:

> In her song, "Lovie Joe," she gave such a close imitation of Dave Montgomery of Montgomery and Stone fame, that one would be justified in thinking that it was that comedian himself dressed up for the occasion were it not for the fact that Miss Brice is much younger and considerably better-looking than the actor whom she imitates.[59]

The *New York Sun* also mentioned Brice's imitation of actor Eddie Foy. The review demonstrates just how talented she was:

> She conquered a Broadway audience last night. She is rather comely, but eccentric in her unintelligible delivery of patter text and possesses above all the element of distinctiveness in action and facial expression. So, the spectators delighted in her originality and her grotesqueness and even forgave her brief imitation of Eddie Foy because it was such a little one.[60]

Brice was already developing the wide-eyed slapstick mugging for which she was to become famous.

Although the 1910 *Follies* was notable for the debuts of Fanny Brice and Bert Williams, critics of the day gave the revue less than favorable notices. The *New York Tribune* said the music was better than the book; "the performance as a whole is crude." Many reviewers felt that Ziegfeld had spent a lot of money on what amounted to only a vaudeville show. In this light the *New York Evening Post* called it "one of the best seen here in a long time." The production's shortcomings were blamed on Ziegfeld. Said the *Dramatic Mirror*: "It is to be regretted that with such an outlay of money, time, and talent, a more consistently entertaining performance could not be devised, for, taking it as a whole, it is really below par."

Variety was equally harsh: "If the *Follies* of 1910 is reframed the way it should have been in the first place, this show will be the best of all the Ziegfeld shows."[61]

It could be surmised that from the number of encores she received that Fanny Brice was considered the hit of the show by the audience. But several critics disagreed. "Mr. Williams ... was the real star of the evening," declared the *New York Herald.*

The *Chicago Examiner* said Williams stood head and shoulders above the rest of the cast. "He was the needed artist in this great assemblage of good-looking nobodies. ... Bert Williams ... is the Mark Twain of his color."[62]

And in the black community Williams was, of course, considered the star of the 1910 *Follies*. The *New York Age* critic observed: "In this pretentious musical review, the work of the colored comedian stands boldly out, from an artistic standpoint, above everybody and everything. ... [He was] the hit of the big white production."[63]

The same year also saw Bert Williams's motion picture debut. It is not widely known that "blacks ... participated in American films in one way or another since the beginning of the industry in about 1888."[64] Williams's foray into movies was connected with black film producer William Foster. Foster is credited with being the first black film producer and distributor. Thomas Cripps records that Foster was

> a clever hustler from Chicago, he had been a press agent for the Williams and Walker revues and Cole and Johnson's "A Trip to Coontown," a sportwriter for the [Chicago] *Defender*, an occasional actor under the name of Juli Jones, and finally, a purveyor of sheet music and Haitian coffee. ... He began in Chicago in 1912, produced *The Railroad Porter* and other films in the Middle West, moved to Los Angeles and tried to raise $25,000 with the encouragement of an officer of the black Golden State Insurance Company ... finally, in 1929, appealed to the NAACP for support.[65]

Although Cripps says that the Foster Photoplay Company started in 1912, other film historians contend that the company began in 1910. In that year William Foster produced an all-black film called *The Pullman Porter*. It starred Jerry Mills, Lottie Grady, the soubrette star of *Mr. Lode of Koal*, and Bert Williams.[66] Nothing is known about the plot of the film, nor does there seem to be any surviving copies of the film. Thomas Cripps observes that this is mainly because "early black pioneers went largely unrecorded, even in the black press."[67] In 1912 Foster produced a film in the Keystone Cops genre called *The Railroad Porter*. Since Mills and Grady were in the cast, it is tempting to suspect that Bert Williams may have been in it as well.[68] Foster went on to film a number of movies, including the Buck and Bubbles series.

In 1914, the *New York Age* reported that the Foster Photoplay Company was going to build a studio in Jacksonville, Florida. Foster wanted blacks to become involved in all aspects of moviemaking. "All the members of the Foster Company will be colored," said the *Age*, "producers, actors, camera men, darkroom men and a regular stock company."[69] It is not known how the Foster Company fared in Florida. But it is clear that by then Williams had decided to go with a white film producer for his motion picture work.

Chapter 18

I n September 1910 Booker T. Washington took time from his busy schedule to pen a tribute to Bert Williams. The article, entitled "Interesting People," was published in *American Magazine*. Washington cited Williams as one of his favorite entertainers. The great orator said:

> When I go to the theatre, which is not often, I generally go to hear the colored comedian, Bert Williams. I go to hear him, however, as often as I have opportunity, and I am seldom in the same city with him that I do not find myself . . . drifting in the direction of the theatre in which he is playing.[1]

Washington said that "vaudeville performances, as a rule, strike me as tiresome. . . . But Bert Williams' humor strikes me as the real thing." He believed that Williams's humor had the quality of being fresh, spontaneous, and yet built on human psychology. Washington recalled watching Williams quietly standing in a crowd studying people's behavior. This, said Washington, was how Williams gathered his material for his songs and stories. "I suppose the best reason I can give for liking his quaint songs and humorous sayings," said Washington, "is that he puts into this form some of the quality and philosophy of the Negro race."[2] Washington then gave a brief biographical sketch of Williams, noting how he had worked his way to the top. Taking a potshot at black intellectuals allied with W. E. B. DuBois, Washington declared:

> During all the years I have known Bert Williams, I have never heard him whine or cry about his color, or about any racial discrimination. He has gone right on, in season and out of season, doing his job, perfecting himself in his work, till he has reached the top-rung in his specialty.[3]

Washington clearly recognized in Williams a follower of his own philosophy. As he stated in his famous Atlanta Exposition address: "It is at the bottom of life we must begin, and not at the top. Nor should we permit our grievances to overshadow our opportunities."[4]

Perhaps it was with this thought in mind that Washington concluded:

> Bert Williams is a tremendous asset of the Negro race. He is an asset because he has succeeded in actually doing something, and because he has succeeded,

145

the fact of his success helps the Negro many times more than he could help the Negro by merely contenting himself to whine and complain about racial difficulties and racial discriminations.[5]

Williams was flattered by Washington's praise, and in December 1910 he replied in an article published in the *Green Book Magazine*. Bert Williams denied that he was any innovator or trailblazer. "Other men of my own color have done the same," he said. "I am a successor, not an originator."[6]

Williams reviewed the contributions of blacks to entertainment up to 1910. He proclaimed: "Our race has taken root upon this soil; after two hundred years of struggle upward, we may be apart here, but not alien. And I firmly believe that we have contributed our share to American entertainment."[7] Williams specifically named two entertainment forms. "The one new stage form which has been developed in this country is of plantation origin; I refer, of course, to minstrelsy. The only music that may be regarded as typically American music is Negro music."[8]

Williams then addressed the question of why comedians portrayed caricatures of ethnic groups on stage. He suggested the sociological theory that mocking nonwhites and immigrants was a way of coping with people of unfamiliar background: "My observation has led me to the theory that when a strange unassimilated element exists in a nation, it almost immediately finds its way to the stage in comic types, usually caricatures."[9] He hastened to point out that "minstrelsy and Negro comedy have been largely in the hands of white men. . . . I may add that the white men who have interpreted our race in this manner have done us no discredit."[10]

He named the blackface comedy team of McIntyre and Heath as an example. Williams differed strikingly from George Walker in appraising white entertainers in blackface; Walker had been known to criticize these minstrels for their unnatural portrayal of blacks. Four years earlier he had complained: "Blackfaced white comedians used to make themselves look as ridiculous as they could when portraying a 'darky' character."[11]

Thinking of his own ambitions for drama, Williams wrote:

> Many people have not found many openings into the theatrical profession. That we have a natural talent for the stage in certain lines of entertainment at least, cannot be denied; but with that talent limited to a few obscure theatres or dance halls of undesirable reputation, it has had no chance to expand according to its promise.[12]

Williams then offered a short review of highlights of black theater, from the African Company in New York in 1820, to black dramatic actor Ira Aldridge, to playwright Alexandre Dumas *père* and Sam Lucas, the first black actor to play Uncle Tom. He ended the essay by paying tribute to his contemporaries: the Black Patti, Bob Cole, and J. Rosamond Johnson, Will Marion Cook, and Alex Rogers.

Meanwhile the health of former partner George Walker was deteriorating. The black newspaper the *Chicago Defender* concluded: "Mr. Walker is not dead, but his dream of *life* is o'er." Walker had visited friends in Chicago recently and they were shocked. Where was the sharp-witted and alert George William Walker who so adeptly handled the business affairs of Williams and Walker? It was reported that "Mr. Walker was unable to recognize his most intimate friends, as his mind is now a blank and his mental force of insanity is now a hopeless cause of mental decay, said by doctors to be incurable." *Chicago Defender* theater critic Sylvester Russell characterized Walker as a victim of Bert Williams's success: "His power to coach his partner to a blunt hilarious episode of laughter robbed him of his own reward in the final climax."[13]

Williams missed his partner but clearly savored the sweet taste of success as a solo entertainer. In an interview with the *Chicago Examiner*, Williams talked about some of his ideas for skits in the *Follies*:

> I'd like to play this old rheumatic character of mine in a white production. But it will take time. The people must become gradually accustomed to my appearance on the stage among white people. You've noticed there is not a white woman on the stage during my appearance in the Follies. I had that put into the contract.[14]

The *Examiner* interview resulted in a serious attack on Bert Williams by another critic. Sylvester Russell attacked both the *Examiner* critic – Ashton Stevens – and Williams, accusing both of hypocrisy and bad taste. What Stevens perceived to be complimentary to Williams was in reality a slap in the face:

> Stevens tells us that Williams draws a Negro character as vivid as "Nigger Jim" in "Huckleberry Finn." . . . Stevens had to wring the "Nigger" in . . . but where any other white man of the highest breeding would have omitted it. . . . Why should Stevens bring up "color," and old out-of-date theory, when white people are ashamed to call a colored person "nigger" . . . knowing that the word is now out of respectable commission.[15]

Russell condemned Stevens for using Williams's alleged Danish ancestry as an explanation for Williams's achievements. He also criticized Williams for not being assertive about his racial pride. If Williams was as courageous as George Walker, said Russell, "he would assert these things in his interviews. He has no backbone."

It was probably in response to critics like Russell that Williams made one of his most famous statements. While by no means a dyed-in-the-wool militant, Williams often spoke of segregation with anger:

> People sometimes ask me if I would give anything to be white. I answer, in the words of the song, most emphatically, "No." . . . I have never been able

to discover that there was anything disgraceful in being a colored man. But I have often found it inconvenient – in America.[16]

Russell also attacked Williams's opinions about theater: "Stevens pays a high compliment to Bert Williams' songs but Stevens don't know if Williams would only give up playing pool that he could fill in his idle time in writing a Negro play in which to star."

Williams had told the *Chicago Examiner* that he thought there was little hope of him ever being in a black show again. Russell said that Williams was wrong about that and about being in the *Follies* with white women. "Now according to Williams' contract, how is he going to ever be able to play his dear old character on the stage with white women? The public don't care three straws who appears on the stage with Williams at all."[17]

Finally Russell concluded that Williams was being "used" by Ziegfeld. He had been placed "in a vaudeville skit-farce drama written for a lot of white actors with no reputation who need somebody for a drawing card." Ziegfeld should let Williams go and star in an all-colored show even if it meant that the *Ziegfeld Follies* would suffer, argued Russell.

Black critics weren't the only ones skeptical of whether Williams belonged in the *Ziegfeld Follies*. Late in 1910 a Washington critic wrote: "Bert Williams, a natural comedian, is genuinely amusing, but the producer is lacking in taste and discretion when he engages a colored man to appear in the same company with white men and women."[18]

That attack prompted a counterattack in Williams's defense by the *Indianapolis Freeman*. It claimed that the *Washington Post* critic ignored the fact that audiences loved Williams. "Mr. Williams' three appearances were applauded to the echo and he was easily the star of the show." However, he was restricted and "does not begin to have an opportunity to utilize the fullness of his powers as a comedian and all-round actor." The *Freeman* agreed with Sylvester Russell that Williams would be better off in an all-colored show. "This suggestion is made," explained the *Freeman*, "not to satisfy critics of the Ralph Graves type, but to enable Mr. Williams to do himself full justice and to afford paying employment to half a hundred of bright colored artists who need the opportunity that such an aggregation would place within their reach."[19]

One Negro artist would, however, never have the opportunity to perform with Williams again: George William Walker. He died Friday, January 6, 1911, at 7:00 P.M. in an Islip, Long Island, sanatorium. Newspapers gave his age as thirty-eight and the cause of death as paresis.[20] Mrs. Walker was in Cincinnati with *His Honor the Barber*. After receiving the telegram, she left immediately for New York City. Bert Williams was in Brooklyn with the *Follies* on that fateful day. As he was preparing to go onstage, his valet entered his dressing room and delivered the news of George's death.

Williams broke down and cried like a baby in his valet's arms. He was unable to go on with the show that evening.[21]

George Walker's funeral was held Monday morning, January 9, 1911, in Harlem. Walker's mother and Bert and Lottie Williams were the only persons present at the service, along with Walker's widow, Aida. The floral pieces were numerous, including a large Masonic-design wreath from Williams. It had a card bearing the inscription: "My Dear Old Pal." After the service, the body lay in state for the public to view until Tuesday afternoon, when it was shipped to Walker's hometown of Lawrence, Kansas, for burial.[22]

The nation's black newspapers saw Walker's death as the end of an era for the black actor. The *Indianapolis Freeman* credited Williams and Walker with helping to break down racial stereotypes on stage.

> During the 16 years Williams and Walker were together, they set a new standard for colored performers that was never before and is not likely again to be attained by colored performers. They caused colored performers to cease to be considered a race, and more, in fact than the Irish, Germans, or just plain American comedians.[23]

The *Chicago Defender* said:

> The death of George Walker of Williams and Walker brings to an end the 17 years of hearty enjoyment the public received from the greatest Negro team of actors who ever lived and the most popular pair of comedy stars America has produced.

The *Boston Guardian* went farther, reflecting that Walker was really part of a trio. Summarizing his career, it said: "After a sixteen year fight, he found himself, his wife and Bert Williams, the most popular trio of colored actors in the world.[24]

In this vein, Sylvester Russell pleaded for a reunion of Aida Overton Walker and Bert Williams onstage. "The name of Williams and Walker is still fresh on the pages of American stage history," Russell wrote in April 1911. "We can scarcely afford to stand aside and see that name go to waste." Russell suggested that if theatrical managers saw the potential for utilizing the "Williams and Walker" name, then "the pathway would be clear for Bert A. Williams and Aida Overton Walker." Furthermore, Russell argued that both of them needed one another professionally:

> They have no doubt discovered that it is better to stand the vicissitudes of life and fight it out together as parties who are used to each other and in one social class than to be humiliated by being thrown into contact with such relations as have existed in companies in which both of these stars have been serving.

Russell thought that if Florenz Ziegfeld could promote playwright Jesse

Shipp and Aida Overton Walker as well as Bert Williams in first-class theaters, "the American public would see more of what they have longed for – another big colored musical comedy affair."[25]

It is not known what Aida Overton Walker and Bert Williams thought of this proposal or even if they discussed it. Anyway, Mrs. Walker had other plans. She had made up her mind to concentrate on vaudeville dance groups, the *New York Age* announced in May, 1911.[26] Bert Williams, apparently set for a stellar career in the *Ziegfeld Follies*, was now reported ready to quit. The *New York Age* carried an article about how Williams wanted to quit the show out west and was coaxed into staying.

Ostensibly Ziegfeld had granted Williams permission to leave the road tour of the 1910 *Follies* once they had played San Francisco. This was to enable the comedian to "come directly East to begin rehearsals for the *Follies* of 1911." But when the theater managers in Los Angeles got wind of this, they refused to play the *Follies* sans Williams in their houses unless Ziegfeld gave them a different contract. If they didn't have Williams, who was the box office draw, they would lose money. So Williams was asked to stay on until the production left California. But the Salt Lake City theaters insisted on the same terms as the Los Angeles theaters, and Williams still couldn't leave. Finally, when Denver theaters also insisted on Williams, Ziegfeld had to make Williams complete the whole tour.[27]

What remains to be explained is this: Why did Williams want to leave the show early? Was he depressed over Walker's death? Maybe. Or was he still encountering difficulties with fellow cast members? That is the most plausible reason. Williams was having problems coping with being a "token black" in an all-white theatrical company. Certainly Williams and Walker had appeared on vaudeville bills with whites, but all their important work had been with all-black companies. Williams had a tendency to withdraw socially when he felt uncomfortable or threatened. Another explanation is that Williams didn't have enough confidence in his ability. But the constant demand for him in the *Follies* should have convinced him that he was a star.

Another possibility is that he was contemplating leaving Ziegfeld altogether. David Belasco's offer was fresh in his mind, and he may have felt frustrated at his own inability to pursue his ambitions. But again, he was grateful to Ziegfeld for recognizing his talent. And in the end he decided to remain with the *Follies*.

Bert Williams often collaborated with others to compose songs for his shows. But perhaps none of his collaborators was as colorful as the newspaper columnist–short story writer Ring Lardner (1885–1933). Lardner was known as a syndicated sports columnist for the *Chicago Tribune*, and later he turned out short stories for magazines such as the *Saturday Evening Post*, *Cosmopolitan* and *The New Yorker*. Lardner influenced a generation of writers. "Probably no other modern American writer, except perhaps Hemingway, has been imitated so much," said one Lardner scholar. "Lardner's recreation of the diction and the rhythms of American dialogue" made him a model for other writers.[28] Lardner liked Bert Williams and hoped to write a song for him. In 1909 Lardner published a song, "Little Puff of Smoke, Good Night," described as "a Southern croon in the Bert Williams manner."[29] Ring Lardner's son later recalled that, though his father did like Bert Williams, he still had racial prejudices.

> I can ... remember hearing him speak, in [a] burst of justified indignation, of "that damn Jew Ziegfeld." And his attitude toward blacks was even more contradictory. He had participated in minstrel shows based on racial stereotypes, and even when he wrote lyrics for Bert Williams, he accepted, as Williams himself did in his public image, cliche conventions like the black man's fear of ghosts. He somehow kept on believing, as he had been brought up to believe, that blacks in general were inferior, even after he had come to admire individuals like Williams and Paul Robeson and the composer J. Rosamond Johnson.[30]

In February 1911 Lardner began contacting Bert Williams concerning possible music for the *Ziegfeld Follies*. Writing to his wife, Lardner reported:

> I walked downtown after supper last night and ran into Bert Williams, who was on his way to the theater. I told him about an idea I had for a song and he approved it. He provided an idea for another one and told me to work on both of them and to report to him later in the week.[31]

A few weeks later Lardner wrote: "I met Mr. Williams last night and was encouraged but I won't tell you any more about it because it's very uncertain."[32]

It is also uncertain what songs Lardner is referring to. In the following letter, which survives from an apparent body of correspondence between Lardner and Williams,[33] Bert Williams suggests that he was composing music to Lardner's lyrics.

> March 14, 1911
>
> Hellow There, Big Boy:
>
> Thanks so much for the laying out. But it was deserved. Have revamped the song, so I am sure it's a positive hit. Will rewrite the music this week while I am in Baltimore. It's not so cold here now, but it's not time yet to leave the overcoat home. Please, during your spring practice, get the KINKS out of your arms—because I am going to beat you bowling and beat you GOOD. I know you're having a GOOD time "mongest the Pines" and when I see you, Bro' Dorey, my regards. This week Baltimore, next, Syracuse. If I hear from you there shall send you all the route into Frisco. Good luck and health are the worst I can wish you.
>
> Bert Williams.[34]

Soon afterward Lardner wrote that Williams appeared to have finished the songs: "He said he would have the music finished for one of my songs this week, and that he was going to sing it, but he didn't say when."[35]

Williams did not use a Lardner song in his act that year. However, the two kept in touch over the following years. . . . In 1917 Bert Williams finally introduced a Ring Lardner song in the *Ziegfeld Follies*, and after that, Lardner was successful in having many of his songs interpolated into the *Follies*.

When the *Ziegfeld Follies of 1911* opened on June 26, 1911, Ziegfeld's name was officially included in the title of the show for the first time. Despite the new title, the new *Follies* featured some of the stars from 1910, including Fanny Brice, Harry Watson, Jr., Lillian Lorraine, and Bert Williams.

The 1911 show also carried over the Ziegfeld habit of burlesquing other Broadway shows. The musical comedy *The Pink Lady*, the Gilbert and Sullivan operetta *H.M.S. Pinafore*, and a play called *Everywife* were the targets of parody this season. It was this last piece, in which Bert Williams appeared, that captured the attention of critics and audiences at the 1911 *Follies*.

The sketch called "Everywife" was sophisticated by Ziegfeld standards insofar as it had a bit of theater history behind it. It was essentially based on the medieval morality play called *Everyman*, which focuses on the theme of man's mortality. The play opens with a messenger speaking a prologue. Death summons Everyman, who is not ready until he asks his friends to join him. Of the friends, only Good Deeds follows Everyman to the grave. In 1908 Walter Browne wrote a play called *Everywoman: Her Pilgrimage in Quest of Love*. The messenger is called "Nobody." "Nobody," of course, is also the title of Bert Williams's signature song. It is not known if the irony was intentional or coincidental. *Everywife*, written in 1911 by Broadway playwright George V. Hobart, is a satire of *Everywoman*. Ziegfeld presented only a short version.

Dramatically, in both *Everywife* and *Everywoman*, a character called "Nobody" acts as a chorus figure. In ancient Greek drama, the chorus commented on the action, serving as the playwright's mouthpiece or expressing the moral issues underlying the play.[36]

So, in the *Follies* skit, Bert Williams acted as "Nobody," or chorus, commenting humorously on the story of the quarrel of Everyhusband and his wife, the departure of Happiness from the home, the meeting of Everyhusband with Rhyme, Drink, Gamble, and the varied attentions of the Great White Way, and his meeting with Reason.[37] Williams took center stage and asked the audience: "What is the plot of the Follies? Nobody knows. What is the moral pointed out by the Follies? Don't ask me – Nobody knows."[38]

Everywife spoofed the trials and tribulations of wives with wayward husbands. Mabel Rowland described Williams as being faithful to the role of chorus. He pointed out to the goodness of Everywife and shook his head at the foolishness of Everyhusband.

> In his introductions to the wanderings of "Everyhusband," Mr. Williams expounds the symbolism of the piece. "A stage door," he says, "is a symbol and symbol is a sumpin' that stands for sumpin' else and believe me, a stage door stands for an awful lot *I* wouldn't stand for." Mr. Williams follows Everyhusband through his more or less chastening experiences in the gay world! "Now," said the dusky and sapient one, "he's down at his club, pourin' *fusel oil* on his troubles." And as he spoke, he wagged a perplexed and anxious head.[39]

The critics were delighted with Williams's acting in the skit. Said the *New York Post*: "He enacted the chorus amid a great deal of merriment. In fact, he was the leader in the fun, which was fast and furious while he was in the scene." The *New York Tribune* observed that "there is little of it that is not acted in a legitimate manner." *Variety*, however, found this approach unsuitable for Ziegfeld's *Follies*. It complained: "The author was so serious that the actors are too. Although the piece was excellently produced and played, it doesn't fit in 'The Follies' for New York." Only the *New York Times* valued the skit itself, recommending that "the clever burlesque of this piece has to be seen to be appreciated."[40]

The other *Follies* role Williams had in 1911 was in a sketch called "Upper and Lower Level." Grand Central Railroad Station in New York City was then under construction. A mock-up version of the construction site served as a set for Williams and his fellow actor, Leon Errol. Errol (1881–1951) was a vaudeville actor originally from Australia. A master of physical comedy, he was dubbed Rubber Legs by critics. Theater historian Gerald Bordman described him: "With his wobbly legs, combined with his funny brows and funny eyes, he was later to become the most hilarious inebriate ever to stagger across a stage."[41]

In "Upper and Lower," however, Errol and Williams had to stagger, if not tiptoe, across dangerous construction girders high above the stage. Errol played an eccentric British tourist who wants to go to the "upper level" of Grand Central. His reluctant guide is a red cap porter played by Bert Williams. As the two men trace their way across the girders, Errol comes close to falling several times. All the while, Errol and Bert Williams engage in some hilarious dialogue:

> *Errol:*　You have a wife and family, I suppose?
> *Williams:* Oh yes, sir; I's married an' I'se got three chil'un.
> *Errol:*　Is that so? Ah, that's very commendable.
> *Williams:* Yes sir, so it is.
> *Errol:*　What are the names of your children?
> *Williams:* Well, I names 'em out de Bible. Dar's Hanna and den dar's Samuel and de las' one name I willa.

Errol: Iwilla? I don't remember that name in the Bible.
Williams: Sure 'tis. Don't you 'member where it say, IWILLA *rise?*[42]

Near the end of the skit, Errol finally falls off the elevation into the pit below. Just when he lands, there is the sound of dynamite exploding. Williams looks up in the air and says: "Thar he goes, way up, up. . . . Ah, there he goes. Now he's near the Metropolitan Tower. Ef he kin only grab that little golden ball on the top. . . . Uh, uh, he muffed it."[43]

In her book *The Ziegfeld Follies,* Marjorie Farnsworth tells of an anecdote concerning this act when the *Follies* was touring Chicago. Errol and Williams worked together well; they both loved to ad-lib and stay onstage as long as possible. Sometimes, in fact, they stalled the show. When this happened in Chicago, the theater manager called Ziegfeld to complain. Ziegfeld agreed to come to Chicago himself and pull the comedians into line. But as he stood backstage watching Williams and Errol, he was laughing too hard to chastise them.[44]

The critics, too, loved the sketch. Williams and Errol "brought down the house," said the *New York World.* The scene was "excruciatingly funny," reported the *New York Post.*[45]

After the "Upper and Lower" scene, Williams returned to the stage with several songs and his inimitable poker-game pantomime. One song was "Woodman Spare That Tree." With music by Irving Berlin and lyrics by Vincent Bryan, the song was a husband's plea to save his arboreal hideout from his wife.

Another comedy song, which won favor with Williams fans when he recorded it, was "Dat's Harmony." Williams composed the music to lyrics by Grant Clarke. Williams occasionally dipped into social commentary, and "Dat's Harmony" had lyrics referring to theater mogul Lee Shubert and composer John Philip Sousa.

> Mister Shubert's serenade is grand
> I certainly love to hear a big brass band
> Play Sousa's marches by the score
> An' I likes good opera, what is more
> Dat pleasing melody in F
> Is sho' some music well I guess
> But folks make a mistake you see
> When dey say dat's all to harmony.[46]

Williams's songs met with a mixed critical reception. Only *Variety* liked "Dat's Harmony," while the *New York Times* regarded Williams's music as "equal to any he has had." The "Harmony" song plus the poker game, said the *New York World,* "brought him twice the amount of applause that any other performer received during the evening." For many Williams was "the big hit of the night," and once again critics admitted that "it is doubtful if there is a more amusing actor of the kind, black or white, on the stage to-day." Williams was one of the reasons why the *New York Times* thought that the 1911 *Follies* seemed to "have more fun and more specialties . . . than those of former years."[47]

Chapter 19

Bert Williams's father, Frederick, died Monday, April 1, 1912, in New York City, "of heart failure after a lingering illness."[1] About sixty-one years old, he left a widow, Julia, and a son, Bert, according to the *New York Age*. Williams was traveling with the *Ziegfeld Follies* company in Pennsylvania when his father died. He returned to New York for the funeral on Thursday, April 4. After the funeral Bert Williams took time off from performing. He decided to renew his Ziegfeld contract for another three years and also to dispose of his father's business.[2] He had bought the building at 2283 Seventh Avenue in Harlem and turned it into a barbershop and poolroom for Frederick Williams; the establishment was known as "Williams' Barbershop." Vaudevillian Tom Fletcher said:

> Fred Williams brought in Jesse Shipp, Jr. [son of Williams and Walker playwright Jesse Shipp], to manage the business. . . . After Bert Williams' father died, Bert gave the business to the junior Shipp and the place soon became the gathering place for practically all of the top-flight figures in athletics and show business.[3]

It has been alleged that in 1912 Williams had an embarrassing experience during a vaudeville turn. Unlike the unpleasant situations of the past, this one seems to have been of Williams's own making. Ostensibly Williams had bet someone, perhaps over a drink, that he could do an imitation of himself masquerading as another person. To top it off, Williams thought that his self-impersonation, as it were, could win him a prize in the amateur-night contest at Miner's Bowery, which offered prizes to the ten or so male amateurs who competed after the regular vaudeville performance on Fridays:

> Each entrant was paid a dollar for his work, and there were first, second and third prizes awarded to the leading performers with the audience as judges. In some theatres, the first prize was a watch. At Miner's Bowery, it was usually a five dollar gold piece.[4]

Amateurs got only five to ten minutes for their spot; if they took longer, they "got the hook." Miner's was notorious for its hook, a long cane. If the

156

audience disapproved of the artist, the hook would appear out of the wings and pull the artist offstage. Marjorie Farnsworth has given an account of Williams's alleged performance at Miner's:

> He was introduced simply as "Joe Martin." Williams strolled onto the stage with the familiar Williams accessories of naive and stumbling awkwardness verging on hidden panic. It very soon became apparent that the rough spectators at Miner's considered that Williams was giving a dreadfully poor imitation of Williams. There were jeers from the floor and catcalls from the balcony. . . . As Williams kept trying, these changed to demands to "give him the hook." The demands became so strident and insistent that in order to prevent violence and riot, Williams literally was given the hook.[5]

The only eyewitness account of the event comes from playwright Channing Pollack in his autobiography, *Harvest of My Years*. Though Pollack claims to have seen Williams perform as an amateur, his account adds little to Farnsworth's: "One evening, seeking amusement, a dozen of us went to a burlesque theatre in the Bowery where Bert Williams appeared on the stage as an amateur giving an imitation of Bert Williams – and was a complete flop."[6]

No reviews of the incident have surfaced. It is likely that since Miner's was a second-class vaudeville house, none of the entertainment trade papers would have covered an amateur-night there. If Williams did appear at Miner's imitating himself, the question of what state of mind drove him to try that stunt is one that should be left to psychologists to answer.

In June 1912 plans were announced for Williams to go to England. The *New York Age* said:

> Negotiations are being made to play Bert Williams for four weeks at the Coliseum, London. The big comedian will not start rehearsals in the Follies of 1912 until August and if Messrs. Erlanger and Ziegfeld say yes, he will coon [sic] sail for Europe.[7]

On June 20 Bert Williams stepped down from the presidency of the Frogs, the black theatrical club. Playwright Jesse Shipp succeeded him as president. Williams was happy to drift into the background and let others have the spotlight. At the Frogs' annual frolic at the Manhattan Casino on June 27, songwriter Henry S. Creamer said Williams kept busy in other ways:

> Ex-President Frog Bert Williams constituted himself chairman of the Dew Committee; he spent most of his spare time providing liquid within which the Frogs splashed – and I noticed that a large degree of the splashing was done in the vicinity of the refreshment counter.[8]

The Frogs' *Frolic* was a rare opportunity for Williams to socialize; normally in June, he would have been hard at work in the *Follies*. But that year's *Follies* had been postponed until October, giving rise to speculation and rumor. Ziegfeld's rivals, the Shubert brothers, made much hay out of the postponement. It was proof, they said, that Ziegfeld was "slipping." Raised in Syracuse, New York, the Shubert brothers – Sam, Lee, and Jake (also known at J. J.) – began to manage theaters in upstate New York in the late 19th century.

After Sam died in 1905, Lee and J. J. Shubert accelerated their acquisition of theaters in New York City. They soon presented a threat to the Syndicate (the theatrical monopoly controlled by Abraham Erlanger and Marc Klaw). The Shuberts refused to bend under the Syndicate's rules, and by shrewd methods of real estate deals, financing, and manipulation, they emerged victorious. By 1920 the Shuberts were indisputably the dominant force in American theater.

The Shuberts' desire to control American theater extended also to the media, and in 1909 they started their own newspaper, the *New York Review*. The *Review* promoted Shubert-produced shows and panned those of Shubert rivals. Maryann Chach noted that: "The majority of articles were not signed which may indicate that they were press releases which the *Review* simply reprinted without editing. Many of the pieces were orchestrated by the Shubert Bros."[9]

It was in the *New York Review* that an article appeared in July 1912, discussing the delay of the *Ziegfeld Follies*. Apparently the article suggested that the tension of an integrated cast led to the postponement of the show. This allegation stirred Jack Shoemaker, former business manager of Williams and Walker, to rise to Bert Williams's defense. Shoemaker worked for Williams and Walker for six years and worked with Williams during the *Mr. Lode of Koal* show. Shoemaker quoted the *New York Review* as claiming that "the reason why Ziegfeld has not produced his Follies this season was because he ha[s] not been able to get white performers to work with this colored man."[10] Shoemaker said that this was not the reason. It was because Ziegfeld already had a show playing at the Moulin Rouge. *The Winsome Widow* opened April 11, 1912, and ran until September. It was a moneymaker, and its popularity in no small way derived from Mae West's debut performance in it.[11] Ziegfeld had common business sense, said Shoemaker; "no man who is sane starts opposition to himself." As for the charge that Williams's presence in the cast prevented the June premiere, Shoemaker said this was nonsense. "Bert Williams is a very easy man to get along with," he said. "No white performer or chorus girl ever had cause to feel that they sacrificed their self-respect by working in the same company with Bert Williams." Williams would do anything to help people. Shoemaker gave the example of how Williams quietly took a loss in his eight-thousand-dollar investment in the *Mr. Lode of Koal* company when the show closed prematurely. Shoemaker said: "That's being white because it's right." Shoemaker implied that since Williams was the star of the show, he could ostensibly have argued for some returns on his investment. Instead he insisted on the debts being paid.

According to Jack Shoemaker another example of Williams's generosity is his treatment of his invalid partner, George Walker:

> When Bert Williams' partner, George Walker, was stricken with his death illness, after he had spent all of his own money, Mr. Williams worked and shared liberally with his sick associate. He sent to Mr. Walker, the first summer of his illness, $600, and during the following season, sent him a check for $50 every week. All of this was Bert Williams' money. The next summer, and until Walker died, he received the same liberal allowance and when he died, his body was sent to Lawrence, Kansas, his home, and buried without regard to cost. Most people will agree that this was white treatment.

Shoemaker next recited an anecdote about a Christmas party that Williams left early. "I went to look for him," said Shoemaker, and found him in his dressing room reading a volume of Emerson's essays. Can any man read Emerson and not be white?" Shoemaker said that Williams never offended him in any way during their relationship. "I am positive that any white lady or gentleman . . . never ever feared that they will have cause for regret on his account."

The Shoemaker letter came to the attention of Aida Overton Walker, who wrote a sharp rebuttal. "After reading and re-reading the article and . . . wishing to know the meaning of Mr. Shoemaker's reference to Mr. Walker, depicting him as a charity patient, I cannot refrain from trying to defend Mr. Walker's memory from misrepresentation."[12] Mrs. Walker thought the claim that Bert Williams was "white" because he was kind to his partner was absurd. "It is," said Mrs. Walker, "a poor way of impressing the readers of the *Age* of Mr. Williams' finer points as a man." She said that it was true that Williams gave Walker six hundred dollars during the first summer of his illness but insisted that Walker was still on the company payroll. George Walker received fifty dollars a week during the run of *Mr. Lode of Koal*. But the payments stopped when the show closed, contended Mrs. Walker. Shoemaker's claim that Walker continued to receive money from Williams after that time was a "delightful untruth," she said. She added that Bert Williams never visited her husband nor gave him any financial assistance during the last summer of his life. As for the funeral and burial arrangments, "that was an act of private friendship on the part of Bert Williams," Mrs. Walker said. "Shoemaker should remember that George Walker was once his employer and his confidant," Mrs. Walker advised Shoemaker:

> Should Mr. Shoemaker need Mr. Walker's memory in the future for reference, or a means by which he might whiten someone's character, let him

remember that MR. WALKER WAS A MAN AT ALL TIMES. . . . HE WAS A TRUE
PARTNER TO HIS PARTNER TO THE END. Died at peace with God and man. Let
him rest!

The preoccupation with skin color was not limited to white men like
Shoemaker. Lester Walton noticed that black entertainers were also
obsessed with this topic. In an October 1912 issue of the *New York Age*,
Walton observed: "Within the last six months, I have noticed that colored
acts have been more prone to ridicule the man or woman with a black face
than ever before. To me, it seems that many have acquired this habit."

Walton gave the example of one black act in which the performers
called each other "black spasms." Walton complained that such black acts,
which mocked black people's skin color, wished to win applause from white
audiences. But such dialogue performed before black people, argued
Walton, was in very poor taste. He pointed out that discriminatory practices by blacks against blacks was common. Walton said there were certain
social circles in which being light-complexioned was the key to admission.
The irony is, said Walton, that "the Negro who seeks to draw the color line
on another [Negro] is the first to yell about the white man's discriminating
attitude toward him."[13] There was no need for black entertainers to engage
in self-ridicule or self-hatred in order to be successful. Walton thought that
these black entertainers needed to consider Bert Williams a role model.

> There is Bert Williams, who is one of the funniest comedians alive. Yet he
> never degrades his race in his work. He makes Negro mannerisms a telling
> feature. So it behooves the colored manager to put a stop to this epidemic
> of ridicule in which the black man is the object of attack.

Williams was in his twelfth year as a recording artist in 1912. He con-
tinued to be one of the only black performers available on recordings. In
September 1912 he recorded two records for Columbia: "How? Fried!," and
"You Can't Do Nothin'."[15] Williams was starting his third year as a Ziegfeld
star. He was said to be a big hit in the 1912 show, which previewed in
Philadelphia, said the *New York Age*.

The Broadway opening of the *Ziegfeld Follies of 1912* on October 21,
1912, was a triumph for Bert Williams. Lester Walton commented that "it
must have been gratifying to him Monday evening when he made his first
appearance, and was given a more enthusiastic reception than all the other
artists combined."[16] This *Follies* edition was also triumphant for Williams
in other ways. He was given more creative freedom. When he had first
signed with Ziegfeld, there was an understanding that Williams would not
appear on stage with white women. Since the female artists and Ziegfeld
Girls were the heart of the Ziegfeld show, this meant that Williams would
be restricted as a performer. But by 1912, Ziegfeld and Williams had put to
rest their fears of a racial backlash. The *New York Age* reported:

In the "Follies of 1912," the colored comedian has lines with women and at the finale of both the first and the second acts is seen with the principals. When the curtain goes down in the second act, Mr. Williams is located on the end of the first line next to Miss [Rae] Samuels, who . . . made a favorable impression as a singer.[17]

The theater program for the *Follies* listed Williams as appearing in three spots as the characters, "Howell Noyes–carriage caller," "Cabman," and "Walker Foote, a roller chair man."[18] The only scene that the critics liked and for which there is documentation was the "Cabman" scene. The skit was one of Williams's all-time best. The players, Williams and Leon Errol, were given the opportunity to write their own comedy material and collect whatever theater props they needed. Williams insisted on realism in his acting. The "Cabman" sketch was to feature a black cabman who drives a hansom cab pulled by a horse. Leon Errol recalled that, "I will never forget the delight that poor Bert exhibited when, after a search of several days, we found an antiquated, dilapidated cab reposing in the storage yard of a West Side dealer in such antiques."[19]

Errol and Williams fixed up the cab to make it stageworthy, and the results would have made any theater scenery designer proud. Errol said of Williams: "He just stood off and burst into a perfect hysteria of guttural guffaws, when the job was completed."[20]

Errol and Williams hired a driver and a horse to take the hansom cab to the Moulin Rouge Theater. They were only one block from the theater when Williams suggested that they let the driver and horse go and pull the chariot the rest of the way themselves. Williams wanted to surprise the *Follies* company, who thought that Williams and Errol were using no props in their act.[21] Errol described what happened:

> As we neared the theatre, I realized that the great double scenery doors were wide open and as we ran, I shouted to Bert: "Right in on the stage!" He got me instantly and the way we wheeled from the roadway, across the sidewalk and right on to the stage in the midst of a hundred rehearsing men and women, was a flourish in *tour de force* that would have done credit to the chariot racers in "Ben Hur," and it created almost as much excitement as that celebrated scene when we tore in and temporarily broke up the rehearsal. It was too much for the risibilities of Williams. He just lay down on the floor and rolled about in ecstatic joy. He certainly did love a joke.[22]

Williams and Errol did not use a real horse in the "Cabman" skit. The "horse" was played by the vaudeville comic team of LeBrun and Queen. When the sketch began, the audience saw "the antiquated horse called Nicodemus, the antique cab and the shabby driver, discovered in front of a drop on which was painted a view of Seventh Avenue at Forty-Seventh Street, New York City."[23]

Bert Williams, as the cab driver, polished his cab in dead seriousness.

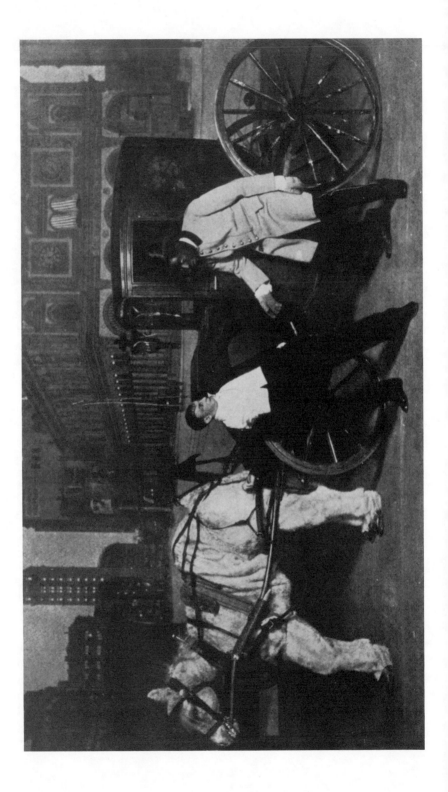

Every time the nervous horse crossed its legs, Williams said "Whoa." Presently Errol stumbled onto the stage in evening clothes and obviously drunk. Rowland records that "Williams recognized him as fair game and their dialogue was screamingly funny."[24]

> *Williams:* "Where do you want to go to, boss?"
> *Errol:* "I want to go *sebalabaloo*."
> *Williams:* "Oh, you want to go to Seventh Avenue?"
> *Errol:* "Yeah, I wanna go sebalabaloo. Y'know where 'tis?"
> *Williams:* "Oh yes, I know where 'tis. Get in an I'll drive you dar. I know where 'tis all right. It's fur!"[25]

It is said that when the horse heard that "the distance was far, ... he commence[d] to shake as if he would drop dead." Williams tries to revive the horse by tempting him. "Oats, Nicodeum, OATS!" This inspires the horse to act differently, as though it were a show horse.[26] Unbeknownst to Errol, the cab is already on Seventh Avenue. Williams is thinking to drive him all around the city, bringing him back to the spot where they started. Thus the cabman, with his inebriated passenger, makes the artificial horse walk in circles around the stage, much to the audience's delight.[27]

The Williams-Errol performance was regarded by many critics as the high point of the show. The *New York Times* said the skit was "the funniest moment of the Follies of 1912." The *New York Tribune* called it "one of the most successful scenes in the whole entertainment." The scene provided "many laughs," reported *Variety*, while the *New York Age* labeled it "genuinely funny."[28] After critiquing the whole show, the *New York World* singled out Bert Williams: "There was just one artist on the stage. He was Bert Williams, who first as a cabman and later in one of his own inimitable specialities, convulsed the audience with his solemn demeanor and droll wit."[29]

Williams's specialty spot in the show permitted him to sing his songs. The *Follies* program did not list the songs, but three were named by reviewers. They were "My Landlady," "You're on the Right Road, but You're Going the Wrong Way," and "Borrow from Me."[30] Williams was the composer of all the songs. *Variety* thought that "On the Right Road" was the best, while the *New York Times* chose "Borrow from Me" as exceptional. As usual, Williams injected his folky humor into the lyrics which described "the conditions under which he could be induced to lend money to a friend."[31] Lester Walton also thought "Borrow from Me" was a good tune for Bert Williams, but he lamented the fact that the other songs were just passable. Walton noted: "Mr. Williams is such a great artist that it would

Bert Williams and Leon Errol in a scene from the 1912 *Ziegfeld Follies*. (*Courtesy Wisconsin Center for Film and Theater Research*)

have to be an awful bad song if he failed in his efforts to make good with it; but I have heard him sing so many songs that were much more meritorious."[32] Walton thought that Williams would have had better luck with his music had he collaborated with his past lyricists, such as Alex Rogers. But Williams had done extremely well, considering that the *Follies of 1912* seemed to offer little more than glamorous women. *Variety* summed it up this way: "Ziegfeld can pick 'em. He's got 'em in this season's Follies. And he better had, for there isn't much else there, excepting some settings, comedians who are wasted, a book that is nil, and music the same. But the girls!"[33]

Chapter 20

I n January 1913 Bert Williams went back into the recording studios of Columbia Records to cut a number of records. They were mostly songs he had composed, which he had performed either in vaudeville or the *Ziegfeld Follies*. On January 3 he recorded the Irving Berlin–Vincent Bryan hit, "Woodman Spare That Tree," which he had introduced in the 1911 edition of the *Follies*. That day, too, Williams cut another recording of the popular "Nobody." On January 13 he recorded "Borrow from Me," with lyrics by Jean Havez. The next day Williams recorded another of his compositions: "You're on the Right Road, but You're Going the Wrong Way" also with lyrics by Jean Havez. Finally, on January 21, he recorded the Henry Creamer–Will Vodery tune, "I Was Certainly Going Some."[1]

Williams's recordings sold well in the United States and in Great Britain. Mostly because of his recordings and performances, there was a demand for blackface entertainers in Europe. Lester Walton said that it gave signs of being a real craze:

> The demand for blackface acts is great, and the leading colored and white teams doing blackface have been booked to appear in London some time during the spring or summer. An offer was recently made Klaw and Erlanger and Flo Ziegfeld, in which a London manager offered them $2,000 a week for the services of Bert Williams. The offer was refused.

Walton worried that the British would see blackface comedians as typical of all American blacks. He noted that most blackface comedians on Broadway were white, and Bert Williams was the only black. "This state of affairs is due in the main to the white comedian copying the work of the colored comedian and then improving and elaborating upon it." Eventually, Walton said, the white artist gets the credit and recognition for his adaptation of what was originally a black product.[2]

Meanwhile Aida Overton Walker continued her work as a choreographer, occasionally doing benefit shows for the black community. In May 1913 she appeared at the New Star Casino in New York. The benefit, for several New York black charities, consisted of eight variety acts. These

165

included the Porto Rico Girls and the Happy Girls, whom Aida Overton
Walker choreographed:

> Miss Walker appeared twice on the bill. In her first number, she sang the
> "Cleopatra Rag" and was compelled to respond to encores. She was next
> heard in "So Different from the Rest," assisted by Miss Pearl Crawford. . . .
> As a fitting finale, Miss Walker, in male attire, rendered several old favorite
> selections, reinforced by the female members of the Porto Rico Girls and the
> Happy Girls act. When the curtain descended, Miss Walker stood out in bold
> relief, with the girls forming an effective background. The picture was a
> pretty one.[3]

About a week after this benefit, the *New York Age* announced that
Williams would not be in the 1913 *Follies*. No reason was given.[4] Williams
was not ill nor had he quarreled with Flo Ziegfeld. A likely reason for his
absence from the *Follies* was the fact that about this time, his sister-in-law
died. Lottie Williams's sister had left behind three girls in Chicago. The
girls – Eunice, Charlotte, and Laura Tyler – were sent for, and Bert probably agreed to stay home and help his wife raise her nieces.[5] Years later one
of the nieces talked to a newspaper reporter about her "Uncle Eggs." "They
called him 'Eggs'" . . . said Charlotte Tyler, "nicknamed for his right
name – 'Egbert.'" She explained that people close to Bert Williams always
called him by that nickname. Charlotte Tyler remembered her uncle as a
very kind and generous man: "Life with 'Uncle Eggs' was wonderful all the
time. . . . It was like living with Santa Claus. . . . He'd give us girls $10 in
gold for every cake or every plate of biscuits we'd bake him, and he'd give
us $100 apiece in gold at Christmas."[6]

Charlotte Tyler said her uncle was more interested in teaching his
nieces than disciplining them:

> He never raised his voice; he was never angry. Always, there were presents,
> but sometimes during the day, he'd sit down with us in his library . . . and
> he'd read to us – serious books, things he thought would be good for us. We
> had to be good in school to please him.[7]

Since Bert Williams and his wife had no children of their own, the arrival of the nieces meant that at last they had a family. Williams enjoyed
being with children and was a special friend of neighborhood children.

> "He always gave them rides – it was just a question of how many . . . could
> find foothold." Mrs. Bert Williams told a reporter that she would watch as
> children gathered on the sidewalk waiting for her husband. They are a little
> bit stubborn in their confidence that same evening, an hour before theatre
> time, he will spin up Seventh Avenue, stop in front of 2309, wink at them,
> and say to his wife in that funny, helpless way: "You can't keep 'em off,
> mother – flies around molasses!"[8]

But he could not stay away from the stage for long. The Frogs, the theatrical club to which Williams belonged, had held a frolic, or variety show, for the public every summer since 1908. In 1913 the Frogs invited Aida Overton Walker to join them in their annual show. Bert Williams leapt at the chance to join his old sidekick, with whom he had not performed since 1909. The *New York Age* reported:

> The Annual Frogs Frolic. Held Every summer since 1908. S. H. Dudley, Aida Overton Walker and Bert Williams to head up a show August 11 at the Manhattan Casino. They will then tour Philadephia, Baltimore, Washington and Richmond. The show was expected to break box office records in all cities especially in Richmond. "For the first time, the citizens of Richmond will have an opportunity to see Bert Williams and other prominent colored acts [about] which they have heard much but have never seen. As Richmond is not included on the theatrical map by the large colored shows, those interested in theatricals . . . never get a chance to see the leading performers of the race.[9]

An ad for the show advertised it as "the greatest collection of Negro Artists that has ever appeared together in the same performance." James Reese Europe was to be orchestra director.

The 1913 Frogs Frolic featured the Frogs and many important black entertainers of the day. The first part of the show was a minstrel show, with playwright Jesse Shipp serving as interlocutor. Williams and Walker company member Theodore Pankey sang "I Don't Want To." Jesse Clipper, of the vaudeville act "The Clippers" performed "Ragtime Violin." Louis Saulsbury, who later worked with Aida Overton Walker in her shows, sang "The Same Old Girl." Although he was seventy-three, the veteran minstrel performer Sam Lucas (1840–1916) brought down the house with an honest song: "I Was Alright in My Younger Days." Bobby Kemp, part of a husband-and-wife vaudeville act, sang "That Going Some." At the close of the minstrel show came S. H. Dudley and Bert Williams – what the audience had been waiting for. Lester Walton described the reaction to Williams:

> Of course, Bert A. Williams was the principal attraction. He had not been seen by many colored playgoers for three or four seasons, and the great interest centered in his appearance was gratifying. Mr. Williams appeared at the end of the minstrel first part with S. H. Dudley, and the two leading comedians were a scream. Mr. Williams was seen for the first time in his career in the role of a dusky damsel, who was all dressed up in a slit skirt and other female toggery. Mr. Dudley appeared as Mr. Williams' gentleman friend. They sang an old song, "Goo Goo Eyes," and then proceeded to tickle the funny bone of all present in a grotesque dance which would have made even old man Groucho himself laugh. At the conclusion of their turn, they were given a big ovation.[10]

The olio, or "afterpiece," as minstrel showmen called it, consisted of a variety of acts. The Sambo Girl dancers; Bobby and Mae Kemp; comedians

Harrison Stewart and Vi, Kelley and Catlin, and Harper and Gillians all appeared before Aida Overton Walker came onstage. Mrs. Walker was dressed in a seductive costume and was assisted in a song and dance by Jesse Shipp. The song was "The International Rag." According to the *New York Age*, Mrs. Walker's clothes commanded as much attention as her performance: "The dance was a big hit. What did Miss Walker wear? Why, a slit skirt, and believe me, the slit could not ride on the street cars for half fair either. Some full-grown slit."[11]

Mrs. Walker was followed by comedian Billy Robinson, of the vaudevile team of Cooper and Robinson—believe it or not, none other than Bill ("Bojangles") Robinson. Around the turn of the century he had met George W. Cooper, and on January 10, 1903, they officially became Cooper and Robinson—Comedians. (Ironically, the greatest dancer in the world was not yet earning his living as one.)[12]

Robinson was followed by vaudeville performers Hodges and Lauchmere, who had known Williams and Walker in their San Francisco days. Next was bandleader Williams Sweatman. In 1903 he and his band had become the first to make a recording, when they played Scott Joplin's "Maple Leaf Rag" (for a cylinder phonograph) in a music store in Minneapolis, Minnesota.[13] On this occasion the bandleader played the clarinet.

The final performers were billed as songwriters "[Alex] Rogers and [Henry S.] Creamer's Negro Players and the Dancing Demons—six men and women dancing "a waltz in syncopated time."[14]

After the successful frolic show in New York, the Frogs had scheduled a series of one-night stands in cities along the Atlantic seaboard. Some performers in the New York Frogs Frolic, including Aida Overton Walker, did not go on tour.[15]

A minor racial episode occurred in Baltimore. Because of the late booking of the tour, the Frogs' manager had a white newspaper advertise the show: "In his desire to secure a large crowd and [re]assure the white theatergoers . . . he caused to be inserted in an advertisement that special sections would be reserved for white people." The Frogs apologized for the manager, stating that it was not their intention to perform for segregated audiences. Many blacks in Baltimore were offended by the ad and boycotted the Frogs' show.[16]

In Richmond the Frogs had the best time of all the cities they visited. The members of the company were given an automobile tour and treated to a banquet at the leading social club. A dance was given in their honor on the roof of the Mechanics Savings Bank. The show, held at the City Auditorium, boasted the largest turnout of the cities on the Frogs' tour. They succeeded in temporarily dropping "the color bar":

For the first time in the history of the place, colored men stood in the box office and helped the while attaches sell tickets to colored and white playgoers alike. . . . So many white people attended the performance, that the section reserved for them became overcrowded and many sat with the colored people – a condition which has never heretofore prevailed in that city.[17]

Critic Douglas Gordon, of the *Richmond Times-Dispatch*, said of the Frogs' show:

In the first place, it was absolutely clean, literally clean. Think of being able to say that of one of our minstrel shows. Secondly, it was hilariously amusing, one of the funniest, cleverest all-round performances that I have ever seen in many a day, and finally, it was at times thoroughly artistic.[18]

Black theater was blossoming all over the country in 1913. As early as 1905 Chicago had had a black theater called the Pekin, founded by Robert T. Motts. It "featured a lively fare of ragtime, cakewalks and 'coon songs.' Proudly billed as 'the only Negro-owned theater in the world,' the Pekin became one of the showplaces of the South Side."[19]

It was at the Pekin Theater that Aida Overton Walker opened for a weeklong engagement with her own large company. The *Chicago Defender* described her show as "a new and novel vaudeville concert entertainment." Though revered as a dancer-choreographer in the Williams and Walker shows, Mrs. Walker had, through the years, earned respect as a serious dancer. The *Defender* observed that she was "the only colored lady that has ever been accepted as a danseuse of the classics in reference to her performance of the dance, 'Salome.'"[20]

Critics complained that "she didn't appear often enough on the bill," only three times. In her first appearance Mrs. Walker performed two dances. In "La Rumba," with music by black composer Tim Brymm, she was supported by Louis Saulsbury. In "Aida Valse," Aida Walker did a solo dance to music by Will H. Vodery (1885–1951). The Chris Smith song "Chalky White Eyes" provided the theme for Mrs. Walker's last solo spot in the show. She did, however, appear in the company's finale number: "Wonderful Girl."[21] The *Defender* praised Aida Overton Walker, observing that she "still remains a luminary of first water in the realms of dramatic art and terpsichore." Later people would reflect that the 1913 Pekin Theater appearance was the "most successful engagement of her career" as a solo vaudeville artist.[22]

Bert Williams was also appearing in vaudeville. In December 1913 he had one of his best runs in vaudeville when he appeared as headliner at New York City's Palace Theater, regarded by many performers as one of the most prestigious vaudeville houses in the country. *Variety* said that Bert Williams's act was nothing short of sensational.

Judging from the Monday evening attendance, the drawing power of Bert Williams is all that the management hoped for. The house was filled to capacity by 8:20 and several hundred late applicants for seats were turned away. Williams did 33 minutes and left the audience shouting for more. Williams sang five songs and told two stories and then [was] called back to do the poker pantomime and sing "Nobody."[23]

Variety only named two of the songs Williams sang, "Darktown Poker Club," which spoofed Hoyle's card game rules, and "Nobody." It seems that Williams didn't want to sing "Nobody," because *Variety* reported that "the audience insisted upon 'Nobody' and refused to let him go until he had sung it."[24]

One of the stories Williams told was about "the man who wouldn't want any fish next Sunday." Williams's storytelling was a real treat. His mellow, baritone voice would rise and dip according to his dramatic recitation. People who heard Bert Williams's stories or songs observed that he had a poetic feeling for words, which made his performances enjoyable. The following story—"Fish"—is taken from Jervis Anderson's *This Was Harlem*:

He would tell his audiences a story in the first person of a young black boy who supported his family by catching and selling fish. One day, he took his catch up a mountain lined with houses of white people. Rebuffed again and again, he finally made his way to the tops where he found a small white man standing in the doorway of a house. "I walks up to him and I bows low to him, ver' polite, and I sez to him, I sez: 'Mister, does you want some fresh feesh?' And he sez to me, he sez: 'No, we don't want no fish today.'" Making his way down the mountain, the boy [was] overtaken by a landslide which carried him painfully to its feet. Digging his way out, he looked up and saw at the top the little man beckoning him. "So I sez to myself: 'Praise God, that w'te man done changed his mind.' So I climbs back again up the mountain, seven thousand feet high, till I come to the plum top, and w'en I gits there, the little white man is still standin' there waitin' for me. He waits till I'm right close to him before he speaks. Then he clears his throat and sez to me, he sez: 'And we don't want none tomorrow either.'"[25]

Critics lamented that Williams's gift of storytelling was not being utilized in the *Ziegfeld Follies*. "Williams has the storytelling gift in a degree possessed by few. It's a pity he puts it to such poor use in his present turn." Williams' version of the Tango was called "screamingly funny," although many people missed the "lazy, loose-jointed stepping" of the old Williams and Walker days.[26]

After this Bert Williams went to Philadelphia to be headliner for a week at the Keith vaudeville house. The *New York Age* said that Williams wanted to do this in order to become "the first colored performer to play this house for a number of years." (A colored comedian had become involved in an altercation at Keith's, and since then the house manager had refused to play colored acts.) "It is thought by some that Bert Williams, by appearing at Keith's this week, will break the ice for other classy colored turns."[27]

In January 1914 Williams was stil at the Palace. But his performance was cut short one night due to a severe cold. *Variety* said: "The colored entertainer worked at a disadvantage, a severe cold manifesting itself to such an extent that he had to beg off. He put in a busy 20 minutes."[28]

That same month, Aida Overton Walker, now with a dance group, played at the Bijou Theater in Minneapolis. Mrs. Walker's company had been scaled down considerably from the ensemble that had played Chicago several months earlier. The *Minneapolis Tribune* said little about Walker or her dance group except that "Walker's Happy Girls is a troupe of girl entertainers with Reed and Marshall as principal comedians."[29]

Bert Williams returned to recording and film work in 1914. In February he recorded for Columbia Records "You Can't Get Away from It," a ditty that copied the call-response trombone trick used in "Nobody" and "Darktown Poker Club." Because Williams worked for Florenz Ziegfeld, who in turn worked for Klaw and Erlanger, the Syndicate, he came to make films for Biograph. Biograph, one of the earliest film companies, is now mostly remembered for the films of D. W. Griffith produced for them, as well as for the early films of Mary Pickford. Terry Ramsaye says that by 1914, "the Protective Amusement Company had been formed and an arrangement had been made for the Biograph to photograph its pictures to be produced from the selected stage successes of the K & E [Klaw and Erlanger] stage productions."[30] But, according to Rowland, not all of Biograph's screenplays were to be made from already-produced plays. Speaking of Bert Williams, Rowland wrote:

> He was approached by Mr. Tarkington Baker, who had great faith in his value as a [film] picture star, especially should he be presented in the scenarios which Mr. Baker was prepared to produce. These were stories by Irvin Cobb and other equally capable workers of Southern Negro material.[31]

Williams agreed to the proposal, and suitable screenplays were written for him. One of these required a graveyard location. "Williams discovered a satisfactory graveyard on Staten Island, where a thrifty sexton locked the gates and held off a funeral while the scenes were photographed."[32]

It is possible that this is the film to which Charters was referring when she cited a film in which "Williams [played] the role of a cringing blackface preacher paralyzed with superstitious fear in a 'haunted' graveyard."[33]

Nothing else of the storyline of the film–*Darktown Jubilee*–is known. Indeed, the film is now lost. "Legend has it that *Darktown Jubilee* started out to be a profound hit, when a wave of race antagonism arose. . . . At a Brooklyn presentation of this picture, a race riot resulted in the death of two men."[34]

Marshall Hyatt, in his book *The Afro-American Cinematic Experience*, suggests that the riot occurred because *Darktown Jubilee* was "an early attempt to star a black actor in a non-stereotyped role." If Hyatt is implying that Williams did not use blackface in the film, his theory would be a plausible explanation. It runs counter, however, to Ann Charters, who argues that Williams was a "blackface preacher" in the film. In 1914 Williams purportedly did another Biograph film, a three-reeler called *The Indian*. Kemp Niven, who lists Bert Williams in the cast of that picture, does not say what Williams's role was.[35] During early film days, it was not unusual for actors to go uncredited in movies.

Meanwhile, Aida Overton Walker was doing trailblazing of her own as a dancer. In May 1914 she was at Hammerstein's for a vaudeville stint. *Variety*'s review of her act revealed how much Mrs. Walker had matured as a dancer, mastering all the styles of vernacular dance.

> Miss Walker now offers the prevailing "ballroom" dancing act, assisted by Lackey Grant. They have their own colored orchestra, just like the others, but their turn differs in that they open with the so-called Maxixe and a Hesitation Tango to follow. They do much more of the away-from-each-other stepping than their Caucasian contemporaries. Then comes a Negro Drag and finally what is called Jiggeree. These latter consist of considerable hip gyrating and swaying, finishing with some jigging and pirouetting. A good pair of dancers, but the act is not sensationally effective.[36]

The 1914 *Ziegfeld Follies* opened on June 1, 1914. Along with Bert Williams, the stars were Ann Pennington, Leon Errol, and Ed Wynn. According to the program of the New Amsterdam Theater, Williams appeared in the show four times. "In act 1, scene 2, Mr. Williams received an uproarious greeting on his appearance from behind a snowbank in front of the public library at 42nd Street and Fifth Avenue."[37] Williams sang a song called, "I'm Cured," as a character named "Onyx, a member of the Alimony Club." *Variety* said, "Mr. Williams didn't do much here."[38]

Many skits in the *Ziegfeld Follies* were topical, drawing their inspiration from current events. In Act 1, Scene 7, for Williams's second appearance, "the borderline between Texas and Mexico" was depicted in scenery. Mexico was in the news in 1914 because of the U.S. government's occupation of Vera Cruz in retaliation for the Mexicans' arrest of American soldiers.

Theater critic Burns Mantle thought Bert Williams did well in this unorthodox setting. "Mr. Bert Williams, the colored comedian . . . contributes his allotted share of the joy by appearing as a caddie to Mr. Errol's amateur golfer."[39]

Act 2, Scene 5, once again paired Williams and Errol. The scene was called "The Skyscraper," an obvious attempt to recapture the brilliant comedy of the 1911 *Follies* sketch "Grand Central Station." The *New York Times* described the skit:

Williams and Errol appear as workmen on the one thousand three hundred and thirteenth story of a skyscraper in course of construction. It wound up, after much funny dialog, by Errol falling off during an electrical storm which was novel and striking.[40]

Williams's dialogue was full of wisecracks and clever comic lines. "'I may be dark,' said Mr. Williams, as he was poised dangerously over a girder on the ninety-ninth story . . . 'but I ain't no crow, and bein' up here is safe so long as you stay up.'"[41] *Munsey's Magazine* said "the attempts of Errol to convince Williams that they are as safe as they would be in bed at home, are highly diverting."[42] The scene provided "some of the best laughs of the night," said the *New York Herald.*[43]

Act 2, Scene 5, "Ziegfeld Danse de Follies," was Williams's last spot in the show. Here he performed several songs. Williams opened with "The Man That Wrote 'The Vampire' Must Have Known My Wife." Williams composed the tune to lyrics by Earl Jones and Gene Buck. Next Williams sang "a poker song wherein with the aid of a razor, Williams told how he had rewritten the rules of the game."[44] The song was "Darktown Poker Club."

Theatre Magazine seemed to sum up the sentiments of many when it remarked that "the 1914 edition is a huge success. . . . Bert Williams is one of the bright spots of the performance."[45]

Aida Overton Walker offered another outing for New York's black community on June 16 at the Manhattan Casino. The event, called "the Tango Picnic," was a dance extravaganza featuring Mrs. Walker:

> As predicted, Aida Overton Walker was the center of attraction and the favorite of the evening. In her five original dances–Maxixe, Hesitation Tango, Southern Drag, and Jiggeree–Mrs. Walker came up to all expectations. The Southern Drag received the greatest applause. She was assisted by Lackaye Grant. Mrs. Walker wore a beautiful gold-colored creation of satin chiffon and spangled net, bringing out the effects of an oriental costume.[46]

During August 1914 Aida Overton Walker again appeared at Hammerstein's Victoria Theater in New York.[47] But that was to be her last stage performance. Around the end of September, Mrs. Walker fell ill. Several weeks later, on Sunday evening, October 11, she died. The cause of death was uncertain, some sources claiming that she died from a nervous breakdown. A more plausible cause–kidney disease–was cited by black newspapers.[48]

Mrs. Walker was believed to have been about thirty-four at the time of her death. The *Chicago Defender* said an uncle was sole survivor. The funeral was held Thursday, October 15, at St. Phillip's Protestant Episcopal Church in Harlem. Aida Overton Walker's death was a great shock to many people. It is not known how Bert Williams reacted to Mrs. Walker's death.

He may have agreed, in fact, that "she was considered the third wheel in the famous Williams and Walker Company."[49] But Aida Walker was more than just a third wheel. "She was the premier dancer of the colored race" and "the greatest female attraction with prestige" in the black community.[50] Many members of the press reviewed Mrs. Walker's career and concluded that "no other colored woman in America was better known or had a more brilliant list of accomplishments in her particular sphere."[51] Had she lived today, she would undoubtedly have been as daring and creative in our time as she was in her own. Aida Overton Walker was seen as a role model for black women. One critic stated: "Her loss in the theatrical world will never be replaced, as she never imitated. ... She simply made history. I hope the young actresses of the race will take her as an example."[52]

Bert Williams was not among the pallbearers at Mrs. Walker's funeral. The press did not mention if he was even present.

Chapter 21

Although Bert Williams continued to perform in the *Ziegfeld Follies* after Aida Overton Walker's death, it was becoming less fun. Aida's passing served to remind Williams of how lonely he felt being in an all-white show. As we have seen, the *Follies* usually opened in New York City in June, played there for the summer, and toured the country in the fall and winter. On these trips Williams constantly came up against racial segregation. Despite his fame, he had to endure the humiliating "separate but equal" accommodations just like other black people of the time. Now that George and Aida were both gone, Williams wanted badly to reach out to white fellow actors. But because he could not eat or travel with them, friendships were hard to come by. W. C. Fields (1880–1946) – whose career spanned vaudeville, Broadway, theater, and motion pictures – was one of the few actors Williams opened up to. Fields appeared in the *Follies* in 1915 for the first time, and he remembered that Bert Williams was a lonely man.

> My good friend, Williams, met with a great many unpleasantly limiting conditions and, as time went on, he seemed to feel that craving for a club, or some place where he could meet those of his own profession, and talk shop as other actor-folk do. With all his philosophy, and he had a well-rounded philosophy, he would occasionally say, "Well, there is no way for me to know this or that thing, which you say is going on – I'm just relegated – I don't belong." It was not said in a bitter tone, but it did sound sadly hopeless and it did seem a pity that any artist who contributed so much that was of the best to our theatre, should be denied even the common comforts of living when on the road in cities like St. Louis and Cincinnati.[1]

Williams apparently did not regard Fields's entry into the *Ziegfeld Follies* as competition. What did upset him, however, was the inability of Ziegfeld's writers to provide good stage material for him. The book and lyrics writers for Ziegfeld in 1915 were Rennold Wolf, Gene Buck, and Channing Pollack. Pollack (1880–1946) was originally a drama critic and later did publicity for Ziegfeld. "Alone or with collaborators, he wrote about thirty shows that saw the footlights, ranging from sketches for several

Ziegfeld Follies and the books of musical comedies to farce and melodrama."[2]

In his autobiography Pollack says that the 1915 *Ziegfeld Follies* was the most difficult show he wrote for. After Pollack wrote his script for the show, the performers proceeded to improvise their parts. Pollack said: "Within the next half hour, each one had rewritten his part, without respect to anyone else."[3] To make matters worse, the stage props and scenery had been designed for the original Pollack script. When the actors "rewrote" their parts, many props and scenes had to be discarded, including Bert Williams's. Pollack described what happened to one Bert Williams skit:

> We had started with the idea of Rip Van Winkle, just awakened after oversleeping a century, and finding everything unfamiliar in New York. We didn't see how we were to get Rip into a submarine, and then into an aeroplane. . . . The submarine was about ten feet long. Bert Williams and Leon Errol were to play a comedy scene in it. There wasn't room for either to sit up straight, or to move, and both were to be in the dark, behind several pieces of gauze, twenty feet back of the footlights.[4]

Pollack rewrote the submarine sketch thirteen times before it was finally dropped from the script. Another Pollack idea was to suspend Bert Williams in a zeppelin above the stage. This scene, "rehearsed, rewritten and [re]rehearsed a dozen times, always in the face of loud protests from Bert Williams, who didn't enjoy being suspended in midair, finally was discarded without ever having been seen by the public."[5]

Pollack's experience with Bert Williams seems to have been repeated with many other *Follies* performers. It is no wonder, therefore, that when the show opened in Atlantic City, Pollack didn't recognize his own work. Speaking of his co-writer, Rennold Wolf, Pollack declared:

> Ren and I had written the *Follies*, and attended every rehearsal, but I'll swear that three-quarters of the performance given that Sunday night we never had heard or seen before. Ren said that the players were "making it up" as they went along, and he may have been right.[6]

One of the scenes in which Williams did appear in the *Ziegfeld Follies of 1915*, was as a West Indian hall boy named Thomas. W. C. Fields and Ann Pennington were also in the sketch. *Variety* provided details of the scene:

> Bert Williams is on a couch at the curtain. It is about one a.m. The switch-board gets busy, the tenants (mostly women) and the callers (mostly men) go in and out when they are not overworking Williams at the phone. He knows them all. It is the class of apartments that may be found all over the west side of Manhattan, between 42nd and 125th Streets. One young woman, as she exits, impresses upon the bell boy he must tell anyone who calls up she had to retire with a severe headache. "Everybody?" asks Williams. "Yes,

everybody," replies the girl. "Even the old gentleman?" he inquires. Answering the phone, Williams in response to supposedly a question as to the whereabouts of one of the female tenants, says, "Oh, she has gone out with her fie-nance-cier."[7]

The *New York Times* raved over Williams in this skit. The critic said: "You should see Bert Williams as a West Indian apartment hall boy."[8] The *New York World* called Williams in this scene "hilariously funny."[9]

In 1915 Bert Williams came as close as he would ever get to performing in a George Bernard Shaw play. The *Follies* lampooned Shaw's play *Androcles and the Lion.* In the play a Christian and his wife, fleeing persecution by the Romans, are accosted by a lion. In the *Ziegfeld Follies*, Will West played the Christian, Phil Dwyer played the lion, and Bert Williams, as O. Shaw, impersonated the playwright. This scene drew mixed reaction from the critics. The *New York Tribune* said the Shaw burlesque was "well done" and that "Bert Williams was as funny as he has ever been." *Variety* panned the piece, claiming that the only line worth anything at all was when West, calling the Lion, said "Come here, Leo." Williams exclaimed, "My God, a Jew Lion!"[10]

In 1915 Williams was upstaged not so much by fellow comedians like W. C. Fields or Leon Errol as by the stage scenery. The *New York Times* critic spoke for many when he said: "The star of the new summer show is . . . Joseph Urban."[11] Urban (1872–1933), an artist–stage designer making his debut with Ziegfeld in 1915, is credited with being "the first major designer to carefully coordinate colors and to employ subtle lighting to enhance his color schemes."[12]

In 1915 World War I was on the minds of many Americans, even though the United States had not entered the conflict yet. This explains why the *Follies* writers wanted to use military items like submarines, zeppelins, and airplanes in the show. President Woodrow Wilson had declared that America was neutral, and Bert Williams picked up this theme in a song recorded in August, 1915: "I'm Neutral." Raymond Hubbell, Dave Stamper, Gene Buck, and George V. Hobart were the songwriters. Williams is believed to have introduced this tune in the 1915 *Follies.* Also in August–September 1915, Williams recorded other songs, including "Everybody," "Indoor Sports," "Samuel," "Hard Times," "Purpotus," "Never 'Mo," and "Eph Calls Up the Boss." It is not known if Williams composed these.[13]

In the *Ziegfeld Follies* Williams had settled into a sort of routine situation-comedy act, called for by playing against white actors. Much of his appeal, his black detractors said, was due to his being the token black in the show. While this status undoubtedly guaranteed his fame, it also meant that Williams was cut off from the creative changes taking place then in black theater. The Lincoln and Lafayette theaters in New York were at the forefront of the new black theater in New York. The Lafayette, at Seventh Avenue and 131st Street, was managed by Eugene Elmore and Lester Walton between 1914 and 1916. By then, Walton claimed, a breakthrough had been achieved for the black actor: "For years, the colored performer has been sadly declaring that his field is limited, color permitting him to appear on stage as a Negro only, maybe occasionally as an Oriental."[14]

But, Walton said, it was possible for black actors to use makeup as white characters on stage. In the 1915 production of Dion Boucicault's *The Octoroon*—a play about "the tragic mulatto"—black actor Charles Gilpin played a white character. Gilpin, who had been in the Williams and Walker show *Abyssinia*, concocted an ingenious mixture of stage makeup that permitted him and other black actors to look white. The makeup was so effective, it is said, that at first friends of the cast members didn't recognize them on stage.[15]

Experiments like the *Octoroon* encouraged black actors to adapt other plays by white playwrights. The year 1916 was the tercentenary of Shakespeare's birth, and black actors joined in the national Shakespeare revival that year. The Lafayette Theater put on a version of *Othello* with Edward Sterling Wright and Marion Toney in the leading roles, for example.

The 1916 *Ziegfeld Follies* parodied a number of Shakespeare's plays, including *Julius Caesar, Henry VIII, Romeo and Juliet*, and *Othello*. Bert Williams appeared in a travesty of the latter; it was his participation in the tercentenary celebration. The scene was called "The Bedroom in Mr. and Mrs. Othello's Apartment."[16]

> In "Othello," Mr. Williams has his broadest chance. ... The travesties are not prolonged and carry more humor in dialog than action. In "Othello," Mr. Williams, as the Moor, says to Desdemona [Mr. Don Barclay], "Who have you been running around with lately, Desperate-money?" "Not a single soul, excepting the 72nd Regiment," is the reply, thereby giving Barclay, of course, credit for the laugh. Mr. Williams seemed to work too slowly in this bit.[17]

Another critic thought that "Bert Williams was an interesting 'Othello,' although hardly screamingly humorous."[18] The *New York Times* was more enthused about Williams. Its critic advised readers:

> You should see the scene from *Othello* with Bert Williams, not to be outdone by any Frank Tinney (a white blackface comedian) as the Moor. He chokes his Desdemona ... till he is tired and then beats her with a sledgehammer, but it only irritates her.[19]

Williams played a reluctant soldier in the 1916 *Follies* skit "Recruiting on Broadway." "He is compelled to enlist as a soldier, much against a Falstaffian preference for running instead of fighting," said the *New York Herald*.[20] Williams's character was appropriately named "Maybe Knott."

Unfortunately, this scene was later dropped from the show, and another of Bert Williams's scenes was moved around to give more space to Fanny Brice.[21]

Brice and Williams performed together in a rare episode during a scene called "The Blushing Ballet," a travesty on "Scheherazade." "Scheherazade," a character in the *Arabian Nights*, was the inspiration for a suite composed in 1888 by Rimsky-Korsakov. In 1910 choreographer Michel Fokine devised a ballet set to Rimsky-Korsakov's music. Dancer-choreographer Vaslav Nijinsky (1890–1950) played the black slave who woos Scheherazade in the ballet. In 1916, Nijinsky's American debut in this dance was the occasion for the *Follies'* burlesque. Many found Nijinsky's portrayal of the slave disturbing. "The part of the Negro who makes love to the princess is a repulsive one, but he tones down some of its unpleasantness. The impulse to jump on the stage and thrash him must be suppressed."[22]

In the 1916 *Follies*, Bert Williams played the black slave Nijinsky and had a field day imitating the many mimes and menacing moves of the dance by Nijinsky. Fanny Brice sang the song "Nijinsky." The *New York Times* thought Williams's performance was novel. "You should see him as 'le Negro,'" it suggested. "While 'The Blushing Ballet' is on, Nijinski has his inexorable day in court."[23]

Another unusual character Bert Williams played in 1916 was that of the bandit-revolutionary Pancho Villa. In 1916 Villa had been chased out of New Mexico for invading the town of Columbus near the Mexican border. Six thousand American soldiers pursued Villa and his men, but he managed to evade capture. Theater audiences must have found Bert Williams's impersonation of this Mexican bandit rather odd, if not hilarious. Bert Williams also impersonated a Hawaiian in another scene. "Here, Bert Williams [was] appearing in a brief straw skirt and an expressing of deep grief to do a few Honolulu steps."[24] Williams was really attempting to broaden his acting range by portraying different nationalities.

But few critics seemed to give Williams credit for being innovative. "He has had," said the *New York Herald*, "better things in other *Follies*."[25] Some thought the writers of the show were to blame: "The dusky Williams, unfortunately, never did succeed in being vastly humorous. There is no inclination, however, to place the blame for the phenomenon upon Mr. Williams."[26]

Other observers thought that this year, Ziegfeld had his priorities mixed up:

> If one-quarter of such ability as is expended upon the stage decorations and the costumes could have been applied to the book and lyrics and the music, praise for the new *Follies* might be almost unlimited. ... This year's show is beneath the standards of some of its predecessors.[27]

During the summer of 1916, while in the *Follies*, Williams recorded two songs for Columbia Records – "The Lee Family" and "I'm Gone Before I Go," as well as several films for Biograph.[28] In June the *New York Age* reported that Williams was to appear in a series of two-reel comedies.[29] One comedy, called *Fish*, featured Williams "as a country boy who, among other things, fishes and hawks his catch to white folks."[30] From this description it appears that the scenario was based on a story that Williams had used in his vaudeville act.

Other elements of Williams's vaudeville stage business, the famous pantomime poker game, showed up in another 1916 film – *A Natural Born Gambler*. The director was G. W. Bitzer. The 16mm film has been recently reissued by the Eastin Phelan Corporation.[31] Their catalog describes it as having a "nickelodeon piano score" and "lasting 14 minutes at 24 fps." The movie is listed as being "2 reels" in length.

In the film Williams is seen seated at a table with other men, playing poker. Everyone is having fun, especially Williams, who cheats by taking a card from between the toes of another player under the table. Suddenly the police burst in, arresting all present. The men are led out to the waiting police paddy wagon. Williams protests, to no avail. When he sees the paddy wagon, he faints. Later, in his jail cell, Williams plays an imaginary poker game. As the camera zooms in on Williams, his face runs the gamut of emotion from suspicion to glee, from ecstasy to disappointment. The game (and the movie) ends with Williams's realization that he has "lost" to himself.

In the only known film review of Bert Williams, the *Moving Picture World* said:

> That celebrated poker game which Bert Williams has so often played the pantomime on the spoken stage, is the inspiration of this two-reel comedy. The characters are all colored persons of the same sex, and they are all addicted to gambling. Williams attempts to annex the roll of a swell sport from the city, but the game is raided and, when last seen, the natural-born gambler is sadly dealing out imaginary hands behind the bars of a prison. The business of some of the scenes could be improved, but Bert Williams' skill at pantomime shows up well on the screen.[32]

Later Williams's lawyer, Henry Herzbrun (who was also an attorney for Biograph and later Paramount Pictures), argued that racial prejudice caused Biograph to shelve his films.

> There is no market. All of the representatives releasing concerns were approached and they were unanimous in their decision that the Southern territory [of the United States] would resent and would not exhibit the pictures of a Negro star; they were also unanimous in regretting that this was so.[33]

In December 1916 there appeared an interview with Bert Williams in *The Soil: A Magazine of Art*. In the interview, Williams talked about his method of acting and his thoughts about racial relations. When asked "What element of your work are you most interested in?" Williams replied: "Character." With this answer Williams advocated a theory of acting that was remarkably similar to that taught by the Russian director Konstantin Stanislavsky (1865–1938). Although Stanislavsky's ideas were not published until 1926 (in *An Actor Prepares*), after Williams's death, it is possible that Williams knew something about the Russian school of acting. In the same interview, Williams confessed: "I like to see how the other fellow works," he said, referring to the fact that he makes a round of the theatres on Sunday."[34] Williams said:

> I try to portray the shiftless darky to the fullest extent, his fun, his philosophy. Show this shiftless darky a book and he won't know what it is about. He can't read or write, but ask him a question and he'll answer it with a philosophy that has something in it. There is nothing about this fellow I don't know. I have studied him; his joys and sorrows. Contrast is vital. If I take up a lazy stevedore, I must study his movements. I have to. He is not in me. The way he walks, the way he crosses his legs, the way he leans up against a wall, one foot forward. I must imagine an idea and find out the way it would strike him, what he would do and think about it at any particular moment, before any particular audience in any particular frame of mind, and imagine how to "put it over" to the audience.[35]

Williams elaborated on the roles of music and dance in his acting:

> Often my dancing is the most important [element] in expressing the characters of the lazy darkey. It all depends in what phase of the character I want to express. Sometimes my voice is of uppermost importance, sometimes my song. I think the movements are always important. I don't believe there are any limitations to what can be expressed through this medium.[36]

Without criticizing Ziegfeld, Williams implied that the *Ziegfeld Follies* did not allow him to explore dramatic character-building. Williams said:

> If I were free to do as I would like, I would give both sides of the shiftless darkey, the pathos as well as the fun. . . . I'd like to take a character and build it up, giving both sides. . . . But I have to do the thing of the moment because time is too short. The present show changes too quickly to lay out for a definite aim, to build up. One can't build up a character in a hurry.[37]

Williams's ideas here seem similar to those articulated by Stanislavsky in his book *Building a Character*. Williams probably was familiar with Stanislavsky's technique through the appearances of the Moscow Art Theater in New York. Stanislavsky wrote:

> Let us agree that the word "perspective" means: the calculated, harmonious inter-relationship and distribution of the parts of a whole play or role. . . . If we stop short at the end of every bit in a role and then start over again with

the next, we never get up momentum in our efforts, our desire, our actions. ... you must have the depth, the perspective the far away beckoning goal in mind.[38]

Williams thought that part of his problem was that white Americans perceived that the "shiftless darkey" stage-character stereotype was real. They expected this stereotypical acting not only of black people in general but of black actors as well:

When a man has no pigment in his skin, it's hard. Just think what I have to do to "get by." The Caucasian believes that every colored man is a "coon," that they are all alike, that they should not live in a modern way. This is a mistake. We have as many differences as the white man and no one characteristic covers us all.[39]

He confessed that he was frustrated. Like many other actors who are identified with a certain successful role or character, he found it difficult to do something different. "The public knows me for certain things—if I attempt anything outside of those things, I'm not Bert Williams."[40]

Chapter 22

On April 2, 1917, the United States declared war on Germany and Austria-Hungary, thus entering World War I on the side of the Allies. Preparations for war, however, had been under way for some time. On June 16, 1916, Governor Whitman of New York had appointed a white man, Colonel Williams Hayward, to head the 15th (Colored) Infantry National Guard Regiment. This regiment was renamed the 369th U.S. Infantry when the United States went to war.[1]

On May 13, 1917, the 369th was ordered to report to Plattsburg, New York to begin training. They paraded through New York City before leaving for Plattsburg. Arthur Little, a veteran of the regiment, which fought in France, later wrote about the parade.[2]

> On Sunday morning, May 13th, we started for Peekskill. Our 2nd Battalion left the Brooklyn armory at about half past eight. We travelled by elevated railroad train across the Brooklyn Bridge and up Third Avenue. At Forty-Second Street, we detrained and marched to Park Avenue where we formed in line to be joined by the 1st and 3rd Battalions, the Machine Gun Company and the Band, which had to come down from the Harlem armory at 132nd Street and Seventh Avenue. There was delay and confusion.[3]

Bert Williams was the grand marshal. He was to ride at the head of the parade on a white horse.[4] He had reserved seats on the reviewing stand, situated on Fifth Avenue, for Lottie Williams and her three nieces. Arthur Little wrote:

> At about half past twelve, midday, we marched up Fifth Avenue. The march was made in the simplest of formations. Many of our men had had no drilling at all; none had much drilling. We took no more chances of disaster, by passing from one formation to another, than were absolutely unavoidable. Our men, however, were natural born marchers and cadence observers. With a band playing or with spectators cheering, they just couldn't be held from keeping step. That bright sunny Sunday morning, we had both – the playing band and the spectators.

Oddly enough, the *New York Age*'s report on the parade said nothing about Bert Williams's participation. His niece Charlotte Tyler explained why.

Once he told his wife and us three nieces to sit in the reviewing stand on Fifth Avenue in New York to see him ride in a military parade. He told us to look for him ride behind his close friend, Colonel William Hayward. He had on his uniform and boots, all dressed up. And we waited, all ready to scream when he'd come past, but he never came. There was the 15th [Regiment] and Colonel Hayward, but no Uncle Eggs, and that evening, we asked where he'd been and he said: "On the way down, my horse just turned out of the parade and went down in a subway entrance. I talked to it when it left the parade and I talked to it down there in the subway, but I never did find out why it wanted to go there or why it didn't want to come out.

Tom Fletcher gave Bert Williams's version of the incident, which was told in the form of a joke.

Bert was in the parade with the regiment, when the horse he was riding got out of control and ran away. The horse didn't stop until it ran into a lady's kitchen. According to Bert, the lady indignantly demanded to know what he meant by bringing a horse into her kitchen, and he told her it wasn't his fault, it was the horse's idea.[7]

Apparently many white New Yorkers thought the parade itself was funny too. Roi Ottley reported: "Some six hundred Negroes marched down Fifth Avenue in celebration of the event. Since they had no guns, they marched with broomsticks. . . . Many whites laughed at these "darkies playing soldiers." But it was this same regiment that became known as the Hell Fighters and was decorated by the French government for bravery.[8]

The next edition of the *Ziegfeld Follies* opened June 12, 1917. Book and lyrics were by George V. Hobart and Gene Buck. Music was provided by Raymond Hubbell and David Stamper. The 1917 *Follies* boasted an astounding array of talent. In addition to the Ziegfeld Girls and Bert Williams, the revue featured such stars as W. C. Fields, Ann Pennington, Will Rogers, Fanny Brice, and Eddie Cantor. Like Al Jolson, Cantor started his show business career as a blackface performer. But unlike Bert Williams, Cantor was able to drop the blackface mask and go on to other modes of performing.

Born Isidore Itzkowitz on New York's East Side on January 31, 1892, Cantor started in show business in 1910 wearing blackface. His earliest breaks came with the 1912 Gus Edwards production of *Kid Kabaret*. He was discovered by Florenz Ziegfeld and put into the 1916 *Ziegfeld Follies*. Anthony Slide noted that "when not in blackface, Cantor was best with Jewish humor."[9] He was famous for his popping eyes and outrageous comic song. Cantor joined a long tradition of white comic performers in blackface, including McIntyre and Heath, Moran and Mack, Frank Tinney, and of course, Al Jolson. As a "new kid on the block," Cantor expected Williams to be resentful and aloof to him. Instead Bert Williams did his best to act as mentor to Eddie Cantor. Cantor later wrote:

Bert Williams helped me a great deal. I'd expected possible resentment from Bert. How would he react to another blackface comedian? I couldn't have been more wrong. . . .

When we were introduced at our first rehearsal, I was overwhelmed. . . . But he flashed me a warm smile, put out his hand, and said, "Young man, you and I are going to be good friends." My doubts as a newcomer were dispelled. It wasn't so much his words – I'd heard them before. It was his voice. It rang true.[10]

If Bert Williams's relationship with Eddie Cantor was based on sincerity, critics of the 1917 *Follies* did not find that emotion in the show's book. The *New York Times* thought that Geogre V. Hobart and Gene Buck had come up with comic situations that were not believable.

Almost all of their comedy has only a Broadway application. . . . While a thing does not have to come within one's personal experience to seem funny, there should be the possibility of its happening to one. . . . The folly of the substitution of the stage-door point of view for a more wholesome one is best illustrated in a scene between Bert Williams and Eddie Cantor.[11]

Eddie Cantor, in his autobiography, *As I Remember Them*, summarized the skit he did with Bert Williams:

In our first sketch together in the Follies, Bert was playing a porter at Grand Central Station. I was his son, who was about to arrive home from college. Bert had bragged to the other porters that I was a big, strong, husky football hero, and they were all on hand to get a look at me. When I stepped off the train, a slim, 116 pounds in a tight pinch-back suit and with almost effeminate manners, my first words were "Look, Dad, I carry matches." All the porters laughed. Bert was humiliated. "Son," he said, "pick up those grips." I pouted, "Dad! Remember, I have a temper." "And I'm gonna show where you got it from," Bert would retort. The scene ran ten minutes. Bert would get more embarrassed every minute. His blackout line was, "Pick up those grips. Today is my graduation and your commencement."[12]

The *Times* complained that the comic sketch was not developed as it should have been and singled out the Eddie Cantor character as a prime reason:

Here surely was an opportunity for a scene of real humor between the illiterate father, dubious to the value of a college education, and [the] representative of the haughtily superior second generation. But the authors missed their chance completely, and made the character of the son an unwholesome and objectionable type too frequently portrayed on the local stage.[13]

Another newspaper, the *New York Herald*, saw nothing apparently wrong with the Williams-Cantor skit:

Bert Williams is now a porter in the Grand Central Terminal who takes the place of the information man, and has a lot of trouble with the time tables and stations with strange names. He also has a son just home from college who has taken a degree in dancing and tries it on father. The son is Eddie Cantor, who sings and talks in an intimate way about everybody, like Frank Tinney, only faster. He, too, made a hit.[14]

Bert Williams, however, knew that the act needed polishing. He took it on himself to counsel Eddie Cantor. Cantor recalled:

> Williams went out of his way not to embarrass a fellow performer. If a mistake was made on stage, even a glaring one, he'd say nothing till the show was over. Then, in the privacy of a dressing room, he'd "discuss" it. . . . We broke in the sketch at the Apollo Theater in Atlantic City. I "camped" all over the stage. Back in the dressing room, Bert, in his quiet, almost professorial manner, said: "Look, son, don't push too hard. You can afford to underplay this character because the situation almost carries the scene."[15]

Although Williams's scene with Cantor was his most memorable in 1917, it was not the only scene he played in. Williams was constantly trying out new comedy ideas that allowed him to expand beyond his regular blackface acting. In the "Subway Episode," Williams played a bear. *The New York Herald* reported:

> In the subway episode, Fred Heider, in the costume of an Alpine guide, led a party of sightseeing girls across the Interborough Mountains. This appealed to everyone who has to walk around town. Bert Williams took part in this scene as a performing bear, who danced and talked and frightened a crowd of workmen in the tunnels.[16]

As usual, Bert Williams had a spot in the *Follies* program in which he sang. He was not using his own music as much as before. A song he sang in the 1917 *Follies*, "entitled 'Home Sweet Home,' in which he explained that the 'little trouble abroad' was not nearly so 'slaughterous' as the battle in his own home, was by Ring W. Lardner."[17]

Lardner, who had been trying to get Bert Williams to introduce one of his songs in the *Follies* since 1911, was elated. After seeing Williams perform his song, Lardner wrote about the performance in a letter to his mother, Lena Lardner. The letter is important since it reveals that Williams's health was declining:

> I enclose a sheet from the Follies program. Contrary to my previous information, the song Bert Williams is singing is one to which I wrote both words and music. He has been sick and didn't do very well with it the night we heard him. It was the only song he sang. He expects to put it on a record this fall.[18]

Although Ring Lardner was to go on to have other songs interpolated into later *Ziegfeld Follies*, he was disappointed with "Home Sweet Home." A Lardner biographer said of the song:

It may be the song of which he much later wrote: "Bert sang a song of mine once and I had it published; it was put on phonograph records, too, and I think the total royalties from sheet music and records amounted to $46.50." Whatever the case, neither the published nor the recorded version has been located.[19]

Although "Home Sweet Home" was not listed in the *Follies* program, a song with a similar title, "No Place Like Home," was recorded in September 1917. This may well have been the Lardner song. The songs listed in the program were: "I Ain't Married No More," music by Les Copland and lyrics by Rennold Wolf, and "Unhappy," music by Henry S. Creamer and lyrics by J. Turner Layton.[20]

Leslie C. Copland (1887–1942) was a Tin Pan Alley writer who wrote popular as well as ragtime songs.[21] Copland's lyricist was the journalist Rennold Wolf, who had interviewed Williams in 1912 for *Green Book* magazine. "Unhappy" was penned by black songwriters John Turner Layton (1894–1978) and Henry Creamer (1879–1930), who are famous for the tune, "After You're Gone," which Sophie Tucker made into a standard.[22]

The critics of the 1917 *Follies* were dazzled by the array of talent the show offered. Fanny Brice made a big hit in the production. One critic noted: "Miss Fannie Brice received a lot of applause when she came out to sing the 'Ziegfeld Follies Rag.' . . . 'The Episode of the Mississippi Levee' gave Mr. Cantor and Miss Brice the centre of the stage as singers and dancers."[23]

The 1917 *Follies* exploited that year's theme of patriotism by featuring a musical finale in the first part of the show that concluded with the playing of the "Star Spangled Banner," and with the unfolding – over the heads of the standing audience – of a huge American flag that canopied the auditorium. [24] The folk philosopher Will Rogers (1879–1935) told jokes that poked fun at a current American preoccupation: the war. One review reported a few of Rogers's jokes:

> "I see that one man claims exemption from military service on the ground that he had a Ford dependent on him," he explained. "I saw a darkey, who said the Kaiser hadn't done anything to him," he continued, "and if he had, he forgave him."[25]

Not all of the criticism of Eddie Cantor's performance was harsh. The *New York Tribune* saw genuine talent in Cantor, observing: "Cantor is a blackface comedian who knows what to do with a song. He runs considerably ahead of the dependable Bert Williams in the new show."[26]

Critics thought that Williams did well in that year's production. "Bert Williams shuffled his feet, rolled his eyes, and got more out of his lines than was in them," said the *New York Times*, and the *New York Tribune* thought

Williams was "funnier than he has been in the several preceding Follies."[27]

In general the critics saw the 1917 *Follies* as being original in stage design but unoriginal in production ideas. The *New York World* credited theater designer Joseph Urban with "much of the spectacular beauty" of the show. The *New York Times* called the 1917 *Follies* "an urban orgy of color."[28] The *New York Tribune* panned the show's unoriginal production sketches.

> The various scenes ... reveal well-worn musical comedy stamping grounds – a Mississippi levee, a roof garden, Grand Central Terminal, the new subway hazards. But it may be that one should lay these delinquincies at the feet of Mr. Hobart rather than Mr. Ziegfeld.[29]

In his 1916 interview with *The Soil* magazine, Bert Williams had complained that the *Ziegfeld Follies* did not allow performers enough time to do a competent job. In 1917 it seemed that nothing had changed. The *New York American* commented on the pacing of the show: "The idea of the thing was rush-rapid transit entertainment that gave you no time to think. Just as you were about to criticize one feature, another happened, and it went that way all through the evening.[30]

After taking stock of the attractions of the show – Bert Williams, the Joseph Urban sets, and the Ziegfeld Girls – the *New York Herald* summarized the *Follies*, calling it "a rainbow of fun, color, and feminine beauty."[31]

Bert Williams continued to record and do film work during 1917. In February *Variety* reported that Williams was "writing scenarios for one-reel comedies in which he may be featured during the coming summer. The pictures are to be made by Selig."[32] This was William Selig, the minstrel-show man who had given Bert Williams his first break in California during the 1890s. Selig was one of the earliest independent film producers, founding the Selig Palyscope Company, which in 1907–8 filmed *The Count of Monte Cristo* near Los Angeles. In 1909 Selig built a studio in the Los Angeles suburb of Edendale.[33]

In August 1917 *Variety* hinted that the Selig films were about to be made. Although *Variety* did not name Selig's company, it is possible that this was the film company Williams was doing business with. It claimed that Williams was to be involved both in front of and behind the camera. "Arrangements [are] underway to have the colored comedian appear in a series of Bert Williams pictures that an independent company is planning to manufacture. Bert ... is willing to take up the camera work."[34]

It is not known whether the Selig pictures with Bert Williams were ever made or released. In September Williams recorded two songs for Columbia Records: "No Place Like Home" and "Twenty Years."[35]

After the traditional New York summer opening, the *Ziegfeld Follies* went on a national tour. It may have been in reference to the 1917 edition of the show that Eddie Cantor wrote about Bert Williams's frustration with segregation. In his autobiography Cantor described one instance:

> One New Year's Eve, after the show, most of the cast headed for parties. Bert and I had arranged to see the New Year in together at the hotel where he was permitted to live, provided he used the back elevator. I was to pick up a turkey we had ordered from a nearby restaurant. As we started out the stage door, I said, "See you at the hotel, okay?"
>
> "Okay," Bert replied, "I'm on my way to the back elevator." This was the first hint of bitterness I'd ever heard from my turn-thine-other-cheek friend. Painfully aware that no words could help his hurt, I said nothing. We stood for a moment in understanding silence. Then Bert added, "It wouldn't be so bad, Eddie, if I didn't still hear the applause ringing in my ears."[36]

In January 1918 an important autobiographical essay, called the "Comic Side of Trouble," appeared in *American Magazine*. Among the many topics Bert Williams discussed was his way of coping with problems like segregation. Williams parlayed his own sorrows into his art and tried to find humor in embarrassing situations. He wrote:

> The sight of other people in trouble is nearly always funny. This is human nature. . . . The man with the real sense of humor is the man who can put himself in the spectator's place and laugh at his own misfortunes. That is what I am called upon to do every day. Nearly all of my successful songs have been based on the idea that I am getting the worst of it. I am the "Jonah Man," the man who, even if it rained soup, would be found with a fork in his hand and no spoon in sight; the man whose fighting relatives come to visit him and whose head is always dented by the furniture they throw at each other.[37]

Williams believed that one of the challenges of a good comic was the ability to make the audience identify with him or her:

> Troubles are funny only when you pin them to one particular individual. And that individual, the fellow who is the goat, must be the man who is singing the song or telling the story. Then the audience can picture him in their mind's eye.[38]

Bert Williams had begun to be more vocal about the evils of racism, and in May 1918 he spoke out in an interview with the *New York Age*. He told Lester A. Walton of his tribulations while traveling as the lone black in the *Ziegfeld Follies* company and how many injustices he had had to endure. Williams denounced the contradictory and humiliating conditions of segregated public accomodations. He asked:

> Why is it a colored passenger can sleep over or under a white passenger on a Pullman and no color question is raised, but just as soon as a citizen of color

applies at a hotel for a room where he would be separated by walls and doors, objection is made to his presence?[39]

Williams's feelings of resentment and estrangement from society now extended to the *Ziegfeld Follies*. The new edition of the *Follies* opened on June 18, 1918. It featured many performers from earlier editions – Eddie Cantor, W. C. Fields, Will Rogers, Lillian Lorraine – but not Bert Williams. Though the book and lyrics for the show were by Rennold Wolf and Gene Buck, they had failed to come up with comedy skits for Williams to perform in. The *New York Age* later explained that Williams quit the show "because of lack of material." Ziegfeld and Williams both denied that there had been any argument between them.[40]

In a move calculated to give himself a sense of pride and identity, he became a naturalized citizen on June 14, 1918. The *New York Age* reported:

> Naturalization papers were issued to Bert A. Williams, the comedian, in the United States District Court Friday of last week. Although one of the country's most prominent and best-known Negroes, it was not until last week that he became a full-fledged American citizen. . . . Four years ago, while playing with the Follies in Boston . . . Mr. Williams applied for his first papers.[41]

The *Age* noted that Williams had formerly been a citizen of the Bahamas, a British colony. Although he did not perform in the *Follies* in 1918, Williams occupied himself by appearing in the *Ziegfeld Midnite Frolic*, which took place on the roof garden of the New Amsterdam Theater in New York. Ziegfeld used the *Frolic* as a training ground for chorus girls and comedians who aspired to get into the *Follies*. Eddie Cantor, a "graduate" of the *Frolic*, described it once: "The Amsterdam Roof was a unique pleasure center, neither theater nor cabaret, but a blend of both. It was a supper club where it cost a person five dollars just to sit down."[42]

According to Cantor, "When you graduated from the *Frolic*, you went down, not up – downstairs into the New Amsterdam Theater to appear in the Follies."[43] Given Cantor's description, it sounds as though this was a comedown for Bert Williams. But it was perhaps a good place for him, since he did not have to compete with performers like W. C. Fields, Will Rogers, and Eddie Cantor. In its review of Williams's act in the 1918 *Frolic*, the *New York Age* said little except that he won the hearts of the audience. Williams was also cheered by congratulatory telegrams from such *Follies* performers as Fields, Frank Carter, Rogers, and Cantor. The *New York Evening Journal* told of Williams's phenomenal reception by the *Frolic* audience at one o'clock in the morning:

> When Bert Williams, one of America's foremost comedians, made his initial bow before the audience of the Ziegfeld Midnite Frolic – on the New Amsterdam Theatre Roof last night, he received, as was expected, a hearty reception – almost an ovation.[44]

Exactly what Williams's act consisted of is not known, but it may have included comic monologues in which he sang his signature song, "Nobody," similar to his vaudeville acts. The *New York Evening Journal* was ecstatic over Williams's performance. Said its critic:

> Never was this dusky comedian revealed to better advantage than last night, when in spendid fashion, he unfolded his quaint monologue in his dry, droll fashion, and gave us some songs which made an instantaneous hit with the capacity audience, earning him a storm of applause, which sounded like a barrage and drumfire in one.[45]

The *New York Age* said the applause lasted almost five minutes.

About a week later, Bert Williams performed in a benefit for the Colored Men's Branch of the YMCA in New York City. Also appearing were Irving Berlin, Miller and Lyles, J. Rosamond Johnson, and the Clef Club. The benefit took place at the vaudeville theater – the Alhambra – at Seventh Avenue and 126th Street. Lester Walton covered the benefit and wrote of Bert Williams's performance.

> Mr. Williams told two funny jokes, sang a tuneful war number and, as an encore, rendered his old hit, "In The Evenings," doing the poker game in pantomime. As he concluded his performance amid salvos of applause, he was presented with a large bunch of flowers, the gift of the "Association," which is composed of young men residing in Harlem. Ford Dabney accompanied Mr. Williams on the piano.[46]

Ford Dabney (1883–1958), a black songwriter, had cowritten "The Pensacola Mooch" with Will Marion Cook for the 1910 *Ziegfeld Follies*.[47] Walton noted that even though Bert Williams had not performed for black audiences for almost a decade, he was still popular with his own people. "Even the cork did not hide the genuine smile of satisfaction that flitted across his countenance," when he walked offstage after receiving the flowers, said Walton.

On August 26, 1918, Bert Williams recorded a song with a Faustian theme: "Oh Death, Where Is Thy Sting?" The song, written by Clarence A. Stout, has been reissued on the Folkways label under the title, "Nobody and Other Songs by Bert Williams." Williams sings in his parlando-rubato style about a "Parson Brown," tempted by the devil, who tells of booze, women, and fun in hell. On August 26, 1918, Williams recorded two more songs – "When I Return" and "You'll Find Old Dixieland in France." The writers of the former song, released by Columbia, are also unknown. Its title suggests that it may have dealt with American soldiers fighting in World War I. The latter was composed by George W. Meyer with lyrics by Grant Clarke. Clarke (1884–1931) was a Tin Pan Alley tunesmith who was famous for Bert Williams's 1911 hit, "Dat's Harmony." George W. Meyer (1884–1959) is known for popular songs like the 1917 tune, "For Me and My Gal" and

"I'm a Little Blackbird," which Florence Mills made into a standard.[48] "You'll Find Old Dixieland in France" was never released by Columbia, although the music was published by Leo Feist in 1918. The sheet music carried the caption, "Introduced by Bert Williams in Ziegfeld Midnite Frolic," over a photo of rural black sharecroppers superimposed over a larger photo of the Eiffel Tower. The lyrics tell of how black southern boys have gone to fight the Germans in France. This song was clearly in the vein of patriotic songs of the day, including "Over There," "We're All Going Calling on the Kaiser," and "Oh, How I Hate to Get Up in the Morning," the Irving Berlin song introduced in the 1918 Broadway musical *Yip Yip Yaphank*.

In December 1918 Williams left the *Ziegfeld Midnite Frolic* temporarily to appear in vaudeville at the Palace in New York. *Variety* said: "The house was jammed and the reception he received was tremendous." Williams began with a comedy song called "Judge Grimes." *Variety* reported:

> Williams had the audience laughing so heartily, he was compelled to stop in the midst of the lyric. It was followed with a couple of short stories, and then another number, something about "You Can't Shake That Shimmy Here," and his burlesque of the dance was a scream from start to finish. "The Panic's On," a typical Williams song, was next, and finally another song about "Evenin'." The latter led up to the "poker game," and the moment Williams started it, there was a thunder of applause and laughter.[49]

The critic noted that when Williams concluded his act, the applause was so extended that he had to stop and make a little speech thanking the audience.[50] The *New York Age* reported that Williams literally stopped the show. "Only the turning out of the theatre's lights convinced those present ... that another act should follow Mr. Williams' offering and that his songs and stories had ended for the time being."[51]

Williams returned to the *Ziegfeld Midnite Frolic* a week later. *Variety* explained:

> The Midnite Frolic was several shows in one, the "Nine O'Clock Frolic" and the "Midnite Frolic." Joining Williams this time were Fannie Brice, who was "a laughing not twice," George Price, who did blackface impersonations of Eddie Cantor and Al Jolson, and Will Rogers dressed up in a cowboy outfit.[52]

Bert Williams and another performer – Hal Hixon – "did a bit of imaginary musical instruments [pantomime], but the moment was too sad," said *Variety*. *Life* magazine said that there was "too little of Bert Williams, who, given a chance, is an irresistable Negro entertainer."[53]

Williams's reaction to this must have been similar to comments he made a few years earlier: "I often think of the old court jesters, how they used to make the guests weep before they made them laugh, but *I have to do the thing of the moment because time is too short*."[54]

Chapter 23

On February 13, 1919, Bert Williams returned to Columbia's studios to record two songs: "Oh, Lawdie" and "Bring Back Those Wonderful Days." (The latter was recently reissued on a Folkways album of Williams's songs.) Although both songs could conceivably be by Bert Williams, it has not been determined who the songwriters actually were.[1]

A few weeks later Williams's wife, Lottie, made society-page headlines nationwide by hosting a party. The *Chicago Defender* ran an item describing the large and lavish affair:

> Mrs. Bert Williams, 2309 Seventh Avenue, New York City, and niece, Miss Lottie Tyler, received in honor of Mrs. Theo Furnell of Berkeley, California, last Tuesday evening. One hundred and fifty beautifully gowned ladies . . . were present to honor Mrs. Furnell, . . . a former resident of Chicago. The palatial home of the hostess was decorated in scarlet and spring flowers, and the stairway was banked with palms and ferns. The artistic decorations overhanging the walks and stairway added much comfort to the guests. . . . An elaborate collation was served by Jarvis, the caterer. The ladies all wore corsages of orchids, sweet peas, and lilies of the valley. Among the handsomely gowned and jeweled were Mrs. Bert Williams, attired in black lace and diamonds; Mrs. Furnell wore a richly embroidered black satin gown and jewels; Mrs. Henderson, grey crepe and duchess lace, and Miss Tyler wore a heavily beaded white crepe gown.[2]

Among the people who read the *Chicago Defender*'s account of Lottie Williams's party was a young blues singer, Alberta Hunter (1895–1987). After recording with Black Swan in New York, Alberta Hunter went to Chicago and picked up her recording career along with singing in nightclubs and touring the vaudeville circuit. About 1927 she went to Europe, where she sang in musicals, including the London production of *Showboat* with Paul Robeson, and in nightclubs all over the Continent. After World War II she returned to the United States and settled in New York. During 1957–77 she worked as a nurse, but she returned at the age of eighty-two to sing in clubs, on television, and at jazz festivals. She is credited with acquainting Europe with the blues of black female singers.[3]

According to Hunter's biographer, she had met Lottie Tyler (Bert

Williams's niece Charlotte), in a Chicago nightclub and was very impressed. Tyler invited Hunter to visit her in New York, and on reading the *Defender*'s account of Mrs. Williams's social affair, Hunter decided it was time to accept the invitation.[4] It seems that Albert Hunter looked forward not only to seeing Lottie Tyler again but also to meeting Bert Williams, who she hoped would give her a hand professionally.

Albert found Lottie at her aunt's house. She went up to the door and knocked.

> "I didn't know you had to meet people formally," Alberta said. "I didn't know you had to at least walk in and say, 'Good morning,' graciously. You don't go knocking on the door and say [as she did to Lottie's uncle], 'Lottie here?' That's how I met Bert Williams, out of the clear blue sky, for no rhyme or reason," Alberta said. "He didn't pay any attention to me. I wasn't even alive. He was a West Indian. They're full of baloney, a lot of them. Thought they were better than God made little apples. Forgive me for saying it, because so many of my friends are West Indians and I love 'em so. But they've always been big shots."[5]
>
> [Alberta Hunter's reaction to Williams was not so much anger as much as the hurt of a fan snubbed by her hero.] "I admired him and was proud of him," she said. "Because at the time, colored people weren't getting the breaks that I thought they deserved. I was happy to see somebody get them, especially those who were ladies and gentlemen."[6]

In March 1919 Bert Williams began the first of a hectic schedule of vaudeville appearances, opening at the Colonial Theatre on the seventeenth. *Variety* said:

> Bert Williams, headlining the bill, held his own easily. He sw[u]ng each number into applause, but perhaps the best liked of the newer selections was "Everybody Wants a Key to My Cellar," having a musical production swing and lyrics good for a laugh. They fit in his droll style.[7]

During the week of March 24, 1919, for some reason, Williams did not headline the show. *Variety* reported:

> Williams earned a hit. He had one or two new stories; that one about his friend who became a lion tamer and started out by tying all the lions to a tree while he washed out their cages, getting the biggest laugh. Williams' song routine is but slightly changed, a new number being "Everybody Wants a Key to My Cellar." He encored with "Nobody," stating [that] it was by request.[8]

The success of "Everybody Wants a Key to My Cellar" caused Williams to record it for Columbia on April 4, 1919.[9]

Williams followed a vaudeville appearance at New York's Riverside Theater in March with an appearance at the Royal Theater on the East Side in April. *Variety* said little about his act except that "he was treated with an ovation on his appearance [and] he went over with a bang."[10] About a week later he recorded the tune "It's Nobody's Business But My Own."

In the song (not to be confused with Billie Holiday's later "'Tain't Nobody's Business If I Do," written by Porter Grainger and Everett Robbins[11]), written by Will E. Skidmore and Marshall Walker, Williams lampoons the stereotype of the black preacher as a womanizer. (The lyrics have the preacher defending his behavior.)

In late April the *Age* reported that Williams was playing at the Orpheum in Manhattan and at the Bushwick in Brooklyn. The two months of nonstop performing and recording took a toll on him. He had to go to a sanatorium to regain his health. It was late May when the *Age* noted that "Bert Williams is back in New York after little more than a week's stay at West Baden, Indiana."[12] (West Baden was a favorite health resort because of its mineral springs.) Williams could probably have used more rest, but he may have been anxious to get back to New York to begin rehearsals for the *Follies*.

In 1919 the *Ziegfeld Follies* were entering their thirteenth year and quickly becoming "an American institution." This latest *Follies*, the critics felt, demonstrated that Ziegfeld was again fortunate in having a hit show.

Part of the key to Ziegfeld's 1919 success was his recruitment of Irving Berlin to compose the music for the *Follies*. Now remembered for such songs as "Alexander's Ragtime Band" and "White Christmas," and for shows like *Annie Get Your Gun*, Berlin was already a legend in 1919.

Ziegfeld's second wife, actress Billie Burke, related an anecdote that described how Berlin composed the most famous song of the 1919 *Follies*:

> Irving had completed his score and, like everyone else who worked for Ziegfeld, was in the state of total collapse, determined to retire to a cave in the hills. But Flo insisted, as he always insisted, on a little more. "Just one more song, Irving," he wheedled. "A little song." "No more," said Irving, "I'm written out." "Oh," [said Ziegfeld], "I just want a small one, just a snatch to bring the girls on. . . ." Badgered and weary, Irving retired to his room and wrote a little song to bring the girls on and it was, of course, that great tune, "A Pretty Girl Is Like a Melody."[13]
>
> The cast of the 1919 Follies was a diverse one. It consisted of Eddie Cantor, the brother and sister comic act of Ray and Johnny Dooley, actor George LeMaire, who later worked in Hollywood, and the popular showgirl Marilyn Miller. Others included singer John Steele, who introduced the above-mentioned Berlin song, vaudeville comedians Gus Van and Joe Schenck, and ballroom dancers Maurice Mouvet and Florence Walton. Although Bert Williams was probably the best known of all the performers in the case, the show's writers gave him little to do.

In Act 1, Scene 7, Williams had a role in a sketch called "The Popular Pests," written by Gene Buck and Dave Stamper. The *New York Herald* wrote:

Manhattan Island's "popular pests" introduced more comedians, Bert Williams being the Janitor, Eddie Dowling the Waiter, Joe Schenck the Bell Boy, Johnny Dooley the Hat Check Boy, Eddie Cantor the Taxi Driver, and Miss Fay [sic] Dooley the Servant Girl who demanded four days "out" every week.[14]

In the only known photograph of this scene, the cast poses with Bert Williams, in the center, wearing a dejected look.[15]

In Scene 9 of the same act, Williams was a human target for a sharpshooter in the scene called "He Seldom Misses." George Lemaire played Sure-Shot Dick, and Williams portrayed Jasper Slocum. The *New York Herald* said "Lemaire in the role of the cowboy marksman [made] life miserable for his unwilling William Tell, alias Williams." The *New York Tribune* thought "Bert Williams was exceedingly funny," while another review said the sketch gave Williams "only a fair opportunity."[16] *Variety* was critical of the sketch, calling it "an elderly bit of burlesque business that has been played to death for years, but given new life through the treatment of Messr. Williams and Lemaire. It made for some laughs, but is far from funny."[17] Williams was also in the final scene of the first "act," which was a minstrel show. One review gossiped that Ziegfeld had spent about thirty-five thousand dollars on this scene alone. The *Post* added: "And a novel minstrel show it was."[18]

The "Follies Minstrels," as the act was called, had the customary end men and interlocutor. Eddie Cantor was Mr. Tambo, Bert Williams played Mr. Bones, and George Lemaire served as Interlocutor. Bert Williams and George Lemaire sang a duet called "I Want to See a Minstrel Show."[19]

In the third episode of Act 2, Williams sang, "It's Nobody's Business But My Own," which he had just recorded.

A trenchant description of Williams's singing style was supplied by Eddie Cantor. Cantor recalled that Williams "had a unique way of rendering songs, injecting his talk between rests and catching up with the melodic phrase after he had let it get a head start."[20] It was his special style of singing that made Williams a popular recording artist. But his success as a singer also depended on getting good music.

In the 1919 *Follies* Bert Williams's songs were not well received. According to the *New York Times*: "Bert Williams was not very liberally supplied with humorous lines, or with humorous songs, but he scored unfailingly thanks to his massive comedy method and his humorous personality."[21]

Variety said: "Mr. Williams sang two, getting little with either."[22] The *New York Tribune* was more perceptive in appraising Williams. The review stated: "None of his songs in the first two-thirds of the performance was in the least effective. It is a long time since we have seen Williams in a good song, but the fault lies entirely with his material."[23]

Williams was painfully aware that his recent stage performances had been mediocre. In an interview with *Theatre Magazine*, June 1919, Williams lashed out bitterly at the theater audience, which he blamed for his troubles. He began to doubt his ability as a comedian.

> There is a period . . . that is the despair of any comedian. It is the age just beyond the years of indiscretion, on the edge of innocuous desuetude. It is the man who is a regular theatre-goer for many years, and who saw you once when you were so funny that he has never forgotten it. . . . Long experience with audiences has taught the hardened comedian to look for happy faces, for smiles that broaden and when he finds these warm spots he feels, rather than sees the icy places, the smiles that seem to crack through a film of ice. They throw out a chill that makes him wish he was a tragedian. They are at every performance, in every theatre, the students of the drama.[24]

Williams complained that there was a certain type of New Yorker, a "morb" who sat through performances with a stone face. He added: "Honestly, it makes your heart ache to look at their faces. They seem to be spending their money like dead men, as though they didn't care what happened."[25]

Later in Act 2, there was one skit that had special meaning for Ziegfeld. The Volstead Act, soon to go into effect, would usher in the Prohibition era in the United States. "The law meant certain death, as Ziegfeld knew at once, to the *Midnight Frolic*, and its world of boozy excitement."[26]

The Prohibition sketch featured a bar scene, with songs by Irving Berlin, about alcohol. The songs were "Syncopated Cocktail," sung by Marilyn Miller, and "You Cannot Make Your Shimmy Shake Shake on Tea," performed by Bert Williams. The Shimmy, a dance that required dancers to shake their shoulders, was then in vogue. The song, lamenting the coming of Prohibition and the drinking of tea,[27] prompted *Variety* to note:

> In a general comedy way, Williams did better than he had done with the "Follies" for a long time. He had the punch Prohibition number in a scene of that description. It was "You Cannot Make Your Shimmy Shake on Tea," by Irving Berlin. The number did fairly. It came late. There [were] three hours of show [preceding it].[28]

Williams was to create for himself a subspecialty of drinking songs with this number and "I Makes Mine Myself," which he sang later in the show *Broadway Brevities of 1920*. Williams's new musical repertoire caused at least one historian to accuse him of suggesting blacks were prone to alcoholism.[29]

But for Bert Williams these kinds of songs fit right into his act. Williams's type of comedy "depended mainly upon either word play or lampooning usually solemn institutions such as churches, marriages or funerals."[30] Williams made a distinction between which current topics or events could be satirized and which could not. He said: "There are, of course, many humorous things which cannot be used because of their sensitive relation to national issues. Much depends upon the delivery of a song, which means the natural humor which the comedian creates."[31]

Another issue that was too sensitive for Bert Williams to satirize was the labor status of the actor in 1919. For a number of years actors had seen the entertainment world transformed by the big business practices of first the Syndicate and later the Shubert brothers. One scholar summed up the situation:

> As theatrical control passed from the hands of the independent manager into the hands of the businessmen, the actor came to realize more fully that he was facing a highly modern business organization intent primarily on protecting neither art nor the artist but its own interest. Not only did the actor begin to have convictions that too many theatres had been built . . . but he also began to feel the pressure of too many inadequate conditions.[32]

In reaction to these conditions, the Actors Equity Association (AEA) was founded on May 16, 1913. The objective of the AEA was to be "a live organization of actors to insist primarily upon a standard, uniform, and equitable contract." During the three years following the formation of the AEA, theatrical managers refused to meet with it to discuss a contract equitable to actor and manager alike. Despite this lack of a contract, AEA "rectified abuses, arbitrated cases, and recovered money" for its members.[33]

In August 1917 the United Managers' Protective Association (UMPA), which represented the managers, and AEA agreed on the details of a standard contract, "including payment by the manager of costumes of actresses receiving less than $150 per week, a definite limitation on free rehearsals, a basic working week," and other items.[34] Formally approved by the UMPA in October 1917 this contract agreement was extended by AEA in 1918. It instructed its members that "no member of the AEA should sign any other than an Equity contract. . . . Such a pledge meant that, once the actors signed, the managers who wanted Equity actors would have to abide by the Equity contracts."[35]

The UMPA was not too worried; it knew the Equity agreement would expire in 1919 and selected this time to begin a new attack on Equity. In the spring of 1919, UMPA dissolved itself, and many of its old members joined a new group called the Producing Manager's Association (PMA). The theater managers feared an Equity strike. Their proposal was therefore aimed at breaking such a strike, "nationwide in scope so that actors striking against the legitimate managers in New York could not hop to vaudeville in Chicago, burlesque in St. Louis or motion pictures in Los Angeles."[36] With all doors of employment closed, the actors would gladly accept anything offered to them, the managers believed.

To the actors this action by the PMA was adding insult to injury. It was not only a standard contract that was at stake, it was also the actor's right to union representation to resolve grievances. Among these were lack of transportation for performers to and from shows, managers' disregard of the two-week notice of termination, failure of managers to compensate actors for extra performances, and unrestricted free rehearsal time.[37]

Actress Ethel Barrymore wrote:

> There was no limit to the period of free rehearsals and no guarantee for any definite period of work – this, of course, is not referring to sporadic individual cases, but to the vast majority [of managers]. Companies would rehearse eight or nine, or even more, weeks and close up with less than one week's salary.[38]

PMA argued that AEA did not represent the actors. Barrymore retorted, "We have between five thousand and six thousand members, numbering ninety percent of all the most prominent professionals."[39]

Efforts to negotiate an agreement between AEA and PMA became hopelessly deadlocked, and AEA finally voted to strike on August 7, 1919. Although Ziegfeld was a former member of UMPA, he had not publicly come out as a member of PMA. However, in writing, Ziegfeld had always let the public know whose side he was on. Ziegfeld thought the theatrical manager was misunderstood and underappreciated by others. He claimed that he treated his actors well and scoffed at those who insisted that the managers were making money at the expense of the performers and stage personnel. Ziegfeld said: "The man who believes that after we have paid the performers and the 'few' theater employees, we have the remainder as 'velvet' should get his thinking apparatus straightened out. He is all wrong."[40]

Ziegfeld had big plans for the 1919 *Follies*. He was planning to increase floor seat prices, because of the huge business, to $3.50 a seat. This would mean a possible thousand dollar increase in gross earnings for the show. Moreover, the *Follies* was booked to go on tour nationally beginning September 14.[41]

Since the *Ziegfeld Follies* were considered musical comedy, the success of Ziegfeld's plans depended on the exemption of the musical comedy units of Equity from the strike. Nevertheless, in a surprise move, these sections of AEA voted to walk out with their comrades.[42] They joined the crowds of striking actors and disappointed theatergoers, who roamed the Broadway theater area on the night of August 7:

> Another crowd collected on Forty-First Street, behind the New Amsterdam Theatre, where the "Ziegfeld Follies" was at work. There, John Charles Thomas and Cyril Chadwick had persuaded Eddie Cantor, Eddie Dowling, and Phil Dwyer to walk out, and the chorus had congregated on the fire escape to watch the street show.[43]

Ziegfeld talked Ray and Johnny Dooley out of striking, explaining that he was not a PMA member. He then went looking for Eddie Cantor. Cantor recalled: "I went to see the [George White's] *Scandals* that evening, but Ziegfeld located me there and called me back an hour later with the assurance that he hadn't joined [PMA]. I promptly returned to the show."[44]

On Friday, August 8, *Variety* said that the main gossip on Broadway was whether Ziegfeld was a PMA member or not. Although several *Follies* members had walked out on Thursday, AEA issued no walkout orders for its members in the show nor did it picket the New Amsterdam Theater. Thus it must have come as a surprise to Ziegfeld when he learned that Cantor was telling AEA people that the *Ziegfeld Follies* would close that night. Ostensibly "Johnny and Ray Dooley and Eddie Dowling and possibly Bert Williams would walk out." Yet, that evening, all the alleged strikers, including Cantor and Bert Williams, were on stage. On Saturday, August 9, it was rumored that Ziegfeld was a PMA member after all. The continued performance of the *Follies* was being touted "as something of a managerial triumph."[45] This was true to a certain extent.

The 1919 *Ziegfeld Follies* grossed $29,000 during its first week and $28,730 the second. It continued to play to packed houses early during the Equity strike, and it was on its way to becoming the season's most successful musical show.[46]

Because of the rumors circulated over the weekend, Equity decided to issue Ziegfeld an ultimatum on Monday, August 11. Ziegfeld was told that Equity was giving him until five-thirty that afternoon to provide "definite and official assurance that he was not a member of the Producing Managers' Association."[47] Ziegfeld was in a dilemma. On the one hand, as a theatrical producer, his real interest lay on the side of the managers. On the other hand:

> Ziegfeld was not in the mood to allow his show to be closed by Equity, and yet he knew that in the face of orders from Equity, he could not hope to keep his cast in line. The events of the first night of the strike had clearly demonstrated that only too clearly. In this crisis, therefore, he turned to the courts to compel his company to continue to work for him whether or not it wished to.[48]

That day Ziegfeld went to New York Supreme Court and got a temporary injunction order restraining Equity from persuading his cast to leave the show and cast members from leaving of their own will. The *Follies* members named in the injunction were Eddie Cantor, Johnny Dooley, Ray Dooley, Gus Van, Joseph Schenck, John Steele, and Eddie Dowling.[49] It is not clear why the other major *Follies* stars, such as Bert Williams and Marilyn Miller, were not cited in the court order. It should be noted that the principals named were actors who had either already walked out once or were suspected of being Equity sympathizers. The defendants were the officers of Equity.

After the restraining order had been issued, Ziegfeld sent a copy of it along with a declaration of his strike status to Equity headquarters. The declaration read: "I feel honored to be able to announce that I have today become a member of the Producing Managers' Association." Court arguments for and against the injunction were to be heard on Wednesday, August 13. When the Ziegfeld injunction was heard in court that day, Equity obtained a modification of the order to the extent that the members of the company were no longer bound to continue to play against their will, as they had been by the preliminary order. In his ruling the judge declared that "he had never intended to restrain the actors from quitting their employers, but only to restrain any persons from influencing [them] to do so."[50] Ziegfeld and the managers believed they had struck a blow at Equity, even though the court had ruled that the actors were "free agents." A final hearing on the injunction case itself was scheduled for Friday, August 15. Ziegfeld believed he could count on his company performing until then.

The events of the last several days had given him cause to believe this. The Equity pickets had refrained from picketing the New Amsterdam Theater on Forty-second Street.[51] A sign at Equity headquarters read: "All members of the *Ziegfeld Follies* cast are members of Actors' Equity and are loyal." Despite this, the union officials told *Follies* members to continue performing because of the injunction.[52]

On the evening of the thirteenth, the *Follies* members took matters into their own hands. Eddie Cantor was the first to strike. He recalled:

> That night, I took my stand on Forty-First Street opposite the stage door of the New Amsterdam Theater, and as the actors of the *Follies* arrived I whistled to them. The first to appear were Van and Schneck. They heard the siren call and turned their heads.
> "What's up, Eddie?"
> "Strike."
> Without a word, they crossed over to my side of the street and struck. As the next actors arrived, all three of us whistled. They halted at the signal and turned. They were Johnny and Ray Dooley.
> "What's the matter?"
> "Strike."
> In a short while, the whole cast was lined up on our side of the block and we marched to the headquarters of Actors' Equity.[53]

Joining the strike line as well were Phil Dwyer, the animal impersonator, and numerous Ziegfeld Girls. "About twenty of the *Follies'* chorus girls joined the group of stars and waded through the rain to Strike Headquarters to report the closing of the New Amsterdam. They were received with a hilarious joy."[54]

According to the *New York Times*, "An audience of nearly 2,000 persons was turned out of the theater at 8:45 o'clock." When the New Amsterdam Theater manager, Malcolm Douglas, realized that the six stars were not going to appear, he had to go before the curtain to announce the show's closing to the packed house. The audience's "sympathetic cheers, jeers and laughter . . . resulted in a double line of patrons several hundred feet long before the box office windows to receive their refunds."[55] The New Amsterdam had to refund $2,740.

Contrary to Cantor's report, several of the *Follies* stars did not strike. Bert Williams was among them. He came to the theater later than the other players because his first stage appearance was not until late in the first act. In an anecdote told to W. C. Fields, Williams related how the historic moment had bypassed him.

> I went to the theater as usual, made up and dressed. Then I came out of my dressing room and found the big auditorium empty and the strike on. I knew nothing of it: I had not been told. You see, I just didn't belong. So then . . . I went back to my dressing room, washed up and went up on the roof. It all seemed like a nightmare. There on the roof stood the manager talking with a small group of men. He saw me and said, "Well Bert, are you with us or against us?" Then I went home. . . . I went into the library and closed the door. . . . Then I arranged some chairs in a semi-circle and held a meeting. I started the *Bert Williams Equity*. I was all the officers and all the members of both sides. . . . First I was the president and opened the meeting, and then I was each succeeding officer and I made little speeches – any way I had my own little equity and that is what I called it. I held briefs for both sides, because you see, I don't belong to either side. Nobody really wants me.[56]

Williams's sad tale illustrates what one observer said of him: "He was in the *Follies*, but he was not allowed to be part of the *Follies*."[57] There is no record in the Equity archives of Williams ever becoming an Equity member.

At the beginning of the strike, the *Ziegfeld Midnite Frolic* was exempted from the pickets because it was considered vaudeville. After the *Follies* closed, Ziegfeld attempted to keep the *Frolic* going. Though Williams could have continued performing then, if he so chose, given his depression over the strike, it is doubtful that he did. When the stagehands and musicians walked out in sympathy with the actors, Ziegfeld finally had to close the *Frolic* too.[58] It was a bitter experience for Williams. He never appeared in a *Ziegfeld Follies* again.

Chapter 24

Within a year, from autumn 1919 to December 1920, Bert Williams made fifteen recordings, more than twice as many as usual. The songs included "I'm Sorry I Ain't Got It," "The Moon Shines on the Moonshine," "Checkers," "Somebody," "Ten Little Bottles," "Unlucky Blues," "Lonesome Alimony Blues," "Get Up," "Save a Little Dram for Me," "I Want to Know Where Tosti Went," "You Can't Trust Nobody," "Eve Cost Adam Just One Bone," "You'll Never Need a Doctor No Mo'," "My Last Dollar," and "I'm Gonna Quit Saturday."[1]

Two of these recordings – "Unlucky Blues" and "Lonesome Alimony Blues" – have the word *blues* in the title. As with the previous craze for ragtime, songwriters injected the word *blues* into song titles irrespective of whether a particular song merited that label musically. On February 14, 1920, Mamie Smith (1883–1946) had become the first of a long line of black female blues singers to record. The songs were "You Can't Keep a Good Man Down" and "This Thing Called Love." Bert Williams's recordings of "Unlucky Blues" and "Lonesome Alimony Blues" were made several months later.

The origin of the blues is very uncertain. According to Eileen Southern: "The dividing line between the blues and some kinds of spirituals cannot always be drawn."[2] Southern says that blues singer Ma Rainey first heard the blues in 1902.[3] But if the blues had always been a "genre" of African American music, what brought them into prominence in the 1920s was the beginning of radio broadcasting and the evolution of "race records," or record labels that offered blues music. Thus blues as well as jazz became accessible to the American public.

The relationship of Bert Williams's music to the blues deserves some comment here because of the similarity of the two.

Although musicologists and musicians agreed that "the blues has few absolute features," there nevertheless are some basic characteristics. Southern says:

> Generally, but not always, the blues reflects the personal response of its inventor to a specific occurrence or situation. By singing about his misery, the

blues singer achieves a kind of catharsis and life becomes bearable again.[4] Almost always, there is a note of irony or humor in the blues, as if the blues singer is audaciously challenging fate to mete out further blues. Sure, he has lost his job, and his woman has left him, and he has the blues; but he will go out the next morning to look for another job, and perhaps his woman will return.[5]

If singing the blues includes singing about hard luck, then certainly Williams had been singing the blues for a long time. His most popular songs – including "Nobody," "Jonah Man," and "When It's All Goin' Out and Nothin' Comin' In" – all utilized this motif.

"Unlucky Blues," a recording fortunately available today on the Folkways label, shows some characteristics of what is called "classic blues." Williams incorporates more bending, scooping, and dipping of notes in his singing of "Unlucky Blues." Also, the song has more quarter tones, or "blues notes," than the normal Williams song.[6]

However, "Unlucky Blues" also seems to lack some important elements of "classic blues": the "three-line stanza" and improvisation. For these reasons, musicians may not consider it true blues. But then, one might argue, is there any such thing as true blues?

Some of the songs Bert Williams recorded in 1920 were interpolated into the show *Broadway Brevities of 1920*. After the Equity strike, which had closed down the *Ziegfeld Follies of 1919*, Eddie Cantor was declared persona non grata by Ziegfeld for being a strike leader. The reasons for Bert Williams's leaving Ziegfeld are unclear, though it is possible that his contract with Ziegfeld had run out and he wished to try something new.

In 1920 the current rage on Broadway was the revue. Almost overnight, a number of revues sprang up – *George White's Scandals, The Passing Show, Greenwich Village Follies, The Music Box Revues*, the *Earl Carroll Vanities*, and so on. All imitated or were at least influenced by the *Ziegfeld Follies*. George LeMaire, who had been in the 1919 *Follies* with Bert Williams and Eddie Cantor, came up with an idea for a revue. It was called *Broadway Brevities of 1920*, in anticipation of annual editions. George LeMaire stood in awe of Bert Williams. He told a Williams biographer:

> I liked the man as well as any man I ever met and better than most men, for he had so many fine qualities. I admired him as an artist, tremendously because he was *a great artist*. . . . I have seen him, silently rise from his chair, while a group of us were sitting, and go to a door, admit a lady in pantomime, bring her down to a table, converse in gesture, order a whole dinner, with various bits of comedy to the waiter, pay the check and escort her out. It would be a perfect gem in its completeness.[7]

Produced by George LeMaire's brother, Rufus, *Broadway Brevities* had many chorus girls and a small group of leading players – Eddie Cantor,

George LeMaire, Edith Haller, and Bert Williams. The producers had
booked the show into a major Shubert house–the Winter Garden–and
recruited a hot new Tin Pan Alley songsmith–George Gershwin.

Gershwin, after his hit song, "Swanee," in *La La Lucille* the year
before, was a formidable catch for Rufus and George LeMaire. Gershwin
contributed seven songs to *Broadway Brevities*, most with lyrics by Arthur
Jackson or Irving Caesar. The remaining songs were by Blair Treymor and
Archie Gottler, with interpolations by Bert Kalmar, Harry Ruby, and Irving
Berlin.

Bert Williams appeared twice during each of the two acts of *Broadway
Brevities*. In Act 1, Scene 1, Williams and George LeMaire played prison in-
mates in a sketch called "Ninety Days from Broadway." Act 1, Scene 8, was
simply entitled "That Inimitable Comedian–Bert Williams." This was
Williams's song spot. The *New York Evening Telegram* said:

> Bert Williams has one or two of his best moments which he fills in his usual
> deliberate style. In one song, he reaches a delightful climax when, after
> boasting of his great knowledge, he confesses reluctantly that after all, he
> does now know where Tosti went, after he said "Goodbye, forever."[8]

The song referred to was the Chris Smith composition "I Want to Know
Where Tosti Went (When He Said Goodbye)."[9]

The other numbers Williams performed included another Chris Smith
song, "You'll Never Need a Doctor No Mo'"; "Save a Little Dram for Me,"
music and lyrics by Will E. Skidmore and Marshall Walker; "I'll Make Mine
Myself," music by Robert Hood Bowes and lyrics by Francis DeWitt; and
"Eve Cost Adam Just One Bone," music and lyrics by Charles Bayha. The
sheet music for these showed Williams in blackface and costume on the
cover, and the music publisher advertised, "As sung by Bert Williams in
'Broadway Brevities.'"

Williams's spot was followed by a comedy scene called "At the Dentist's
Office." Eddie Cantor played the patient and George LeMaire played the
dentist. Florenz Ziegfeld alleged that the sketch resembled one used the
year before in his *Follies*. A Ziegfeld biographer elaborated:

> Cantor and George LeMaire had jointly presented a comic sketch by Ziegfeld
> and Rennold Wolf called "The Osteopath's Office" in the 1919 *Follies*.
> Ziegfeld claimed that Cantor and LeMaire had rewritten the number and
> represented it as *The Dentist's Office* in LeMaire's new Shubert show, *Broad-
> way Brevities*. Ziegfeld won the suit and the act was dropped from the
> Shubert show.[10]

In Act 2, Scene 1, a dance-pantomime with music conceived by Bert
Williams, was performed by Ula Sharon and Alexis Kosloff, who staged it.
The program described the pantomime:

An officer of the Guards, craves the Kiss of Youth, but she hides from him. Insensate, he invades the sanctuary, coaxes, pleads, implores, but Youth defeats even force, seeking refuge on an outer balcony. Mad, with desire, he drags her back and ravishes the Kiss from Youth. Defiled, Youth, with unconscious courage, drives to his base heart, the pin from her corsage. He will never kiss again.[11]

Reviewers felt that dancer Ula Sharon was the true hit of the show: "When she appeared in a brief, clever pantomime, 'The Kiss,' . . . composed by Bert Williams, her work with Alexis Kosloff was equal to the traditions of the Ballet Russe."[12] The *Evening Post* also praised the pantomime: "One mighty good thing came, however, at the beginning of the second act, in the pantomime, 'The Kiss,' which with the music, was by Bert Williams, and which was remarkably well danced by Ula Sharon and Alexis Kosloff."[13]

Williams appeared in two more scenes: In "The Smart Bootery" Williams played a customer in George LeMaire's store and in the finale of the show, Williams joined the rest of the cast in a promenade down "The Marble Steps."

Critics of *Broadway Brevities* were disappointed in Bert Williams's performances. Reviews by the *Times* and the *Evening Post* were typical: "Bert Williams, not quite so well-treated as Cantor in the matter of material, nevertheless contrives to be more than amusing upon occasions."[15]

Theatre Magazine was kinder than most reviewers when it stated: "Bert Williams and Eddie Cantor, engaging clowns both, provide a few entertaining minutes, but for the most part, the grade of comedy is on a par with the number two burlesque shows."[16]

Broadway Brevities opened in Philadelphia on September 6, 1920. The *Philadelphia Inquirer* critic liked both the show and Bert Williams:

> Bert Williams, who well deserves the name, inimitable comedian, finds a right place in this entertainment. He is given a free hand and takes advantage of the chances which are given to him. There is so much that is good in "Broadway Brevities 1920" that it is difficult to report it all.

But his opinion was in the minority.

General critical remarks about *Broadway Brevities* panned the show. "As poor a show as the big [Winter] Garden has ever staged," said *Theatre Magazine*. Heywood Broun of the *Tribune* said, "we think that it is the worst musical show we ever saw."[17]

The word *vulgar* appeared in several press notices, as did comparison with burlesque. In particular, Eddie Cantor and the song "Stage Door Blues" were cited as inappropriate for Broadway. The *New York Evening Post* complained:

> Eddie Cantor was cordially greeted, but he had little that was new in his acts and his language and actions were often vulgar in the extreme. . . . "The

Stage Door Blues" . . . has no place among decent people. Moreover, it is cheap – very cheap – vulgarity.[18]

The *Tribune* concurred that the comedy was in poor taste. "None of the wit is honest enough to be called vulgar." The *Times* did not apply the adjective *vulgar* to the show but alluded to it. "There is here and there an idea in a lyric," said the critic, "and now and then, there is a stretch which could stand the censor's pencil."[19]

Broadway Brevities played for thirteen weeks, or 105 performances, hardly making Broadway history.[20] A show that was to make Broadway history, however, was *The Emperor Jones*, by the great playwright Eugene O'Neill. It is the story of a former Pullman porter named Brutus Jones who becomes emperor of a West Indian island and sets up a dictatorship. Jones flees to escape the natives' revolt and is killed by a silver bullet.

Despite O'Neill's broad use of what he considered black dialect, many saw *The Emperor Jones* as not a typical "Negro" role.

> For here was no stereotype of Negro character. Emperor Jones' ultimate fall, although superstition is involved, occurs because the artifices that have propped him up have been removed. So, exposed and defenseless, Jones – like any other man – falls victim to his fear and his essential, primitive nature. In certain ways, therefore, this is only incidentally a Negro play, it could well have used any man.[21]

The original plan for casting of *The Emperor Jones* called for a white cast. Eugene O'Neill's biographers have stated: "The roles of various natives, spirits and ghost-prisoners were played by such members of the group as Charles Ellis, Christina Ell, and Slim Martin, who blackened their bodies as required."[22] (These were all white actors.) O'Neill, George Cram ("Jig") Cook, the play's director, and Jasper Deeter, who played the supporting role of Cockney trader Smithers, were involved in the decision to cast the main character Brutus Jones.

Since many cast members had to wear blackface in the play, it was thought that the leading character should also do so – a train of thought that should have opened up the possibility of considering Bert Williams for the role. There is no record of Eugene O'Neill having considered this. He apparently envisaged Brutus Jones being played by a white actor, but the play's director disagreed:

> There are people who recall that . . . Cook was determined from the beginning to cast a Negro in the role – a decision which, as little as five years later, would probably have been an automatic one. But, in 1920, no Negro had ever played a major role in an American tragedy, and Jasper Deeter has maintained that Cook at first thought Charles Ellis should undertake the part, playing it in blackface. O'Neill, Deeter said, raised no objection. "I was the one who insisted that a Negro play Jones," Deeter added.[23]

And so a search was conducted for a black actor to play Brutus Jones. One of the actors approached was Paul Robeson, who read the script and was offended by O'Neill's portrayal of "Negro dialect" and excessive use of the word "nigger." (Ironically, in 1924 Robeson consented to play Brutus Jones, and the role helped propel him to stardom.[24])

Another actor considered for the role was Charles Gilpin. He had gotten favorable reviews in a supporting role as the black clergyman, William Curtis, in the play *Abraham Lincoln*, which had opened at the Cort Theater in New York on December 15, 1919. Gilpin was working odd jobs while not acting, and it took the Provincetown Players a while to locate him.

Gilpin later told an interviewer that he had almost no time to prepare for his part in *The Emperor Jones*:

> They asked me to come down to a rehearsal – the play had not been produced then – and look it over. I found that this was the dress rehearsal and that the play was to open the very next night in Stamford [Connecticut]. Could I learn the lines immediately and go on at the first performance? I said I could, if they would settle it with the other actor. I had no rehearsal with the company. The next day, through a mistake, I went to New Haven instead of Stamford; and when I finally reached the theatre in the latter town, it was after seven o'clock, and I had only time to dress and make up before the performance began. But I got through it all right.[25]

Alexander Woollcott, writing in the *New York Times*, praised Gilpin's performance. Woollcott said the play

> weaves a most potent spell, thanks partly to the force and cunning of its author, thanks partly to the admirable playing of Charles S. Gilpin in a title role so predominant that the play is little more than a dramatic monologue. His is an uncommonly powerful and imaginative performance, in several respects unsurpassed this season in New York. Mr. Gilpin is a Negro.[26]

The Emperor Jones and Charles Gilpin became famous overnight. Soon Gilpin was being asked for opinions on blacks in theater, just as Bert Williams had been years before. In an interview with the *New York Age*, for example, Gilpin gave his opinion about what Broadway audiences wanted:

> People want dramatic stock, but they want plays that are up-to-date Broadway successes. ... They want to see these plays done. People realize that they must have students of the drama and those with talent but no training; but they do object to a whole show done by amateurs. They like musical shows and will pack the house, but the week following must have a doubly strong show to attract. They like comedies, in a word, variety. But let each change be of the best of its kind.[27]

Charters reports that "Bert Williams saw Gilpin's Brutus Jones and admired the performance very much." But others report that Williams was envious, if not jealous, of Gilpin. Here was a role that he would have liked to have played. Here was the type of acting he wanted to do under the direction of someone like David Belasco. Tom Fletcher wrote:

> One of the things Bert couldn't understand, and it worried him slightly, was about Charles Gilpin becoming a star before him. Charley, he would point out, was just a chorus boy in one of the Williams and Walker shows, and now he had stardom. We would tell him that he had been a star for years, but he would always answer, "Yes, but that was when George was living. The team of Williams and Walker was the star of our productions. When you are the star of the show and unable to appear, the company closes until the star can appear. If you can't come back, then the company stays closed. When Gilpin was unable to appear, the show would close. I have been with the *Follies* for years. If I am unable to appear in the *Follies* the show must still go on. The big hit I am in the *Follies* doesn't mean that my leaving will make any difference, because I am only one of the stars."[28]

Several factors militated against Williams being selected to play in *The Emperor Jones*. First, he simply wasn't available: *Broadway Brevities* had opened September 29, 1920, and *The Emperor Jones* opened November 1, 1920. Also, Williams was too closely identified with comedy. Except for certain moments in the Williams and Walker shows, Williams had never done any "dramatic" acting. Furthermore, Williams was unaware that the Provincetown Players were considering casting Brutus Jones in blackface. Had he known this, he could conceivably have gone after the part. But even then, it seems unlikely that he would have won it. For instance, Charlie Chaplin was said to have been interested in a minor part in *The Emperor Jones*. But Eugene O'Neill, fearing that a box office name in the cast would steal attention from his play, put his foot down. Chaplin backed out.[29]

With the success of Gilpin in *The Emperor Jones*, however, Williams realized that the time was right for him to make his dramatic debut. Williams got hold of a play script that he thought would be the perfect dramatic vehicle for him. Mrs. Bert Williams stated later that her husband was obsessed with the idea of branching out into dramatic acting. He carried the play script around with him all the time. Mrs. Williams called it "his Bible." She said:

> He hoped that it might do for him what "The Emperor Jones" did for Mr. Gilpin. They were very good friends, and my husband knew what a fight Mr. Gilpin had – and how much courage the producers needed. This piece that he hung his hopes on was very sombre. There was a voodoo theme; a jealous husband, a half-caste, tortures his wife's child inside a charmed circle that she cannot cross, and she dies of horror. The part of the husband might seem the opposite of any one would choose for Bert, who adored children and his home, but that may have been just the reason he wanted to play it. He worshipped that manuscript.[30]

Williams wanted to make a clean break with his comedy image. In order to do this, Mrs. Williams claimed, he wanted the play to open in Europe. "And the next year, his heart was set on that – he was going to London to open in a serious play. He chose London because he was afraid that at first New York wouldn't be able to disassociate him from his old type of work."[31]

The "serious play" that Mrs. Williams claimed her husband wanted to act in was possibly a play called *Taboo*. The playwright was Mary Hoyt Wiborg, a white woman who was the daughter of wealthy financier Frank Wiborg. The playscript of *Taboo* appears not to have been published. But a review of the play, which opened in New York April 5, 1922, gave a detailed description of the plot. Thus it is possible to compare this description of *Taboo* with Mrs. Williams's account. *Taboo* is about the ancient rites of certain Louisiana Negroes whose most important invocations were offered on June 24 – St. John's Eve.

> The story seems centered about The Child (Master Junior Tierman), a little white boy, seven years old, who had from birth been dumb, and whose mind had never developed normally. His grandmother, Mrs. Gaylord (Margaret Wycherly) and a young man (Henry O'Neill), apparently her son, were the child's guardians. They had exhausted the resources of medical science in a fruitless effort to restore the boy to normalcy. In the meantime, from a talk between Aunt Angy (Marie Jackson Stuart) and Mammy Dorceas (Fannie Bell Deknight), the child's nurse, it was brought out that among the half-declosed legends of "The Circle," there was one which hinted darkly of some connection between this ancient cult and the present afflictions of the white child.

> There was prevailing at the time, a drought which continued for many years. It was intended that the rites of St. John's Eve should be directed toward an appeal to the spirits of voodoo for relief through the bringing of rain.

> The power of superstition was shown when Mrs. Gaylord, in despair over the failure of the doctors to cure The Child, agreed to a suggestion made by Mammy Dorceas, that the white woman personally go to the meeting of "The Circle" that night and ask for voodoo charms that could remove the bewitchment which held The Child's mind in thrall.

> Tom (Alex Rogers), the family coachman, was king of "The Circle" and his principal assistants were Aunt Angy, Mammy Dorceas, Lemuel Johnson (Milton Dees), Joseph (F. H. Wilson), and Sadie (Ruth Taylor). Men and women laborers from the neigborhood plantations made up the membership of the voodoo circle.

> Jim (Paul Robeson) and Steve (Harold Simmelkjaer) are two wandering Negroes, strangers in the community. They come by accident to the scene of the impending rites just prior to the coming of the voodoo king and his followers. Jim goes to sleep behind a neighboring tree, where he remained undiscovered throughout the entire night. Steve, rambling around, runs into the group of voodooists, but is chased way from the scene. Then the voodoo rites begin.

The officers, headed by Tom the king, Aunt Angy and Mammy Dorceas, with Sadie, Joseph and Lemuel following, came first upon the scene and after dismissing the stranger Steve, proceeded to engage in wordy and hilarious converse. This turned at times, to angry disputation when the value of Joseph's Indian luckstone was compared with the roots and dead skins on which Aunt Angy pinned her faith.

Before the others were finally assembled, the white woman – Mrs. Gaylord – was made to appear and the king formed the Luck Ball which was to be the means of of restoring The Child's lost faculties. As she took the Luck Ball and left to return home, the membership assembled and the voodoo incantations began. The secret snake was brought in its box to the altar and the king began an invocation to the gods for rain. Under the spell of his fervid pleadings, Ruth Taylor as Sadie, stepped from among the worshippers, disclosed herself as being half-clothed, bare as to shoulders and bust, and from thighs to toes. As the king invoked the voodoo spirits and the *boula* (drum) was thumped, this girl proceeded to do a dance of sorts...

As the play transpired, the scene following, representing a "Juju compound along the Guinea coast, Africa," is the materializing of a dream, which came to the sleeping stranger, Jim . . . In that African country, the dream showed that a drought was prevailing and Jim was the black king with Mrs. Gaylord as the white Queen, paralleling the legend hinted at by Aunt Angy in the first act. The people demanded a sacrifice for the propit[i]ation of the angry rain gods and the child, mentally defective as in reality, was surrendered by the Queen to the Beze (witch doctor) for that purpose...

The following morning, when he awakes, Jim is discovered by the two plantation hands: Joseph and Lemuel, who have The Child with them. Tom recognizes The Child as one of his dream creatures and is mystified. The two hands finally entrust The Child with Jim to be taken home.

In the meantime, Mrs. Gaylord has prepared a feast day for her hands and those from neighboring plantations. Her houseguests include three white neighbors: Cartwright (Harold McGee) and Wheeler (Walker Dowling) both planters, and a minister – Dr. Elder (David A. Leonard). These men reached home before the colored people assembled and Wheeler commenting on the drought from which the land is suffering, told a story of fifty years before, when a similar condition was experienced and a white child afflicted as was The Child, disappeared with a strange Negro and was never found, giving rise to the belief that it had been offered to the voodoo worshipers as a sacrifice to the rain gods.

This story so affects Mrs. Gaylord that she become[s] greatly distressed later when she learns that her grandchild had been placed in the charge of a stranger and that neither had been seen since. As her worry reached its highest pitch, The Child returned, accompanied by Jim, and again does the Negro discover the living replica of an image of his dream, for in Mrs. Gaylord, he sees again his white Queen consort of the African Juju compound. But the strain upon the white woman's emotions has been great and when she sees the stranger in person and recalls the story told a few minutes earlier by Wheeler, her heart is not strong enough to carry the burden, and she collapses. Then when the white men rush out to seize the strange Negro (Jim) in the belief that he had injured the dead woman, The Child speaks for the first time in its life, saying: "Don't hurt him!"

As the final curtain descends, there is grief over the death of the grandmother, but this is tempered by wonder at the miracle of the boy's cure and rejoicing at an impending rain which is being heralded by flashes of lightning and crashes of thunder.

It is clear that Mrs. Williams's description of the play is not quite the same as the review of *Taboo*. There are, nevertheless, some similarities in topics: a child who is tortured or bewitched, a voodoo "circle" or theme, a woman character who dies of horror. Also significant is the fact that it is a drama rather than a musical comedy, making it a radical departure for Bert Williams. Furthermore, *Taboo* later played in London where Mrs. Patrick Campbell played the role of Mrs. Gaylord. The role of Jim, played in New York by Paul Robeson, was possibly the part in *Taboo* that Bert Williams was to play. It is conceivable though that Mrs. Williams only had a vague idea of the play *Taboo*; this would explain why she described the piece as focusing on a husband-wife conflict. But here again, one could argue that she is alluding to an entirely different play. Because there is no extant correspondence between the playwright Mary Wiborg and Bert Williams, we will never know for certain the identity of Williams's "serious play" or "Bible."

Chapter 25

T he cultural climate that made possible shows like *The Emperor Jones* and *Shuffle Along* is sometimes referred to as the Harlem Renaissance. "The thing that happened did not appear at first glance as a development; it seemed like a sudden awakening, an instantaneous change."[1] The nation became aware of the astonishing accomplishments of black Americans in the fields of music, art, theater, and literature. The Harlem Renaissance must be studied within the context of the larger social changes in American society during the 1920s. Nathan Irvin Huggins, in his book, *Harlem Renaissance*, argues that "The aura of the postwar decade, epitomized in F. Scott Fitzgerald's 'younger generation' and the Jazz Age, was reflected among Negro intellectuals too. They created the 'New Negro.'"[2]

This "New Negro" was, on the one hand, the result of a new black generation's celebration of its racial heritage, and on the other, the product of young white Americans' thirst for the exotic and unconventional. In the 1920s:

> The factors for a significant cultural development in the American popular theatre were all present: a white audience fascinated by the Negro, though in many ways obviously misinformed, critics and writers interested in the possibilities of seeing Negro themes and actors on the stage; and a great pool of Negro talent, trained in cabarets, vaudeville houses, and Negro theatres.[3]

The landmark black musical comedy *Shuffle Along*, with music and lyrics by Eubie Blake and Noble Sissle, was one of the first black shows to capitalize on this audience. After it opened at the 63rd Street Theater in New York in June, 1921, Lester Walton called it "the cleanest and most ambitious colored musical attraction to command the respectful attention of New York theatergoers in recent years."[4] Alan Dale of the *New York American* praised the dancing in the show: "Talk of pep! These people made pep seem something different to the tame thing we know further downtown. Every sinew in their frames responded to their extreme energy."[5]

Eubie Blake later said: "It was Alan Dale's review that really made people want to see the show."[6] Critics were conscious of how the pioneering work of Bert Williams and George Walker had prepared the way for Eubie Blake's success. Lester Walton recalled:

> It has been more than a decade since a colored musical attraction figured in a long run in New York. During the season of 1907–8, Williams and Walker, in *Bandanna Land*, held forth for several months at the old Majestic Theatre. To parallel this record was the burning ambition of many a colored performer. . . . Now comes "Shuffle Along," faithfully functioning as a steam-roller. It has knocked over and crushed to earth many of the barriers that stood in the path of the colored show's progress. Precedents have been established. Not only has the old Williams and Walker record been equalled, it has been surpassed.[7]

But before starting a new show of his own, Bert Williams completed a series of recordings in 1921 for Columbia Records. On July 12 he recorded "Tain't No Disgrace to Run When You're Skeered." The following day he recorded a similar tune: "I Ain't Afraid of Nothin' Dat's Alive." In October Williams cut two more records: "Brother Low Down" and "Unexpectedly." His last recording, which was made on February 24, 1922, was called "Not Lately." The writers of these songs are unknown, although it is conceivable that Bert Williams composed them.

Williams signed with A. H. Woods, a producer associated with the Shuberts, to do a musical comedy. Originally *The Pink Slip*, the title was later changed to *Under the Bamboo Tree*. Bert Williams was to be the main star of the show, unlike his position in *Broadway Brevities*.

John E. Nail tells of Williams's dedication to making *Under the Bamboo Tree* more successful than his previous solo show, *Mr. Lode of Koal*: "It was Bert's determination to bring 'The Bamboo Tree,' to New York and his passionate faith in that piece wore him out – and finally killed him, I think."[8]

Nail said that Williams yearned to branch out and show Broadway audiences that he could do new things. "Bert longed to do real comedy," said Nail, "and 'The Bamboo Tree' had a little comedy in it. . . . He wanted New York, that knew him only in the *Follies* and in vaudeville and the music hall, to see him in that new light."[9]

The Shuberts hired the famous American operetta composer, Sigmund Romberg, to write music for the show. But strangely enough, *Under the Bamboo Tree* is not mentioned in Romberg's biography or in the forty-five volumes of Romberg musical manuscripts held by the University of California at Berkeley.[10] It is clear, however, from records of the Shubert Organization that $250 was paid to "Bert Williams a/c Sigmund Romberg rewriting music."[11] In 1921 Romberg was preoccupied with his huge operetta hit, *Blossom Time*, and the black composer Will Vodery was called in to complete the score for *Under the Bamboo Tree*. Vodery had been musical director for *Bandanna Land* and for the *Ziegfeld Follies* since 1913. The book and lyrics for *Under the Bamboo Tree* were by Walker DeLeon (1884–1947), who later became a Hollywood screenwriter. The Shuberts also paid $200 to a lyricist named Matthew Woodward.[12] The choreography of the Bert Williams show was by Canadian-born choreographer Allan K. Foster (1890–1937), noted for the dance group the Foster Girls.

Williams's costars were mostly actors from vaudeville: Harry K. Morton, Zella Russell, Sammy White, Eva Puck, Esther Howard, and Spencer Charters. Unlike *Mr. Lode of Koal*, *Under the Bamboo Tree* was a vehicle for Bert Williams at the head of an all-white company.

In the opening scene of the play, the audience is told that a "wealthy old gentleman named Coglan, who died several weeks ago, left a buried treasure on this island. Before he died, Mr. Coglan wrote directions for finding the treasure on a piece of pink paper. He then tore the paper into six pieces and hid the pieces."[13] The porter of the island's hotel, Anania Washington, played by Bert Williams, overhears this story and plots to deceive people by planting phony pink slips (the source of the play's original title) around the hotel. Washington then causes excitement among the hotel guests by suggesting that the real pink slips and treasure are in the hotel.

A fortune-teller, Madame LeCorez, believes that she has an advantage over the other hotel guests by utilizing her psychic powers to find the treasure. This serves as the background for the first musical number of the show, "If What She Sees Comes True,"[14] performed by Zella Russell and chorus.

When the stage is empty, Bert Williams emerges and calls after the departing chorus: "And I certainly wish you luck with what you will find." Then he takes some pink wrapping paper from his pocket and, hearing a noise, looks cautiously around the stage. A bellboy enters from the left and exits carrying a trunk. At this, Williams hurriedly puts the paper back in his pocket, and says: "There goes my dollar tip. Never mind, I'm going to make it faster than that now." Resolved to fabricate the legendary pink slips, Williams once again takes the paper out of his pocket and is forced to conceal it again when a bird whistle is heard offstage. Williams becomes paranoid about being discovered. He says: "That's a signal. It must be a signal. Because we ain't got that kind of birds around here. Can't be too careful, these big investigations going on every day; never know when they are getting ready to John Doe you."[15]

During this monologue, Williams is gradually folding the pink wrapping paper. "The man said six." He starts tearing the paper. After this, the script directions call for two songs sung by Williams, "Mixed Up" and "Judge Grimes."[16] Jack Newton and Williams then engage in a discussion about the mechanics of flying. The script indicates that this dialogue leads into the song "Gravitation." As Act 1 ends, Williams is forced into hiding when the hotel guests become suspicious of his behavior.

In Act 2, Williams is found in the garden of the hotel talking to a puppy. To save himself, he surmises that it might be wise to get rid of all the bogus pink slips. Williams says to the puppy: "Ain't no use in talking, puppy – much as I love you, I got to git rid of you. That pink slip in yo' collar is too much proximity for me."[7] The distraught porter then sings the song "Puppy Dog," considered the most memorable tune of the show.[18]

In an interview, Williams told Chicago theater critic Ashton Stevens that he used a real dog in the play. Williams also reflected that he believed that the show was a good play because of this scene:

> "I'm a porter at Catalina Island; an awful liar; but a character. And I've got a song coming along that ought to have character in it, too. I sing it with a dog; with a gangling-legged out-cast dog. A lady has given me a dollar to take this dog out and feed him, and her husband has given me five dollars to take the dog and drown him. There ought to be some character in that song, not to say problem. I'm working it out – slow-way I do everything, Brother Stevens. But I think I ought to be able to understand the way that old black porter feels. Yes," He added, in that mellow and melancholy bass, "and I think I ought to be able to understand how the dog feels too."[19]

The play ends with Williams confessing to his sham. But the hotel guests forgive him, realizing that money is not the most important thing in life.

Under the Bamboo Tree was apparently scheduled for a Philadelphia tryout in November, 1921.[20] But it never played in Philadelphia. The Shuberts records for the show do not mention a Philadelphia opening. The Shuberts decided the piece needed "play-doctoring," and ostensibly at this time, the title of the play was changed and Vodery and Woodward were brought in to help with the music.

The production opened in Cincinnati, Ohio, on December 4, 1922. In a newspaper preview notice, it was explained that "after a brief road tour, it is the intention of the Shuberts to take the production into New York."[21] The advertisement for the show in the Cincinnati press attempted to paint the musical as glamorous, claiming that it offered "a dazzling array of artists and a breezy bevy of Broadway beauties." The opening night at the Cincinnati Shubert Theatre, at Seventh and Walnut streets, was attended by a capacity audience, and J. J. Shubert himself, who was seen taking notes during the performance.

The critics were kind to the show. The *Cincinnati Enquirer* commented: "The show should be in for a long run. ... The story is farci[c]al in its nature, so too much in the way of inconsistency for plausibility was not to be expected." In respect to the staging and direction, the *Enquirer* said: "*Under the Bamboo Tree* has been tastefully staged. There were remarkably few hitches."[22]

Bert Williams was saluted for his acting ability. The press noted:

In the role of the porter, Williams has a part that fits him like a glove. He is a droll entertainer and he has the faculty of feeling the pulse of his audience well. Thus, he was able to gloss over the few uncertain places that were bound to creep into a new production.[23]

Nevertheless, Williams's singing talent was seen as the show's main attraction. The Cincinnati critic noted that:

> Bert has a way of his own when it comes to "putting over" a song and such numbers as "Gravitation" and "Puppy Dog" are likely to become popular before the week's engagement is up. That is, people will go to the theater to hear him sing them. No one else could do it quite as he does.[24]

Other performers in the production, such as Sammy White, Zella Russell, and James Marlowe were also complimented.

But the show lost money in Cincinnati—more than two thousand dollars the first week and more than seven thousand dollars the second.[25] Because the show was in trouble, the Shuberts were loath to pay the writers their royalties. In a letter dated December 18, 1921, and signed "Billy," Will Vodery wrote to Bert Williams: "No royalties paid of which violate contracts. Can you adjust these matters or must I take action at once? Tony Heindl to write score of 'Puppy Dog' to use as trombone solo."[26] No extant Williams correspondence reveals whether the problem was solved.

On December 11, 1921, *Under the Bamboo Tree* opened at the Studebaker Theater in Chicago. That city's critics were harsher in their judgment of the musical. Particularly the book writer, Walter DeLeon, was taken to task. The *Chicago Tribune* said: "It is not much of a plot, and since the librettist has strung it out at some length, it involved frequent desolate stretches in an entertainment that otherwise does its best to be lively."[27] The *Chicago Daily News* charged that the plot was not new at all. "Something reminiscent of Mark Twain's 'Pink Slip for 10 Cent Fare' is at the bottom of it," said the critic.[28]

It was noted that Williams's recent theater appearances in the *Ziegfeld Follies* had not been long enough to truly showcase his talents. Therefore the Chicago critics were pleased with the idea of *Bamboo Tree* as a vehicle for Williams. Said the *Tribune*: "Here he is not exactly omnipotent, but frequently on the stage, involved in the distressing perplexities of a full-grown plot, and as always, the very personification of comic woe."[29]

The *Daily News* admired Williams's manner of utilizing his body in acting. Amy Leslie wrote:

> His face is his fortune, from the big, uncanny eyes to that expressive vat of expression. Bert's mouth, with its white teeth and catching smile. There is a little pathos in his long simian arms and splay feet as he swings lazily into a shuffle or idles along his thieving way as the porter. He stopped the show a couple of times last night.[30]

Bert Williams in stage costume for *Under the Bamboo Tree* (1921–22). (*Courtesy Wisconsin Center for Film and Theater Research*)

Williams's performance of the song "Puppy Dog" was called "the most engaging moment of the show. . . . This is funny and not without its note of searching pathos – the representative comedian at his best."[31] The *Daily News* also liked the song: "He croons melodiously as the orchestra plays a lovely obligato."[32]

The Chicago press cited other actors, such as James Marlowe and Spencer Charters, for their fine performances but panned that of Esther Howard. The *Daily News* complained: "Miss Howard dawdles through a somewhat uncouth ingenue role and seems to have lost her gait."[33] The song "In the Movies," performed by Sammy White, Harry Morton, and Eva Puck, was singled out as a highlight of the show. This spoof on Hollywood filmmaking allowed them to "exploit the rapid-fire film episode and the new slow-red movement in which is demonstrated crucial points of the actor's activities."[34]

While *Under the Bamboo Tree* was in Chicago, Bert Williams became irritated by a number of problems connected with the production. The contract he had with the Shuberts called for him to be paid $1,250 a week plus 10 percent of the gross at the box office.[35] Williams claimed that he was not being paid according to contract. In a letter discussing the show's New Year's Eve engagement in Chicago, Williams brought up the salary issue:

> My misunderstanding, if there be one, is with Mr. Bryant. He came into my dressing room and offered me the salary of $600 for each of the houses I played and that he would try to get me something to go along with that. . . . It was a verbal agreement between he and I. The check I received called for $1,000, and when I asked for the other $200, there has been no satisfaction. Mr. Bryant has not even had the courtesy to tell me which he will settle.[36]

Williams was also upset about changes in the management of *Under the Bamboo Tree*. The song "Puppy Dog" had been given a jazzlike scoring by the show's orchestra conductor, Anton Heidl, and had charmed the critics and audience. But now the Shuberts wanted to replace Heidl. Williams protested. He sent a telegram to J. J. Shubert: WISH YOU WOULD CONSIDER THE DECISION OF MOVING TONY HEIDL. HE IS VERY SATISFACTORY TO ME. I HATE TO MAKE CHANGES. ADVISE EVANS. – LITTLE BERT WILLIAMS[37] Williams's pleas to retain Heidl were in vain. By the time the show moved to Detroit, Heidl had been replaced by J. Albert Hurley as musical director for *Under the Bamboo Tree*.[38] Possibly because of the removal of his musical director, Williams seems to have dropped his hit song from the show temporarily. In a letter to songwriter Mabel Rowland, dated January, 1922, Williams wrote: "We close here in Chicago the 19th. Extra Sunday night. I think it would have been wonderfull [sic] to have sung 'Puppy Dog.' Beside[s] the dog is from the Bide A Wee [an animal shelter]."[39]

Williams was worried about the success of the show. Since the opening of *Under the Bamboo Tree*, it had played for twelve weeks – from the week of December 10, 1921 to the week of February 18, 1922 – during six of which it had lost money.[40] Williams must have sensed the similarity between this show and *Mr. Lode of Koal*. He was determined that *this* show would not close prematurely, and that he *could* be a success on his own, no matter what.

Chapter 26

W illiams's disputes with the Shuberts were not his only problems. His health had begun to decline. Henry Herzbrun (1885–1953),[1] Williams's lawyer, came to visit him in Chicago. After Williams's death, Herzbrun gave the following account of his meeting with Williams:

> I saw Bert a month or so ago in Chicago. He was lying on the couch in his dressing room when I entered. He told me that his stomach was bad, "but that's the way I am, feeling fine one day and not so good the next." . . . During the course of our talk, I suggested that he close for a few weeks after the Chicago engagement and take a rest. He was obviously in ill health. He refused to think of the suggestion. "Throw a lot of people out of work? Never. I feel a lot better today."[2]

So, although he was sick, Williams insisted on going to Detroit with his show. The *Detroit News* disclosed that Williams "had been ill for several weeks with a painful attack of neuritis. He was advised not to go give a performance, but when he was told that a capacity audience was assured . . . he insisted on appearing."[3]

Despite this note in the press, no one except the company and theater staff knew exactly how seriously ill Williams was. For his comfort, a cot was placed in his dressing room and between the acts he rested.[4]

In Detroit *Under the Bamboo Tree* was to play at the Garrick Theater, which the Shuberts had decorated in the colors of money, green and gold. The Garrick's theme was mainly green: The color was found in the wall hangings, the seats, the wallpaper, and in the drop curtain. The latter featured a large monogram in the center – the letter *G* in majestic gold.[5]

Equally golden to the ears of the critics was the singing of Bert Williams. The *Detroit Times* remarked:

> His role of a porter in a Pacific Coast resort hotel is not without its possibilities, so that he is better off than he has been in the last couple of years. . . . He is allotted several good songs, took all of them, attempts at the topical sort of semi-narrative, semi-philosophical ditties that he does so well – but only one of them, addressed to a lap dog which he holds, has any

of the truly human touch essential to a successful Williams song. That, and the encore about what makes the wild cat wild, are [of] a piece with the Williams tradition.[6]

The *Detroit News* also found this group of Williams tunes quite "meritorious." It cited the aviation song, the Judge Grimes song, and the wildcat song as acceptable but reserved its praise for the fourth number, calling it

> a masterpiece of writing and singing. . . . With Bernice (that's the name of the mutt) on his lap, he sings a plaintive little address entitled "Puppy Dog," in which he finds himself as lonely as the dog. It is a gem of artful acting that inspires much laughter and that at the same time brings the listener close to tears.[7]

The pathos of Williams's acting suggested to one critic that Williams had matured as an actor. In an eloquent description of Williams's performance, the *Detroit Free Press* observed

> It is not altogether the meatiest part that ever fell to Williams, but what he does with the role whenever the opportunities offer. . . . It is as much what he does as what he says that brings laughs, and in those moments when he glimpses the yawning jail door, there is eloquence in every move, every expression of those dusky features, a depiction of fear that is striking in its genuineness. There is the same old slouch, the sonorous drawl that turns every word to such good account, the recitative method of delivering a song that proves as effective, the touch of a real actor that finds expression when he snuggles a mongrel in his lanky arms and commiserates the canine on the ill-fortune that spared it from drowning as a puppy.[8]

Under the Bamboo Tree seemed to resemble other 1920s musicals in offering displays of snappy, attractive choreography. Because Detroit was not a usual tryout town for a Broadway-bound musical, the critics were mesmerized by the choreography of Allan K. Foster. Exclaimed the *Detroit Free Press*: "It has been quite some time since so many good dancers were assembled under one banner hereabout." The *Detroit News* also admitted that "the show [was] particularly fortunate" in the area of dance.

The player whose dancing attracted the most attention was Harry Morton. One critic wondered how Morton's "eccentric and acrobatic steps . . . do not, strangely enough, leave him at the final curtain with a broken neck." Another reviewer also stated that "Mr. Morton does quite a bit of his [dancing] on the back of his neck."[9] Other performers noted for their choreography were Sammy White and Eva Puck. The *Detroit Times* said these two definitely had "to be listed among the steppers," while the *Detroit Free Press* found White to be as eccentric a dancer as Morton.[10]

According to the Detroit press, the choreography was the main merit of the production. The *Detroit News* thought *Under the Bamboo Tree* was "a fast and dapper entertainment, alive with agile dancing."[11] The *Detroit Times* was more critical of the musical because it did not have a book to support a huge star like Bert Williams.

> As for the vehicle itself, it perhaps isn't remarkable save for the number of good dancers it includes among its players and for the fact that it starts off with a rush that would be wonderful if it lasted. But the plot about the hidden treasure to be found by means of six slips of pink paper is completely Shubertized by the time the second act curtain goes up though it has more novelty of idea than one expects in such a show. . . . A fair entertainment but by no means good enough for such an extraordinar[il]y good comedian as Mr. Williams.[12]

A third Detroit review judged that *Bamboo Tree* had plenty of dancing and song and "the other ingredients that help to make musical comedy popular." But, said the *Detroit Free Press*, "it is Williams, as he puts a word of meaning into his assertion that 'whenever it comes to picking up money, I can stoop as low as anybody,' who is the chief contributor to three hours of merriment."[13]

The following day, Monday, February 27, 1922, Bert Williams still felt sick but decided to perform anyway.[14] The press reported that "Williams became ill early in the evening and the company did its stuff . . . half an hour waiting on him to get better. He then went on for a few minutes, but was compelled to quit after about 10 minutes."[15] Sammy White recalled what happened:

> I was playing a Harold Lloydish part, the role of a tourist. Bert Williams was the porter, and as I came on stage, I'd say: "Come, come, porter – roll that trunk along faster or I'll miss my train." Williams, rolling the trunk along, would roll his eyes at the audience and say: "Uh-huh, boss – Yassuh, yassuh," and then he'd do a mincing strut that would send the audience into a[n] uproar. On this particular night, I made my entrance, offstage, and went into my lines. As soon as Bert came on stage, I could feel that Death was walking by his side. "Uh-huh, boss," he said, and there was the most terrible sound in his voice that I've ever heard. He wiped his brow with his big kerchief, and he was perspiring so that when he removed his handkerchief, his makeup was splotched. The audience start[ed] howling. They thought this was part of his antics. Williams gamely went along with his lines, but each time, it was a terrible effort. His voice had a curious croak in it, and at the sound of this old voice, the hysteria of the audience mounted. Like the great trouper that he was, Bert finished the scene and then they rang down the curtain.[16]

John C. Dancy, a friend of Williams and director of the Detroit Urban League, was also there. Dancy claimed: "I was the first to see him falter, and I told the man who controlled the curtain to lower it because Bert Williams could not go on."[17] After Williams left the Garrick stage, "the management put on some stories and dance acts while a doctor was called.

Then it was announced that Bert was too sick to continue. An understudy stepped out . . . but the audience rose like one man and went to the window for the refund."[18]

Meanwhile, backstage, the cast hovered around Bert Williams's room. Sammy White and John Dancy helped the comedian out of the wings. White said:

> When he laid him out on a couch in his dressing room, I whispered to him: "Bert, the audience laughed because they didn't know you were sick." He looked up at me and said, "Mistuh White, that's a nice way to die – they was laughing when I made my last exit."[19]

According to Mrs. Williams, her husband's health had been declining for some time before the *Bamboo Tree* tour. When Williams was at home in New York, his wife used to wait for his chauffeur to bring him home from the theater.

> As the ailment which was to carry him off took a firm hold upon him (for, while it is not generally known, my husband was a sick man for two years), he became less hearty in his greetings to the children on the block and they noticed it. Indeed, sometimes he would have to hold on to the railing while he pulled himself up the front steps. The chauffeur would walk directly behind him. He was so sensitive he would not be helped up, because he did not want anyone to know how ill he was. Once inside the door, he would sink into a chair even before he took off his overcoat. He was very, very brave up to the last.[20]

Robert M. Evans, the manager of the *Under the Bamboo Tree* company, said that Williams first became ill in Chicago:

> The play was a great success in Chicago, but the star was a very sick man and played under the greatest difficulties. . . . All day, every day, he stayed in bed. He called me his "jailor and turnkey" because I saw to it personally that no one disturbed him or, in fact, reached him at all. His valet and I dressed and undressed him all the time like a baby. The mere effort of moving enough for us to adjust his collar, tired and winded him, so that he had to rest between times and the process of dressing took a very long time.[21]

John Dancy said:

> I accompanied him back to his hotel. . . . This was the Wolverine, then very new, and regarded as one of the finest in town. Other Negroes, particularly those with extremely light skins, had been able occasionally to find accommodations at some good hotels, but to my knowledge, this was the first time a Negro had been openly accepted at one.[22]

Williams had caught a cold in Chicago, and being the trouper that he was, insisted upon performing instead of getting well. The cold developed into pneumonia and was compounded by heart problems, dating back several years. John Dancy said that Williams "knew he would not last much longer. He asked that I mail his checks for his Detroit performances to his wife, and advise her to deposit them immediately."[23]

On Tuesday, February 28, the Michigan Central Railroad sent wheelchairs, blankets, and porters to transport Bert Williams to the train depot in Detroit. Rowland reported that "the trip was a tedious vigil for his attendants, but he slept most of the way."[24] Mrs. Williams had been called and was to meet her husband's train in New York. "Arriving in New York, he tried to appear cheerful when they were met by Mrs. Williams, but it was no use. She saw that he was very sick and feared the worst. He was put to bed at their home and sank steadily."[25]

Dr. Herbert Cornwell diagnosed Williams's condition as being complicated by "degenerative myocarditis," a heart condition. A heart specialist, Dr. Charles Schramm, was called in.[26]

On Saturday, March 4, Williams took a turn for the worse. His lungs had been weakened by lumbar pneumonia, and his condition was critically anemic: "His young friend and protégé, Will H. Vodery, the composer, was called upon for a transfusion. He gave his blood gladly and the big man rallied and opened his eyes. To the doctor's question, 'How do you feel?' he replied: '80% better.'"[27]

But the rally was only temporary. A will was composed, leaving his entire estate to his wife, Lottie. Williams was apparently conscious long enough to endorse his will by signing it with "a mark."[28] At 11:30 P.M., Saturday, March 4, 1922, Bert Williams breathed his last. He was forty-six years old. His mother, Julia, and his wife, Lottie, and her three nieces were the only survivors.

Three funerals were held for Bert Williams – one, family; one, public Masonic; and one, private Masonic. The public funeral was held at St. Phillip's Protestant Episcopal Church in Harlem. On Tuesday, March 7, Williams's body was on view from 10:00 A.M. to noon for thousands to view. Then "the family services were held at 12:30 P.M., at which Hutchins C. Bishop officiated. . . . Musical numbers were rendered by the St. Phillip's choirs." The *New York Times* said that more than five thousand people paid their last respects to Bert Williams and thousands more could not get in to the church.[29]

The funeral wreaths were from those who were closest to Bert Williams or admired him:

> The metallic casket was covered with a blanket of white roses, orchids and lilies, a floral offering from his widow. Other beautiful floral pieces were from Eddie Cantor, member of the *Ziegfeld Follies*, The Frogs, members of the *Shuffle Along* company, Nora Bayes (vaudeville singer), Florenz Ziegfeld, and Miller and Lyles (comedians).[30]

Similarly, the honorary pallbearers included men whose lives had been touched by Bert Williams and who were among his close friends. Many of them were outstanding men in their own right:

John B. Nail – Harlem real estate broker
Leon Errol – comedian
Ford Dabney – songwriter
Harry T. Burleigh – musician
Lester A. Walton – drama critic
R. C. McPherson – songwriter
Henry Troy – singer with the Williams and Walker company
James Lightfoot – singer with the Williams and Walker company
Edward Johnson, a.k.a. "Black Carl" – performer with Williams and Walker's company
Noble Sissle – songwriter and performer
Chris Smith – songwriter
Harry H. Pace – Black record company owner[31]

The *New York Age* said that the sadness of the occasion was compounded by the miserable weather the day of the funeral:

When the body was carried from the church after the services, the rain began to fall in torrents as if the heavens were weeping for the loss of so bright a star. Despite this heavy downpour, the honorary pallbearers walked behind the hearse to the undertaking establishment of J. W. Duncan, 2303 Seventh Avenue . . . where it lay in state until 10:30 Wednesday morning when it was removed to the Masonic Temple, 71 East 23rd Street.[32]

Although Bert Williams held life membership in Lodge Waverly #567 in Edinburgh, Scotland (which he had joined in 1903), an agreement was reached with St. Cecile Lodge in New York to have them conduct private Masonic rites for Williams.[33] From noon until 1:00 P.M. on Wednesday, March 8, a private Masonic rite was held. "The Lambs skin presented to Williams by the Waverly Lodge of Edinburgh, Scotland was placed in the coffin, with the customary sprigs of acacia, symbols of the Mason's faith in the immortality of the soul."[34]

From 1:00 to 2:00 P.M., the public Masonic services were held. The *New York Times* said: "Two thousand persons, the majority members of the colored race, crowded the Grand Lodge room which contains seats for 1,200."[35] Handel's "Largo" and Chopin's "Funeral March" were played by the orchestra of the *Shuffle Along* company: "At the close of the ceremony, Mrs. Lottie Williams, the widow, fainted, but was quickly revived. She finally left the room supported by two of her husband's friends, Alex Rogers and Will Vodery."[36] Bert Williams was buried in Woodlawn Cemetery in New York City.

The tributes to Bert Williams reveal different perceptions of why he was important and what his contributions were. Many people cited his status as a unique black comedian who possessed genius. The *New York Tribune* called Williams "a creator of a comedy character possessing originality that amounted to genius."[37] The *Detroit Times* said Williams was "one of the premier funsters of the American stage."[38]

The *New York Times* praised Williams as a comedy actor: "Williams had a comedy method of his own. . . . Although not really a great singer, he could put over with great effect a song that was really a funny story told to music."[39]

The editor of the *New York Star* stressed that "repeating the formula that there is no one to replace Bert Williams is merely the stark truth. There is no one to take his place."[40]

After Williams's death, people said how much the comedian had touched or enriched their lives – perhaps one of the greatest tributes one can pay a comedian. David Belasco, theater producer, observed: "What he did, he did perfectly well, and in the doing of it, he performed an important work, rendering a valuable service to society – for he made this world a happier, brighter place to live than it would have been without him."[41]

The style and manner in which Bert Williams made people laugh was recalled by many. Emmett Scott, secretary-treasurer for Howard University, remembered that Williams had standards about comedy.

> To my mind, the biggest and best thing that can be said about Bert Williams' comedy is that it was always clean, and this is a lesson from which many present-day comedians may learn much. He never found it necessary to bring his comedy to the gutter level in order to produce laughter.[42]

Another contribution that Williams made and which is almost forgotten today is the fact that he was the first black American comedian to appear to all segments of society, regardless of race. The *Chicago Defender* summed it up when it declared: "No other performer in the history of the American stage enjoyed the popularity and esteem of all races and classes of theater-goers to the remarkable extent gained by Bert Williams."[43]

With his unique gift of mime and uncanny talent at being both tragic and comic at once, Williams fitted clearly into the heritage of world theater. The drama critic of the Washington, D.C., *Star* made an important observation:

> The death of Bert Williams removes an influence in public entertainment whose importance is greater than the public that seeks to be amused is likely to realize. . . . His school was the theatre . . . broad as the comparison must seem, the school of Aeschylus, Euripides, and Sophocles. As these old poets adapted themselves to their day and excelled in the sublime, Bert Williams adapted himself to his era and excelled in the ridiculous.[44]

In 1922 (as there are today) there were those who chose to focus not on what Bert Williams had done but on what he could have been. For them Williams was a victim of his times. Because of racism, they said, he could not realize his ambition to become a dramatic actor. Among those who portrayed Williams as a bitter man was Heywood Broun of the *New York World*. After Williams's death, Broun wrote: "Bert Williams found prosperity and success in the theatre, but his high talents were largely wasted."[45]

Frustrated, yes, Williams would have said, but not wasted. To those who sought to appraise what his life was about, Williams had this to say: "I don't want people to say of me when I am dead: 'How much did he leave?,' but rather–[if] they say anything at all–'How much did he enjoy?'"[46]

Throughout his life, Williams admitted that he had been hurt by racism. But instead of being angry about it, he laughed about it and made others see the stupidity of racial prejudice. In his song "Nobody," Bert Williams brought out the basic needs of every human being: the need for food and shelter, the need for companionship, the need to be loved. In singing "Nobody," Bert Williams made people feel that they were "Somebody." Bert Williams felt that it was his mission to do that and he enjoyed doing it. He said: "I have no grievance whatever against the world or the people in it; I'm having a grand time."[47]

Appendix A

George William Walker

The career of George William Walker is almost synonymous with that of Bert Williams. Williams's partner for sixteen years, Walker was born in Lawrence, Kansas, around 1873. About 1893 Walker traveled from Kansas to San Francisco via a medicine show run by Dr. Waite. He was offered a job in the Selig and Mastodon Minstrel Show by Bert Williams as one of the end men. Originally, Walker was more of a comedian than Williams, and it must be speculated how much Williams was influenced by Walker in his use of comedy.

After playing in the Midway Plaisance, a dive in downtown San Francisco, Williams and Walker took to the road. They were en route to Chicago with a medicine show when they encountered racism in a Colorado mining town. This caused them to leave the medicine show and strike out for Chicago on their own. Rejected by the management of the new black show—*The Octoroons*—Walker and Williams revised their act. The result was that with Williams as comic and Walker as a foil, the act was more successful. They were recruited for a Broadway show—*The Gold Bug*—in Indiana in 1896. Two other shows—Eugene Sandow's and *A Good Thing*—followed. But Walker's biggest break was his record-breaking appearance with Williams at Koster and Bial's vaudeville hall in 1896. This performance made New York critics take note of the comedy team.

Walker was proud of being black and had big plans for a national black theater in the United States. He allied himself with the most creative black people of his day—Will Marion Cook, Alex Rogers, and Jesse Shipp—to produce high-class black musical comedies. Among the Williams and Walker shows were: *Senegambian Carnival, A Lucky Coon, The Policy Players, The Sons of Ham, In Dahomey, Abyssinia*, and *Bandanna Land*. Walker was far ahead of his time in utilizing African themes in several of these plays and also in portraying African characters.

Walker was responsible for bringing Aida Overton Walker into the

229

Williams and Walker company. He recognized her talent and was deeply devoted to her. The couple married in 1899. They had no children.

George Walker was one of the first black recording artists, cutting records with Bert Williams for Victor Talking Machine Records in 1901. A member of the National Negro Businessmen's League and a founding member and first president of the Frogs, a black theatrical club, George Walker was also a songwriter (see Appendix B). Walker crusaded for civil rights and fought to get first-class bookings in theaters for Bert Williams and himself. He succeeded in breaking down segregation laws in several cities. Walker spoke out against racism. (See Bibliography for articles by Walker.)

In short, if Bert Williams was the artistic persona of the Williams and Walker team, then George Walker was its business persona. Said the *Indianapolis Freeman*:

> Mr. Walker's executive ability was known only to the manager with whom he had dealings, and they inwardly disliked him because he was bold and fearless enough to stand up for what the services of Williams and Walker were worth. (16 Jan. 1911)

During the run of *Bandanna Land,* Walker became ill. His illness was diagnosed as paresis, a late stage of syphilis. Because penicillin was not available in 1909, the disease was fatal. George Williams Walker died January 6, 1911, in Islip, New York, at the age of thirty-eight.

Aida Overton Walker

She was born Ada Wilmon Overton on February 14, 1880, in New York City. She later changed her name to Aida. The daughter of Moses Overton and Pauline Whitfield, Aida Overton studied dance as a youngster and at age 16 joined the Black Patti Troubadours. She left that company when Bob Cole and other blacks asked for more pay and better working conditions. A friend asked Aida to join her in posing for an advertisement for a tobacco product with Williams and Walker. Aida posed, collected her pay, and went home. George Walker had to beg her to return to the stage as one of the cakewalk dancers in Williams and Walker's vaudeville act. Before long, the couple was married; they had no children.

Aida Overton Walker was an original member of the Williams and Walker organization, from 1899 to 1908. She was regarded as the "third wheel" in the company, right after her husband and Bert Williams in popularity. Mrs. Walker's signature song was "I'm Miss Hannah from Savannah," which she taught to a very young Florence Mills.

Aida Overton Walker was noted for her dancing first with her husband, George, and later as a single in vaudeville. During her lifetime, she was regarded as the best black female dancer in the United States and was often compared with white female modern dancers. Mrs. Walker won praise for cakewalking in Great Britain during the run of *In Dahomey*. This critical acclaim was topped by numerous invitations to social affairs at Buckingham Palace, among British high society, and at schools like Oxford.

Mrs. Walker must be regarded as the first black female choreographer. She was known for her renditions of classical dances like "Salome," as well as ballroom and black dances. Aida Overton Walker choreographed the Williams and Walker shows, *Abyssinia* and *Bandanna Land*. It is said that she had a financial as well as artistic interest in several dance groups she performed with in vaudeville.

When her husband fell ill during the run of *Bandanna Land*, Mrs. Walker took over his role, rendering an acceptable male impersonation and comedy acting with Bert Williams. She left the Williams and Walker organization in 1909 to join Bob Cole and John Rosamond Johnson's company. Mrs. Walker played one of the female leads in their effort *The Red Moon*. She also had a leading role in the 1910–11 show, *His Honor the Barber*. Her reviews for both shows were outstanding.

Mrs. Walker wrote several articles advising black women aspiring to the theater (see Bibliography). She gave numerous benefits for black people, and these were always big social events. She performed in vaudeville with Bobby Kemp in 1911 and Lackaye Grant in 1914. Her act at the Pekin Theater in Chicago was said to be her greatest professional triumph. Aida Overton Walker rejoined Bert Williams in 1913 as part of the Frogs Frolic but did not tour with him.

The strain of overworking took its toll on Mrs. Walker, who was exhausted after losing both her husband and mother to death in a short time. Her last stage appearance was on August 16, 1914, in New York City. Friends said that she had been not well for some time but refused to rest. Aida Overton Walker died October 11, 1914, in New York City, of a kidney ailment. She was reportedly only thirty-four.

Appendix B

Musical Compositions of Bert Williams

"Believe Me." Lyrics by Alex Rogers. Chicago: Will Rossiter, 1909.

"Blackville Strutters Ball." Lyrics and music with George W. Walker. New York: Hurtig and Seamon, 1900.

"Borrow from Me." Lyrics by Jean Havez. New York: Jerome H. Remick, 1912.

"By-Gone Days in Dixie." Lyrics by Alex Rogers. Chicago: Will Rossiter, 1909.

"Chink, Chink Chinaman." Lyrics by Alex Rogers. Chicago: Will Rossiter, 1909.

"Dance of the Toads." Lyrics by Bert Williams. New York: P. F. Howley, 1898.

"Darktown Poker Club." Lyrics by Jean Havez. Music with Will Vodery. New York: Jerome H. Remick, 1914.

"Dat's Harmony." Lyrics by Grant Clark. New York: Jerome H. Remick, 1911.

"Dora Dean." Lyrics by Bert Williams. Arranged by George W. Hertzel, San Francisco: Broder & Schlam, c. 1895–96.

"Fas', Fas' World." Lyrics by Alex Rogers. New York: Gotham-Attucks, 1907.

"Forget It! Don't You Care?" Lyrics by Bert Williams. New York: Howley, Haviland, 1899.

"Fortune Telling Man." Music and lyrics with George W. Walker. New York: Joseph W. Stern, 1901.

"Ghost of a Coon." Music and lyrics with George W. Walker. Arranged by William H. Tyers. New York: Joseph W. Stern, 1900.

"Hannah, You Won't Do!" Music and lyrics with George W. Walker. New York: M. Witmark, 1896.

"Harbor of Lost Dreams." Music and lyrics with George W. Walker. Chicago: Will Rossiter, 1909.

"He's Up Against the Real Thing Now." Lyrics by Edward Furber. New York: Joseph W. Stern, 1898.

"Here It Comes Again." Lyrics by Earle C. Jones and Alex Rogers. New York: Gotham-Attucks, 1906.

"Honey You Made a Hit with Me." Music and lyrics with Ernest Hogan, New York: Broder & Schram, 1897.

"I Don't Like No Cheap Man." Music and lyrics with George W. Walker. Arranged by William H. Tyers. New York: Joseph W. Stern, 1897.

"I Got de Headache Now." (A Darkey Lamentation) Music and lyrics with George W. Walker. Arranged by William H. Tyers. New York: Joseph W. Stern, 1897.

"I Got Money Locked Up in a Vault." Original music and lyrics by Irving Jones. Revised 1899 by Bert Williams and George W. Walker.

"I Guess That Will Hold You for a While." Music and lyrics with Walter Smart, New York: Howley, Haviland & Co.,1897.

"I Thought I Was a Winner." (Comic Song and Refrain with Coon Parody) Lyrics by Bert Williams. Chicago: S. Brainard's Sons, 1896.

"I'd Rather Have Nothing All of the Time (Than Something for a Little While)." Lyrics by John B. Lowitz. New York: Gotham-Attucks, 1908.

"If I Should Die Before I Wake (How Will I Know I'm Dead?)." Lyrics by Thomas J. Gray. New York: Joseph W. Stern, 1910.

"If You Love Your Baby, Make Goo Goo Eyes." Music and lyrics with George W. Walker. New York: Hurtig and Seamon, 1900.

"I'm a Cooler for the Warmest Coon in Town." Music and lyrics with George A. Walker. New York: Joseph W. Stern, 1897.

"I'm Cured." Lyrics by Jean Havez. New York: Jerome H. Remick, 1914.

"Island of By and By." Lyrics by Alex Rogers. New York: Gotham-Attucks, 1906.

"It Ain't No Use to Sing Dem Songs to Me." Music and lyrics with George W. Walker. New York: Joseph W. Stern, 1902.

"It's Hard to Find a King Like Me." Lyrics by Alex Rogers. New York: Gotham-Attucks, 1906.

"I've Been Livin' Moderate All My Life." Lyrics by George W. Walker. Arranged by William H. Tyers. New York: Joseph W. Stern, 1900.

"Jig." London: F. F. Keith. Prowse, 1903.

"Jolly Jungle Boys." Lyrics by Earle C. Jones. New York: Gotham-Attucks, 1906.

"Late Hours." Lyrics by David Kempner. New York: Gotham-Attucks, 1907.

"Let It Alone." Lyrics by Alex Rogers. New York: Gotham-Attucks, 1906.

"Little Moses." Lyrics by Earle C. Jones. New York: Gotham-Attucks, 1905.

"Look Down Dar Below." Music and lyrics with George W. Walker. New York: W. B. Gray, 1897.

"Lorraine." Lyrics by Earle C. Jones. New York: Gotham-Attucks, 1905.

"Ma South Car'lina Gal." Music and lyrics with George W. Walker. Arranged by William H. Tyers. New York: Joseph W. Stern, 1898.

"Mammy's Little Pickaninny Boy." (Ethiopian Lullaby) Music and lyrics with George W. Walker. Chicago: M. Witmark, 1896.

"Medicine Man." Music and lyrics with George W. Walker. New York: Joseph W. Stern, 1899.

"Miss Brown's Cakewalk." Lyrics by Bert Williams. Chicago: S. Brainard's Sons, 1896.

"Miss Georgia." Lyrics by Alex Rogers. New York: Attucks, 1905.

"My Landlady." Lyrics by Fred E. Mierisch and James T. Brymm. New York: Leo Feist, 1912.

"My Old Man." Lyrics by Alex Rogers. Chicago: Will Rossiter, 1909.

"No Coon Can Come Too Black for Me." Lyrics by Walter Smart. New York: Howley, Haviland & Co., 1898.

"Nobody." Lyrics by Alex Rogers. New York: Attucks, 1905.

"Not a Coon Came Out the Way That He Went In." Music and lyrics with George W. Walker. New York: Joseph W. Stern, 1899.

"Oh, I Don't Know, You're Not So Warm." (Comic Song and Refrain with Coon Parody) Lyrics by Bert Williams. Arranged by D. A. Lewis. Chicago: S. Brainard's Sons, 1897.

"Rastus Johnson, U.S.A." Lyrics by Alex Rogers. New York: Gotham-Attucks, 1906.

"She's Getting More Like the White Folks Every Day." Music and lyrics with George W. Walker. New York: Shapiro, Bernstein and Von Tilzer, 1901.

"Snap Shot Sal." Music and lyrics with George W. Walker. New York: Feist and Frankenthaler, 1899.

"Tale of the Monkey Maid (or Die Trying)." Lyrics by Alex Rogers. New York: Gotham-Attucks, 1906.

"That's a Plenty." Lyrics by Henry S. Creamer. Chicago: Will Rossiter Co., 1909.

"Trip to Coontown." Lyrics by Bob Cole and Billy Johnson. New York: Haviland, 1897.

"The Vampire." Lyrics by Earle C. Jones and Gene Buck. New York: Jerome H. Remick, 1914.

"The Voodoo Man." (Coon Chant) Music and lyrics with George W. Walker. New York: Hurtig and Seamon, 1900.

"When It's All Goin' Out and Nothin' Comin' In." Music and lyrics with George W. Walker. Lyrics revised by James W. Johnson. New York: Joseph W. Stern, 1902.

"When Miss Maria Johnson Marries Me." (Negro Song) Music and lyrics with George W. Walker. New York: Hurtig and Seamon, 1900.

"When Zacharias Lead the Band." Music and lyrics with George W. Walker. New York: Joseph H. Stern, 1901.

"Where My Forefathers Died." Lyrics by Alex Rogers. New York: Gotham-Attucks, 1906.

"White Folks Call It Chantecler, but It's Just Plain Chicken to Me." Lyrics by Andrew B. Sterling. New York: Harry Von Tilzer, 1910.

"Why Don't You Get a Lady of Your Own?" Music and lyrics with George W. Walker. New York: Joseph W. Stern, 1901.

"You're Gwine to Get Somethin' What You Don't Expect." Lyrics by Vincent Bryan. New York: Leo Feist, 1910.

"You're on the Right Road, but You're Going the Wrong Way." Lyrics by Jean Havez. New York: Jerome H. Remick, 1912.

Notes

Abbreviations Used in Notes

Age	*New York Age*
AMT	Bordman, Gerald. *American Musical Theatre: A Chronicle*. New York: Oxford University Press, 1978.
BIB	Sampson, Henry T. *Blacks in Blackface: A Sourcebook on Early Black Musicals*. Metuchen, New Jersey: Scarecrow Press, 1980.
COC	Bordman, Gerald. *The Concise Oxford Companion to American Theatre*. New York: Oxford University Press, 1987.
DM	*New York Dramatic Mirror*
Freeman	*Indianapolis Freeman*
GW	Sampson, Henry T. *The Ghost Walks: A Chronological History of Blacks in Show Business, 1865-1910*. Metuchen, New Jersey: Scarecrow Press, 1988.
JBJ	Riis, Thomas L. *Just Before Jazz: Black Musical Theater in New York, 1890-1915*. Washington: Smithsonian Institution Press, 1989.
MOBA	Southern, Eileen. *The Music of Black Americans: A History*. 2nd ed. New York & London: W. W. Norton & Co. 1983
NOB	Charters, Ann. *Nobody: The Story of Bert Williams*. New York: Macmillan, 1970.
NYMA	Municipal Archives of the City of New York.
NYPL	Clipping files of the Billy Rose Theater Collection, New York Public Library.
NYT	*New York Times.*
ROW	Rowland, Mabel, ed. *Bert Williams: Son of Laughter*. New York: English Crafters, 1923.

Preface

1. Joseph Boskin, *Sambo: The Rise & Demise of an American Jester*. (New York: Oxford University Press, 1986), pp. 10–11. Ironically, the illustration chosen for the *New York Times* book review of Boskin's book was a photograph of Williams and Walker in 1895. See Robert G. O'Meally, "An Icon Through History," *New York Times Book Review*), 4 Jan. 1987, p. 8.
2. Allen Woll, *Black Musical Theatre from Coontown to Dreamgirls*. (Baton Rouge: Louisiana State University Press, 1989), p. xiii.

Chapter 1

1. *Chicago Record-Herald*, "Bert Williams: Boy-Gentleman, Comedian," 25 Sept. 1910, sec. 6, p. 7; Paul Asbury, *The Story of the Bahamas*. (London: Macmillan/Macmillan Caribbean, 1975), p. 123.

2. Asbury, p. 124.

3. Other Bert Williams biographers have claimed his grandfather's name was Svend Eric Williams. But "Svend Eric" may have been a nickname. See ROW, p. 1, and *NOB*, p. 15. On both the birth and death certificates of Frederick Williams, Jr., Frederick Williams (Sr.) and Emiline Armbrister are named as parents. See death certificate, Frederick Williams (Jr.), 1 April 1912 NYMA; *Register of Births*, 5 Oct. 1850, Registrar General's Office, Nassau, N.P. Bahamas.

4. Bert A. Williams, "The Comic Side of Trouble," *American Magazine* 85 (January 1918), p. 34.

5. Booker T. Washington, "Interesting People," *American Magazine* 70 (September 1910), p. 600; Rennold Wolf, "The Greatest Comedian of the American Stage," *Green Book Magazine* 7 (June 1912), p. 1174.

6. Lloyd Lewis, "Life with Uncle Eggs," *Chicago Sun*, 21 April 1946 (weekly book supplement, p. 3). Frederick Williams, Sr.'s occupation is given as "jeweler" on his son's birth certificate. See birth certificate, *Register of Births*, 5 Oct. 1850, Registrar General's Office, Nassau, N.P. Bahamas.

7. Wolf, p. 1174.

8. Asbury, pp. 79–80.

9. *NOB*, p. 15.

10. Williams, *American Magazine*, p. 34; see also *NOB*, p. 15, for a similar citation.

11. ROW, pp. 4–5.

12. Lewis, p. 3.

13. ROW, p. 2; see also *NOB*, p. 15.

14. Ibid.

15. Charles Ives, *The Isles of Summer; or Nassau and the Bahamas*, ill. ed. (New Haven, Conn.: published by the author, 1880), p. 268.

16. Asbury, pp. 150, 153.

17. Ives, p. 269.

18. Wolf, p. 1174

19. Washington, p. 600.

20. On the birth certificate of Bert Williams, his father's occupation is given as: "Waiter, R. V. Hotel." *Register of Births*, 12 Nov. 1874, Registrar General's Office, Nassau, N.P. Bahamas.

21. Asbury, p. 223.

22. ROW, p. 2; see also *NOB*, p. 15.

23. Al Rose, *Eubie Blake*. (New York: Schirmer Books, 1979), p. 34.

24. *Register of Births*, 12 Nov. 1874, Registrar General's Office, Nassau, N.P. Bahamas.

25. Williams, p. 34. See also parallel quotation in *NOB*, p. 15.

26. *NYT*, "Ivory Williams," 27 March 1933, p. 15.

27. Death certificate of Ivory Williams. Vermillion County, Illinois, Department of Public Health, Vital Records Division, 27 March 1933.

28. Bert A. Williams, "Keeping Up with the New Laughs," *Theater Magazine* 29, no. 220 (June 1919), p. 346.

29. Washington, p. 600.

30. See *Age*, "Bert Williams Now a Full-Fledged Citizen," 22 June 1918, p. 1.

31. ROW, pp. 7–8.

32. Asbury, p. 169.

33. *Chicago Record-Herald*, "Bert Williams: Boy-Gentleman, Comedian," 25 Sept. 1910, sec. 6, p. 7.

34. Williams, *American Magazine*, p. 34.

35. Merlin Stonehouse, *John Wesley North and the Reform Frontier*. (Minneapolis: University of Minnesota Press, 1965), p. 225. See *NOB*, p. 17.

36. Obituary of Bert A. Williams, *Riverside Daily Press*, 8 March 1922, p. 3.

37. Williams, *American Magazine*, p. 34.

38. ROW, p. 9. See also *NOB*, p. 16 for same account.

39. Lewis, p. 3.

40. *Chicago Record-Herald*, 25 Sept. 1910, p. 7.

41. Lewis, p. 3.

42. *Chicago Record-Herald*, 25 Sept. 1910, p. 7. Williams's school records are difficult to trace. Although the Riverside Press credits Williams with graduating from the 14th Street School, the present-day Riverside school district ironically has no records of this school. Personal communication to the author from Riverside Unified Schools, 10 September 1990.

43. *Riverside Daily Press*, 8 March 1922, p. 3.

44. Washington, pp. 600–601.

45. Williams, *American Magazine*, p. 34.

46. Personal communication to the author from Stanford University Libraries, Special Collections Department, 5 Sept. 1989.

47. Bert Williams, "My Trip Abroad," "Diary," circa 1900. Cited courtesy of San Francisco Performing Arts Library and Museum.

48. Williams, *American Magazine*, p. 34.

49. Washington, pp. 601, 603.

50. Williams, *American Magazine*, p. 34.

51. Ibid.

52. ROW, pp. 11–12. See similar quotation in *NOB*, p. 18.

53. William Selig is described as having been the "owner of a traveling minstrel show." Benjamin B. Hampton, *History of the American Film Industry from Its Beginnings to 1931*. (New York: Dover Publications, Inc., 1970), p. 24.

54. Terry Ramsaye, *A Million and One Nights*. (New York: Simon & Schuster, 1964), p. 303.

Chapter 2

1. Bert A. Williams, "Bert Williams Tells of Walker," *Freeman*, 14 Jan. 1911, p. 5.

2. See *MOBA*, p. 229.

3. Ibid., pp. 88–89.

4. Ibid., p. 90.

5. Ibid., p. 232.

238   BERT WILLIAMS

6. Ibid., p. 92.

7. Robert C. Toll, *Blacking Up: The Minstrel Show in Nineteenth Century America.* (New York: Oxford University Press, 1974), p. 54.

8. *MOBA*, p. 92.

9. Terry Ramsaye, *A Million and One Nights.* (New York: Simon & Schuster, 1964), pp. 303–304.

10. Williams, *Freeman*, 14 Jan. 1911, p. 5. See also similar citation in *NOB*, p. 21.

11. *Age*, "Bert Williams' Stage Career," 11 March 1922, p. 2.

12. Ibid.

13. Williams, *Freeman*, 14 Jan. 1911, p. 5.

14. George W. Walker, "Bert and Me and Them," *Age*, 24 Dec. 1908, p. 4.

15. Herbert Asbury, *The Barbary Coast: An Informal History of the San Francisco Underworld.* (New York: Alfred A. Knopf, 1923), p. 131.

16. Walker, *Age*, 24 Dec. 1908, p. 4.

17. William Issel, *San Francisco, 1865–1932: Politics, Power and Urban Development* (Berkeley: University of California Press, 1986), p. 111.

18. *San Francisco Examiner*, "Thousands at the Fair," 2 Jan. 1894, p. 10.

19. George W. Walker, "The Negro on the American Stage," *Colored American Magazine* 11, no. 4 (August 1906), p. 248.

20. *San Francisco Examiner*, "Samuel in the Bear Pit," 3 May 1894, p. 4.

21. Walker, *Colored American Magazine*, p. 248.

22. Rennold Wolf, "The Greatest Comedian on the American Stage," *Green Book Magazine* 7 (June 1912), pp. 1175, 1177.

23. David A. Jasen, *Tin Pan Alley.* (New York: Donald I. Fine, Inc., 1988), p. 10.

24. Tom Fletcher, *100 Years of the Negro in Show Business.* (New York: Burdge, 1954), p. 229. See also *JBJ*, p. 167.

25. Williams, *Freeman*, 14 Jan. 1911, p. 5.

26. Howard R. Lamor, ed., *Reader's Encyclopedia of the American West.* (New York: Thomas Y. Crowell, 1977), p. 275.

27. Benjamin McKie Rastall, "The Labor History of the Cripple Creek District: A Study in Industrial Revolution," *Bulletin of the University of Wisconsin* 3, no. 1 (1908) (economics and political science series), p. 16.

28. Ibid., p. 63.

29. ROW, p. 156. See also *NOB*, pp. 25–26.

30. Williams, *Freeman*, 14 Jan. 1911, p. 5.

31. James Haskins, *Black Theater in America.* (New York: Thomas Y. Crowell, 1982), p. 34.

32. *JBJ*, p. 20.

33. Toll, p. 76.

34. *Freeman*, 3 July 1897. Quoted in *BIB*, p. 62.

35. *NOB*, pp. 26–27.

36. ROW, p. 34.

37. Williams, *Freeman*, 14 Jan. 1911, p. 5.

38. Bert A. Williams, "The Comic Side of Trouble," *American Magazine* 85 (January 1918), p. 60. See also *NOB*, p. 28.

39. Walker, *Age*, 24 Dec. 1908, p. 4.

40. William Foster, "Memoirs of William Foster: Pioneers of the Stage." In Theophilus Lewis, ed. *The Official Theatrical World of Colored Artists.* (New York: Theatrical World Publishing Company, 1928), p. 44.

41. Williams, *American Magazine*, p. 60. See also parallel passage in *NOB*, p. 28.

Chapter 3

1. Richard Traubner, *Operetta: A Theatrical History*. (New York: Oxford University Press, 1983), pp. 366–367.

2. *AMT*, p. 139.

3. Ibid, p. 46.

4. Edward N. Waters, *Victor Herbert: A Life in Music*. (New York: Macmillan, 1955), pp. 116–117.

5. *AMT*, p. 146.

6. George Lederer interview, *Variety*, 17 March 1922, p. 14.

7. Ibid.

8. The history of the Casino Theater is given in Mary C. Henderson, *The City and the Theatre*. (Clifton, N. J.: James T. White and Company, 1973).

9. *Variety*, 17 March 1922, p. 14.

10. Ibid.

11. Ibid.

12. *DM*, "Casino – The Gold Bug," 26 Sept. 1896, p. 14.

13. For Victor Herbert, says Gerald Bordman, *The Gold Bug* was "one of the worst failures of his career." *AMT*, p. 146.

14. Edward A. Dithmar, "The Theatres," *NYT*, 27 Sept. 1896, sec. 3, p. 12.

15. Bert A. Williams, "Bert Williams Tells of Walker," *Freeman*, 14 Jan. 1911, p. 5.

16. *Boston Globe*, "Mr. Dailey's Success in a McNally Farce," 6 Oct. 1896, p. 2.

17. Ibid. See also program, Hollis Street Theatre, Boston, 5 Oct. 1896, *A Good Thing*, in NYPL.

18. Williams, *Freeman*, 14 Jan. 1911, p. 5.

19. Anthony Slide, *The Vaudevillians: A Dictionary of Vaudeville Performers*. (Westport, Conn.: Arlington House, 1981), p. 134.

20. George W. Walker, "The Negro on the American Stage," *Colored American Magazine* 11, no. 4 (August 1906), p. 246.

21. *DM*, Vaudeville Jottings," 17 Oct. 1896, p. 18.

22. Ibid.

23. George W. Walker, "Bert and Me and Them," *Age*, 24 Dec. 1908, p. 4.

Chapter 4

1. Martin W. Laforse and James A. Drake, *Popular Culture and American Life*. (Chicago: Nelson-Hall, 1981), p. 107.

2. Douglas Gilbert, *American Vaudeville: Its Life and Times*. (New York: Dover Publications, Inc., 1940), p. 4.

3. Frank B. Copley, "The Story of a Great Vaudeville Manager," *American Magazine* 94 (December 1922), p. 153.

4. Bernard Sobel, *A Picture History of Vaudeville*. (New York: Citadel Press,

1961), pp. 58–59; John E. DiMeglio, *Vaudeville, U.S.A.* (Bowling Green, Ohio: Bowling Green Popular Press, 1973), p. 35.

    5. DiMeglio, pp. 35–36.

    6. Sobel, pp. 58–59.

    7. DiMeglio, p. 19.

    8. Mary C. Henderson, *The City and the Theatre.* (Clifton, N.J.: James T. White and Company, 1973), p. 147.

    9. Laforse, p. 131.

    10. *DM*, 7 Nov. 1896, p. 17.

    11. *DM*, 9 Jan. 1897, p. 17.

    12. *DM*, 16 Jan. 1897, p. 19.

    13. William Foster, "Memoirs of William Foster: Pioneers of the Stage." In Theophilus Lewis, ed., *The Official Theatrical World of Colored Artists.* (New York: Theatrical World Publishing Company, 1928), p. 47.

    14. Ibid.

    15. Ibid.

    16. James Haskins with Kathleen Benson, *Scott Joplin.* (Garden City, N.Y.: Doubleday, 1978), p. 102.

    17. Personal communication to the author from David A. Jasen.

    18. Terry Waldo, *This Is Ragtime.* (New York: Hawthorn Books, Inc., 1976), pp. 25–26.

    19. Lynne Fauley Emery, *Black Dance in the United States from 1619 to 1970.* (New York: Dance Horizons, 1980), p. 92.

    20. Waldo, pp. 25–26.

    21. Jack Donahue, "Hoofing," *Saturday Evening Post* 202, no. 11, 14 Sept. 1924, p. 29; Carl Van Vechten, *In the Garret.* (New York: Knopf, 1920), pp. 313–14.

    22. Marshall and Jean Stearns, *Jazz Dance: The Story of American Vernacular Dance.* (New York: Schirmer Books, 1979), p. 197.

    23. Ibid., p. 54.

    24. W. E. B. DuBois, *The Philadelphia Negro: A Social Study* (together with a special report on domestic service by Isabel Eaton). (New York: Benjamin Blom, 1899), p. 320.

    25. *DM*, 27 Feb. 1897, p. 17.

    26. *Freeman*, 29 Feb. 1897. Cited in *GW*, p. 125.

    27. *DM*, "Philadelphia Vaudeville Correspondence," 27 March 1897, p. 20.

    28. *NYT*, "Notes of the Week," 4 April 1897, p. 16.

    29. Ethel Barrymore, *Memories: An Autobiography.* (New York: Harper & Brothers, 1955), p. 178.

    30. *DM*, 17 April 1897, p. 17.

    31. Advertisement in *Pall Mall Gazette* (London), 19 April 1897, p. 1; Bert A. Williams, "The Comic Side of Trouble," *American Magazine* 85 (January 1918), p. 60.

    32. Advertisement in *Boston Globe*, 18 July 1897, p. 19.

    33. *Boston Globe*, "Keith's Theatre," 20 July 1897, p. 7.

    34. *Boston Globe*, 25 July 1897, pp. 18–19.

    35. *DM*, "San Francisco," April 30, 1898, p. 18.

    36. *DM*, "Proctor's," 1 Jan. 1898, p. 16; "I Don't Like No Cheap Man." Music and lyrics by Bert A. Williams and George W. Walker. Arranged by W. H. Tyers. Copyright 1897 by Joseph W. Stern & Company. Copyright assigned to Edward B. Marks Music Co. Copyright renewed 1924 by Lottie Williams.

37. James Weldon Johnson, *Black Manhattan*. (New York: Alfred A. Knopf, 1930), p. 105. The Vanderbilt letter is also cited in *NOB*, p. 36.

Chapter 5

1. *MOBA*, p. 268.
2. *JBJ*, pp. 42–43.
3. Edward Kennedy Ellington, *Music Is My Mistress*. (Garden City, N.Y.: Doubleday, 1973), pp. 96–97.
4. Will Marion Cook, "Clorindy, the Origin of the Cakewalk," *Theatre Arts* 31 (September 1947), p. 61. Among African Americans, "Harry T. Burleigh (1866–1949) was the first to achieve national distinction as a composer, arranger, and concert artist" (*MOBA*, p. 266).
5. For a description of "Black Bohemia," see James Weldon Johnson, *Along This Way: The Autobiography of James Weldon Johnson*. (New York: Viking Penguin, 1933), p. 171.
6. George W. Walker, "The Negro on the American Stage," *Colored American Magazine* 11, no. 4 (August 1906), p. 247.
7. Ibid., p. 61.
8. Ibid., p. 62.
9. Ibid.
10. Ibid., p. 65.
11. Addison, Gayle, *Oak and Ivy: A Biography of Paul Laurence Dunbar*. (Garden City, N.Y.: Doubleday, 1971), p. 86.
12. *Boston Globe*, "Drama and Music," 4 Sept. 1898, p. 18.
13. *Cincinnati Enquirer*, "The Theaters," 20 Sept. 1898, p. 3.
14. *Boston Globe*, "Senegambian Carnival," 2 Sept. 1898, p. 2.
15. *Cincinnati Enquirer*, 20 Sept. 1898, p. 3.
16. *Boston Globe*, 2 Sept. 1898, p. 2.
17. *Washington Post*, "Williams and Walker's Senegambian Carnival at the Academy," 11 Oct. 1898, p. 7.
18. *Cincinnati Enquirer*, 20 Sept. 1898, p. 3.
19. Robert C. Toll, *Blacking Up: The Minstrel Show in Nineteenth Century America*. (New York: Oxford University Press, 1974), p. 68.
20. Ibid., p. 69.
21. *Boston Globe*, "Music and Drama," 2 Sept. 1898, p. 2; *Boston Globe*, 4 Sept. 1898, p. 18.
22. See advertisement re *Clorindy* in *DM*, 20 August 1898, p. 6, for a list of *Clorindy*'s songs.
23. *Boston Globe*, 2 Sept. 1898, p. 2.
24. The birth name, place of birth, names of parents, and date of arrival in New York are from the death certificate of Charlotte Louise Williams, 17 March 1929, Dept. of Health, City of New York, NYMA.
25. *NOB*, p. 60; ROW, p. 37.
26. *NOB*, p. 60. Theater reviews that show Mrs. Williams's name change include *Boston Globe*, 13 March 1901, p. 9, and *Newark Evening News*, 12 Nov. 1901, p. 3. The nonexistence of a marriage certificate in Manhattan c. 1899–1901 is authenticated by

a personal communication to the author from NYMA, 1990. A similar communication from the county clerk of Cook County, Illinois, to the author in 1990, asserted that there is no marriage certificate there for the Williamses.

27. ROW, p. 194.

28. "Who Dat Say Chicken in Dis Crowd?" Music by Will Marion Cook. Lyrics by Paul Laurence Dunbar. New York: M. Witmark & Sons, 1898.

29. *Cincinnati Enquirer*, 20 Sept. 1898, p. 3.

30. Ibid., 20 Sept. 1898, p. 3.

31. *Washington Post*, 11 Oct. 1898, p. 7.

32. *COC*, p. 232.

33. *Brooklyn Eagle*, "The Gayety," 17 Jan. 1899, p. 5.

34. *Washington Post*, "Williams and Walker in A Lucky Coon at the Academy," 9 May 1899, p. 7.

35. "Hottest Coon in Dixie." Music by Will Marion Cook. Lyrics by Paul Laurence Dunbar, New York: M. Witmark & Sons, 1898.

36. *DM*, "Dewey," 14 Jan. 1899, p. 18.

37. *Cleveland Plain Dealer*, "The Star," 18 April 1899, p. 3; *Washington Post*, "Williams and Walker in A Lucky Coon at the Academy," 9 May 1899, p. 7.

38. *Brooklyn Eagle*, "The Gayety," 17 Jan. 1899, p. 5.

39. *Cleveland Plain Dealer*, 18 April, 1899, p. 3.

40. *Washington Post*, 9 May 1899, p. 7.

41. *DM*, 11 March 1899, p. 7; *Brooklyn Eagle*, 17 Jan. 1899, p. 5.

42. *Cleveland Plain Dealer*, 18 April 1899, p. 3.

Chapter 6

1. Tom Fletcher, *100 Years of the Negro in Show Business*. (New York: Burdge, 1954; New York: Da Capo Press, 1984), p. 230.

2. ROW, p. 37.

3. *BIB*, p. 278.

4. Program, *The Policy Players*, Lyceum Theater, Detroit, 17 Dec. 1899.

5. *NYT*, "At Koster and Bial's," 3 April 1900, p. 9.

6. *Louisville Courier-Journal*, "At the Theaters," 27 Nov. 1899, p. 5; *DM*, "Star," 21 Oct. 1899, p. 16; *Brooklyn Eagle*, "The Bijou," 20 March 1900, p. 6.

7. *Boston Globe*, "Music and Drama," 13 March 1900, p. 9.

8. Program, *The Policy Players*, Lyceum Theater, Detroit, 17 Dec. 1899. Although it is certain that the show underwent some changes during its run, the Detroit program is cited as an example of what the show was like.

9. "The Medicine Man." Music and lyrics by Bert A. Williams and George W. Walker. Arranged by William H. Tyers. Copyright 1899 by Joseph W. Stern. Copyright reassigned 1922 to Edward B. Marks Company.

10. *Louisville Courier-Journal*, "At the Theaters," 27 No. 1899, p. 5.

11. "The Ghost of a Coon." Music and lyrics by Bert A. Williams and George W. Walker. Arranged by William H. Tyers. New York: Joseph W. Stern, 1900.

12. *Boston Globe*, 13 March 1900, p. 9.

13. *Brooklyn Eagle*, 20 March 1900, p. 6.; *Boston Globe*, 13 March 1900, p. 9.

14. *Boston Globe*, 13 March 1900, p. 9.

15. *Brooklyn Eagle*, 13 March 1900, p. 9.

16. *Baltimore Sun*, "Farce at the Holliday," 7 Nov. 1899, p. 7.

17. *Brooklyn Eagle*, 13 March 1900, p. 9.

18. *Louisville Courier-Journal*, 27 Nov. 1899, p. 5.

19. *Louisville Courier-Journal*, 7 Nov. 1899, p. 5.

20. *Boston Globe*, 13 March 1900, p. 9.

21. *Detroit Free Press*, "The Stage," 18 Dec. 1899, p. 4.

22. *Cleveland Plain Dealer*, "The Policy Players," 12 Dec. 1899, p. 5.

23. *Detroit Free Press*, 18 Dec. 1899, p. 4.

24. *DM*, "Star," 21 Oct. 1899, p. 16.

25. *Louisville Courier-Journal*, 27 Nov. 1899, p. 5; *DM*, "Harlem Music Hall," 21 Oct. 1899, p. 18.

26. *Philadelphia Inquirer*, "The Policy Players – Auditorium," 27 March 1900, p. 5.

27. *DM*, "Star – Sons of Ham," 20 Oct. 1900, p. 17.

28. "Miss Hannah from Savannah." Music by Richard C. McPherson (Cecil Mack). Lyrics by Tom Lemonier. New York: Joseph W. Stern Co., 1901.

29. "Hard-Hearted Hannah." Music by Milton Ager. Lyrics by Bob Bigelow, Charles Bak and Jack Yellen, 1929.

30. *Salt Lake Herald*, "Amusements," 17 May 1902, p. 4; *NYT*, "Sons of Ham Pleases," 4 March 1902, p. 4.

31. *New York Telegraph*, cited in *GW*, p. 238.

32. *Cleveland Plain Dealer*, "Lyceum Theatre," 11 Feb. 1902, p. 4; *Denver Post*, "The Sons of Ham," 25 May 1901, sec. 2, p. 1; *San Francisco Chronicle*, "The Playbills For This Week," 7 April 1902, p. 2. *Kansas City Star*, "Grand – Williams and Walker," 6 Jan. 1902, p. 3.

33. The identity of the song is uncertain. It may have been "I Wants to Be the Leading Lady," music by Harry Van Tilzer, lyrics by George Totten Smith (1901), or "I Am de Leading Lady ob de Town," music and lyrics by Theodore Lane (1902).

34. "The Phrenologist Coon." Music by Will Accooe, lyrics by Ernest Hogan. New York: Joseph W. Stern Co., 1901.

35. *San Francisco Chronicle*, 7 April 1902, p. 2.

36. *Detroit Free Press*, 3 Feb. 1902, p. 4.

37. "My Castle on the Nile." Music by John Rosamond Johnson. Lyrics by Bob Cole and James Weldon Johnson. New York: Joseph W. Stern Company, 1901.

38. *New York Telegraph*, 20 September 1901 cited in *GW*, pp. 237–238.

39. "When It's All Goin' Out and Nothin' Comin' In." Music and lyrics by Bert A. Williams and George W. Walker. New York: Joseph W. Stern, 1902.

40. Bert A. Williams, "Keeping Up with the New Laughs," *Theatre Magazine* 29, no. 220 (June 1919), p. 348.

41. *Detroit Free Press*, 3 Feb. 1902, p. 4.

42. *Philadelphia Inquirer*, "Auditorium – Sons of Ham," 9 April 1901, p. 5.

43. *Brooklyn Eagle*, 1 Oct. 1901, p. 6; *Cincinnati Enquirer*, 9 Dec. 1901, p. 6; *Salt Lake Herald*, 17 May 1902, p. 4; *Denver Post*, "The Sons of Ham," 25 May 1901, sec. 2, p. 1; *San Francisco Chronicle*, 7 April 1902, p. 2.

44. *Brooklyn Eagle*, 1 Oct. 1901, p. 6.

45. *Chicago Tribune*, "The Sons of Ham," 15 June 1902, p. 40.

46. *Kansas City Star*, "Grand – Williams and Walker," 6 Jan. 1902, p. 40.

47. *Freeman*, 15 Dec. 1900, p. 2.

48. *Freeman*, 18 May 1901, p. 5; *Freeman*, 27 April 1901, p. 5.

49. *DM*, "Vaudeville," 22 June, 1901, p. 16.

50. "Good Morning, Carrie." Music by Richard C. McPherson. Lyrics by Elmer Bowman and Chris Smith. Windsor Music Company, 1901.

51. Jim Walsh, "Favorite Pioneer Recording Artists: Bert Williams, a Thwarted Genius," *Hobbies*. (September 1950), p. 25.

52. "Discography," in *NOB*, pp. 150–1.

53. *JBJ*, p. 114. Bert Williams can be heard today on the following available LPs: *Follies, Scandals and Other Diversions from Ziegfeld to the Shuberts*, New World Records, NW 215, 1977; and *Nobody and Other Songs*, Folkways Records RBF 602, 1981. The original Williams recordings from 1901 to 1922 are now collectors' items.

54. See Appendix A, "White Shows with Individual Songs by Black Composers, 1895-1914," in *JBJ*, p. 192; and Jack Burton, *Blue Book of Broadway Musicals*. With additions by Larry Freeman. (Watkins Glen, N.Y.: Century House, 1952; reprint: 1969), p. 47.

Chapter 7

1. Helen Armstead-Johnson, "Themes and Values in Afro-American Librettos and Book Musicals, 1898-1930," In Glenn Loney, ed., *Musical Theatre in America: Papers and Proceedings of the Conference on the Musical Theatre in America*. (Contributions in Drama and Theatre Studies, no. 8.) (London: Greenwood, 1984), p. 136.

2. James Weldon Johnson, *Along This Way: The Autobiography of James Weldon Johnson*. (New York: Viking Penguin, 1933), p. 175.

3. Armstead-Johnson, p. 136.

4. Ibid.

5. Tom Fletcher, *100 Years of the Negro in Show Business*. (New York: Burdge, 1954), p. 231.

6. For more information, see Edwin S. Redkey, *Black Exodus: Black Nationalist and Back to Africa Movements, 1890-1910*. (New Haven, Conn.: Yale University Press, 1969).

7. Harold R. Issacs, *The New World of Negro Americans*. (New York: John Day Co., 1963), p. 179.

8. S. J. Pryor, "S. J. Pryor Gives Impressions of In Dahomey," *NYT*, 19 July 1903, p. 3.

9. During the 1904-5 season, *In Dahomey* played at the Globe Theater in Boston.

10. *Boston Globe*, 21 Sept. 1902, p. 23.

11. *Boston Globe*, "Music Hall – In Dahomey," 23 Sept. 1902, p. 10; *Boston Globe*, "Boston Music Hall – In Dahomey," 23 Sept. 1902, p. 8.

12. "Grand – In Dahomey," 1 Nov. 1902, in NYPL.

13. *Boston Globe*, 23 Sept. 1902, p. 8.

14. *Boston Herald*, 23 Sept. 1902, p. 10.

15. Ibid.

16. *JBJ*, p. 95.

17. "Molly Green." Music by Will Marion Cook. Lyrics by Cecil Mack (Richard C. McPherson). Copyright by Will Marion Cook, 1902.

18. *Boston Herald*, 23 Sept. 1902, p. 10.

19. Fletcher, p. 236.

20. *Boston Globe*, 23 Sept. 1902, p. 8.

21. *Boston Herald*, 23 Sept. 1902, p. 10.

22. Ibid.

23. "Grand – In Dahomey," in NYPL.

24. *JBJ*, p. 97; "Society." Music by Will Marion Cook. Copyright 1903 by Keith Prowse and Co. Ltd.

25. *Boston Globe*, 23 Sept. 1902, p. 8.

26. In both the New York Theater and Shaftesbury Theatre programs, Hattie McIntosh is assigned this song.

27. "Leaders of the Colored Aristocracy." Music by Will Marion Cook. Lyrics by James Weldon Johnson. Copyright 1902 by Will Marion Cook.

28. *Boston Globe*, 23 Sept. 1902, p. 8.

29. *Boston Herald*, 23 Sept. 1902, p. 10.

30. *Boston Evening Transcript*, "Boston Music Hall – In Dahomey," 23 Sept. 1902, p. 7.

31. Marianna W. Davis, ed., *Contributions of Black Women to America*, 2 vols. (Columbia, S.C.: Kenday Press, 1982), vol. 1, p. 341. Madame Walker became the country's first black female millionaire through her sale of beauty products for black women.

32. *Boston Globe*, 23 Sept. 1902, p. 8.

Chapter 8

1. *AMT*, p. 190.

2. *NOB*, p. 71.

3. William C. Young, *Famous American Playhouses: Documents of American Theatre History*, 2 vols. (Chicago: American Library Associations, 1973), vol. 1, p. 243.

4. Milo L. Smith, "The Klaw-Erlanger Bogeyman Myth," *Players* 44, no. 2 (January 1969): pp. 70–71.

5. Alfred L. Bernheim et. al., *The Business of the Theatre: An Ecomomic History of the American Theatre, 1750–1932*. (New York: Benjamin Blom, Inc. 1932), p. 47.

6. Smith, p. 73.

7. Bernheim, p. 51.

8. *DM*, 30 Nov. 1895, p. 17.

9. Young, pp. 244–246.

10. *NYT*, "Dahomey on Broadway," 13 Feb. 1903, p. 9.

11. *New York World*, "Negro Show Made Stir on Broadway." 19 Feb. 1903, p. 3.

12. *NYT*, 13 Feb. 1903, p. 9.

13. *New York World*, 19 Feb. 1903, p. 3.

14. *New York Mail and Express*, "Stage and Foyer," 19 Feb. 1903, p. 4.

15. *NYT*, 13 Feb. 1903, p. 9.

16. *New York Mail and Express*, 19 Feb. 1903, p. 4.

17. *New York Clipper*, 28 Feb. 1903, p. 6.

18. *NYT*, 13 Feb. 1903, p. 9.

19. *New York Mail and Express*, "News of the Drama," 19 Feb. 1903, p. 4.

20. *New York World*, 19 Feb. 1903, p. 3.

21. Ibid.

22. *New York Mail and Express*, 19 Feb. 1903, p. 4.

23. Anonymous clipping, c. 1903, "A Health Cure in 3 Acts," NYPL.

24. *New York Mail and Express*, 19 Feb. 1903, p. 4.

25. "Broadway in Dahomey By and By." Music by Al Johns. Lyrics by Alex Rogers. New York: Harry Von Tilzer Music Publishing Co., 1902.

26. *New York World*, 19 Feb. 1903, p. 3; *New York Clipper*, 28 Feb. 1903, p. 6.

27. *Freeman*, 4 April 1903. Cited in *GW*, p. 291.

28. *New York World*, 19 Feb. 1903, p. 3; *New York Clipper*, 28 Feb. 1903, p. 6; *GW*, p. 290.

29. *NYT*, 13 Feb. 1903, p. 9.

30. *New York World*, 19 Feb. 1903, p. 3.; *New York Clipper*, 28 Feb. 1903, p. 6.

31. *NYT*, 13 Feb. 1903, p. 9.

32. "A Health Cure in 3 Acts, NYPL; *New York World*, 19 Feb. 1903, p. 3; *New York Mail and Express*, 19 Feb. 1903, p. 4.

33. *New York Herald*, "In Dahomey Is Full of Music," 19 Feb. 1903, p. 13.

34. "I'm a Jonah Man." Music and lyrics by Alex Rogers. New York: M. Witmark & Sons, 1903.

35. *New York World*, 19 Feb. 1903, p. 3; *New York Mail and Express*, 19 Feb. 1903, p. 4; Augusta DaBubna, "The Negro on the Stage," *Theatre Magazine* 3, no. 26 (April 1903), p. 98.

36. *New York Clipper*, 28 Feb. 1903, p. 6.

37. *New York Mail and Express*, 19 Feb. 1903, p. 4.

38. James Montague, "Mister Coon in Town," *New York Evening Journal*, 19 February 1903, editorial page.

Chapter 9

1. *NOB*, p. 77. *In Dahomey* played at the Crown Theatre in Peckham the week of April 4, 1904. Theater program, Crown Theatre, Peckham, England, in Theatre Museum, National Museum of the Performing Arts, London, England. The Oxford engagement is mentioned in Aida Overton Walker's "Colored Men and Women on the Stage," *Colored American Magazine* 9, nos. 4–5 (October 1905), p. 573.

2. Raymond Mander and Joe Mitchenson, *The Lost Theatres of London*. (New York: Taplinger Publishing Company, 1968), p. 493.

3. Ibid., p. 502.

4. ROW, p. 52. See also *NOB*, pp. 71, 76.

5. ROW, p. 53. See also *NOB*, p. 76. The number of people in the Williams and Walker company was cited in *Daily News* (London), "The Dawn of New Music: Negro Aspirations," 16 May 1903, p. 6. With the exception of the *Times* (London), all British reviews of *In Dahomey* are quoted from: Jeffrey Green, "In Dahomey in London in 1903," *The Black Perspective In Music* 11, no 1 (Spring 1983), pp. 23–40.

6. *Daily Mail* (London), "In Dahomey Amusing Production at the Shaftesbury Theatre," 18 May 1903, p. 3. *St. James Gazette* (London), 18 May 1903.

7. *The Star* (London), 17 May 1903, p. 1.

8. "In Dahomey, a musical comedy at the Shaftesbury," *In Dahomey* file, NYPL; *In Dahomey* review, 18 May 1903.

9. *Sunday Sun* (London), 17 May 1903, p. 6.

10. *Daily Mail* (London), 18 May 1903, p. 3.; *Sunday Sun* (London) 17 May 1903, p. 6.

11. *The Times* (London), "Shaftesbury Theater," 18 May 1903, p. 12.

12. *The Star* (London), 18 May 1903, p. 1.

13. *The Standard,* 18 May 1903, p. 5.

14. *St. James Gazette* (London), 18 May 1903; *The Globe* (London), 18 May 1903, p. 8.; *Daily News* (London), 18 May 1903, back page.

15. *The Era* (London), 23 May 1903, p. 16.

16. *The Star* (London), 18 May 1903, p. 1; *The Playgoer,* "In Dahomey at the Shaftesbury Theatre," 1903, p. 469, in NYPL.

17. *Pall Mall Gazette,* 18 May 1903, p. 11; *The Sphere* (London), 23 May 1903, p. 162; *The Globe* (London), 18 May 1903, p. 8.

18. *The Times* (London), 18 May 1903, p. 12.

19. "Annie Laurie" by Williams Douglas. From Margaret Bradford Boni, ed., *Fireside Book of Folksongs* (New York: Simon & Schuster, 1947), p. 110.

20. "Dahomean Queen." Music by John Leubrie Hill. Lyrics by Frank B. Williams. Copyright 1903 by M. Witmark and Sons Co.

21. "Swing Along." Copyright 1902 by Will Marion Cook. Copyright 1912 by G. Schirmer.

22. *The Playgoer,* p. 466.

23. Harry Von Tilzer was a famous Tin Pan Alley publisher and composer. His best-known songs include "Shine On, Harvest Moon," "Wait Till The Sun Shines, Nelly," and "I Want a Girl (Just Like the Girl That Married Dear Old Dad)."

24. Thomas L. Riis, "Black Musical Theater in New York, 1890–1915," Ph.D dissertation, University of Michigan, 1981, p. 176.

25. James Weldon Johnson, *Along This Way: The Autobiography of James Weldon Johnson.* (New York: Viking Press, 1933), p. 177.

26. A reference to Mrs. Leslie Carter, who appeared in the 1903 David Belasco production of "Du Barry."

27. A reference to Williams and Walker's famous song – "Good Morning Carrie" – composed in 1901 by Chris Smith, J. Timm Brymm, and R. C. McPherson.

28. "I Wants to Be an Actor Lady." Music by Harry Von Tilzer. Lyrics by Vincent Bryan. Copyright 1902 by Harry Von Tilzer Music Publishing Co.

29. The biographical sketch of Abbie Mitchell is compiled from Henry T. Sampson, *BIB,* pp. 279, 358; Eileen Southern, *Biographical Dictionary of Afro American and African Musicians.* (Westport, Conn.: Greenwood, 1982), p. 275; Allen Woll, *Dictionary of the Black Theater.* (Westport, Conn., Greenwood, 1983), p. 235.

30. *The Times* (London), 18 May 1903, p. 12.

31. *St. James Gazette* (London), 18 May 1903; *Daily News* (London), 18 May 1903, back page.

32. "Brown Skin Baby Mine." Music by Will Marion Cook. Lyrics by Harry B. Smith and Cecil Mack (Richard C. McPherson). Copyright 1902 by Will Marion Cook as "Gypsy Maid." Copyright 1903 as "Brown Skin Baby Mine."

33. *The Playgoer,* p. 469.

34. *Sunday Sun* (London), 17 May 1903, p. 6.

35. *The Times* (London), 18 May 1903, p. 12.

36. *The Playgoer*, p. 465.

37. *The Times* (London), 18 May 1903, p. 12.

38. *The Globe* (London), 18 May 1903, p. 8.

39. *Pall Mall Gazette*, 18 May 1903, p. 11.

40. *The Times* (London), 18 May 1903, p. 12.

41. *The Era* (London), 23 May 1903, p. 16; *The Star* (London), 18 May 1903, p. 1; *JBJ*, p. 101.

42. "The Czar." Music by Will Marion Cook. Lyrics by Paul Laurence Dunbar. Copyright 1902 by Will Marion Cook.

43. *The Era* (London), 23 May 1903, p. 16.

44. J. G. Riewald, *Sir Max Beerbohm: Man and Writer*. (The Hague; Martinus Nijhoff, 1953), p. 148.

45. Max Beerbohm, *Around Theaters*, 2 vols. (New York: Alfred A. Knopf, 1930), Vol. 2, p. 405.

46. Raymond Mander and Joe Mitchenson. *Theatrical Companion to Shaw*. (London: Folcroft Library Editions, 1971), p. 62.

47. George Bernard Shaw to Johnston Forbes-Robertson, 21 and 22 Dec. 1903. In Dan H. Lawrence, ed., *Bernard Shaw; Collected Letters, 1898-1910*. (New York: Dodd, Mead, and Co., 1965), pp. 384-85.

48. Mander, *Theatrical Companion*, p. 58.

49. *Sunday Dispatch* (London), 20 May 1903. Cited in *GW*, p. 296.

50. *The Playgoer*, p. 469.

51. *The Times* (London), 18 May 1903, p. 12.

52. *Pall Mall Gazette* (London), 18 May 1903, p. 11.

53. *Sunday Sun* (London), 17 May 1903, p. 6.

54. *The Sphere* (London), 23 May 1903, p. 162.

55. *Pall Mall Gazette*, 18 May 1903, p. 11.

56. *The Times* (London), 18 May 1903, p. 12.

57. *New York Herald*, 17 May 1903. Cited in *GW*, p. 294.

58. *New York Clipper*, 20 May 1903. Cited in *GW*, p. 296.

59. *The Sphere* (London), 23 May 1903, p. 162.

60. Review, 18 May 1903. In NYPL.

61. *The Globe* (London), 18 May 1903, p. 8.

62. *NYT*, "Invasion of London Stage by American Playwrights," 9 Aug. 1903, sec. 3, p. 21.

Chapter 10

1. *Pall Mall Gazette* (London), 18 May 1903, p. 11. This review of *In Dahomey* and other British reviews are cited from Jeffrey Green, "In Dahomey In London In 1903," *The Black Perspective in Music* 11, no. 1 (Spring 1983), pp. 23-40.

2. Green notes: "This custom of playing the [British national] anthem at the end of performances obtained for many years in theaters and movie houses, but fell into neglect in the 1960's" (p. 24).

3. *The Times* (London), 18 May 1903, p. 12; *St. James Gazette* (London), 18 May 1903, p. 12.

4. *Denver Post*, "Williams and Walker Conquered the English," 27 Nov. 1904, p. 9.

5. *Sunday Sun* (London), 17 May 1903, p. 6; *St. James Gazette* (London), 18 May 1903, p. 12.

6. *The Era* (London), 24 May 1903, p. 14.

7. Ibid.

8. *The Era*, 20 June 1903, p. 12.

9. Green, p. 35.

10. *The Playgoer* (London), c. 1903, p. 465.

11. Terry Waldo, *This Is Ragtime* (New York: Hawthorn, 1976), pp. 25–26.

12. ROW, p. 61.

13. *The Playgoer* (London), c. 1903, p. 465.

14. *Weekly Dispatch* (London), "Plays and Players," 24 May 1903, p. 8.

15. "That's How the Cakewalk's Done." Music and lyrics by John Leubrie Hill. Copyright 1903 by Keith Prowse & Co. Ltd., London.

16. James Haskins, *Black Theater in America* (New York: Thomas Y. Crowell, 1982), p. 50.

17. Lynne Fauley Emery. *Black Dance in the United States from 1619 to 1970.* (New York: Dance Horizons, 1980), p. 213.

18. Ted Fox, *Showtime at the Apollo* (New York: Holt, Rinehart & Winston, 1983), p. 52.

19. Ian Bevan, *Royal Performance: The Story of Royal Theatregoing.* (London: Hutchinson, 1954), pp. 200, 202.

20. Bevan, p. 202.

21. Edward, Duke of Windsor, *A King's Story: The Memoirs* of the Duke of Windsor. (New York: G. P. Putnam's Sons, 1947), pp. 5–6. Edward does not mention Bert Williams or *In Dahomey* in his book.

22. Green, p. 36.

23. Ibid.

24. Bevan, pp. 202–203.

25. Doris Saunders, "The Command Performance of Williams and Walker Before the King and Queen of England, June 23, 1903," *Negro Digest* 11 (March, 1962), p. 17.

26. ROW, p. 54; Saunders, pp. 17–18.

27. Green, p. 36.

28. *The Era* (London), 27 June 1903.

29. Saunders, p. 18.

30. ROW, p. 55.

31. *St. James Gazette* (London), 24 June 1903, p. 7.

32. *The Era* (London), 27 June 1903.

33. Saunders, p. 19.

34. Ibid.

35. ROW p. 54.

36. ROW, pp. 57–58.

37. Ibid.

38. *The Era*, 27 June 1903.

39. *NOB*, p. 76.

40. "Evah Darkey Is a King." Music by John H. Cook. Lyrics by E. P. Moran and Paul Laurence Dunbar. Copyright 1902 by John H. Cook.

41. Bert A. Williams, "The Comic Side of Trouble," *American Magazine* 85 (January 1918), p. 34.

42. Green, p. 37.

43. Ibid.

44. *BIB*, p. 80.

45. *NOB*, p. 59; Williams, *American Magazine*, p. 34. The author did not search Edward VII's papers in London. In some correspondence and papers which are published, the correspondants are his family members, political friends and mistresses. The great majority of Edward's papers appear to be diplomatic in nature, discussing political matters.

46. *Age*, 22 Oct. 1914, p. 6.

47. Aida Overton Walker, "Colored Men and Women on the Stage," *Colored American Magazine* 9, no. 4–5 (October 1905), p. 573.

48. Jim Walsh, "Favorite Pioneer Recording Artists: Bert Williams: A Thwarted Genius, I," *Hobbies* (September 1950), p. 25. See also *NOB*, p. 149, for matrix numbers of Williams's British recordings.

49. Lester A. Walton, "Thousands of All Races Mourn Bert Williams' Death," *Age*, 11 March 1922, p. 6.

50. ROW, p. 62. See also similar passage in *NOB*, p. 77.

51. George W. Walker, "The Negro on the American Stage," *Colored American Magazine* 11, no. 4 (August 1906), p. 573.

52. Ibid.

Chapter 11

1. Program, *In Dahomey*, New York Theater, 18 Feb. 1903, in NYPL.

2. *San Francisco Chronicle*, "Hit of Williams and Walker at the Grand," 5 Dec. 1904, p. 9.

3. Ibid.

4. "John Russell Coryell," in W. J. Burke and W. D. Howe, *American Authors and Books, 1640 to the Present Day*, 3rd ed., rev. by Irving and Anne Weiss. (New York: Crown Publishers, 1972), p. 138.

5. *Baltimore Sun*, "In Dahomey at the Lyric," 14 Sept. 1904, p. 8; Rowland, pp. 46–47.

6. *San Francisco Chronicle*, 5 Dec. 1904, p. 9.

7. ROW, p. 46.

8. The *In Dahomey* script excerpt from the Library of Congress is cited in John Graziano, "Sentimental Songs, Rags, and Transformations: The Emergence of the Black Musical, 1895–1910," in Glenn Loney, ed., *Musical Theatre in America: Papers and Proceedings of the Conference on the Musical Theatre in America*. (Contributions in Drama and Theatre Studies no. 8) (London: Greenwood Press, 1984), pp. 212–13.

9. Reading with Rowland: "The robbers have coolly seated themselves in the smoking car and are playing pinochle" (ROW, p. 47).

10. Reading with Rowland: "He seizes a bottle of Scotch from one of the robbers who is just about to take a drink" (Ibid.).

11. *San Francisco Chronicle*, 5 Dec. 1904, p. 9.

12. ROW, p. 47.

13. *Baltimore Sun,* 14 Sept. 1904, p. 8.

14. *San Francisco Chronicle,* 5 Dec. 1904, p. 9.

15. *Baltimore Sun,* 14 Sept. 1904, p. 8; *San Francisco Chronicle,* 5 Dec. 1904, p. 9.

16. "I May Be Crazy but I Ain't No Fool." Music and lyrics by Alex Rogers. Copyright 1904 by Attucks Music Publishing Co. Copyright 1932 by Lavinia Rogers.

17. Graziano, p. 217.

18. Ibid.

19. The songs were subtle social comments on current events. The Philippines were incorporated as a United States territory in 1902.

20. *Brooklyn Daily Eagle,* "Many kinds of fun at Brooklyn theaters," 18 April 1905, p. 10; *Daily State Gazette* (Trenton, N.J.), "In Dahomey at State St.," 3 May 1903, p. 8.

21. Ibid.

22. "Me an' de Minstrel Band." Music by James Vaughn. Lyrics by Alex Rogers. Copyright 1904 by Attucks Music Publishing Company.

23. Sylvester Russell, *Freeman,* 1 Oct. 1904. Cited in *GW,* p. 328.

24. "When the Moon Shines." Music by James Vaughn. Lyrics by Alex Rogers. Copyright 1904 by Attucks Music Publishing Company.

25. Sylvester Russell, *Freeman,* 1 Oct. 1904, cited in *GW,* p. 328.

26. "Why Adam Sinned." Music and lyrics by Alex Rogers. Copyright 1904 by Attucks Music Publishing Company.

27. *Chicago Tribune,* "In Dahomey," 17 Oct. 1904, p. 6; *Denver Post,* 28 Nov. 1904, p. 2; *New York Evening Post,* "In Dahomey," 28 August 1904, p. 7.

28. *Baltimore Sun,* 14 Sept. 1904, p. 8.

29. *Brooklyn Eagle,* 18 April 1905, p. 10.

30. *Boston Transcript,* "Globe Theatre – In Dahomey," 21 March 1905, in NYPL.

31. *San Francisco Chronicle,* 5 Dec. 1904, p. 9.

32. *Denver Post,* 28 August 1904, p. 2.

33. Ibid.

34. *Brooklyn Eagle,* 18 April 1905, p. 10; *Chicago Tribune,* 17 Oct. 1904, p. 6; *Boston Transcript,* 21 March 1905; *San Francisco Chronicle,* 5 Dec. 1904, p. 9; *Daily State Gazette* (Trenton, NJ), 3 May 1903, p. 8.

35. Eleanora Duse was appearing in a play in London in 1903; hence she could have seen Bert Williams in *In Dahomey.*

36. Sandra Richards, "Bert Williams: The Man and the Mask," *Mime, Mask and Marionette* 1 (Spring 1978), p. 19.

37. *GW,* p. 337.

38. David A. Jasen, *Tin Pan Alley* (New York: Donald I. Fine, Inc., 1988), p. 32.

39. Ibid.

40. Jasen describes these firms in his book, *Tin Pan Alley.*

41. Rennold Wolf, "The Greatest Comedian on the American Stage," *Green Book Magazine* 7 (June, 1912), pp. 1183–84.

42. Ibid., p. 1182.

43. See *Chicago Tribune,* 29 May 1906, p. 8.

44. Marian Storm, "All 135th Street Is Missing Bert Williams," *New York Evening Post,* 7 April 1922, p. 16.

45. Bert A. Williams, "The Comic Side of Trouble," *American Magazine* 85 (January 1918), p. 34.

46. Ibid. See also *NOB* for similar quotation, p. 107.

47. *NOB*, p. 107. Charters is wrong here. The lyrics of "Nobody" were not "Jesse Shipp's words" but Alex Rogers's.

48. Mary C. Henderson, *The City and the Theatre* (Clifton, N.J.: James T. White and Company, 1973), p. 246. This theater should not be confused with the present-day Majestic at 245 West Fortieth Street in New York City.

49. Lester A. Walton, "Williams and Walker on Broadway," *Colored American Magazine* 14, no. 4 (April 1908), p. 228.

50. "The New National Theatre," *Colored American Magazine* 9, no. 5–6 (1905), p. 667.

51. ROW, pp. 21–22.

52. *Benjamin Hurtig, Jules Hurtig, Harry T. Seamon v. Bert A. Williams and George W. Walker*, June 19, 1905, New York Supreme Court, NYMA.

53. *F. Ray Comstock v. Egbert A. Williams*, May 10, 1910, New York Supreme Court, NYMA.

54. Douglas Gilbert, *American Vaudeville: Its Life and Times* (New York: Dover Publications, Inc., 1940), p. 283.

55. Walton, *Colored American Magazine*, p. 228.

56. "Abyssinia Postponed," *Colored American Magazine* 9, no. 5 (November 1905), p. 607.

Chapter 12

1. *Variety*, "Will Williams Quit?" 16 Dec. 1905, p. 6.

2. *Variety*, "Alhambra," 16 Dec. 1905, p. 6.

3. *Freeman*, 9 Dec. 1905. Cited in *GW*, pp. 125, 353.

4. *GW* p. 353.

5. *NOB*, p. 88.

6. Bert A. Williams, "Williams Tells of Walker," *Freeman*, 14 Jan. 1911, p. 5.

7. Williams's biographers have been mistaken about *Abyssinia*. Rowland incorrectly names it as the last show in which Williams and Walker appeared together; Charters says the show opened in 1908 instead of 1906. See ROW, p. 68; *NOB*, p. 83.

8. Allen Woll, *Dictionary of the Black Theater*. (Westport, Conn.: Greenwood Press, 1983), p. 3.

9. Thomas L. Riis, "Black Musical Theater in New York, 1890–1915," Ph.D dissertation, University of Michigan, 1981, pp. 209, 212.

10. Riis, p. 212.

11. ROW, pp. 189–190.

12. *NYT*, "Williams and Walker Again," 21 Feb. 1906, p. 9.

13. *DM*, "Majestic – Abyssinia," 3 March 1906, p. 3.

14. "The Isle of By and By." Music by Bert A. Williams. Lyrics by Alex Rogers. New York: Gotham-Attucks, 1906.

15. Riis, p. 127.

16. Ibid.

17. *Chicago Tribune*, "News of the Theaters," 29 May 1906, p. 8; *Brooklyn Eagle*, "The Folly," 19 February 1907, p. 4.

18. *Chicago Tribune*, 29 May 1906, p. 8.

19. Ibid.

20. "Here It Comes Again." Music by Bert A. Williams. Lyrics by Alex Rogers and Earle C. Jones. New York: Gotham-Attucks, 1906.

21. *NYT*, 21 February 1906, p. 9.

22. *DM*, 3 March 1906, p. 3.

23. *Chicago Tribune*, 29 May 1906, p. 8.

24. ROW, p. 71

25. *Boston Globe*, "Williams and Walker, Globe Theatre," 3 April 1906, p. 13; *New York Evening Post*, "Abyssinia," 21 Feb. 1907, p. 7.

26. *Chicago Tribune*, 29 May 1906, p. 6.

27. *New York Tribune*, "Abyssinia at the Majestic," 21 Feb. 1906, p. 7; *NYT*, 21 Feb. 1906, p. 9; *Age*, "Abyssinia," 22 Feb. 1906, p. 1.

28. *New York Herald*, "Abyssinia Only Good in Spots," 21 Feb. 1906, p. 10.

29. *New York Evening Post*, 21 Feb. 1906, p. 7.

30. *DM*, 3 March 1906, p. 3.

31. Rae D. Henkle, "What Is Going On at the Theaters – Lyceum," *Cleveland Plain Dealer*, 15 Jan. 1907, p. 4.

32. *Globe-Democrat* (St. Louis, MO), 24 Nov. 1906, cited in *GW*, p. 380.

33. *Philadelphia Inquirer*, "Abyssinia at the Park," 10 April 1906, p. 4.

34. Jim Walsh, "Favorite Pioneer Recording Artists – Bert Williams, A Thwarted Genius, I," *Hobbies* (September 1950), pp. 25, 36.

35. Walsh, p. 36.

36. Lester A. Walton, "Williams and Walker on Broadway," *Colored American Magazine* 14, no 4 (April 1908), p. 228.

37. *F. Ray Comstock* v. *Egbert A. Williams*, New York Supreme Court, May 10, 1910, NYMA.

38. The biographical sketch of F. Ray Comstock is compiled from *Who Was Who in the American Theater, 1912–1976*. (Detroit: Gale Research, 1978), p. 506; and Jerry Stagg, *The Brothers Shubert*. (New York: Random House, 1968), p. 58.

39. Theatrical contract, F. Ray Comstock, Egbert A. Williams, and George W. Walker, March 1, 1907, NYMA.

Chapter 13

1. Alain Locke (1886–1954), a Rhodes scholar at Oxford University in 1910, received a Ph.D in the United States and taught philosophy at Howard University. He was a major figure in the promotion of the Harlem Renaissance movement in the 1920s.

2. Albert Ross to Bert Williams and George Walker, 16 October 1907. Reprinted in *Variety*, 14 Dec. 1907, p. 30.

3. Bert Williams and George Walker to Albert Ross, 18 October 1907. Reprinted in *Variety*, 14 Dec. 1907, p. 30.

4. *DM*, "Majestic – Bandanna Land," 15 Feb. 1908, p. 3. The representative musical program described here is derived from the program of Lyceum Theater, Detroit, 5 Jan. 1908.

5. "Dinah, Be My Little Dinah." Music by Will Marion Cook. Lyrics by Alex Rogers. New York: Gotham-Attucks, 1907.

6. "Until Then." Music by Will Marion Cook. Lyrics by Alex Rogers. New York, Gotham-Attucks, 1907.

7. "It's Hard to Love Somebody (Who's Loving Somebody Else)." Music by Chris Smith. Lyrics by Richard C. McPherson (Cecil Mack). New York: Gotham-Attucks, 1907.

8. *DM*, 13 Feb. 1908, p. 3.

9. "Late Hours." Music by Bert A. Williams. Lyrics by David Kempner. New York: Gotham-Attucks, 1907.

10. *Toronto Star*, "Music and Fun at the Grand," 14 Jan. 1908, p. 9.

11. *Age*, "Bandanna Land," 6 Feb. 1908, p. 10.

12. Tom Fletcher, *100 Years of the Negro in Show Business*. (New York: Burdge, 1954), pp. 239–40. See also parallel citation in *NOB*, pp. 106–7.

13. Bert A. Williams, "The Comic Side of Trouble," *American Magazine* 85 (January 1918), p. 60.

14. "Bon-Bon Buddie," Music by Will Marion Cook. Lyrics by Alex Rogers. New York: Gotham-Attucks, 1907.

15. *Age*, 6 Feb. 1908, p. 10; *Toronto Star*, 14 Jan. 1908, p. 9.; *New York Sun*, "Bandanna Land Pleases," 4 Feb. 1908, p. 7.

16. *NYT*, "Bandanna Land Pleases," 4 Feb. 1908, p. 7; *New York Tribune*, "Williams and Walker in Bandanna Land," 4 Feb. 1907, p. 7.

17. *NYT*, 4 Feb. 1908, p. 7.

18. "Somebody Lied." Music by Jeff T. Branen. Lyrics by Evans Lloyd. Adapted by Bert A. Williams. Chicago: Will Rossiter, 1907.

19. *Toronto Star*, 14 Jan. 1908, p. 9.; *Chicago Tribune*, "News of the Theaters," 11 Nov. 1907, p. 8.

20. *Cincinnati Enquirer*, "Colored Comedians," 1 March 1909, p. 8; *New York Herald*, "New Play Full of Music," 4 Feb. 1908, p. 10; *DM*, 15 Feb. 1908, p. 3.

21. DeWolf Hopper (1858–1935) was noted for the role of Don Medigua in John Philip Sousa's *El Capitan*. Hopper starred in many plays, including *Mr. Pickwick* and several Gilbert and Sullivan revivals.

22. *Baltimore Sun*, "Comedy of Color at Academy," 11 August 1908, p. 7.

23. *Chicago Tribune*, 11 Nov. 1907, p. 8.

24. *DM*, 13 Feb. 1908, p. 3; *Toronto Star*, 14 Jan. 1908, p. 9; *Detroit Free Press*, "Lyceum – Williams and Walker in Bandanna Land," 6 Jan. 1908, p. 4.

25. *Age*, 6 Feb. 1908, p. 10.

26. *Age*, "Dr. Washington Stops Show," 13 Feb. 1908, p. 6.

27. Lester A. Walton, "Morris Letter Causes Comment," *Age*, 13 Feb. 1908, p. 6.

28. *Age*, "Mr. Shoemaker Wake Up!" 13 Feb. 1908, p. 6.

29. *Age*, "George W. Walker's letter to the Thirteen Club," 20 Feb. 1908, p. 6.

30. *Age*, "The Secret of Williams and Walker's Success," 27 Feb. 1908, p. 6.

31. Lester A. Walton, "Controversy over Williams and Walker," *Age*, 5 March 1908, p. 6.

32. *Age*, "Anniversary Celebration of Williams and Walker – A Gala Event," 2 April 1908, p. 6.

33. *Variety*, "Orpheum," 13 June 108, p. 5; *Variety*, "Alhambra," 20 June 1908, p. 17; *Variety*, 27 June 1908, p. 5.

34. *F. Ray Comstock* v. *Egbert Williams*, New York Supreme Court, 10 May 1910, p. 11, NYMA.

35. *Age*, "Williams and Walker in Vaudeville," 4 June 1908, p. 6.

Chapter 14

1. Robert Kimball and William Bolcom, *Reminiscing with Sissle and Blake.* (New York: Viking Press, 1973), p. 86.

2. ROW, p. 181.

3. Tom Fletcher, *100 Years of the Negro in Show Business.* (New York: Burdge, 1954), pp. 246, 249. See also *NOB*, p. 116, for similar quotation.

4. *Age*, "Vaudeville Nine Defeats Williams and Walker Team," 4 June 1908, p. 6.

5. Ibid.

6. Ibid.

7. Ibid.

8. Aristophanes, *The Complete Plays of Aristophanes*, ed. Moses Hadas. (New York: Bantam Books, 1962), p. 375.

9. *Age*, "Well Known Performers Organize the Frogs," 9 July 1908, p. 6.

10. Ibid.

11. Ibid.

12. Theatrical contract, F. Ray Comstock, Egbert A. Williams, and George W. Walker, 1 March 1907.

13. *NYT*, "New Combine Born in Theatre Land," 28 April 1907, p. 9.

14. Ibid.

15. *NYT*, "Belasco Maintains His Independence," 30 April 1907, jp. 9.

16. *Age*, "Two Theatrical Successes," 17 Oct. 1907, p. 1.

17. *Age*, "Bandanna Land at Academy of Music," 14 May 1908, p. 6.

18. Lester A. Walton, "The Coming Season," *Age*, 30 July 1908, p. 6.

19. *DM*, 20 Nov. 1908, cited in *GW*, p. 444.

20. *Age*, "Williams and Walker at Grand Opera House," 20 August 1908, p. 6.

21. Lester A. Walton, "Salome," *Age*, 27 Aug. 1908, p. 6.

22. *Age*, "Bandanna Land in New England," 3 Sept. 1908, p. 6.

23. *Age*, "Mrs. Lottie Williams Convalescent," 7 May 1908, p. 6; *Age*, "Retirement of Lottie Williams," 24 Dec. 1908, p. 6.

24. Ann Charters writes: "When Bert became a star performer in the *Ziegfeld Follies*, she retired from the stage," *NOB*, p. 60.

25. Lester A. Walton, "About the Stars and Shows," *Age*, 8 Oct. 1908, p. 6.

26. Loften Mitchell, *Black Drama: The Story of the American Negro in the Theatre.* (New York: Hawthorn Books, 1967), p. 53.

27. Louis J. Vorhaus, M.D., "Paresis," *Encyclopedia Americana*, 30 vols. (Danbury, Conn.: Grolier Inc., 1990), vol. 21, p. 427.

28. *Age*, "Theatrical Jottings," 3 Dec. 1908, p. 6.

29. George W. Walker, "Bert and Me and Them," *Age*, 24 Dec. 1908, p. 4.

30. Veronica Adams, "The Dramatic Stage as an Upbuilder of the Races," *Chicago Interocean*, 17 Jan. 1909, p. 6; 25 Feb. 1909, p. 6.

31. *Age*, "From Bandanna Land," 21 Jan. 1909, p. 6; *Age*, "Theatrical Jottings," 18 Feb. 1909, p. 6; *Age*, "Theatrical Comment," 25 Feb. 1909, p. 6.

Chapter 15

1. *F. Ray Comstock v. Egbert A. Williams*, New York Supreme Court, 10 May 1910, NYMA; hereafter cited as *"Comstock v. Williams."*

2. Ibid.

3. *Variety*, "Williams Alone Next Season," 22 May 1909, p. 5.

4. This and the following quotations are cited from theatrical contract, F. Ray Comstock and Egbert A. Williams, 8 May 1909, NYMA.

5. Buster Keaton with Charles Samuels, *My Wonderful World of Slapstick* (Garden City, New York: Doubleday, 1960), pp. 78–79.

6. *Variety*, "New Acts – Bert Williams," 22 May 1909, p. 15.

7. Lester A. Walton, "Music and the Stage," *Age*, 26 May 1909, p. 6.

8. *Variety*, "Fifth Avenue," 5 June 1909, p. 16.

9. *Detroit Free Press*, "Temple-Vaudeville," 22 June 1909, p. 4.

10. Lester A. Walton, "Music and the Stage," *Age*, 15 July 1909, p. 6.

11. *BIB*, pp. 344–5.

12. Lester A. Walton, "Music and the Stage," *Age*, 22 July 1909, p. 6.

13. Lester A. Walton, "Music and the Stage," *Age*, 5 August 1909, p. 6; *BIB*, pp. 116–117.

14. *Comstock* v. *Williams*, New York Supreme Court, 10 May 1910, p. 4., NYMA.

15. Ibid., pp. 4–5.

16. Ibid., p. 7.

17. Ibid., p. 5.

18. Lester A. Walton, "Mr. Lode of Koal, a Broadway Show," *Age*, 16 Sept. 1909, p. 6.

19. *BIB*, p. 264.

20. *Freeman*, "Bert A. Williams & Co. in Mr. Lode of Koal," 20 Nov. 1909, p. 6.

21. "The Harbor of Lost Dreams." Music by Bert A. Williams. Lyrics by Alex Rogers. Arranged by John Rosamond Johnson. Chicago: Will Rossiter, 1909.

22. *Freeman*, 20 Nov. 1909, p. 6.

23. Ibid.

24. *BIB*, p. 264.

25. *Freeman*, 20 Nov. 1909, p. 6.

26. "That's a Plenty." Music by Bert A. Williams. Lyrics by Henry S. Creamer. Chicago: Will Rossiter Co., 1909. Contrary to Rowland, the song was not performed in *Bandanna Land* (see ROW, p. 65).

27. "Chink, Chink Chinaman." Music by Bert Williams. Lyrics by Alex Rogers. Arranged by John Rosamond Johnson. Chicago: Will Rossiter, 1909.

28. *Freeman*, 20 Nov. 1909, p. 6.

29. "Believe Me." Music by Bert A. Williams. Lyrics by Alex Rogers. Chicago: Will Rossiter, 1909.

30. *Comstock* v. *Williams*, New York Supreme Court, 10 May 1910, pp. 7–7A, NYMA; *Age*, "Bert Williams Celebrates 35th Birthday, 18 Nov. 1909, p. 6.

31. *Age*, "Shows of the Season," 16 Sept. 1909, p. 6.

32. *NYT*, "Bert Williams in Mr. Lode of Koal," 2 Nov. 1909, p. 9; *St. Louis Post Dispatch*, "Bert Williams at the Garrick," 6 Sept. 1909, p. 6.

33. Bonney Royal, "What Bonney Royal Saw at the Great Northern," *Chicago Tribune*, 6 Oct. 1909, p. 4; *Toledo Blade*, 30 August 1909, p. 5; *Quincy* (Illinois) *Daily Herald*, cited in *Age*, 23 Sept. 1909, p. 6; *Chicago American*, cited in *Age*, 7 Oct. 1909, p. 6.

34. *DM*, "Majestic: Mr. Lode of Koal," 13 Nov. 1909, p. 7.

35. *Comstock* v. *Williams*, New York Supreme Court, 10 May 1910, pp. 5–6, NYMA.

36. Ibid., p. 7.
37. Lester A. Walton,"Have Williams and Walker Separated?" *Age*, 27 Jan. 1910, p. 6.
38. Ibid.
39. "Profit and Loss Statement – *Mr. Lode of Koal* Company, 1909–1910," Exhibit C in *Comstock* v. *Williams*, New York Supreme Court, 10 May 1910, NYMA.
40. Lester A. Walton, "Closing of Mr. Lode of Koal Co.," *Age*, 24 Feb. 1910, p. 6.

Chapter 16

1. Lester A. Walton, "Theatrical Comment," *Age*, 10 March 1910, p. 6.
2. Ibid.
3. Ibid.
4. Sylvester Russell, "Musical and Dramatic," *Chicago Defender*, 12 March 1910, p. 4.
5. Ibid.
6. *NOB*, p. 108.
7. *Comstock* v. *Williams*, New York Supreme Court, 17 May 1910, p. 3., NYMA.
8. Ibid., p. 2.
9. Lester A. Walton, "Bert Williams in Vaudeville," *Age*, 21 April 1910, p. 6.
10. Ibid.
11. Ibid.
12. *Variety*, "New Act ... Bert Williams," 23 April 1910, p. 12.
13. *Age*, "Legislature Passes African Dodger Bill," 3 May 1917, p. 1.
14. Walton, *Age*, 21 April 1910, p. 6.
15. *Variety*, "Hammerstein's," 30 April 1910, p. 22.
16. *Variety*, "Hammerstein's," 7 May 1910, p. 21.
17. John E. DiMeglio, *Vaudeville, U.S.A.* (Bowling Green, Ohio: Bowling Green State University Press, 1973), p. 116.
18. *Variety*, "Alhambra," 14 May 1910, p. 19.
19. *Comstock* v. *Williams*, New York Supreme Court, 6 May 1910, p. 4, NYMA.
20. Ibid.
21. Ibid.
22. Ibid., pp. 1–2.
23. Ibid., pp. 2–3.
24. Ibid., p. 2.
25. *Comstock* v. *Williams*, New York Supreme Court, 13 May 1910, pp. 1–2, NYMA.
26. Theatrical contract, *Comstock, Williams, and Walker*, 1 March 1907, NYMA.
27. *Comstock* v. *Williams*, New York Supreme Court, 13 May 1910, pp. 2–3, NYMA.
28. *Comstock* v.*Williams*, New York Supreme Court, 6 May 1910, p. 4, NYMA.
29. *Comstock* v. *Williams*, New York Supreme Court, 13 May 1910, p. 3, NYMA.
30. *Comstock* v. *Williams*, New York Supreme Court, 6 May 1910, p. 5, NYMA.
31. *Comstock* v. *Williams*, New York Supreme Court, 10 May 1910, p. 4, NYMA.
32. Ibid., p. 6.
33. Ibid., pp. 6–7.

34. Ibid., p. 7a.

35. *Comstock* v. *Williams*, New York Supreme Court, 17 May 1910, p. 9, NYMA.

36. Ibid.

37. *Comstock* v. *Williams*, New York Supreme Court, 10 May 1910, p. 9, NYMA.

38. Ibid., p. 10.

39. Ibid., p. 11.

40. Ibid., p. 13.

41. Ibid., p. 8.

42. Ibid., p. 10; *Comstock* v. *Williams*, New York Supreme Court, 17 May 1910, p. 4, NYMA.

Chapter 17

1. *Age*, "Bert Williams Turns Philosopher," 1 Dec. 1910, p. 6.

2. Ibid.

3. *NOB*, p. 115.

4. Bert A. Williams, "The Comic Side of Trouble," *American Magazine* 85 (January 1918), p. 61.

5. Charles Higham, *Ziegfeld*. (Chicago: Henry Regnery Co., 1972), p. 10; Randolph Carter, *The World of Flo Ziegfeld*. (New York: Praeger Publishers, 1974), p. 13.

6. See Carter, p. 27, and Harry B. Smith, *First Nights and First Editions*. (Boston: Little, Brown & Co., 1931), pp. 241–42.

7. Florenz Ziegfeld, Jr., "How I Pick Beauties," *Theatre Magazine* 30, no. 233 (September 1919), p. 158.

8. Florenz Ziegfeld, Jr., "Picking Out Pretty Girls for the Stage," *American Magazine* 88, no. 6 (December 1919), p. 34.

9. Ziegfeld, *Theatre Magazine*, p. 160.

10. Williams, *American Magazine*, p. 61.

11. Joel A. Rogers, *World's Great Men of Color*. Edited with an introduction, commentary and new bibliographical notes by John Henrik Clarke. 2 vols. (New York: Macmillan, 1972), Vol. 2, pp. 379–80.

12. Williams, *American Magazine*, pp. 60–61.

13. *Variety*, 28 May 1910, p. 7.

14. Oscar G. Brockett, *History of the Theater*, 4th ed. (Boston: Allyn and Bacon, Inc., 1982), pp. 583–84.

15. ROW, p. xii.

16. Ibid., p. xiii.

17. Ibid., p. 105.

18. Veronica Adams, "The Dramatic Stage as an Upbuilder of the Races," *Chicago Interocean*, 17 Jan. 1909, magazine sec., p. 2.

19. ROW, p. 105.

20. Ibid., p. 106.

21. Ibid., p. 107.

22. Ibid., pp. 107–108.

23. Ibid., pp. 108–109.

24. David Belasco, *The Theatre Through Its Stage Door*, Louis V. Defoe, ed. (New York: Harper & Brothers, 1919), p. 20.

25. ROW, pp. 109–10.

26. David Belasco, "Rosemary, a Preface to the Life of Bert Williams," in ROW, p. xiii.

27. Williams, *American Magazine*, p. 61.

28. The Fanny Brice biographical sketch here is compiled from *COC*, pp. 102–3; Marjorie Farnsworth, *The Ziegfeld Follies*. (New York: Putman, 1956), pp. 47–49; and Daniel Blum, *Great Stars of the American Stage: A Pictorial Record*. (New York: Greenberg Publishers, 1952), p. 99.

29. Farnsworth, pp. 46, 49.

30. Norman Katkov, *The Fabulous Fanny: The Story of Fanny Brice*. (New York: Alfred A. Knopf, 1953), p. 65; Farnsworth, p. 50.

31. Katkov, pp. 65–66.

32. "Lovey Joe." Music by Will Marion Cook. Lyrics by Joe Jordan. Copyright 1910 by Harry Von Tilzer Music Company.

33. Katkov, p. 67.

34. Higham, p. 79.

35. Katkov, p. 68.

36. Ward Morehouse, "The Ziegfeld Follies—A Formula with Class," *Theatre Arts* (May 1956), p. 68; *NYT*, "In Vaudeville and Roof Gardens," 19 June 1910, p. 12; *Variety*, "Follies of 1910," 25 June 1910, p. 15.

37. "Goodbye Beckie Cohn." Music by Fred Fisher. Lyrics by Harry Breen. Copyright 1910 by Maurice Shapiro. From *Delaney's Songbook*, no. 59 in Music Collection, at Lincoln Center. Irving Berlin did not have a song in the *Ziegfeld Follies* until 1911, when Bert Williams introduced "Woodman Spare That Tree."

38. Jack Burton, *The Blue Book of Tin Pan Alley*. (Watkins Glen, N.Y.: Century House, 1951), p. 88; *Variety*, 25 June 1910, p. 15.

39. Al-Tony Gilmore, *Bad Nigger! The National Impact of Jack Johnson*. (Port Washington, N.Y.: Kennikat Press, 1975), p. 72, no. 1.

40. *NYT*, "Eight Killed in Fight Riots," 5 July 1910, pp. 1, 4.

41. Rennold Wolf, "The Greatest Comedian on the American Stage," *Green Book Magazine* 7 (June 1912), p. 1181. See also ROW, p. 181.

42. ROW, pp. 180–181.

43. *Washington Post*, "The Follies of 1910," 27 Dec. 1910, p. 11.

44. Program, Oliver Theater, Lincoln, Nebraska, *Follies of 1910*, 29 May 1910, NYPL.

45. *New York Evening Post*, 21 June 1910, p. 9; *New York Tribune*, 21 June 1910, p. 7.

46. Gerald Bordman, *American Operetta: From H.M.S. Pinafore to Sweeney Todd*. (New York: Oxford University Press, 1981), p. 83; see also David A. Jasen, *Tin Pan Alley*. (New York: Donald I. Fine, Inc., 1988), pp. 84–85.

47. Ashton Stevens, "Bert Williams in the Follies of 1910," *Chicago Examiner*, cited in *GW*, pp. 529, 531.

48. *Variety*, 25 June 1910, p. 15.

49. *New York Sun*, 21 June 1910, p. 9; *New York Tribune*, 21 June 1910, p. 7.

50. *NYT*, "Chantecler Wins Financial Success," 13 Feb. 1910, sec. 3, p. 1.

51. Edmond Rostand, *Chantecler: Play in Four Acts*, trans. by Gertrude Hall (New York: Duffield and Company, 1921), p. 39.

52. *NOB*, pp. 115–116. See photograph in Bernard Sobel, *A Pictorial History of Vaudeville* (New York: Citadel Press, 1961), p. 206.

53. "White Folks Call It Chantecler, but It's Just Plain Chicken to Me." Music by Bert A. Williams. Lyrics by Andrew B. Sterling. Copyright 1910 by Harry Von Tilzer Music Company.

54. *Variety*, 23 June 1910, p. 15.

55. *DM*, 2 July 1910, p. 10.

56. Katkov, pp. 68–69.

57. Terry Waldo, *This Is Ragtime*. (New York: Hawthorn Books, Inc., 1976), p. 129.

58. *New York World*, 21 June 1910, p. 7; *Leslie's Weekly*, 7 July 1910, p. 21.

59. *Leslie's Weekly*, 7 July 1910, p. 21.

60. *New York Sun*, 21 June 1910, p. 9.

61. *New York Tribune*, 21 June 1910, p. 7; *New York Evening Post*, 21 June 1910, p. 9; *DM*, 2 July 1910, p. 10; *Variety*, 26 June 1910, p. 15.

62. *New York Herald*, 21 June 1910, p. 12; Lester A. Walton, "Music and the Stage," *Age*, 23 June 1910, p. 6. *Chicago Examiner*, cited in *GW*, p. 529.

63. Walton, *Age*, 23 June 1910, p. 6.

64. Henry T. Sampson, *Blacks in Black and White: A Source Book on Black Films*. (Metuchen: N.J.: Scarecrow Press, 1977), p. 1.

65. Thomas Cripps, *Slow Fade to Black*. (London: Oxford University Press, 1977), pp. 79–80, 179.

66. Phyllis Rauch Klotman, *Frame by Frame: A Black Filmography*. (Bloomington: Indiana University Press, 1979), p. 695. Klotman doesn't name Williams as cast member of *Pullman Porter* but Sampson does. See Sampson, pp. 246–66.

67. Cripps, p. 76.

68. Klotman, p. 422. The discussion here of Bert Williams's films is by no means a definitive one. Many factors remain to be documented; this is a potential area for film scholars.

69. *Age*, "To Build Movie Studio," 9 April 1914, p. 6.

Chapter 18

1. Booker T. Washington, "The Greatest Comedian the Negro Race Has," *American Magazine* 70 (Sept. 1910), p. 601.

2. Ibid.

3. Ibid.

4. Booker T. Washington, *Up from Slavery: An Autobiography*. (New York: Doubleday, 1901; Bantam: 1963), p. 155.

5. Washington, *American Magazine*, pp. 603–4.

6. Bert A. Williams, "The Negro on the Stage," *Green Book Magazine* 4 (December 1910), pp. 1341–42.

7. Ibid., p. 1342.

8. Ibid.

9. Ibid.

10. Ibid.

11. George W. Walker, "The Negro on the American Stage," *Colored American Magazine* 11, no. 4 (October 1906), p. 248.

12. Williams, *Green Book Magazine*, p. 1342.

13. Sylvester Russell, "George W. Walker of Williams and Walker," *Chicago Defender*, 2 July 1910, p. 4.

14. *Chicago Examiner*, 2 Oct. 1910, cited in Sylvester Russell, "The Bert Williams Interviews," *Chicago Defender*, 8 Oct. 1910, p. 2.

15. Ibid.

16. *Chicago Defender*, 8 Oct. 1910, p. 2; Bert A. Williams, "The Comic Side of Trouble," *American Magazine* 85 (January 1918), p. 34.

17. *Chicago Defender*, 8 Oct. 1910, p. 2.

18. Ralph Graves, "Drew, Ruth St. Denis and Marshall," *Washington Post*, 1 Jan. 1911, magazine sec., part 3, p. 2.

19. R. W. Thompson, "Theatrical Chit-Chat of Washington," *Freeman*, 14 Jan. 1911, p. 5.

20. *NYT*, "George Walker Dead," 8 Jan. 1911, p. 13.

21. *Chicago Defender*, 14 Jan. 1911, p. 2.

22. Sylvester Russell, "George William Walker of Williams and Walker," *Freeman*, 14 Jan. 1911, p. 5.; *NYT*, "George Walker's Funeral Today," 9 Jan. 1911, p. 13.

23. *Freeman*, "Bert Williams Tells of Walker," 14 Jan. 1911, p. 5.

24. *Chicago Defender*, 14 Jan. 1911, p. 2; *Boston Guardian*, "New York State News – George Walker," 14 Jan. 1911, p. 2.

25. Sylvester Russell, "The Williams and Walker of the Future," *Chicago Defender*, 22 April 1911, p. 4.

26. *Age*, "To Appear in Vaudeville," 25 May 1911, p. 4.

27. *Age*, "Bert Williams in Demand," 25 May 1911, p. 4.

28. Clifford M. Caruthers, *Ring Around Max: The Correspondence of Ring Lardner and Max Perkins*. (DeKalb, Ill.: Northern Illinois University Press, 1973), pp. xv–xvi.

29. Jonathan Yardley, *Ring: A Biography of Ring Lardner*. (New York: Random House, 1977), p. 101.

30. Ring Lardner, Jr., *The Lardners: My Family Remembered*. (New York: Harper & Row, 1976), p. 27.

31. Ring Lardner to Ellis Lardner, 26 Feb. 1911. Cited in Clifford M. Caruthers, ed., *Letters from Ring*. (Flint, Mich.: Walden Press, 1979), p. 104.

32. Ring Lardner to Ellis Lardner, 1 March 1911, cited in ibid., p. 106.

33. Ibid., p. 105.

34. Bert A. Williams to Ring Lardner, 14 March 1911, cited in ibid., p. 109.

35. Ring Lardner to Ellis Lardner, 15 March 1911, cited in ibid., p. 109.

36. Whitney J. Oates and Eugene O'Neill, Jr., ed., *The Complete Greek Drama*, 2 vols. (New York: Random House, 1938), vol. 1, pp. xix–xx.

37. *New York Herald*, "Follies of 1911 Is a Great Big Colorful Show," 27 June 1911, p. 10.

38. *New York Tribune*, "Follies of 1911 Here," 27 June 1911, p. 7.

39. *Chicago Record-Herald*, cited in ROW, pp. 91–92.

40. *Variety*, "Follies of 1911," 1 July 1911, p. 20; *NYT*, "Girls and Glitter in Follies of 1911," 27 June 1911, p. 9.

41. *AMT*, p. 267.

42. ROW, p. 125. See also similar passage in *NOB*, p. 118.

43. ROW, p. 126.

44. Marjorie Farnsworth, *The Ziegfeld Follies*. (New York: Bonanza, 1966), p. 39.

45. *New York World*, "New Follies Both Pretty and Amusing," 27 June 1911, p. 4; *New York Evening Post*, 27 June 1911, p. 9.

46. "Dat's Harmony." Music by Bert A. Williams. Lyrics by Grant Clark. New York: Jerome H. Remick, 1911.

47. *NYT*, 27 June 1911, p. 9; *New York Herald*, 27 June 1911, p. 4; *New York Evening Post*, 27 June 1911, p. 7.

Chapter 19

1. *Age*, "Bert Williams' Father Dead," 4 April 1912, p. 6. The official cause of death was given as "chronic endocarditis." Death certificate of Frederick Williams, Jr., Dept. of Health, City of New York, 1 April 1912, NYMA.

2. *Age*, "Theatrical Jottings," 11 April 1912, p. 6.

3. Tom Fletcher, *100 Years of the Negro in Show Business*. (New York: Burdge, 1954), pp. 243, 246.

4. Alvin Fay Harlan, *Old Bowery Days: The Chronicle of a Famous Street*. (New York: O. Appleton and Company, 1931), pp. 468, 470.

5. Marjorie Farnsworth, *The Ziegfeld Follies*. (New York: G. P. Putnam and Sons, 1956), p. 39.

6. Channing Pollack, *Harvest of My Years: An Autobiography*. (Indianapolis: Bobbs-Merrill, 1943), p. 219.

7. *Age*, "Theatrical Jottings," 13 June 1912, p. 6. I have been unable to substantiate whether Bert Williams actually traveled to London to perform at the Coliseum.

8. Henry S. Creamer, "The Frogs' Frolic," *Age*, 4 July 1912, p. 6.

9. Maryanne Chach, "The New York Review," in Barbara Naomi Cohen-Stratyner, ed., *Performing Arts Resources* 14 (New York: Theatre Library Association, 1989), p. 95. For the history of the Shuberts and their companies, see Jerry Stagg, *The Brothers Shubert*. (New York: Random House, 1968). Microfilm copies of the *New York Review* are preserved in NYPL but lack issues for 1912.

10. These and the following citations are from Jack Shoemaker, "White Is as White Does," *Age*, 25 July 1912, p. 6.

11. *AMT*, p. 276.

12. The following quotations are from Aida Overton Walker, "Respect Memory of the Dead," *Age*, 1 August 1912, p. 6.

13. Lester A. Walton, "Burlesquing the Black Man," *Age*, 17 Oct. 1912, p. 6.

14. Ibid.

15. See "Discography" in *NOB*, p. 150. The writers of these songs are unknown. See *Age*, 17 Oct. 1912, p. 6, re Williams in *1912 Follies* in Philadelphia.

16. Lester A. Walton, "The Follies of 1912," *Age*, 24 Oct. 1912, p. 6.

17. Ibid.

18. Program, *Ziegfeld Follies of 1912*, New Amsterdam Theater, NYPL.

19. ROW, p. 118. See also *NOB*, p. 20, for approximate quotation.

20. ROW, p. 118.

21. Ibid., pp. 118–19. See also *NOB*, p. 121.

22. Ibid.

23. Ibid.

24. Ibid., p. 122. See also *NOB*, p. 119.

25. Ibid., p. 122–23. See also *NOB*, p. 119.

26. Ibid., p. 123. See also *NOB*, pp. 119–20.

27. Ibid.

28. *NYT*, "Follies of 1912 Is a Beauty Show," 22 Oct. 1912, p. 11; *New York Tribune*, "Follies of 1912," 22 Oct. 1912, p. 9; *Age*, 24 Oct. 1912, p. 6; *Variety*, "Ziegfeld's Follies," 25 Oct. 1912, p. 22.

29. *New York World*, "Broadway Belated Night of Follies," 22 Oct. 1912, p. 5.

30. See Appendix B, "Musical Compositions of Bert Williams."

31. *Variety*, 25 Oct. 1912, p. 22; *NYT*, 22 Oct. 1912, p. 11.

32. *Age*, 24 Oct. 1912, p. 6.

33. *Variety*, 25 Oct. 1912, p. 22.

Chapter 20

1. See "Discography" in *NOB*, p. 150.

2. Lester A. Walton, "Outlook Much Brighter," *Age*, 27 February, 1913, p. 6.

3. Lester A. Walton, "An Exceptional Bill," *Age*, 22 May 1913, p. 6.

4. *Age*, "Theatrical Jottings," 22 May 1913, p. 6.

5. Lloyd Lewis, "Life with Uncle Eggs," *Chicago Sun*, 21 April 1946 (weekly book supplement, p. 3); *Chicago Defender*, "Death Ends Career of Stage Idol," by Tony Langston, 11 March 1922, p. 1.

6. Lloyd Lewis, "Life with Uncle Eggs," *Chicago Sun*, book week supplement, 28 April 1946, p. 3.

7. Lewis, *Chicago Sun*, book supplement, 21 April 1946, p. 3.

8. Marian Storm, "All 135th Street Is Missing Bert Williams," *New York Evening Post*, 7 April 1922, p. 16.

9. Lester A. Walton, "Historic Pilgrimage," *Age*, 7 August 1913, p. 6.

10. 14 August 1913, p. 6.

11. Ibid.

12. Jim Haskins and N. R. Mitgang, *Mr. Bojangles: The Biography of Bill Robinson*. (New York: William Morrow and Company, Inc., 1988), pp. 58–59.

13. *MOBA*, pp. 304, 305.

14. Lester A. Walton, "An Unusual Bill," *Age*, 14 August 1913, p. 6.

15. *Age*, "The Frogs in Philly," 14 August 1913, p. 6.

16. Walton, *Age*, 21 August 1913, p. 6.

17. Ibid.

18. *Age*, "A Southern View," 21 August 1913, p. 6.

19. Allan H. Spear: *Black Chicago: The Making of a Negro Ghetto 1890–1920*. (Chicago and London: University of Chicago Press, 1967), p. 76.

20. *Chicago Defender*, Aida Overton Walker at the Pekin Theatre," 1 Nov. 1913, p. 8.

21. *Chicago Defender*, "Aida Overton Walker and Company," 8 Nov. 1913, p. 6.

22. Juli Jones, Jr., *Chicago Defender*, "Chicago Mourns for Noted Artist," 17 Oct. 1914, p. 1.

23. *Variety*, "Palace," 26 Dec. 1913, p. 18.

24. Ibid.

25. Jervis Anderson, *This Was Harlem: A Cultural Portrait 1900–1950*. (New York: Farrar, Straus and Giroux, 1982), pp. 39–40.

26. *Variety*, "New Acts," 26 Dec. 1913, p. 17.

27. *Age*, "Williams in Philly," 8 Jan. 1914, p. 6.

28. *Variety*, "Palace," 2 Jan. 1914, p. 20.

29. *Minneapolis Tribune*, 18 Jan. 1914, p. 14.

30. Terry Ramsaye, *A Million and One Nights*. (New York: Simon & Schuster, 1964), p. 608.

31. ROW, p. 150.

32. Ramsaye, pp. 609–610.

33. *NOB*, pp. 130–131.

34. Ramsaye, p. 610.

35. Marshall, Hyatt, comp. and ed. *The Afro-American Cinematic Experience: An Annotated Bibliography and Filmography*. (Wilmington, Del.: Scholarly Resources, 1983), pp. 192–93; Kemp R. Niven, *Klaw and Erlanger Present Famous Plays in Pictures*, Bebe Bergston, ed. (Los Angeles: John D. Roche, 1939), p. 40.

36. *Variety*, "New Acts – Aida Overton Walker Dancing," 8 May 1914, p. 14.

37. *New York Herald*, "Follies Come to Amuse New York," 2 June 1914, p. 9.

38. *Variety*, "Ziegfeld Follies," 5 June 1914, p. 15.

39. Burns Mantle, "The Stage: Some Early Season Misadventures," *Munsey's Magazine* 53 (October 1914), pp. 1, 90.

40. *NYT*, "Follies Begin Summer Capers," 2 June 1914, p. 11.

41. *New York Herald*, 2 June 1914, p. 9.

42. Mantle, *Munsey's Magazine*, p. 90.

43. *New York Herald*, 2 June 1914, p. 9.

44. *Variety*, 5 June 1914, p. 15.

45. "At the Theatres," *Theatre Magazine*, 20 (July 1914), p. 37.

46. L. P. Williams, "The Tango Picnic," *Age*, 23 July 1914, p. 6.

47. *Age*, "Theatrical Jottings," 6 August 1914, p. 6.

48. N. H. Jefferson, "Aida Overton Walker ... Dies," *Chicago Defender*, 17 Oct. 1914, p. 1; Sylvester Russell, "Aida Overton Walker," *Freeman*, 17 Oct. 1914, p. 5.

49. Juli Jones, Jr., "Chicago Mourns for Noted Artist," *Chicago Defender*, 17 Oct. 1914, p. 7.

50. Jefferson, *Chicago Defender*, 17 Oct. 1914, p. 1; Russell, 17 Oct. 1914, p. 5.

51. *Age*, "Aida Overton Walker Is Dead," 15 Oct. 1914, p. 1.

52. Columbus Bragg, "Chicago Mourns for Noted Artist," *Chicago Defender*, 17 Oct. 1914, p. 5.

Chapter 21

1. ROW, p. 128. See also *NOB*, p. 132.

2. *COC*, p. 340.

3. Channing Pollack, "Building the Follies," *Green Book Magazine* 14 (September 1915), p. 388.

4. Ibid., p. 394.

5. Ibid.

6. Ibid., p. 402.

7. *Variety*, "Ziegfeld Follies of 1915," 25 June 1915, p. 15.

8. *NYT*, "Ziegfeld Follies Here Resplendent," 22 June 1915, p. 15.

9. *New York World*, "New Model of Follies Is Easily Best of All," 22 June 1915, p. 9.

10. *New York Tribune*, "Follies of 1915 Fly into Town," 22 June 1915, p. 9.; *Variety*, 25 June 1915, p. 15.

11. *NYT*, 22 June 1915, p. 15.

12. *COC*, p. 422.

13. See "Discography" in *NOB*, p. 151.

14. *Age*, 13 June 1916, p. 6.

15. Sister Mary Francesca Thompson, "The Lafayette Players, 1915-1932," Ph.D. Dissertation, The University of Michigan, 1972, p. 32.

16. Program, *Ziegfeld Follies of 1916*, New Amsterdam Theater, NYPL.

17. *Variety*, "Ziegfeld Follies," 16 June 1916, p. 13.

18. *New York Tribune*, 13 June 1916, p. 9.

19. *NYT*, 13 June 1916, p. 9.

20. *New York Herald*, "Mr. Ziegfeld's New Follies a Hit in Which Beauty, Art and Melody Mingle," 13 June 1916, p. 14.

21. *Variety*, 16 June 1916, p. 13.

22. Richard Buckle, *Nijinsky*. (New York: Simon & Schuster, 1971), p. 360.

23. *NYT*, 13 June 1916, p. 9.

24. Ibid.

25. *New York Herald*, 13 June 1916, p. 14.

26. *New York Tribune*, 13 June 1916, p. 9.

27. *New York World*, 13 June 1916, p. 9.

28. See "Discography" in *NOB*, p. 151.

29. *Age*, "Theatrical Jottings, 29 June 1916, p. 6.

30. Phyllis Rauch Klotman, *Frame by Frame: A Black Filmography*. (Bloomington: Indiana University Press, 1970), p. 177.

31. See Eastin Phelan Corporation, sales flyer, vol. 22, c. 1990, P.O. Box 4528, Davenport, IA, 52808.

32. *Moving Picture World*, "Comments on the Films," 12 August 1916, p. 1103.

33. ROW, p. 150.

34. "Bert Williams," *The Soil: A Magazine of Art*, 1, no. 1 (December 1916), p. 22.

35. Ibid., p. 19. See also parallel quotation in *ROW*, p. 94.

36. Ibid.

37. Ibid., pp. 20–21.

38. Konstantin Stanislavsky, *Building a Character*, trans. by Elizabeth Reynolds Hapgood. (London: Eyre Methuen, 1950), pp. 173, 175.

39. *The Soil*, pp. 21–22.

40. Ibid., p. 19.

Chapter 22

1. *Age*, "Negro Troops for NYNG," 29 June 1916, p. 1; Roi Ottley and William Weatherby eds. *The Negro in New York: An Informal Social History*. (New York: New York Public Library/Dobbs Ferry, N.Y.; Oceana Publications, Inc. 1967), p. 201.

2. *Age*, "Twenty-five Go to Plattsburg," 17 May 1917, p. 1.

3. Arthur W. Little, *From Harlem to the Rhine: The Story of New York's Colored Volunteers*. (New York: Covici Friede Publishers, 1930), pp. 9–10.

4. Ottley, p. 201.

5. Little, pp. 9–10.

6. Lloyd Lewis, "Life with Uncle Eggs," *Chicago Sun*. Book week supplement, 28 April 1946, p. 3.

7. Tom Fletcher, *100 Years of the Negro in Show Business*. (New York: Burdge, 1954), p. 249.

8. Ottley, p. 201.

9. Anthony Slide, *The Vaudevillians: A Dictionary of Vaudeville Performers*. (Westport, Conn.: Arlington House, 1981), p. 23.

10. Eddie Cantor with Jane Kesner Ardmore, *Take My Life*. (Garden City, N.Y.: Doubleday, 1957, pp. 124–125; Eddie Cantor, *As I Remember Them*. (New York: Duell, Sloan and Pearce, 1963, p. 48.).

11. *NYT*, 17 June 1917, p. 5.

12. Cantor, *As I Remember Them*, pp. 48–49.

13. *NYT*, "The Follies of 1917; Hitchy-Koo," 13 June 1917, sec. 8, p. 5.

14. *New York Herald*, "Ziegfeld Follies Here Again," 13 June 1917, p. 5.

15. Cantor, *As I Remember Them*, p. 49.

16. *New York Herald*, 13 June 1917, p.3.

17. Ibid.

18. Donald Elder, *Ring Lardner: A Biography*. (Garden City, N.Y.: Doubleday and Company, Inc.), p. 147.

19. Jonathan Yardley, *Ring: A Biography of Ring Lardner* (New York: Random House, 1977, pp. 199–200). See "Discography" in *NOB*, p. 151, for listing of "No Place Like Home."

20. Program, *Ziegfeld Follies of 1917*, New Amsterdam Theater, NYPL.

21. See David A. Jasen and Treber Jay Trehener, *Rags and Ragtime, a Musical History*. (New York: Dover Publications, Inc., 1978), pp. 55–56.

22. David A. Jasen, *Tin Pan Alley*. (New York: Donald I. Fine, Inc., 1988), p. 110.

23. "Follies of 1917 Is a Fine Spectacle," *New York Herald*, 13 June 1917, p. 17.

24. *NYT*, 13 June 1917, p. 11.

25. *New York Herald*, 13 June 1917, p. 7.

26. *New York Tribune*, "The Follies Revealed in All Their Pristine Glory at the New Amsterdam," 13 June 1917, p. 11.

27. *NYT*, 13 June 1917, p. 11; *New York Tribune*, 13 June 1917, p. 11.

28. *NYT*, 17 June 1917, sec. 8, p. 5; *New York World*, 13 June 1917, p. 9.

29. *New York Tribune*, 13 June 1917, p. 11.

30. *New York American*, "Beauty Revel in Ziegfeld Follies," 13 June 1917, p. 7.

31. *New York Herald*, 13 June 1917, p. 7.

32. *Variety*, "Bert Williams Scenarios," 9 February 1917, p. 18.

33. Andrew Rolle, *California: A History*, 4th ed. (Arlington Heights, Ill.: Harlan Davidson, Inc., 1987), p. 428.

34. *Variety*, 27 August 1917, p. 24.

35. "Discography," *NOB*, p. 151.

36. Cantor, *As I Remember Them*, p. 50.

37. Bert A. Williams, "The Comic Side of Trouble," *American Magazine* 85 (January 1918), p. 33.

38. Ibid.

39. Lester A. Walton, "Bert Williams on Race Problem," *Age*, 4 May 1918, p. 6.

40. *Age*, "Bert Williams a Hit in Midnite Frolic," 20 June 1918, p. 6.

41. *Age,* "Bert Williams Now a Full-Fledged Citizen," 22 June 1918, p. 1.

42. Cantor, *My Life Is in Your Hands,* p. 153.

43. Cantor, *As I Remember Them,* p. 25.

44. *New York Evening Journal* review quoted in *Age,* 20 July 1918, p. 6.

45. *Age,* 20 July 1918, p. 6.

46. Lester A. Walton, "Benefit at Alhambra a Big Success," *Age,* 6 August 1918, p. 6.

47. Jasen, *Tin Pan Alley,* p. 60.

48. Ibid., pp. 89–90.

49. *Variety,* "New Acts This Week," 6 Dec. 1918, p. 16.

50. *Variety,* "Palace," 6 Dec. 1918, p. 17.

51. *Age,* "Theatrical Chit-Chat," 7 Dec. 1918, p. 6.

52. *Variety,* "The Ziegfeld Frolics," 13 Dec. 1918, p. 16.

53. "One Man's Meat," *Life,* 26 Dec. 1918, p. 972.

54. "Bert Williams," *The Soil, a Magazine of Art* 1, no. 1 (December 1916), p. 21; see also ROW, p. 95.

Chapter 23

1. See "Discography" in *NOB,* p. 151.

2. *Chicago Defender,* "Mrs. Bert Williams Entertains," 1 March 1919, p. 5.

3. *MOBA,* p. 367.

4. Frank C. Taylor with Gerald Cook, *Alberta Hunter: A Celebration in Blues.* (New York: McGraw-Hill), 1987, pp. 33–34.

5. Ibid., pp. 44–45.

6. Ibid., p. 45.

7. *Variety,* "Colonial," 21 March 1919, p. 20.

8. *Variety,* "Palace," 28 March 1919, p. 61.

9. See "Discography" in *NOB,* p. 151.

10. *Variety,* "Royal," 11 April 1919, p. 22.

11. "It's Nobody's Business but My Own." Music and lyrics by Will E. Skidmore and Marshall Walker. Copyright 1919 by Skidmore Music Co.

12. *Age,* "Theatrical Jottings," 24 May 1919, p. 6.

13. Billie Burke with Cameron Shipp, *With a Feather in My Cap.* (New York: Appleton-Century Crofts, Inc., 1949), pp. 196–97.

14. *New York Herald,* "Thirteenth Ziegfeld Follies Eclipses Predecessors in Beauty, Color and Action," 17 June 1919, p. 10.

15. The photograph is reproduced in ROW, pp. 104–5, and *NOB,* p. 142.

16. *New York Herald,* 17 June 1919, p. 10; *New York Evening Post,* "Ziegfeld Follies," 17 June 1919, p. 19.

17. *Variety,* "Ziegfeld Follies," 20 June 1919, p. 14.

18. *Variety,* "Minstrel Show in Follies," 6 June 1919, p. 13; *New York Evening Post,* 17 June 1919, p. 9.

19. "I Want to See a Minstrel Show." Music and lyrics by the Leighton Brothers and Ren Shields. Copyright 1913 by M. Witmark and Sons. In *Delaney's Songbook,* no. 66, Music Collection, New York Public Library.

20. Eddie Cantor, *My Life Is in Your Hands.* (New York: Harper & Brothers, Publishers, 1928), p. 159.

268   BERT   WILLIAMS

21. John Corbin, "Aphrodisiac Follies," *NYT*, 17 June 1919, p. 20.

22. *Variety*, 20 June 1919, p. 14.

23. Heywood Broun, "New Edition of the Follies Lives Up to Tradition of Beauty," *New York Tribune*, 17 June 1919, p. 13.

24. Bert A. Williams, "Keeping Up with the New Laughs," *Theatre Magazine* 29, no. 220 (June 1919), p. 346.

25. Ibid.

26. Charles Higham, *Ziegfeld*. (Chicago: Henry Regnery Co., 1972), pp. 134–135.

27. "You Cannot Make Your Shimmy Shake on Tea." Music by Irving Berlin. Lyrics by Rennold Wolf.

28. *Variety*, 20 June 1919, p. 14.

29. Sam Dennison, *Scandalize My Name: Black Imagery in American Popular Music*. (New York: Garland Publishing, 1982), p. 456.

30. William M. Stowe, Jr., "Damn Funny: The Tragedy of Bert Williams," *Journal of Popular Culture* 10, no. 1 (Summer 1976), pp. 5–6.

31. Williams, *Theatre Magazine*, pp. 346–348.

32. Robert Edgar Faulkender, "Historical Development and Basic Policies of the Actor's Equity Association," Ph.D. diss., University of Pittsburgh, 1954, p. 15.

33. Actor's Equity Association, *The Actor's Equity Association: A Voluntary Association*. (New York: AEA, 1915), p. 9; Faulkender, pp. 25–26; Milton Sills, "Shall Actors Unionize," *DM*, 25 March 1916, p. 6.

34. Faulkender, p. 34.

35. Ibid.

36. Alfred Harding. *The Revolt of the Actors*. (New York: William Morrow and Co., 1929), p. 76.

37. Alfred Harding, "A Brief History of the Actor's Equity Association," in Alfred L. Bernheim et al., *The Business of the Theatre: an Economic History of the American Theatre, 1750–1932*. (New York: Benjamin Blom, 1932), p. 134.

38. Ethel Barrymore, "The Actor's Strike," *The Outlook* 123 (3 Sept. 1919), p. 11.

39. Ibid., p. 12.

40. Florenz Ziegfeld, Jr., "And on the Other Hand," *Theatre Magazine* 25, no. 191 (January 1917), p. 12.

41. *Variety*, "Biggest Takings Thus Far…," 9 Aug. 1919, pp. 25–26.

42. Harding, pp. 80–81.

43. Ibid., p. 83.

44. Cantor, *My Life Is in Your Hands*, pp. 207–8.

45. *Variety*, "Ziegfeld Out and In," 11 August 1919, p. 29; Harding, p. 105.

46. *Variety*, "Summer Season Now in Full Swing," 27 June 1919, p. 14; *Variety*, "New Producing Season Starts Before Out Season Has Passed," 4 July 1919, p. 13.

47. Harding, p. 105.

48. Ibid.

49. Ibid.

50. Ibid., pp. 105, 106, 121.

51. *Variety*, "Follies Gives Performance by Injunction," 12 August 1919, p. 33.

52. *Variety*, "All Working in Follies," 13 August 1919, p. 36.

53. *NYT*, "Chicago Theatres Closed by Strike; Bitter Fight Here," 13 August 1919, p. 12; Cantor, *My Life Is in Your Hands*, p. 208.

54. *NYT*, "Strike Closes Two More Playhouses," 14 August 1919, p. 1; Harding, p. 127.

55. *NYT*, 14 August 1919, p. 1; Harding, p. 127.
56. ROW, pp. 129–130.
57. Dempsey J. Travis, *An Autobiography of Black Jazz.* (Chicago: Urban Research Institute, 1983), p. 18.
58. Cantor, *My Life Is in Your Hands*, p. 208; *Variety*, "Ziegfeld Paying Full Salaries," 15 August 1919, p. 19; *Variety*, "Five Other Shows Closed by Stagehands' Walkout," 19 August 1919, p. 31.

Chapter 24

1. See "Discography" in *NOB*, p. 151.
2. *MOBA*, p. 331.
3. Ibid., p. 330.
4. Ibid., p. 331.
5. Ibid., p. 333.
6. Folkways Records #RBF602, "Nobody and Other Songs by Bert Williams," 1981.
7. ROW, pp. 137–138.
8. *New York Evening Telegram*, "George LaMaire Brings New Production – Broadway Brevities – into Winter Garden," 30 Sept. 1920, p. 20.
9. "I Want to Know Where Tosti Went (When He Said Goodbye)." Music and lyrics by Chris Smith. Copyright 1920 by Shapiro and Berstein and Co., Inc., New York. Tosti probably is a reference to popular art song composer Paolo Tosti, who composed the tune "Goodbye!" See *JBJ*, p. 61.
10. Charles Higham, *Ziegfeld.* (Chicago: Henry Regnery Co., 1972), p. 138.
11. Theater program, *Broadway Brevities of 1920*, Winter Garden File, NYPL.
12. *New York Evening Telegram*, 30 Sept. 1920, p. 20.
13. *New York Evening Post*, "George LaMaire's Broadway Brevities of 1920," 30 Sept. 1920, p. 9.
14. *NYT*, "Broadway Brevities of 1920," 30 Sept. 1920, p. 12.
15. *New York Evening Post*, 30 Sept. 1920, p. 9.
16. "Winter Garden," *Theatre Magazine* 32 (December 1920), p. 371.
17. Heywood Broun, "Broadway Brevities Is Produced at the Winter Garden," *New York Tribune*, 30 Sept. 1920, p. 8; *Theatre Magazine* (December 1920), p. 371; *Philadelphia Inquirer*, "Lyric," 12 Sept. 1920, p. 8.
18. *New York Evening Post*, 30 Sept. 1920, p. 9.
19. *NYT*, 30 Sept. 1920, p. 12.
20. *AMT*, p. 354; Jack Burton, *The Blue Book of Broadway Musicals*; with additions by Larry Freeman. (Watkins Glen, N.Y.: Century House, 1952; 1969), p. 306.
21. Nathan Irvin Huggins, *Harlem Renaissance.* (London: Oxford University Press, 1971), pp. 296–297.
22. Arthur and Barbara Gelb, *O'Neill* (New York: Harper & Brothers, 1960; 1962), p. 445.
23. Ibid.
24. Martin Bauml Duberman, *Paul Robeson.* (New York: Alfred A. Knopf, 1988), pp. 580–582.
25. Mary B. Mullett, "Where Do I Go from Here?" *American Magazine*, vol. 91 (June 1921), p. 134.

26. Alexander Woollcott, "The New O'Neill Play," *NYT*, 7 Nov. 1920, sec. 7, p. 1.

27. *Age*, "Charles S. Gilpin Is Optimistic as to Future Success of Dramatic Stock," 19 March 1921, p. 6.

28. Tom Fletcher, *100 Years of the Negro in Show Business*. (New York: Burdge, 1954), p. 242.

29. See Gelb, pp. 445–446, for a description of this episode.

30. Marian Storm, "All 135th Street Is Missing Bert Williams," *New York Evening Post*, 7 April 1922, p. 16.

31. Ibid.

32. Lucien H. White, "A Review of *Taboo*," *New York Age*, 13 April 1922, p. 6.

Chapter 25

1. Roi Ottley and William Weatherby, ed., *The Negro in New York*. (New York: New York Public Library/Dobbs Ferry, N.Y.: Oceana Publications, 1967), p. 245.

2. Nathan Irvin Huggins, *Harlem Renaissance*. (London: Oxford University Press, 1971), p. 52.

3. Peter S. Woods, "The Negro on Broadway: The Transition Years, 1920–1930," Ph.D. dissertation, Yale University, 1965, pp. 4–5.

4. Lester A. Walton, "Shuffle Along Latest Musical Gem to Invade Broadway," *Age*, 4 June 1921, p. 6.

5. Alan Dale, "Shuffle Along Full of Pep and Real Melody, *New York American*, quoted in Robert Kimball and William Bolcom, *Reminiscing with Sissle and Blake* (New York: Viking Press, 1973), p. 99.

6. Ibid., p. 94.

7. Lester A. Walton, "Shuffle Along Is in Its Sixth Month Run," *Age*, 15 October 1921, p. 6.

8. Marian Storm, "All 135th Street Is Missing Bert Williams," *New York Evening Post*, 7 April 1922, p. 16.

9. Ibid.

10. See Elliott Arnold, *Deep in My Heart: A Story Based on the Life of Sigmund Romberg*, New York: Duell, Sloan and Pearce, 1949; personal communication from John A. Emerson, University of California at Berkeley, Music Library, to the author, 1 Nov. 1985.

11. "Statement of Operations, 1921–1922," *Under the Bamboo Tree/Pink Slip* files, Shubert Archive.

12. Ibid.

13. Typescript of *Under the Bamboo Tree*, *Under the Bamboo Tree/Pink Slip* files, Shubert Archive, pp. 1–2.

14. "If What I See Comes True." Music by Sigmund Romberg. Lyrics by Will Vodery and Matthew Woodward, c. 1921. *Under the Bamboo Tree*, music manuscripts, Shubert Archive.

15. Typescript, *Under the Bamboo Tree*, p. 21, Shubert Archive.

16. "Mixed Up" was written by Will Vodery, but the composer of "Judge Grimes" is unknown.

17. Typescript, *Under the Bamboo Tree*, p. 12, Shubert Archive.

18. "Puppy Dog." Music by Will H. Vodery. Lyrics by Walter DeLeon. Cited in ROW, p. 171.

19. Ashton Stevens, "Bert Williams' Last Interview," in George Oppenheimer, ed., *The Passionate Playgoer* (New York: Viking Press, 1958), p. 157.

20. Charters is mistaken in stating that *Under the Bamboo Tree* went to rehearsal in January 1922, *NOB*, p. 146. It played in Cincinnati and Chicago in December 1921.

21. *Cincinnati Enquirer*, "Shubert–Bert Williams," 4 Dec. 1921, sec. 3, p. 2.

22. *Cincinnati Enquirer*, "Under the Bamboo Tree," 5 Dec. 1921, p. 13.

23. *Cincinnati Enquirer*, 5 Dec. 1921, p. 13.

24. Ibid.

25. "Statement of Operations, 1921–1922," *Under the Bamboo Tree/Pink Slip*, files, Shubert Archive.

26. Will H. Vodery to Bert Williams, 13 Dec. 1921. *Under the Bamboo Tree/Pink Slip* files, Shubert Archive.

27. Sheppard Butler, "Bert Williams with a Plot," *Chicago Tribune*, 12 Dec. 1921, p. 21.

28. Amy Leslie, "Bert Williams in Under the Bamboo Tree," *Chicago Daily News*, 12 Dec. 1921, p. 14.

29. *Chicago Tribune*, 12 Dec. 1921, p. 21.

30. *Chicago Daily News*, 12 Dec. 1921, p. 14.

31. *Chicago Tribune*, 12 Dec. 1921, p. 21.

32. *Chicago Daily News*, 12 Dec. 1921, p. 14.

33. Ibid.

34. Ibid.

35. "Financial Records," *Under the Bamboo/Pink Slip* files, Shubert Archive.

36. Bert Williams to David Beecher, 26 Jan. 1922, *Under the Bamboo Tree/Pink Slip* files, Shubert Archive.

37. Telegram, Bert A. Williams to J. J. Shubert, 22 January 1922, *Under the Bamboo Tree/Pink Slip* files, Shubert Archive.

38. Program, Garrick Theatre, Detroit, *Under the Bamboo Tree*, Detroit Public Library.

39. Letter, Bert A. Williams to Mabel Rowland. Reprinted in ROW, pp. 170–171.

40. "Statement of Operations, 1921–1922 Season," *Under the Bamboo Tree/Pink Slip* files, Shubert Archive.

Chapter 26

1. *NYT*, "Henry Herzbrun" (obituary), 17 Oct. 1953, p. 15.

2. ROW, pp. 153–54.

3. Al Weeks, "Bert Williams–It's His Show," *Detroit News*, 27 Feb. 1922, p. 16.

4. *Detroit Free Press*, "Bert Williams Dies in New York," 6 March 1922, p. 3.

5. *Detroit Journal*, "Garrick Theater a Revelation of Beauty and Utility," 2 Sept. 1909, p. 5.

6. Ralph Holmes, "Bert Williams Jovial in *Under the Bamboo Tree*," *Detroit Evening Times*, 27 Feb. 1922, p. 4.

7. *Detroit News*, 27 Feb. 1922, p. 16.

8. Len G. Shaw, "The Theatre," *Detroit Free Press*, 27 Feb. 1922, p. 2.

9. *Detroit News*, 27 Feb. 1922, p. 16.

10. *Detroit Times*, 27 Feb. 1922, p. 4; *Detroit Free Press*, 27 Feb. 1922, p. 2.

11. *Detroit News*, 27 Feb. 1922, p. 16.

12. *Detroit Free Press*, 27 Feb. 1922, p. 2.

13. Ibid.

14. Ann Charters mistakenly gives the date of Bert Williams's collapse as Feb. 25 instead of Feb. 27. See *NOB*, p. 146.

15. *Detroit Evening Times*, "Bert Williams Ill, May Play Tonight at Garrick," 28 Feb. 1922, p. 4.

16. Ed Sullivan, "Manhattan," *Detroit Free Press*, January 29, 1935, page number unknown, clipping in Bert Williams file, E. Azalia Hackley Collection, Detroit Public Library.

17. John Dancy, "John Dancy Recalls His Friends: Bert Williams, That Ziegfeld Man in Detroit," *Detroit Free Press*, 22 May 1966, p. 7.

18. *Detroit Evening Times*, "News of Williams' Death Shock to Theater Men," 6 March 1922, p. 11.

19. Sullivan, *Detroit Free Press*, January 29, 1935.

20. ROW, p. 192. See also parallel account in *NOB*, p. 145.

21. Ibid., pp. 166, 168.

22. John C. Dancy, *Sands Against the Wind: The Memoirs of John C. Dancy* (Detroit: Wayne State University Press, 1968), p. 118.

23. Ibid., p. 119.

24. ROW, p. 172.

25. Ibid., p. 172–173.

26. Death certificate of Bert Williams, Dept. of Health, City of New York, March 6, 1922; *New York World*, "Bert Williams, Comedian, Dead," 5 March 1922, p. 4.

27. ROW, p. 175.

28. *NYT*, "Bert Williams' Will Signed," 19 March 1922, p. 21.

29. Lester A. Walton, "Thousands of All Races Mourn Bert Williams' Death," *New York Age*, 11 March 1922, p. 1; *NYT*, "Throng at Bert Williams' Funeral," 8 March 1922, p. 15.

30. Walton, *Age*, 11 March 1922, p. 2.

31. Ibid.

32. Ibid.

33. Ibid.

34. *NYT*, "Masons Honor Williams," 9 March 1922, p. 18.

35. Ibid.

36. Ibid.

37. *New York Tribune*, "Theater Critics Lament Death of Bert Williams," 6 March 1922, p. 9.

38. *Detroit Evening Times*, "News of Williams' Death Shock to Theater Men," 6 March 1922, p. 11.

39. *NYT*, "Bert Williams, Negro Comedian Dies Here After Collapse on Detroit Stage," 5 March 1922, p. 1.

40. *New York Star*, quoted in ROW, p. 20.

41. David Belasco, "Rosemary, a Preface to the Life of Bert Williams," in ROW, p. xi.

42. ROW, p. 207.

43. Tony Langston, "Death Ends Career of Stage Idol," *Chicago Defender*, 11 March 1922, p. 1.

44. ROW, p. 199.

45. Heywood Broun, "It Seems to Me," *New York World*, 7 March 1922, p. 11.

46. Bert A. Williams, "The Comic Side of Trouble," *American Magazine* 85 (January 1918), p. 34.

47. Ibid., p. 61.

Annotated Bibliography

General Sources

Adams, Veronica. "The Dramatic Stage as an Upbuilder of the Races." *Chicago Interocean*, 17 Jan. 1909, magazine sec., p. 2. In an interview, Williams and Walker discuss their work and the prospect for black actors in the future.

Beerbohm, Max. "Some Irish Plays and Players." 9 Apr. 1904. In *Around Theatres*. 2 vols. New York: Alfred A. Knopf, 1930. Beerbohm criticizes the musical *In Dahomey* in a passing referrence.

Bordman, Gerald. *American Musical Theatre: A Chronicle*. New York: Oxford University Press, 1978. Extensive chronological examination of most of Williams's shows. Names contemporary shows, interpolating Williams's songs.

_____. *The Concise Oxford Companion to American Theatre*. New York: Oxford University Press, 1984. Provides entries for Williams, *In Dahomey*, and the *Ziegfeld Follies*.

Broun, Heywood. "It Seems to Me." *New York World*, 9 Mar. 1922, p. 11. Journalist questions Ring Lardner's appraisal of Bert Williams.

Brown, Janet. "The 'Coon Singer' and the 'Coon-Song': A Case of the Performer-Character." *Journal of American Culture* 7, no. 1–2 (Spring–Summer 1984), pp. 1–8. Detailed study of the sociology of blackface singers compares Bert Williams with Sophie Tucker.

Cantor, Eddie. "Bert Williams – the Best Teacher I Ever Had." *Ebony* 13, no. 8 (June 1958), pp. 103–6. Illustrated article on Williams by *Follies* costar.

_____. *My Life Is in Your Hands (As told to David Freedman)*. New York and London: Harper & Brothers, 1928. Comedian cites anecdotes about Bert Williams.

_____. *The Way I See It*. Edited by Phyllis Rosenteur. Englewood Cliffs, N.J.: Prentice-Hall, 1959. Passing reference to Williams as mime artist.

Cantor, Eddie, and David Freedman. *Ziegfeld, the Great Glorifier*. New York: Alfred H. King, 1934. Cantor recalls his *Follies* act with Williams.

Carter, Randolph. *The World of Flo Ziegfeld*. New York: Praeger 1974. Cites chronology of *Follies* series, with useful cast and production information.

Caruthers, Clifford M., ed. *Letters from Ring*. Flint, Mich.: Walden Press, 1979. Correspondence of journalist-songwriter Ring Lardner refers to songwriting efforts with Bert Williams in five letters. A letter from Williams to Lardner circa 1911 is also cited.

Charters, Ann. *Nobody: The Story of Bert Williams*. New York: Macmillan, 1970; DaCapo Press, 1983. Biography of Williams with emphasis on the entertainment milieu of his day. Includes a discography and sheet music of several songs by Williams.

Chicago Record Herald. "Bert Williams: Boy-Gentleman-Comedian." 25 Sept. 1910, sec. 6, p. 7. Interview with Bert Williams.

Cook, Will Marion. "Clorindy, or the Origin of the Cakewalk." *Theatre Arts* 31 (September 1947), pp. 61–65. Black composer claims he wrote the show *Clorindy* for Williams and Walker.

Cripps, Thomas. *Slow Fade to Black: The Negro in American Films, 1900–1942.* New York: Oxford University Press, 1977. Passing reference to Williams's film career, concerning William Foster, producer of Williams's first film, *The Pullman Porter.*

Dancy, John C. *Sands Against the Wind: The Memoirs of John C. Dancy.* Detroit: Wayne State University Press, 1968. Former head of the Detroit Urban League and friend of Williams recalls Williams in anecdotes, especially concerning Williams's last show, *Under the Bamboo Tree.*

Detroit Free Press, "John Dancy Recalls His Friends," 22 May 1966, p. 7. The head of the Detroit Urban League remembers his friend Bert Williams.

Dictionary of American Biography. Edited by Dumas Malone. 20 vols., with supplements. New York: Charles Scribner's Sons, 1936. Volume 10 entry for Williams gives wrong year of birth but general account is accurate.

Donahue, Jack. "Hoofing," *Saturday Evening Post* 202, no. 11 (14 Sept. 1929), pp. 29, 233, 234, 237. Vaudeville dancer reminisces about the dancing of Williams and Walker.

Elder, Donald. *Ring Lardner: A Biography.* Garden City, N.Y.: Doubleday, 1956. Journalist friend of Williams describes their friendship and joint songwriting in detail. Cites letter from Williams to Lardner.

Emery, Lynne Fauley. *Black Dance in the United States from 1619 to 1970.* New York: Dance Horizons, 1980. Contains detailed discussion of the place of Williams and Walker in the history of black dance.

Enciclopedia Dello Spettacolo. 10 vols. and supplement. Rome: Casa Editrice le Maschere, 1954–56. Includes biography of Williams in Italian.

Fabre, Genevieve. *Le Theatre Noir aux Etats-Unis.* Paris: Editions du Centre National de la Récherche Scientifique, 1962. Includes detailed account in French of Williams and Walker's career in vaudeville and musical comedy.

Fauset, Jesse. "The Symbolism of Bert Williams." *Crisis,* 24 May 1922, pp. 12–15. Tribute to Williams stresses his San Francisco period. Illustrated.

Feingold, Michael. "Bert Williams: The Clown Who Quoted Aristotle." *Village Voice,* 14 Jan. 1971, pp. 55, 62–63. Retrospective look at Williams.

Fletcher, Tom. *100 Years of the Negro in Show Business.* New York: Burdge, 1954. Contains extensive information on Williams's shows. Cites early influences on Williams.

Gilbert, Douglas. *American Vaudeville: Its Life and Times.* London: Whittlesey House, 1940; 2d edition, New York: Dover Publications, 1963. Detailed biographical sketch contains many errors about Williams's life. Cites a typical Williams and Walker "crossfire" vaudeville routine of minstrel-show origin.

Giorgiady, Nicholas P., et al. *Bert Williams: American Negro Actor.* Illustrated by Robert Swan and Joseph S. Ferrara. Milwaukee: Franklin Publishers, Inc., 1969. The only entire book or booklet about Williams for young readers. Draws upon Cantor book and Rowland biography.

Graziano, John. "Sentimental Songs, Rags, and Transformations: The Emergence of the Black Musical, 1895–1910." In Glenn Loney, ed., *Musical Theatre in America: Papers and Proceedings of the Conference on the Musical Theatre in America*. (Contributions in Drama and Theatre Studies, No. 8) London: Greenwood Press, 1984. Extensive examination of black musicals, including the Williams and Walkers show *In Dahomey*.

Green, Jeffrey P. "In Dahomey in London in 1903," *The Black Perspective in Music* 11, no. 1 (Spring 1983), pp. 23–40. A thoroughly researched study of the British production of *In Dahomey*, citing many British reviews.

Haskins, Jim. *Black Theater in America*. New York: Thomas Y. Crowell, 1982. Chapter on Williams and Walker, including photos of the two.

Higham, Charles. *Ziegfeld*. Chicago: Henry Regnery Company, 1972. Detailed account of hiring of Williams and passing references to his appearances in the 1916 and 1917 *Follies*.

Hirsch, William. "Bert Williams," *Negro History Bulletin* 11 (1941), p. 45. Brief but correct biography.

Hyatt, Marshall, comp. and ed. *The Afro-American Cinematic Experience: An Annotated Bibliography and Filmography*. Wilmington, Del.: Scholarly Resources, 1983. *Darktown Jubilee* and *A Natural Born Gambler* are cited.

Jasen, David A. *Tin Pan Alley: The Composers, the Songs, the Performers and Their Times*. New York: Donald I. Fine, Inc., 1988. Biography of Bert Williams is accurate treatment of the comedian as a songwriter.

Jet. "Bert Williams? He Was Greatest, Most Imitated Comic in U.S." 59 (12 Feb. 1981), pp. 60–62. Detailed story on Williams's life quotes one of his last letters. Illustrated.

Johnson, Helen Armstead. "Themes and Values in Afro-American Librettos and Book Musicals, 1898–1930." In Glenn Loney, ed. *Musical Theatre in America: Papers and Proceedings of the Conference on the Musical Theatre in America* (Contributions in Drama and Theatre Studies, No 8). London: Greenwood Press, 1984. Extensive study of early black musicals, including *In Dahomey*, traces and reconstructs their original scores and librettos.

Johnson, James Weldon. *Along This Way*. New York: Viking Press, 1933. Detailed account of the milieu of Williams's early career touches on his relationships with Belasco and Ziegfeld.

————. *Black Manhattan*. New York: A. A. Knopf, 1930; Atheneum, 1975. Chapter 10 focuses on Williams and Walker, includes photo of the pair as young men.

Keaton, Buster. *My Wonderful World of Slapstick* (With Charles Samuels). Garden City, N.Y.: Doubleday, 1960; DaCapo Press, 1982. Passing reference to Williams and Aida Overton Walker.

Kees, Uncle Rad. "Williams and Walker: Or the Passing of Two of the World's Greatest Entertainers." *Indianapolis Freeman*, March 12, 1910, p. 5. Extensive examination of Williams and Walker's act focuses on Walker's contribution.

Kimball, Robert, and William Bolcom. *Reminiscing with Sissle and Blake*. New York: Viking Press, 1973. Passing references to Williams and the theatrical club the Frogs.

Klotman, Phyllis Rauch. *Frame by Frame: A Black Filmography*. Bloomington: Indiana University Press, 1979. *Fish*, *Darktown Jubilee*, and *A Natural Born Gambler* are named as Bert Williams's motion pictures.

Laforse, Martin, and James A. Drake. *Popular Culture and American Life: Selected Topics in the Study of American Popular Culture*. Chicago: Nelson-Hall, 1981.

Detailed account of Williams's career given in chapter on vaudeville images of blacks.

Lardner, Ring, Jr. *The Lardners: My Family Remembers*. New York: Harper & Row, 1976. Anecdotes about Ring Lardner, Sr.'s, friendship with Bert Williams.

Laurie, Joe, Jr. *Vaudeville from the Honky-Tonks to the Palace*. New York: Holt and Co., 1953. Many passing references to Williams and Walker.

Lewis, Lloyd. "Life with Uncle Eggs." *Chicago Sun Book Week*, 21 Apr. 1946, p. 3. First part of interview with Williams's niece, Charlotte Tyler.

_____. "A Great Stage Artist." *Chicago Sun Book Week*, 28 Apr. 1946, p. 3. Second part of interview with Charlotte Tyler.

_____. "Life with Uncle Eggs." *Negro Digest*, July 1946, pp. 19–22. Reprint of the April 21, 1946 interview.

Literary Digest. "Genius Defeated by Race." 72 (25 May 1922), pp. 28–29. Retrospective look at Williams's life argues that Williams was a victim of Jim Crow society.

The Messenger. "Bert Williams." 4, no. 4 (April 1922), p. 394. Posthumous article criticizes Williams for perpetuating racial stereotypes.

Mitchell, Lofton. *Black Drama*. Clifton, N.Y.: Hawthorn Books, Inc., 1967. Includes overview of Williams and Walker's career.

Monfried, Walter. "Bert Williams, the modern Pagliaccio," *Negro Digest* 11, no. 1, November 1961, pp. 28–32. Biography of Bert Williams gives wrong birthplace. Reprinted from the *Milwaukee Journal*.

Morath, Max. "The Vocal and Theatrical Music of Bert Williams and His Associates." In *Contributions in Drama and Theatre Studies* 1. Westport, Conn.: Greenwood Press, 1979, pp. 11–20. Despite its title, article focuses on milieu of Williams's music rather than his style of performing.

Moving Picture World 29, no. 7 (12 Aug. 1916), p. 1103. Review of *A Natural Born Gambler* is only known film review for Bert Williams.

Murray, R. C. "Williams and Walker, Comedians: Being An Appreciation Of Their Talents," *Colored American Magazine* 9, no. 3 (October 1903), pp. 496–502. Tribute to Williams and Walker, with biographical sketches of some members of the *In Dahomey* company.

Music Memories. "Bert Williams Cyclography." September 1962, p. 10. Includes British-label recordings made in 1904.

Negro History Bulletin. "Egbert Austin Williams." January 1939, p. 28. A detailed review of Bert Williams's career.

New York Age. "Bert Williams Celebrates 35th Birthday." 18 Nov. 1909, p. 6. The cast of *Mr. Lode of Koal* gives surprise party for the star.

_____. "Bert Williams Now a Full-Fledged Citizen." 22 June 1918, p. 1. Sole item documenting that Williams became a naturalized U.S. citizen in 1918.

New York Times. "Would Enjoin Bert Williams." 13 May 1910, p. 9. Lawsuit filed by F. Ray Comstock against Williams for breach of contract.

Niver, Kemp R. *Klaw and Erlanger Present Famous Plays in Pictures*. Edited by Bebe Bergston. Los Angeles: John D. Roche, 1939. Williams is said to have appeared in the 1914 Biograph film *The Indian*.

Osofsky, Gilbert. *Harlem: The Making of a Ghetto: Negro New York, 1890–1930*. New York: Harper Torchbooks, 1971. Detailed account of Williams's life.

Pollock, Channing. "Building the Follies." *Green Book* 14 (September 1915), pp. 388–403. A book writer for the *Ziegfeld Follies* discusses the plans for and rehearsals of Bert Williams skits for the 1915 *Follies*.

_____. *Harvest of My Years: An Autobiography*. Indianapolis: Bobbs-Merrill, 1943. Preparations for the 1915 *Follies* are described in one chapter.

Ramsaye, Terry. *A Million and One Nights: A History of the Motion Picture*. New York: Simon & Schuster, 1964. Detailed report of the filming and critical reception of *A Natural Born Gambler* and *Darktown Jubilee*.

Reed, Joseph W. "A Tribute to the Black Thespian." *Colored American Magazine* 10, no. 1, 1907, pp. 753–55. The contributions of Williams and Walker are cited.

Richards, Sandra. "Bert Williams: The Man and the Mask." *Mime, Mask and Marionette* 1 (Spring 1978), pp. 7–24. A critique of Williams's use of mime and the effect of Jim Crow on his life. Includes photos of Williams.

Riis, Thomas Laurence. "Black Musical Theatre in New York, 1890–1915." Ph.D. dissertation, University of Michigan, 1981. Extensive study of the songs and musicals of the Williams and Walker heyday are included in this important work.

_____. *Just Before Jazz: Black Musical Theater in New York, 1890–1915*. Washington and London, Smithsonian Institution Press, 1989. A music history scholar analyzes the music and productions of black theater, including those of Williams and Walker.

Rogers, Joel A. *World's Great Men of Color*. Edited with an introduction, commentary, and new bibliographical notes by John Henrik Clarke. 2 vols. New York: Macmillan, 1972. Extensive biography of Williams, with picture of Williams and Walker.

Rose, Al. *Eubie Blake*. New York: Schirmer Books, 1979. Composer Eubie Black cites many anecdotes about Williams.

Rowland, Mabel. *Bert Williams – Son of Laughter*. New York: English Crafters, 1923; Negro Universities Press, 1969. Along with Charters's book, it is considered a seminal work on Williams. Contains anecdotes and tributes by many of Bert Williams's acquaintances and friends.

Sampson, Henry T. *Blacks in Blackface: A Sourcebook on Early Black Musicals*. Metuchen, N.J.: Scarecrow Press, 1980. Extensive information about Williams and Walker shows, including casts, plots, musical numbers, and story lines. Biography sections cover Williams and many of his associates. Contains reprint of Williams's article in *American Magazine* and several photos from his career.

_____. *Blacks in Black and White: A Source Book on Black Films*. Metuchen, N.J.: Scarecrow Press, 1977. Credits Williams with the motion pictures *Darktown Jubilee*, *A Natural Born Gambler*, and *The Pullman Porter*.

_____. *The Ghost Walks: A Chronological History of Blacks in Show Business, 1865–1910*. Metuchen, N.J.: Scarecrow Press, 1988. Williams and Walker cited in numerous excerpts from obscure newspaper reviews.

Saunders, Doris. "Command Performance of Williams and Walker." *Negro Digest* 11, March 1962, pp. 16–21. Story about the *In Dahomey* company in England in 1903.

Slide, Anthony, ed. *Selected Vaudeville Criticism*. Metuchen, N.J.: Scarecrow Press, Inc., 1988. Includes excerpts from two vaudeville reviews of Williams as well as Ashton Stevens's *Actorviews*.

Slide, Anthony. *The Vaudevillians, a Dictionary of Vaudeville Performers*. Westport, Conn.: Arlington House, 1981. Includes a full and accurate biographical entry for Bert Williams along with several photographs.

Smith, Eric Ledell. "In Dahomey: The History of a Bert Williams and George Walker Musical Comedy, 1902-1905." M.A. thesis, New York University, Performance Studies Dept., 1985. Extensive study of *In Dahomey* is only known thesis or dissertation ever written on Bert Williams. It cites many reviews and songs as well as firsthand accounts by Williams and Walker.

Snow, Richard F. "American Characters: Bert Williams," *American Heritage* 31, no. 5 (August–September 1980), pp. 46–47. Biographical article borrows from Rowland book and George Walker articles.

The Soil, a Magazine of Art. "Bert Williams." 1, no. 1 (December 1916), pp. 19–23. Although the article is signed "J. B.," Rowland argues that the writer was the magazine's editor: R. J. Coady. Williams talks about his acting and race relations.

Southern, Eileen. *Biographical Dictionary of Afro-American and African Musicians*. Westport, Conn.: Greenwood Press, 1982. Biographies of Williams and Walker and many of their associates.

_____. *The Music of Black Americans: A History*. 2d edition. New York and London: W. W. Norton, 1983. Short overview of Williams and Walker's career, useful in context of black musical theater history.

Stevens, Ashton. "Bert Williams' Last Interview." In George Oppenheimer, ed., *The Passionate Playgoer*. New York: Viking Press, 1958, pp. 154–57. Williams talks about his life and his show *Under the Bamboo Tree*.

_____. *Actorviews*. Chicago: Corici-McGee Co., 1923. Includes "Bert Williams' Last Interview."

Storm, Marian. "All 135th Street Is Missing Bert Williams." *New York Evening Post*, 7 Apr. 1922, p. 16. Important interview with Mrs. Bert Williams and Williams's friend John Nail. Topics discussed include the show *Under the Bamboo Tree*, Williams's home rehearsals, and his dream of starring in a serious play.

Stowe, William M., Jr. "Damn Funny: the Tragedy of Bert Williams," *Journal of Popular Culture* 10, no. 1 (Summer 1976), pp. 5–13. The impact of segregation on Williams's life and career is stressed.

Taylor, Frank C. (With Gerald Cook). *Alberta Hunter: A Celebration in Blues*. New York: McGraw-Hill Book Company, 1987. Hunter's close relationship with Williams's niece Lottie Tyler and Hunter's impressions of Williams are included in this biography.

Toll, Robert C. *On with the Show: The First Century of Show Business in America*. New York: Oxford University Press, 1976. Essay on Williams in Chapter 5 is historically accurate but basically draws on Ann Charters's biography.

_____. *Blacking Up – The Minstrel Show in Nineteenth Century America*. New York: Oxford University Press, 1974. Contains brief comments on Williams's minstrel-show roots.

Travis, Dempsey J. *An Autobiography of Black Jazz* (With an introduction by Studs Terkel). Chicago: Urban Research Institute, 1983. Detailed chapter on black show business describes some Bert Williams performances and Ben Vereen's impersonation of Williams.

Van Doren, Charles, ed. *Webster's American Biographies*. Springfield, Mass.: G. and C. Merriam, 1974. Brief biography of Williams included. Gives wrong year of birth.

Van Vechten, Carl. *In the Garret*. New York: Alfred A. Knopf, 1920. Anecdotes about the dancing of Williams and Walker.

Variety. 27 Aug. 1917, p. 24. Williams's interest in doing film work for independent company is noted.

Varhoff, Edward, and Rima Shore. *The International Dictionary of 20th Century Biography*. New York/Scarborough, Ontario: New American Library, 1987. Entry for Williams gives birthplace as the Bahamas.

Walker, Aida Overton. "Colored Men and Women on the Stage." *Colored American Magazine*, October 1905, pp. 571–75. Mrs. Walker discussed the situation of blacks in theater with comments on Williams and Walker. Includes photo of Mrs. Walker.

_____. "Opportunities the Stage Offers Intelligent and Talented Women." *New York Age*, 24 Dec. 1908, p. 1. Mrs. Walker offers advice to young black women considering careers in theater.

Walker, George. "Bert and Me and Them." *New York Age*. 24 Dec. 1908, p. 4. Walker traces his partnership with Williams from the late 1890s up to 1908.

_____. "The Real Coon on the American Stage," *Theatre Magazine* 6, no. 66 (August 1906), p. 224. Walker talks about Bert Williams and the future for blacks in the American theater. Illustrated.

_____. "The Negro on the American Stage." *Colored American Magazine* 11, no. 4 (October 1906), pp. 243–48. Reprint of *Theatre Magazine* article.

Walsh, Jim. "Favorite Pioneer Recording Artists – Bert Williams, a Thwarted Genius, Part 1," *Hobbies*, September 1950, pp. 23–25, 36. First of a series of articles describing Williams's career as a recording artist.

_____. "Favorite Pioneer Recording Artists – Bert Williams, a Thwarted Genius, Part II." *Hobbies*, October 1950, pp. 19–20. Williams's recording career is evaluated from 1906 to 1909.

_____. "Favorite Pioneer Recording Artists – Bert Williams, a Thwarted Genius, Part III." *Hobbies*, November 1950, pp. 19–22. A discography of Williams's recordings concludes a discussion of some of Williams's final records.

Walton, Lester A. "The Future of the Negro on the Stage," *Colored American Magazine* 6, no. 6 (May 1903), pp. 439–42. Discussion of the impact of Williams and Walker on the black theater of their time.

_____. "Bert Williams on Race Problems." *New York Age*, 4 May 1918, p. 6. Williams speaks out on racism and the role of black soldiers in World War I.

Washington, Booker T. "Interesting People: Bert Williams." *American Magazine* 70, September 1910, pp. 600, 601, 603, 604. Tribute to Williams by the great black leader.

_____. "Dr. Washington Likes Bert Williams' Work," *Chicago Defender*, November 19, 1910, p. 3. Washington salutes the work of Bert Williams.

Who Was Who in America with World Notables. 6 vols. (Chicago: Marquis/Who's Who Inc., 1968). Vol. 4 contains entry for Williams. Notes Williams's study of pantomime with Pietro.

Williams, Bert A. "My Trip Abroad," c. 1900–11. Notebook in San Francisco Performing Arts Library and Museum. Not a travel diary but a notebook kept by Williams as a combination memobook, address book, and record book of road-show dates and routes. It contains some useful information about Williams.

_____. "Williams Tells of Walker." *Indianapolis Freeman*, 14 Jan. 1911, p. 5. Williams tells his life story.

_____. "The Negro on the Stage." *Green Book Album*, 4 Dec. 1910, pp. 1341–44. Williams traces the history of blacks in theater.

_____. "The Negro on the Stage." *New York Age*, 24 Nov. 1910, p. 6. Reprint of the *Green Book Album* article.

_____. "Keeping Up with the New Laughs." *Theatre Magazine* 29, no. 220 (June 1919), pp. 346–48. Williams elaborates his theories about comedy and music.

_____. "Comic Side of Trouble." *American Magazine* 85 (January 1919), pp. 35–36, 58. Williams reflects on his life as a comedian.

Wolf, Rennold. "The Greatest Comedian on the American Stage." *Green Book Magazine* 7 (June 1912), pp. 1173–84. Songwriter-playwright pays tribute to Williams.

Woll, Allen. *Black Musical Theatre from Coontown to Dreamgirls.* Baton Rouge and London: Louisiana State University Press, 1989. Chapter 3 deals with the musicals of Williams and Walker.

_____. *Dictionary of the Black Theatre.* Westport, Conn.: Greenwood Press, 1983. Gives play synopses, production facts, and song titles for many Williams shows. Individual entries include Aida Overton Walker, George Walker, and Bert Williams. Williams's entry fails to cite his appearance in the 1916 *Ziegfeld Follies, Broadway Brevities,* and *Under the Bamboo Tree.*

Yardley, Jonathan. *Ring: A Biography of Ring Lardner,* New York: Random House, 1977. Duplicates material found in Elder and Lardner.

Theater Reviews

Abyssinia

Boston Globe. "Williams and Walker." 3 Apr. 1906, p. 13.

Brooklyn Daily Eagle. "The Folly." 19 Feb. 1907, p. 4.

Chicago Tribune. "News of the Theaters." 29 May 1906, p. 8.

Cleveland Plain Dealer. "Lyceum–Abyssinia." 15 Jan. 1907, p. 4.

Louisville Courier-Journal. 2 Oct. 1906, p. 6.

New York Age. "Abyssinia." 22 Feb. 1906, p. 1.

New York Clipper. "Grand Opera House." 25 Aug. 1906, p. 8.

New York Clipper. "Majestic Theatre." 3 March 1906, p. 55.

New York Daily Tribune. "Abyssinia at the Majestic." 21 Feb. 1906, p. 7.

New York Dramatic Mirror. "Grand Opera House–Abyssinia," 25 Aug. 1906, p. 9.

New York Dramatic Mirror. "Majestic–Abyssinia." 3 March 1906, p. 3.

New York Evening Post. "Abyssinia." 21 Feb. 1906, p. 7.

New York Herald. "Abyssinia Only Good in Spots." 21 Feb. 1906, p. 8.

New York Times. "Williams and Walker Again." 21 Feb. 1906, p. 9.

Philadelphia Inquirer. "Abyssinia at the Park." 10 Apr. 1906, p. 4.

Theatre Magazine. 6, no. 62, April 1906, p. xiv.

Toronto Globe. "Music and the Drama," 12 Feb. 1907, p. 11.

Bandanna Land

Baltimore Sun. "Comedy in Color at the Academy." 11 Aug. 1908, p. 7.

Boston Globe. "Bandanna Land–Best of All the Williams and Walker Shows." 6 Sept. 1908, p. 2.

Chicago Tribune. "News of the Theatres." 11 Nov. 1907, p. 8.

Cincinnati Enquirer. "Colored Comedians." 1 March 1909, p. 8.

Detroit Free Press. "Lyceum–Williams and Walker in 'Bandanna Land.'" 6 Jan. 1908, p. 4.

Louisville Courier-Journal. "At the Masonic." 23 Feb. 1909, p. 4.

New York Clipper. "Grand Opera House." 22 Aug. 1908, p. 1395.

New York Clipper. "Majestic Theatre." 8 Feb. 1908, p. 1395.
New York Daily Tribune. "Majestic Theatre." 4 Feb. 1908, p. 7.
New York Dramatic Mirror. "Majestic – Bandanna Land." 15 Feb. 1908, p. 3.
New York Herald. "New Play Full of Music." 4 Feb. 1908, p. 10.
New York Sun. "Bandanna Land Pleases." 4 Feb. 1908, p. 7.
New York Times. "Bandanna Land Pleases." 4 Feb. 1908, sec. 7, p. 2.
Toledo Blade. "Williams and Walker's Show." 30 Dec. 1907, p. 5.
Toledo News-Bee. "Bandanna Land Is Liked." 30 Dec. 1907, p. 4.
Toronto Star. "Music and Fun at the Grand." 14 Jan. 1908, p. 9.
Walton, Lester A. "Williams and Walker on Broadway," *Colored American Magazine* 4 (1908), pp. 226–30.

Broadway Brevities

New York Evening Post. "Musical Plays." 30 Sept. 1920, p. 9.
New York Evening Telegram. "George Le Maire Brings New Production, 'Broadway Brevities,' into Winter Garden." 30 Sept. 1920, p. 20.
New York Times. "Broadway Brevities, 1920." 30 Sept. 1920, p. 12.
New York Tribune. "'Broadway Brevities' Is Produced at the Winter Garden." 30 Sept. 1920, p. 8.
Philadelphia Inquirer. "Lyric." 12 Sept. 1920, p. 8.
Theatre Magazine. "Winter Garden." Vol. 32, December 1920, p. 371.

Follies of 1910

Indianapolis Freeman. "At the Chicago Theatres: Burt *[sic]* Williams," 1 Oct. 1910, p. 5. Quotes interview with Williams by the Chicago *Record-Herald.*
Indianapolis Freeman. "The Follies of 1910, Bert Williams a Hit." 29 Oct. 1910, p. 5. Includes excerpt from a review by the *Indianapolis News.*
Leslie's Weekly. "Follies of 1910." Vol. 111, 7 July 1910, p. 11.
New York Evening Post. "Follies of 1910." 21 June 1910, p. 9.
New York Herald. "New Set of Follies in Jardin de Paris." 21 June 1910, p. 12.
New York Sun. "Follies of 1910 Arrives." 21 June 1910, p. 9.
New York Times. "Follies of 1910 On New York Roof." 21 June 1910, p. 9.
New York Tribune. "The Follies of 1910 Is Presented at New York Theatre." 21 June 1910, p. 7.
New York World. "Great Crowd Hails Follies Of 1910." 21 June 1910, p. 7.
Percy, Hammond. "The Follies Not Good But Reasonably Careful," *Chicago Tribune,* 6 Sept. 1910, p. 10.
Renaud, Ralph E. "Ziegfeld Offers Big Attraction." *San Francisco Chronicle,* 17 Apr. 1911, p. 2.
Russell, Sylvester. "Bert Williams in a White Show Makes a Big Hit at the Colonial." *Chicago Defender,* 10 Sept. 1910, p. 7. Review of the *Follies of 1910* in Chicago.
The Theater 12. "Jardin de Paris Follies of 1910," August 1910, p. 35.
Walton, Lester A. "Bert Williams Turns Philosopher." *New York Age,* 1 Dec. 1910, p. 6. Walton comments on the hiring of Williams by Ziegfeld.
_____. "Chicago Critics on Bert Williams." *New York Age,* 15 Sept. 1910, p. 6.

_____. *"Theatrical Comments, Bert Williams Feature of Follies of 1910."* New York Age, 23 June 1910, p. 6. Excerpts from New York reviews cited.

Washington Post. "National – The Follies of 1910." 27 Dec. 1910, p. 11.

In Dahomey

Baltimore Sun. "In Dahomey at the Lyric." 13 Sept. 1904, p. 8.

Boston Evening Transcript. "Boston Music Hall – In Dahomey." 23 Sept. 1902, p. 7.

Boston Globe. "Boston Music Hall – In Dahomey." 23 Sept. 1902, p. 8.

Boston Herald. "Music Hall – In Dahomey." 23 Sept. 1902, p. 10.

Boston Transcript. "Globe Theatre – In Dahomey." 21 March 1905.

Brooklyn Daily Eagle. "Many Kinds of Fun at Brooklyn Theatres." 18 Apr. 1905, p. 10.

Chicago Daily Tribune. "In Dahomey." 17 Oct. 1904.

Da Bubna, August. "The Negro on the Stage." *Theatre Magazine* 3, no. 26, April 1903, pp. 96–98.

Daily Mail (London). "In Dahomey Amusing Production at the Shaftesbury Theatre." 18 May 1903, p. 3.

Daily News (London). 18 May 1903, back page.

Daily State Gazette (Trenton, N. J.). 3 May 1905, p. 8.

Denver Post. "Williams and Walker at the Tabor Grand Yesterday." 28 Nov. 1904, p. 2.

Era (London). 23 May 1903, pp. 14, 16.

Globe (London). 18 May 1903, p. 8.

New York Clipper. 28 Feb. 1903, p. 6.

_____. 21 Mar. 1903, p. 96.

_____. 4 Apr. 1903, p. 44.

New York Evening Post. "In Dahomey." 28 August 1904, p. 7.

New York Herald. "In Dahomey Is Full of Music." 19 Feb. 1903, p. 13.

New York Mail and Express. "News of the Drama." 19 Feb. 1903, p. 4.

_____. "Stage and Foyer." 19 Feb. 1903, p. 4.

New York Times. "Dahomey on Broadway." 19 Feb. 1903, p. 9.

_____. "Invasion of London Stage by American Playwrights." 9 Aug. 1903, sec. 3, p. 21.

New York World. "Negro Show Made Stir on Broadway." 19 Feb. 1903, p. 3.

Pall Mall Gazette (London). 18 May 1903, p. 11.

Playgoer (London). "In Dahomey at the Shaftesbury Theatre, 1903," pp. 465–70.

Portland (Oregon) *New Age.* 31 Dec. 1904, sec. 5, p. 1.

Pryor, S. J. "S. J. Pryor Gives Impression of In Dahomey." *New York Times*, 19 July 1903, p. 3.

St. James Gazette (London). 18 May 1903.

St. Louis Republic. 25 Sept. 1904, p. 11.

San Francisco Chronicle. "Hit of Williams and Walker at Grand." 5 Dec. 1904, p. 9.

_____. "To Be Seen in Theatres," 11 Dec. 1904, p. 25.

Sphere (London). 23 May 1903, p. 162.

Standard (London). 18 May 1903, p. 5.

Times (London). "Shaftesbury Theatre." 18 May 1903, p. 12.

Weekly Dispatch (London). "Plays and Players." 24 May 1903, p. 6.

A Lucky Coon

Brooklyn Daily Eagle. "The Gayety." 17 Jan. 1899, p. 5.

Cleveland Plain Dealer. "The Star." 18 Apr. 1899, p. 3.

New York Dramatic Mirror. "The Burlesque Houses." 14 Jan. 1899, p. 18.

Washington Post. "Williams and Walker in 'A Lucky Coon' at the Academy." 9 May 1899, p. 7.

Mr. Lode of Koal

Boston Globe. "Mr. Lode of Koal." 25 Jan. 1910, p. 6.

Cleveland Plain Dealer. "Lyceum." 18 Jan. 1910, p. 4.

Howard, J. D. "Mr. Lode of Koal." *Indianapolis Freeman,* 6 Nov. 1909, p. 5. Review of Bert Williams's show in New York City.

Indianapolis Freeman. "Bert A. Williams at Kansas City, Mo." 2 Oct. 1909, p. 5.

Indianapolis Freeman. "Bert A. Williams & Co. in 'Mr. Lode of Koal,' a Hit on Broadway." 20 Nov. 1909, p. 6.

Kansas City Times. "Bert Williams at the Shubert." 20 Sept. 1909, p. 14.

New York Dramatic Mirror. "Majestic: Mr. Lode of Koal." 13 Nov. 1909, p. 7.

New York Evening Telegram. 2 Nov. 1909, p. 6. Review of *Mr. Lode of Koal* in New York.

New York Tribune. "Stage Affairs." 2 Nov. 1909, p. 6.

Philadelphia Inquirer. "Mr. Lode of Koal Wins Favor Up Town." 14 Dec. 1909, p. 12.

Royal, Bonney. "What Bonney Royal Saw at the Great Northern." *Chicago Tribune,* 6 Oct. 1909, p. 4.

Russell, Sylvester. "Bert A. Williams in *Mr. Lode of Koal*." *Indianapolis Freeman,* 16 Oct. 1909, p. 5.

St. Louis Post-Dispatch. "Bert Williams at the Garrick." 6 Sept. 1909, p. 6.

Swann, Thomas Wallace. "Bert Williams Wins West." *Indianapolis Freeman,* 9 Nov. 1909, p. 6. Critic judges the success of *Mr. Lode of Koal.*

Toledo Blade, 20 August 1909, p. 5. Review of the opening of *Mr. Lode of Koal.*

Walton, Lester A. "Music and the Stage," *New York Age,* 9 Sept. 1909, p. 6. Excerpts from Toledo, Ohio, reviews.

_____. "Music and the Stage." *New York Age,* 16 Sept. 1909, p. 6. Review of *Mr. Lode of Koal* in St. Louis.

_____. "Music and the Stage." *New York Age,* 7 Oct. 1909, p. 6. Interviews with performers along with excerpts from Chicago reviews of the show.

_____. "Music and the Stage." *New York Age,* 4 Nov. 1909, p. 6. Review of *Mr. Lode of Koal* in New York City.

_____. "Music and the Stage." *New York Age,* 9 Dec. 1909, p. 6. Review of *Mr. Lode of Koal* in Providence, Rhode Island.

The Policy Players

Baltimore Sun. "Farce at the Holliday." 7 Nov. 1899, p. 7.

Boston Daily Globe. "Music and Drama – Williams and Walker." 13 Mar. 1900, p. 9.

Brooklyn Daily Eagle. 31 Oct. 1899, p. 9.

_____. "The Bijou." 20 Mar. 1900, p. 9.

Chicago Tribune. "The Policy Players Again." 8 Feb. 1900, p. 8.
Cleveland Plain Dealer. "The Policy Players." 12 Dec. 1899, p. 5.
Detroit Free Press. "Lyceum – Williams and Walker." 18 Dec. 1899, p. 4.
Louisville Courier-Journal. "At the Theatres." 27 Nov. 1899, p. 5.
New York Clipper. "Star Theatre." 21 Oct. 1899, p. 698.
New York Dramatic Mirror. "Harlem Music Hall." 21 Oct. 1899, p. 18.
_____. "Star – Williams and Walker." 14 Oct. 1899, p. 16.
New York Times. "The Policy Players at Koster and Bial's." 3 Apr. 1900, p. 9.
Philadelphia Inquirer. "The Policy Players – Auditorium." 27 Mar. 1900, p. 5.

Senegambian Carnival

Boston Globe. "Senegambian Carnival." 2 Sept. 1898, p. 2.
Cincinnati Enquirer. "At Other Houses." 20 Sept. 1898, p. 5.
Philadelphia Inquirer. "At Other Houses." 13 Sept. 1898, p. 5.
Washington Post. "Williams and Walker's Senegambian Carnival at the Academy."
    11 Oct. 1898, p. 7.

The Sons of Ham

Brooklyn Daily Eagle. "The Bijou." 1 Oct. 1901, p. 6.
Chicago Tribune. "Popular Price Performances – The Sons of Ham." 17 Dec. 1901, p. 4.
Chicago Tribune "The Sons of Ham." 15 June 1902, p. 40.
Cincinnati Enquirer. "Sons of Ham." 9 Dec. 1901, p. 6.
Cleveland Plain Dealer. "Lyceum Theater – 'Sons of Ham,'" 11 Feb. 1902, p. 4.
Denver Post. "The Sons of Ham." 25 May 1902, sec. 2, p. 1.
Detroit Free Press. "Lyceum Theatre – Williams and Walker in 'Sons of Ham,'" 4
    Feb. 1902, p. 4.
Eaton, Henry. "The Stage." *Indianapolis Freeman,* 18 May 1901, p. 5. Review of the
    Sons of Ham in Boston.
Indianapolis Freeman. "The Stage." 27 Apr. 1901, p. 5. The manager of the *Sons of
    Ham* company comments on business.
_____. "The Stage." 21 Sept. 1901, p. 5. Passing reference to the first performance
    of the *Sons of Ham*'s second season, in Mount Vernon, New York.
Kansas City Star. "Grand – Williams and Walker." 6 Jan. 1902, p. 3.
New York Clipper. "Hurtig and Seamon's." 26 Oct. 1901, p. 756.
New York Dramatic Mirror. "Hurtig and Seamon's." 19 Oct. 1901, p. 18.
_____. "Hurtig and Seamon's." 26 Oct. 1901, p. 18.
_____. "Star – Sons of Ham." 20 Oct. 1900, p. 17. Review of the first-season New
    York opening of the show.
New York Times. "Sons of Ham Pleases." 4 Mar. 1902, p. 6.
Newark Evening News. "Sons of Ham." 12 Nov. 1901, p. 3.
Philadelphia Inquirer. "Auditorium." 8 Oct. 1901, p. 16.
_____. "National." 11 Mar. 1902, p. 7.
Salt Lake Herald. "Amusements." 17 May 1902, p. 4.
San Francisco Chronicle. "The Play Bills for This Week." 7 Apr. 1902, p. 2.
Seattle Republican. "Williams and Walker." 25 Apr. 1902, p. 4.

Under the Bamboo Tree

Butler, Sheppard. "Bert Williams with a Plot." *Chicago Tribune*, 12 Dec. 1921, p. 21.
Cincinnati Enquirer. "Under the Bamboo Tree." 5 Dec. 1921, p. 13.
Holmes, Ralph. "Bert Williams Jovial in 'Under the Bamboo Tree.'" *Detroit Times*, 27 Feb. 1922, p. 4.
Leslie, Amy. "Bert Williams in 'Under the Bamboo Tree.'" *Chicago Daily News*, 12 Dec. 1921, p. 14.
Shaw, Len G. "The Theatre." *Detroit Free Press*, 27 Feb. 1922, p. 2.
Weeks, Al. "Bert Williams–It's His Show." *Detroit News*, 27 Feb. 1922, p. 16.

Ziegfeld Follies of 1911

New York Age. "The Star Among Stars." 6 July 1911, p. 6.
New York Dramatic Mirror. "Jardin de Paris–Follies of 1911." 28 June 1911, p. 14.
New York Evening Post. "Follies of 1911." 27 June 1911, p. 9.
New York Herald. "Follies of 1911 Is a Great Big Colorful Show." 27 June 1911, p. 10.
New York Times. "Girls and Glitter in 'Follies of 1911.'" 27 June 1911, sec. 9, p. 3.
New York Tribune. "Follies of 1911 Here." 27 June 1911, p. 8.
Variety. "Follies of 1911." 1 July 1911, p. 20.

Ziegfeld Follies of 1912

New York Age. "The Follies of 1912." 24 Oct. 1912, p. 6.
New York Dramatic News 26, 1912, p. 21. *Frogs' Frolic of 1913*.
New York Times. "Follies of 1912 Is a Beauty Show." 22 Oct. 1912, sec. 11, p. 1.
New York Tribune. "Follies of 1912." 22 Oct. 1912, p. 9.
New York World. "Broadway Belated Night of Follies." 22 Oct. 1912, p. 5.
Variety. "Ziegfeld's Follies." 25 Oct. 1912, p. 22. *Frogs' Frolic of 1913*.
Walton, Lester A. "A Big Undertaking." *New York Age*, 21 Aug. 1913, p. 6. The Frogs' tour of Washington, D.C., Baltimore, Philadelphia, and Richmond, Virginia, is described.
_____. "The Frogs in Philly." *New York Age*, 14 Aug. 1913, p. 6. Review of Williams and the Frogs at Philadelphia's Academy of Music.
_____. "Music and the Stage." *New York Age*, 3 July 1913, p. 6.
_____. "Music and the Stage; Frogs Entertain," *New York Age*, 17 July 1913, p. 6.
_____. "An Unusual Bill." *New York Age*, 14 Aug. 1913, p. 6. Review of the appearance of Williams with Aida Overton Walker at the Manhattan Garden.

Ziegfeld Follies of 1914

Green Book. "The Ziegfeld Follies." Vol. 12 (August 1914), pp. 322–25.
Mantle, Burns. "The Stage: Some Early Season Misadventures." *Munsey's Magazine* 8, no. 1 (October 1914), pp. 88, 90, 92.
New York Dramatic Mirror. 3 June 1914, p. 8.

New York Herald. "'Follies' Come to Amuse New York with Dance, Mirth, and Melody." 2 June 1914, p. 9.
New York Times. "'Follies' Begin Summer Capers." 2 June 1914, sec. 11, p. 3.
Theatre Magazine. "Ziegfeld Follies." Vol. 20, July 1914, p. 37.
Variety. "Ziegfeld Follies." 5 June 1914, p. 15.

Ziegfeld Follies of 1915

Hackett, Frances. "Musical Comedy Evolves." *New Republic* 3, July 31, 1915, p. 336.
New York American. "Follies of 1915 Opens at Shore." 16 June 1915, p. 17. Review of the *1915 Follies* in Atlantic City.
New York Dramatic Mirror. 25 June 1915, p. 8.
New York Times. "Ziegfeld Follies Here Resplendent." 23 June 1915, sec. 15, p. 1.
New York Tribune. "Follies of 1915 Fly into Town." 22 June 1915, p. 7.
New York World. "New Model of Follies Is Easily Best of All." 22 June 1915, p. 9.
Theatre Magazine. "Ziegfeld Follies." Vol. 22 (August 1915), p. 66.
Variety. "Ziegfeld Follies." 31 July 1915, p. 15.

Ziegfeld Follies of 1916

New York American. "Broadway Gives a Rousing Greeting to the 1916 Ziegfeld Follies at the New Amsterdam." 13 June 1916, p. 9.
New York Dramatic Mirror. 17 June 1916, p. 8.
New York Herald. "Mr. Ziegfeld's New Follies a Hit in Which Beauty, Humor, Art and Melody Mingle." 13 June 1916, p. 14.
New York Times. "The 1916 Follies Full of Splendor." 13 June 1916, p. 9.
New York Tribune. "Follies Have Beauty Galore." 13 June 1916, p. 9.
New York World. "New Follies Show in Visions of Beauty." 13 June 1916, p. 9.
Theatre Magazine. "Ziegfeld Follies." Vol. 24 (July 1916), pp. 11, 41.
Variety. "Ziegfeld Follies." 16 June 1916, p. 13.
Walton, Lester A. "Bert Williams," *New York Age,* 15 June 1916, p. 6. Review of Williams's Shakespearean parody in the *Ziegfeld Follies of 1916* and excerpts from reviews of the show from the New York press.

Ziegfeld Follies of 1917

Dale, Alan. "Beauty Revel in Ziegfeld Follies." *New York American,* 14 June 1917, p. 7.
Hackett, Frances. "After the Play." *New Republic,* 11, 7 July 1917, p. 278.
New York Herald. "Ziegfeld Follies Here Again; Beauty, Fun, and Patriotism Meet in Beautiful Production." 13 June 1917, p. 5.
New York Times. "The Follies of 1917 Hitchy-Koo." 17 June 1917, sec. 8, p. 5.
_____. "'Follies of 1917' Is a Fine Spectacle." 14 June 1917, p. 11.
New York Tribune. "The Follies Revealed in All Their Pristine Glory at the New Amsterdam." 13 June 1917, p. 11.
New York World. "Ziegfeld Follies Welcomed with Joy." 13 June 1917, p. 9.

Ziegfeld Follies of 1919

Broun, Heywood. "New Edition of the Follies Lives up to Tradition of Beauty." *New York Tribune*, 17 June 1919, p. 13.
Corbin, John. "Aphrodisiac Follies." *New York Times*, 17 June 1919, p. 20.
New York Evening Post. "Ziegfeld Follies." 17 June 1919, p. 19.
New York Evening Telegram. "Getting Ready for John Barleycorn's Last Night." 17 June 1919, p. 10.
New York World. "The New 'Follies' Loveliest of All." 17 June 1919, p. 11.
Theatre Magazine. "Ziegfeld Follies." Vol. 30 (August 1919), p. 81.
Variety. "Ziegfeld Follies." 13 June 1919, p. 14. Review of the Atlantic City tryout.
_____. "Ziegfeld Follies." 20 June 1919, p. 14.

Ziegfeld's Midnite Frolic of 1918

Life. "Drama: One Man's Mean." Vol. 72 (26 Dec. 1918), p. 972. Review of the *Frolic* carries passing reference to Bert Williams's limited appearance.
New York Age. "Bert Williams a Hit in Midnite Frolic." 20 Aug. 1918, p. 6.
Variety. "The Ziegfeld Follies." 13 Dec. 1918, p. 15.

Vaudeville Reviews
(in chronological order)

New York Dramatic Mirror. "Koster and Bial's." 31 Oct. 1896, p. 9.
_____. "Proctor's." 19 Dec. 1896, p. 17.
_____. "Koster and Bial's." 9 Jan. 1897, p. 17.
_____. "Koster and Bial's." 16 Jan. 1897, p. 19.
_____. "Koster and Bial's." 23 Jan. 1897, p. 17.
_____. "Koster and Bial's." 6 Feb. 1897, p. 19.
_____. "Koster and Bial's." 27 Feb. 1897, p. 17.
Philadelphia Inquirer. "Bill at Keith's Bijou." 23 Mar. 1897, p. 5.
New York Dramatic Mirror. "Philadelphia Vaudeville Correspondence." 27 Mar. 1897, p. 20.
_____. "Keith's Union Square." 10 Apr. 1897, p. 17.
_____. "Keith's Union Square." 17 Apr. 1897, p. 17.
Boston Globe. "Keith's Theatre." 25 July 1897, p. 18.
New York Dramatic Mirror. "Proctor's." 1 Jan. 1898, p. 16. Review of Williams and Walker with Hyde's Comedians.
_____. "Vaudeville Correspondence." 30 Apr. 1898, p. 18. Review of Hyde's Comedians at the Orpheum Theater in San Francisco.
_____. "Vaudeville Correspondence." 18 June 1898, p. 18. Review of Williams and Walker with a stock company at the Hopkins Theater in Chicago.
_____. "Keith's Union Square." 22 June 1901, p. 16.
Walton, Lester. "Music and the Drama." *New York Age*, 2 May 1909, p. 6. Cites headlining dispute with the White Rats and includes excerpts from *New York Telegraph* review.

Walton, Lester A. "Music and the Drama." *New York Age*, 13 May 1909, p. 6. Reviews a Williams vaudeville act in Boston.
Pittsburgh Post. "In the Theaters Last Evening." 25 May 1909, p. 6.
Detroit Times. "Temple." 22 June 1909, p. 4.
Detroit Free Press. "Temple – Vaudeville." 22 June 1909, p. 4.
_____. "Music and the Stage." *New York Age*, 24 June 1909, p. 6. Williams in vaudeville at Detroit's Temple Theatre.
_____. "Music and the Stage." *New York Age*, 21 Apr. 1910, p. 6. Review of Williams's vaudeville act at the Hammerstein Theater cites excerpts from the *Morning Telegram* review and describes White Rats dispute.
Variety. "New Acts of the Week." 23 Apr. 1910, p. 12. Williams at the Hammerstein Theater in New York.
_____. "Hammerstein's." 30 Apr. 1910, p. 22.
_____. "Hammerstein's." 7 May 1910, p. 21.
_____. "Hammerstein's." 14 May 1910, p. 19.
_____. "Alhambra." 14 May 1910, p. 19.
_____. "New Acts Next Week." 26 Dec. 1913, p. 17. Williams at the Palace Theater in New York.
_____. "Palace." 26 Dec. 1913, p. 18.
_____. "Palace." 2 Jan. 1914, p. 20.
Walton, Lester A. "Theatrical Comment." *New York Age*, 12 March 1914, p. 6. "Bert Williams Is Headliner at Keith's [Theater in] Cleveland."
_____. "Benefit at Alhambra a Big Success." *New York Age*, 6 Aug. 1918, p. 6. Review of Williams at a benefit for the Colored Men's branch of the New York YMCA on July 27, 1918.
_____. "New Acts – Palace." 6 Dec. 1918, pp. 16–17. Review of Williams at the Palace in New York.
New York Age. "Theatrical Chit-Chat." 7 Dec. 1918, p. 6. Review of Williams at the Palace in New York.
Kingsley, Walter. "Vaudeville Volleys." *New York Dramatic Mirror*, 14 Dec. 1918, p. 867. Review of Williams at the Palace.
Gentz, Will T. "In the Vaudeville Field." *New York Dramatic Mirror*, 14 Dec. 1918, pp. 869–70. Review of Williams at the Palace.
Variety. "Palace." 28 Mar. 1919, p. 61. Williams at the Palace in New York.
_____. "Royal." 11 Apr. 1919, p. 22. Review of Williams in vaudeville act at the Royal Theater in New York City.

Obituaries and Estate Items
(in chronological order)

New York Times. "Bert Williams, Negro Comedian, Dies Here After Collapse on Detroit Stage." 5 March 1922, p. 1.
New York World. "Bert Williams, Comedian, Dead." 5 March 1922, p. 4.
New York Times. "Bert Williams' Funeral: Masonic Services to Be Part of It at His Request." 6 March 1922, p. 13.
New York Tribune. "Theatre Critics Lament Death of Bert Williams." 6 March 1922, p. 9.

————. "Respect of White Associates Won by Williams' Modesty." 6 March 1922, p. 9.

New York World. "Bert Williams' Memory Honored." 6 March 1922, p. 7.

Detroit Free Press. "Bert Williams Dies in New York." 6 March 1922, p. 3.

Detroit Times. "News of Williams' Death Shock to Theatre Men." 6 March 1922, p. 11.

Toledo Blade. "Comedian's Death Brings Loss to Stage." 7 March 1922, p. 10.

Detroit Times. "Negro Comedian to Be Buried in New York Today." 7 March 1922, p. 4.

New York Clipper. 8 March 1922, p. 307.

New York Times. "Throng at Bert Williams' Funeral." 8 March 1922, p. 15.

New York World. "Whitest Man He Ever Dealt With, Says Ziegfeld." 8 March 1922, p. 12.

Riverside (California) *Daily Press.* "Famous Colored Comedian Was Graduate of Riverside High School." 8 March 1922, p. 3. The obituary in Williams's hometown newspaper throws light on Williams's obscure early life.

New York Times. "Masons Honor Williams: Dean Trader Conducts Funeral Services in Grand Lodge Room." 9 March 1922, p. 17.

Variety. 10 March 1922, p. 18.

Langston, Tony. "Death Ends Career of Stage Idol," *Chicago Defender,* 11 March 1922, p. 1.

Walton, Lester A. "Thousands of All Races Mourn Bert Williams' Death." *New York Age,* 11 March 1922, pp. 1, 6.

New York Age. "Bert Williams' Stage Career." 11 March 1922, p. 6. Summary of Williams's life in show business claims Williams was originally part of a trio act.

New York Times. "Bert Williams' Will Signed." 19 March 1922, p. 21.

————. "Sue Comedian's Estate for Taxes." 5 March 1926, p. 3. The state of New York seeks back taxes from the Williams estate.

————. "Bert Williams Net Estate $18,300." 27 Apr. 1928, p. 16.

New York Age. "Bert Williams' Widow Is Dead, Sick Long Time." 23 March 1929, p. 1.

Index

293